Derrida's Marrano Passover

COMPARATIVE JEWISH LITERATURES

Bloomsbury's **Comparative Jewish Literatures** series creates a new venue for scholarship and debate both in Jewish Studies and Comparative Literature as it showcases the diversity of a nascent field with unique interdisciplinary footprints. It offers both a new way of looking at Jewish writing as well as insights into how Jewish literature is looked at by scholars indifferent to or sympathetic with these texts. Through its focus on the diversity of these groups' perspectives, the series suggests that disciplinary location informs how comparative Jewish literatures are understood theoretically, and it establishes new sectors that abut and intersect with the field in the twenty-first century.

Series Editor
Kitty Millet, San Francisco State University, USA

Advisory Board
Sarah Phillips Casteel, Carleton University, Canada
Bryan Cheyette, University of Reading, UK
Agata Bielik-Robson, University of Nottingham, UK
Nan Goodman, University of Colorado at Boulder, USA
Vivian Liska, University of Antwerp, Belgium
Orly Lubin, Tel Aviv University, Israel
Susan McReynolds, Northwestern University, USA
Paul Mendes-Flohr, University of Chicago, USA
Anna Parkinson, Northwestern University, USA
Na'ama Rokem, University of Chicago, USA
Maurice Samuels, Yale University, USA
Axel Stähler, University of Kent, UK
Ilan Stavans, Amherst College, USA

Volumes in the Series
Jewish Imaginaries of the Spanish Civil War: In Search of Poetic Justice, edited by Cynthia Gabbay
Derrida's Marrano Passover: Exile, Survival, Betrayal, and the Metaphysics of Non-Identity, by Agata Bielik-Robson
Kabbalah and Literature, by Kitty Millet (forthcoming)
Holocaust Literature and Representation: Their Lives, Our Words, edited by Phyllis Lassner and Judith Tydor Baumel-Schwartz (forthcoming)

Derrida's Marrano Passover

Exile, Survival, Betrayal, and the Metaphysics of Non-Identity

Agata Bielik-Robson

BLOOMSBURY ACADEMIC
NEW YORK • LONDON • OXFORD • NEW DELHI • SYDNEY

BLOOMSBURY ACADEMIC
Bloomsbury Publishing Inc
1385 Broadway, New York, NY 10018, USA
50 Bedford Square, London, WC1B 3DP, UK
29 Earlsfort Terrace, Dublin 2, Ireland

BLOOMSBURY, BLOOMSBURY ACADEMIC and the Diana logo are trademarks of Bloomsbury Publishing Plc

First published in the United States of America 2023
This paperback edition published 2024

Copyright © Agata Bielik-Robson, 2023

For legal purposes the Acknowledgements on p. viii constitute an extension of this copyright page.

Cover design by Eleanor Rose
Cover image: Photo of the French philosopher Jacques Derrida answering questions from journalists on January 02, 1982 at the Gare de l'Est in Paris on his return from Prague.
© Joel Robine / AFP/ Getty Images

All rights reserved. No part of this publication may be reproduced or transmitted in any form or by any means, electronic or mechanical, including photocopying, recording, or any information storage or retrieval system, without prior permission in writing from the publishers.

Bloomsbury Publishing Inc does not have any control over, or responsibility for, any third-party websites referred to or in this book. All internet addresses given in this book were correct at the time of going to press. The author and publisher regret any inconvenience caused if addresses have changed or sites have ceased to exist, but can accept no responsibility for any such changes.

Library of Congress Cataloging-in-Publication Data
Names: Bielik-Robson, Agata, author.
Title: Derrida's Marrano Passover : exile, survival, betrayal, and the metaphysics of non-identity / Agata Bielik-Robson.
Description: New York : Bloomsbury Academic, [2023] | Series: Comparative Jewish literatures | Includes bibliographical references and index. | Summary: "The first book devoted to Derrida's Marranism - his paradoxical 'non-Jewish Jewishness' – connecting it to the Derridean themes of exile, survival, betrayal and autobiography"–Provided by publisher.
Identifiers: LCCN 2022025095 (print) | LCCN 2022025096 (ebook) | ISBN 9781501392610 (hardback) | ISBN 9781501392658 (paperback) | ISBN 9781501392634 (epub) | ISBN 9781501392627 (pdf) | ISBN 9781501392641
Subjects: LCSH: Derrida, Jacques–Criticism and interpretation. | Philosophers–France–Biography. | Jewish philosophers–France–Biography. | Jews–Identity. | Crypto-Jews–France–Biography. | France–Biography.
Classification: LCC B2430.D484 B535 2023 (print) | LCC B2430.D484 (ebook) | DDC 194.092 [B]–dc23/eng/20220810
LC record available at https://lccn.loc.gov/2022025095
LC ebook record available at https://lccn.loc.gov/2022025096

ISBN: HB: 978-1-5013-9261-0
PB: 978-1-5013-9265-8
ePDF: 978-1-5013-9262-7
eBook: 978-1-5013-9263-4

Series: Comparative Jewish Literatures

Typeset by Deanta Global Publishing Services, Chennai, India

To find out more about our authors and books visit www.bloomsbury.com and sign up for our newsletters.

Emblème d'une nature morte: la grenade entamée, un soir de Pâques, sur un plateau...

Jacques Derrida, *Foi et Savoir*

Figure 0.1 Willem Kalf, *Still Life with Ewer, Vessels, and Pomegranate,* oil on canvas, mid-1640s, Gift of J. Paul Getty, Courtesy of the Getty Museum.

Contents

Acknowledgements		viii
List of abbreviations		ix
Introduction: The Marrano uncanny: The last and the first of Jews		1
1	*Betray, betray again, betray better*: Marrano theology of survival	51
2	Secret followers of the hiding god: Marrano a-theism	95
3	The nameless still life: Marrano metaphysics of non-presence	137
4	Two serious Marranos: Derrida and Cixous (with constant reference to Poldy Bloom)	169
5	Ana-community: Marrano 'living together'	219
Bibliography		261
Index of names and terms		274

Acknowledgements

This publication was made possible thanks to the support of NCN Opus 13 Grant: *The Marrano Phenomenon: The Jewish 'Hidden Tradition' and Modernity*, registered in the OSF system as 2017/25/B/HS2/02901.

Abbreviations

Works of Jacques Derrida

A   *Aporias*, trans. Thomas Dutoit, Stanford: Stanford University Press, 1994.

ADL   *Adieu to Emmanuel Lévinas*, Translated by Pascale-Anne Brault and Michael Naas, Stanford: Stanford University Press, 1999.

ADV   *Advances*, trans. Philip Lynes, Minneapolis: Minnesota University Press, 2017.

AF   *Archive Fever. A Freudian Impression*, trans. Eric Prenowitz, Chicago: The Chicago University Press, 1996.

AEL   *Adieu to Emmanuel Lévinas*, Translated by Pascale-Anne Brault and Michael Naas, Stanford: Stanford University Press, 1999.

AL   *Acts of Literature*, ed. Derek Attridge, trans. Avital Ronnel, Routledge: London & New York, 1992.

AO   'Abraham, the Other', in *Judeities: Questions for Jacques Derrida*, ed. Bettina Bergo, Joseph Cohen, and Raphael Zagury-Orly, trans. Bettina Bergo and Michael B. Smith, New York: Fordham University Press, 2007.

APO   'Of an Apocalyptic Tone Recently Adopted in Philosophy', trans. John P. Leavey, Jr., *Oxford Literary Review*, Vol. 6 No.2/1984.

AR   *Acts of Religion*, ed. Gil Anidjar, New York and London: Routledge, 2002.

BS1   *The Beast and the Sovereign*, vol. 1, trans. Geoffrey Bennington, Chicago: The University of Chicago Press, 2009.

BS2   *The Beast and the Sovereign*, vol. 2, trans. Geoffrey Bennington, Chicago: The University of Chicago Press, 2011.

C   *Circumfession*, in Jacques Derrida and Geoffrey Bennington, *Jacques Derrida*, Chicago: The University of Chicago Press, 1993.

CP   with Catherine Malabou, *Counterpath. Traveling with Jacques Derrida*, trans. David Wills, Stanford: Stanford University Press, 2004.

CS   'Christianity and Secularization', trans. David Newheiser, Critical Inquiry 47 (Autumn 2020), 138-148.

D   *Demeure. Fiction and Testimony* (postscript to Maurice Blanchot, *The Instant of My Death*), trans. Elizabeth Rottenberg, Stanford: Stanford University Press, 2000.

DIS   *Dissemination*, trans. B. Johnson. Chicago: The University of Chicago Press, 1981.

DJ   *Derrida and Joyce. Texts and Contexts*, ed, Andrew Mitchell and Sam Slote, Albany: SUNY Press, 2013.

DP1   *The Death Penalty*, vol. 1, trans. Peggy Kamuf, Chicago: The University of Chicago Press, 2014.

DP2	*The Death Penalty*, vol. II, trans. Elizabeth Rotenberg, Chicago: The University of Chicago Press, 2016.
F	'Fors', in Nicolas Abraham and Maria Torok, *Wolf Man's Magic Word: A Cryptonymy*, trans. N. Rand, Minneapolis: Minnesota University Press, 1986.
FK	'Faith and Knowledge: The Two Sources of 'Religion' at the Limits of Reason Alone', trans. Samuel Weber, in *Acts of Religion*, ed. Gil Anidjar, London and New York: Routledge, 2002.
FK-F	*Foi et Savoir. Les deux sources de la « religion » aux limites de la simple raison*, Paris: Editions du Seuil, 1996.
FWT	with Elisabeth Roudinesco, *For What Tomorrow . . .: A Dialogue*, trans. Jeff Fort, Stanford: Stanford University Press, 2004.
G	*Glas*, trans. John P. Leavey and Richard Rand, Lincoln: Nebraska University Press, 1986.
GD	*The Gift of Death. The Literature in Secret. Second Edition*, trans. David Willis, Chicago: The Chicago University Press, 2008.
GGG	*Geneses, Genealogies, Genres, and Genius. The Secrets of the Archive*, trans. by Beverley Bie Brahic, New York: Columbia University Press, 2006.
GRAM	*Of Grammatology*, trans. Gayatri Chakravorti Spivak, Baltimore: Johns Hopkins University Press, 1997.
GT	*Given Time: I. Counterfeit Money*, trans. Peggy Kamuf, Chicago: The University of Chicago Press, 1994.
HAS	'How to Avoid Speaking: Denegations', in *Derrida and Negative Theology*, ed. Harold Coward, Albany, NY: SUNY, 1992.
HC	*H.C. for Life, That Is to Say . . .*, trans. Laurent Milesi and Stefan Herbrechter, Stanford, CA: Stanford University Press, 2006.
LD	*Life Death*, trans. Pascale-Anne Brault and Michael Naas, Chicago: The University of Chicago Press, 2020.
LG	'The Law of Genre', in *Glyph* nr 7/ 1980.
LLF	*Learning to Live Finally. The Last Interview*, trans. Pascal-Anne Brault, New York: Melville House, 2011.
LO	'Living On: Borderlines', in *Deconstruction and Criticism*, ed. Harold Bloom, New York: Continuum, 1979.
LT	*Living Together: Jacques Derrida's Communities of Violence and Peace*, ed. Elisabeth Weber, New York: Fordham University Press, 2012.
M	*Margines of Philosophy*, trans. Alan Bass, Chicago: The University of Chicago Press, 1982.
MB	*The Memoirs of the Blind*, trans. Michael Nass, Chicago: The University of Chicago Press, 1993.
MO	*Monolingualism of the Other Or the Prosthesis of Origin*, trans Patrick Mensah, Stanford: Stanford University Press, 1998.
MS	'Marx & Sons', trans. G. M. Goshgarian, in *Ghostly Demarcations. A Symposium on Jacques Derrida's 'Specters of Marx'*, London: Verso, 1999.
OH	*Of Hospitality*, ed. Ann Dufourmantelle, trans. Rachel Bowlby, Stanford: Stanford University Press, 2000.

ON	*On the Name*, ed. Thomas Dutoit, trans. John P. Leavey, Stanford: Stanford University Press, 1995.
OS	*Of Spirit. Heidegger and the Question*, trans. Geoffrey Bennington and Rachel Bowlby, Chicago: The University of Chicago Press, 1989.
P	*The Postcard. From Socrates to Freud and Beyond*, trans. Alan Bass, Chicago: University of Chicago Press, 1987.
PF	*Politics of Friendship*, trans. George Collins, London: Verso, 2006.
PM	*Paper Machine*, trans. Rachel Bowlby, Stanford: Stanford University Press, 2005.
PS1	*Psyche. Inventions of the Other, Volume 1*, trans. Peggy Kamuf and Elizabeth Rottenberg, Stanford: Stanford University Press, 2007.
PS2	*Psyche. Inventions of the Other, Volume 2*, trans. Peggy Kamuf and Elizabeth Rottenberg, Stanford: Stanford University Press, 2008.
R	*Rogues. Two Essays on Reason*, trans. Michael Naas, Stanford: Stanford University Press, 2005.
RM	'The Retrait of Metaphor', trans. Peggy Kamuf, *Enclitic*, vol. 2, no. 2, 1978 ('Le retrait de la métaphore (To Michel de Guy),' *Poe&sie* N°7 (1978).
RP	*Resistances of Psychoanalysis*, trans Peggy Kamuf, Pascale-Anne Brault & Michael Naas, Stanford: Stanford University Press, 1998.
S	*Spurs. Nietzsche's Styles (Eperons. Les Styles de Nietzsche)*, trans. Barbara Harlow, Chicago: The University of Chicago Press, 1979.
SM	*Specters of Marx. The State of Debt, the Work of Mourning, and the New International*, trans. Peggy Kamuf, London: Routledge, 1994.
SQ	*Sovereignties in Question. The Poetics of Paul Celan*, trans. Thomas Dutoit, New York: Fordham University Press, 2005.
TG	'A Testimony Given . . .', in Elisabeth Weber, *Questioning Judaism*, Stanford: Stanford University Press, 2004.
TM	with Safaa Fathy, *Tourner les mots. Au bord d'un film*, Paris: Galilee, 2000.
TS	*A Taste for the Secret*, with Maurizio Ferraris, trans. Giacomo Donis, ed. Giacomo Donis and David Webb, Cambridge: Polity Press, 2001.
V-D	with Hélène Cixous, *Veils*, trans. Geoffrey Bennington, with drawings by Ernest Pignon-Ernest, Stanford: Stanford University Press, 2001.
WD	*Writing and Difference*, trans. Alan Bass, London: Routledge & Kegal Paul, 1978.
WM	'White Mythology: Metaphor in the Text of Philosophy', trans. F. C. T. Moore, *New Literary History*, Vol. 6, No. 1/ 1974, 5-74.
WO	*Without Alibi*, ed. and trans. Peggy Kamuf, Stanford: Stanford University Press, 2002.

Other

CP-M	Catherine Malabou, in *Counterpath. Traveling with Jacques Derrida*, trans. David Wills, Stanford: Stanford University Press, 2004.

HS	Giorgio Agamben, HS: *Homo sacer. Sovereign Power and Bare Life*, trans. Daniel Heller-Roazen, Stanford: Stanford University Press, 1998.
IJD	Hélène Cixous, *Insister of Jacques Derrida*, trans. Peggy Kamuf, Edinborough: Edinburgh University Press, 2007.
JD	Gideon Ofrat, *The Jewish Derrida*, New York: Syracuse University Press, 2001.
MCP	Theodor W. Adorno, *Metaphysics: Concepts and Problems*, trans. Edmund Jephcott, London: Polity Press, 2001.
MIJ	Gershom Scholem, *The Messianic Idea in Judaism. And Other Essays on Jewish Spirituality*, New York: Schocken Books, 1991.
MM	Michael Naas, *Miracle and Machine*, New York: Fordham University Press, 2012.
MF	Michel de Certeau, *The Mystic Fable. Volume One: The Sixteenth and Seventeenth Centuries*, trans. Michael B. Smith, Chicago: The University of Chicago Press, 1992.
MARS	*The Marrano Spectre. Derrida and Hispanism*, ed. Erin Graff Zivin, New York: Fordham University Press, 2019
ND	Theodor W. Adorno, *Negative Dialectics*, trans. E. B. Ashton, London: Routledge, 2004.
OT	*Derrida and Religion. Other Testaments*, eds. Yvonne Sherwood & Kevin Hart, London: Routledge, 2005.
OW	Yirmiyahu Yovel, *The Other Within: The Marranos – Split Identity and Emerging Modernity*, Princeton: Princeton University Press, 2009.
PB	David Farrell Krell, *The Purest of Bastards: Works of mourning, Art, and Affirmation in the Thought of Jacques Derrida*, Philadelphia: The Pennsylvania State University Press, 2000.
PJD	Hélène Cixous, *Jacques Derrida as a Young Jewish Saint*, trans. Beverly Bie Brahic, New York Columbia University Press, 2004.
PS	G. W. F. Hegel, *Phenomenology of Spirit*, trans. A. V. Miller, Oxford: Oxford University Press, 1977.
RA	Martin Hägglund, *Radical Atheism. Derrida and the Time of Life*, Stanford: Stanford University Press, 2008.
SR	Franz Rosenzweig, *The Star of Redemption*, trans. Barbara Galli, Madison: University of Wisconsin Press, 2005.
TSB	Hélène Cixous, 'This Stranjew Body', in *Judeities: Questions for Jacques Derrida*, ed. Bettina Bergo, Joseph Cohen, and Raphael Zagury-Orly, trans. Bettina Bergo and Michael B. Smith, New York: Fordham University Press, 2007.
USH	Franz Rosenzweig, *Understanding the Sick and the Healthy: A View of World, Man, and God*, trans. Nahum Glatzer, Cambridge, MA: Harvard University Press, 1999.
V-C	Hélène Cixous, *Savoir*, in *Veils*, trans. Geoffrey Bennington, with drawings by Ernest Pignon-Ernest, Stanford: Stanford University Press, 2001.

Introduction

The Marrano uncanny: The last and the first of Jews

Look, look, he's a marrano, lower than dust.
Juan de Lucena, De Vita Beata¹

I once said, perhaps rightly: The earlier culture will become a heap of rubble, and finally a heap of ashes, but spirit will hover over the ashes.
Ludwig Wittgenstein²

This book is the first monograph wholly devoted to the issue of Derrida's *marranismo*. It can also be regarded as a 'sort of' (*une sorte*) Marrano midrash: one long commentary on Derrida's famous confession in Toledo –

> I confided it to myself the other day in Toledo, [that] is that if I am a sort [*une sorte*] of marrano of French Catholic culture, and I also have my Christian body, inherited from SA in a more or less twisted line, *condiebar eius sale* ['seasoned with His salt', St. Augustine], I am one of those marranos who no longer say they are Jews even in the secret of their own hearts, not so as to be authenticated marranos on both sides of the public frontier, but because they doubt everything, never go to confession or give up Enlightenment, whatever the cost, ready to have themselves burned, almost, at the only moment they write under the monstrous law of an impossible face-to-face. (C, 170–1)

The place of this confession, Toledo, is far from accidental. Inspired by its *genius loci*, Derrida cannot but recollect the fate of the 'Hebrew citizens of Toledo', the first Iberian *conversos* who underwent compulsory conversion to Christianity. 'Baptized Jews' – a new category of people, neither purely ethnic nor purely religious – emerged in Visigoth Spain as early as in 613 when the king Sisebut issued a decree forcing the Spanish Jews to convert or else leave his realm. Many Jews emigrated, but also many stayed and formed a problematic group eventually to be called *marrane*, 'pigs': *neither* Jewish, because baptized, *nor* Christian, because not eating pork – and, simultaneously,

---

¹ ed. Govert Westerveld (Blanca [Murcia], Spain, 2012), 28.
² Ludwig Wittgenstein, *Culture and Value, A Selection from the Posthumous Remains*, ed. G. W. von Wright and H. Nyman, trans. P. Winch (Oxford and Cambridge, MA: Blackwell Publishers, 1998), 5e.

both Jewish, because keeping major Judaic holidays, and Christian, because attending church masses. And although the subsequent Visigoth lords soon revoked Sisebut's decree, the problem remained:

> How were they to be treated? It took some time and several bishopric councils before a doctrine could take shape. In essence, it drew a rigid distinction between ordinary Jews and baptized Jews. Ordinary Jews, though Christ's opponents, owed him no allegiance; they could practice their rites in private while keeping a low profile. Yet baptized Jews were full-fledged Christians; by practicing Judaism in secret they became rebels and renegades, desecrating the sacrament of baptism and cheating not only the king, but Christ himself. That was a tragic pit, a one-way street with no U-turn allowed. (OW, 7)

The 'baptized Jews' knew from the start that this is a no-win situation: either they become 'full-fledged Christians' or they would never evade persecution. They thus wrote a petition to King Recceswinth – Yirmiyahu Yovel calls it a 'pathetic manifesto' (OW, 7) – in which they tried to convince the Christian lord that they are as fervently Christian as he is himself and that they are going to eat pork on every occasion. It bears a collective signature: 'the Hebrew citizens of Toledo'.

Though indeed pathetic and extremely self-humiliating, this document remains curiously ambivalent, which did not escape Yovel's attention: 'Thus, in promising to keep away from 'the sect of unbaptized Jews', they imply there is also a sect of baptized Jews – their own' (OW, 8). This implication, insisting on the existence of the third party with its *own* separate identity (or, as it will become clear soon, non-identity), goes against the overt meaning of the manifesto in the manner of performative contradiction. By openly claiming to have become 'full-fledged Christians', the Hebrew citizens of Toledo nonetheless secretly assert their distinct status of 'baptized Jews'. This is, historically speaking, the first occurrence of the Marrano aporia of which Derrida will become a true master fourteen centuries later: the aporia of an insoluble tension, which simultaneously pledges allegiance to the host culture and secretly withdraws it; overtly subscribes to the officially accepted identity and refuses the identitarian closure. While it seemingly says no to the Jewish ancestry, it still preserves it; it remains paradoxically faithful in perjury.[3]

---

[3] Toledo is not only the place of the Marranos coming to existence *avant la lettre*: it is also the place of the 1449 rebellion against the *conversos* which brought accusations of Judaizing, trials, and new racially based laws that aimed at the exclusion of the New Christians from the Catholic community. According to David Nirenberg, the *entencia-Estatuto* issued by the Toledo rebel government on the 5th of June 1449 can be called 'the earliest act of racist legislation in Europe. The statute decreed that descendants of converts be barred from holding office or exercising power over Christians, so that Christian society could be freed from Jewish tyranny and corruption': David Nirenberg, *Anti-Judaism: The Western Tradition* (New York: W.W. Norton, 2013), 352. Both these events – the birth of the New Men defying classification and the crisis leading to their extermination – are equally important to Derrida when he locates his confession in this particular city. See also Javier Castaño, '*Cleanse Me from My Sin*: The Social and Cultural Vicissitudes of a Converso Family in Fifteenth-Century Castile', in *Bastards and Believers: Jewish Converts and Conversion from the Bible to the Present*, ed. Theodor Dunkelgrün and Paweł Maciejko (Philadelphia: University of Pennsylvania Press, 2020), 89–111 for a detailed description of the Toledo persecutions.

Derrida dates and maps his Marrano confession in a Celanesque manner, but it is hard to tell when exactly he begins to think about himself as 'a sort of Marrano'. In *Archive Fever*, Derrida mentions 'the Marranos, with whom I have *always* secretly identified (but don't tell anyone)' (AF, 46; emphasis added), which would suggest that his *marranismo* is not just a late affair of the 1990s. In *D'ailleurs, Derrida*, a 1999 film directed by Safaa Fathy, Derrida refers to the Marrano persistency in keeping secrets as an art of resistance to politics understood as a terror of transparency and identity, which he began to practice already in the late 1960s:

> It has concerned me not only in relation to the unconscious, to the political dimension of secrecy, secrecy being that which resists politics, that which resists politicization, citizenship, transparency, phenomenality. Wherever we seek to destroy secrecy or keeping secrets, there is a threat of totalitarianism. Totalitarianism is a crusher of secrecy: you will admit, you will confess, you will say what you really think. So the secret mission, the discreet mission of the Marrano is to teach the secret that secrets should be kept, should be respected. Secrecy should be held in respect. What is an absolute secret? I was obsessed with this question quite as much as that of my supposed Judeo-Spanish origins. *These obsessions met in the figure of the Marrano*. I gradually began to identify with someone who carries a secret that is bigger than himself and to which he does not have access. *As if I were a Marrano's Marrano* [. . .] a lay Marrano, a Marrano who has lost the Jewish and Spanish origins of his Marranism, a kind of universal Marrano.

Derrida says this in the Toledo former synagogue, once also a mosque, and now the church, Santa Maria la Blanca. In his commentary to Fathy's film, 'Lettres sur un aveugle. *Punctum caecum*', Derrida mentions also a blind man in Toledo, who was shot unconsciously to himself by a camera in February 1999. While he distances himself from the Derrida-Actor, letting himself be put on display, he secretly identifies with the Toledan *aveugle*: the one bent on his absolute secret that cannot be either seen or shown.

> When camera turned towards him and during the filming, he remained himself, in his infinite solitude, turned elsewhere [*ailleurs*], turned towards himself in the inwardness of his secret. *His* secret. A secret of which now and forever we will know that we know nothing. A secret of which we also know, once and for all [une fois pur toutes], that it will never come out. (TM, 77)

In French, 'to turn' (*tourner*) refers also to filming, so the blind man in Toledo is at once 'turned/ filmed' and 'turned/bent' towards his inner self which even he cannot see: *Il semble tourné vers le dedans, tourné en vue du dedans qu'il ne voit pas – et c'est tourné vers le dedans qu'il est aussi tourné* (TM, 80). The secret, therefore, stays absolutely safe:

> The blind man is *au secret* [at his secret]. He is devoted to secret. He belongs to secret. He holds to secret, the one of the Marranos of whom one speaks here

everywhere. A Marrano who knows how to hide and a Marrano who, because of that hiding, forgets himself – a little like me. (TM, 81–2)

Is it possible 'to appropriate the absolute knowledge of the blind spot *punctum caecum*'? (TM, 86-7). Derrida warns us against such attempt: 'There is no metalanguage that would be capable of not perjuring on the issue of perjury, there is no truth of the betrayal' (TM, 89). Even if the blind spot is the place of the secret which organizes all discourse and knowledge, it cannot be told, shown, displayed, *tourné*: there is no absolute metalanguage capable to divulge the secret in its entirety. The blind man of Toledo becomes thus a personification of the blind spot, *punctum caecum* – the Marrano secret – which itself cannot be 'turned': while it determines all the twists and turns of Derrida's idiom, all the *tropes* of his complex rhetorical strategies, it itself remains unturned and unmoved. Then, while commenting on another Toledo scene, in which he throws a letter to the yellow Spanish mailbox, Derrida states: '*Among other things, but once for all*, this movie *is* a mailbox full of the letters from Toledo' (TM, 88; emphasis original). This movie, therefore, would be Derrida's quasi-Pauline 'Epistle to the Marranos': a letter sent, but not meant to be received and read, a message in a bottle, written in a strange alphabet, a Marrano *braille* (we shall yet see how important it will be for the Marrano to cultivate the sense of touch). Gradually, the film itself begins to mime Derrida's life, turns into a real autobiography, but not because it is so genuine or truthful. Identifying stronger with the blind man than with the Actor, Derrida states: 'The divorce between the Actor and me, between all the personae which I play and me, has begun long before this movie. It has multiplied and proliferated through the whole of "my-life" [*ma-vie*]' (TM, 75). 'All the world's a stage, and all the men and women merely players', Derrida seems to be repeating after another Jacques, the one from Shakespeare's *As You Like It*, but also after Calderon de la Barca, the Spanish playwright of the Marrano origin, who famously compared life to a dream and a theatrical spectacle.[4] Life is a theatre and *ma-vie* is a *movie*, a parade of masks which 'disperse, multiply' (FK, 100); there is always a performance that involves a gap of irremediable inauthenticity 'between me and the images of me' (TM, 75) – the deep self remaining in *hastara*/concealment, and the me-actors on display – and, as such, is beyond the possibility of an ultimate authentication or SA, the *savoir absolu*. There is no blind spot for the blind spot.

It is precisely this absolute concealment – *hastara* – as opposed to the Hegelian absolute knowledge, which occupies Derrida in Toledo: the difference between the Jewish God of Hiding, which the Marrano cryptofaith merely exacerbates – and the Christian God of light and revealability, belonging to what Hegel called

---

[4] On the Marrano implications of Calderon's sentence, see Norman Simms who interprets it in the Freudian manner and connects it with a censorship forbidding the Marrano secret to come out: 'The dream is life, and life is a dream, as Calderon de Barca writes; and yet also, at the same time, there is a highly complex and censored dream inside a conventionally conceived dream as much as there is a secret life inside a professed and practiced life': Norman Simms, *Masks in the Mirror: Marranism in Jewish Experience* (London and New York: Peter Lang, 2006), 23.

die veroffenbarte Religion, religion made fully visible, apocalyptic, denuded of all secrets. By taking on a mask of 'another Jacob' (akin to Kafka's another Abraham), Derrida glosses over his own performance at the synagogue turned (*tourné*) into Catholic church:

> The Actor meditates on the Marrano mislaid by his own simulacre [...] Dreaming of the Judo-Andalousian diaspora, lost among the synagogues and the mosques of Toledo, he says to himself, just as Jacob terrified of his dream: 'Indeed, IHVH was here and I did not know about it.' He is overwhelmed by fear and says: 'How terrifying is this place! For this is the House of Elohim and the Gateway to Heaven'. (TM, 99)

At once alluding to Jacob's stairway to heaven and Abraham Cohen de Herrera's *Las Puertas del cielo*, a Marrano-Kabbalistic treatise avidly read by Spinoza, the paradigmatic 'Marrano of reason', Derrida-Actor begins to speak of 'The One God': 'His presence *is* his absence. He is where he is not, He is out there, *d'ailleurs* (otherwise and elsewhere; besides and furthermore, TM, 105) *in order* not to be here' (TM, 99; emphasis original). The world, contracted to the synecdochal Toledo, appears thus 'deserted by God, transformed into a desert by God' (TM, 100). It is a terrifying place of the universal exile in which we all are but 'universal Marranos': restlessly wandering through the desert, for ever cut off from the origin which withdrew into *hastara*, the irreversible concealment, the blind spot of everything. The highest mystery or *sod* from the Derridean Marrano version of *Pardes*: the absolute secret. But the secret identification with the blind man of Toledo suggests also a microcosmic interpretation: watch this unwatchable man, says Derrida, for the Marrano *punctum caecum* is also the spot from which everything begins for me.

By augmenting the Marrano figure to the second power, Derrida deepens his commitment to absolute secrecy which now also excludes the 'authenticated marranos': those who can be publicly and officially classified as the descendants of the Sephardic *conversos*. Even his Judeo-Spanish origins are merely 'supposed', forming a part of the play beyond any authentication: he refuses to accept them as a biographical *factum brutum* that would determine his identity, by imposing it on him from the outside and by force. Thus, the Marrano's Marrano becomes the ultimate figure of protestation against any form of the 'apo-calyptic' – veil-tearing – thought which has no respect for the secret and wants to drag it into the light. As Erin Graff Zivin very aptly comments on Derrida's monologue in the Toledo synagogue-church: 'Thus the marrano enters Derrida's work to name an anti-identitarian category with which he can, paradoxically, express a certain identification' (MARS, 4). The Marrano's Marrano figure indeed appears as an aporetic identity, the goal of which is to destabilize all identity – even the already shaky one of the so-called authenticated marranos. Derrida not only is 'the last of Jews': he also wishes to be 'the last of Marranos'. The least, the worst, 'lower than dust', the most lost in his labyrinthine secret, which he carries in the blind inner crypt without doors, windows, and keys – but also because of that 'the first': the 'true Marrano', the real guardian of unavowable secrecy.[5] As he himself comments on the Marrano non-identity: it is 'the identification in the rupture of identification, the same melancholy jubilation, the same analysis finite infinite' (TM, 104): the same reaching, again and again, of the unbridgeable limit – the blind spot which can never become *veroffenbart* and *sonnenklar*, fully revealed and clear as the light of the sun.

My Marrano midrash, therefore, must have a respect for the absolute secret: it cannot make Derrida's *marranismo* 'non-mysterious', in the apocalyptic manner of denudation stripping things naked in the light either of revelation or of reason; it cannot give us *Derrida Denudata*.[6] It must itself belong to the secret-protecting literary genre: *littérature au secret*. According to Hélène Cixous, Derrida *imagines* himself as a Marrano, which leads him towards a literary auto-fiction with a secret embedded in the very centre of his own 'art of telling' (TSB, 69).[7] By applying the critical terms of Frank Kermode – 'propriety', which accounts for a smooth and accessible story, versus 'secrecy', which disturbs the narrative sequence – we can say that, in Derrida's auto-fictional writings, 'struggle between propriety and secrecy is especially intense [. . .] This measure of collusion between novelist and public [. . .] helps one to see why the secrets are so easily overlooked and why – given that the problems only begin when the secrets are noticed – we have hardly, even now, found decent ways to speak of these matters'.[8] Fifty years later, things haven't much improved in this respect, but with Kermode's warning in mind, I will definitely try to be 'decent' in exposing Derrida's secret. This decency entails a certain *retrait* or 'reticence' – Derrida's favourite word in *Faith and Knowledge* – in stating bold hypotheses as to what his secret might cover, but also a speculative tone in which those hypotheses are put forward. Hence the idea of the *Marrano midrash*. Similarly to the traditional rabbinic mode of commentary which rather adds to the interpreted text than tears it apart in pursuit of the hidden meaning,

---

[5] In what follows, I will often resort to Abraham's and Torok's concept of cryptophoria, which I find particularly apt to describe the Marrano condition of carrying the unavowable secret: 'How indeed could one put the unnamable into words? If cryptophores were to do so, *they would die of it, thunderstuck*; the whole world would be swallowed up in this cataclysm, the police and the analyst's coach included [. . .] *The crypt is there with its fine lock, but where is the key to open it?*': Nicolas Abraham and Maria Torok, 'The Topography of Reality: Sketching a Metapsychology of Secrets', in *The Shell and the Kernel*, vol. 1, ed. and trans. Nicholas T. Rand (Chicago: The University of Chicago Press, 1994), 158–9; emphasis added.

[6] For the elucidation of this pun deriving from Christian Knorr von Rosenroth's *Kabbala Denudata*, see my: 'Derrida Denudata: Tsimtsum and the Derridean Metaphysics of Non-Presence', in *Tsimtsum and Modernity: Lurianic Heritage in Modern Philosophy and Theology*, ed. Agata Bielik-Robson and Daniel H. Weiss (Berlin: de Gruyter, 2020), 389–418.

[7] See also David Farrell Krell's commentary on *Circumfession*, which emphasizes the poetic licence implied by the very identification with the Marrano polymorphy: 'it is not so much true as a *makingtrue*, a made-up true, a circumfabulation, avowed with all the force of faith, with the full conviction of the faithful witness. Faithful witness? Perhaps more like a perjured witness, a Marrano, a "pig." Marrano, "pig," too slippery and too catholic to be either Jew or Christian; Echo, too protean and too polymorphous to be Narcissus as either man or woman in either thigh or jaw or throat' (PB, 196).

[8] Frank Kermode, 'Secrecy and Narrative Sequence', in Frank Kermode, *The Art of Telling: Essays on Fiction* (Cambridge, MA: Harvard University Press, 1972), 139.

my *midrash* will also proceed in the additive manner: it will 'disperse and multiply' Derrida's Marrano message in the same way in which Derrida sees the Spanish Marranos 'disperse and multiply' the secret messianic message of the Abrahamic revelation (FK, 100).

According to Derrida's Toledo confession, the 'true Marranos', with their Marranism raised to the second power – and we shall see that in Derrida's rendering, this is indeed an affirmative *power*, not a disempowering affliction – are the lay, universal, and deliberately anti-identitarian individuals who 'doubt everything, never go to confession or give up Enlightenment, whatever the cost, ready to have themselves burned, almost, at the only moment they write under the monstrous law of an impossible face-to-face' (C, 171). Yet, Derrida's Marranism is not as lay as he claims: the Toledo confession is still a confession of sorts, even if the Marrano's Marrano doubts *everything*, including his own Marranism. This all-doubt is his claim to Enlightenment – or what Yovel, apropos Spinoza, calls 'Marranism of reason': a belief in the power of rational skepsis which doubts everything methodically except the very right to doubt, for which the 'Marrano of reason' is ready to almost-burn in the fire of *auto da fé*. *Foi et savoir*, faith and knowledge, confession and methodical doubt, religion and secularization, come here entangled in one aporetic figure, a paradigmatic modern subject.[9] The confession, therefore, does not come easy: it has to be forced by the unavowable monstrous secrecy which the Marrano inherited without choice and which he buried in the deepest crypt of his self. It can never be told, only written:

> Derrida doesn't tell us, he writes it. Writing, however, is not telling. The key of *Circumfession* is precisely that: what is written is not said. Never in his life would Derrida say such a thing, never in his life would he be caught in a 'confession' scene. Never will he be caught in a Catholic situation, he is not Catholic, there will never be a confession. This is not a confession, it is a circumfession, *it's written, not said*. (PJD, 102; emphasis added)

Many commented on the famous Marrano passage from *Circumfession* and they will all sooner or later appear in this book, but when it comes to subtlety and congeniality of spirit (or the 'Marrano spectre'), nothing surpasses Hélène Cixous's literary midrash

---

[9] To what extent, therefore, does Derrida fit Carl Gebhardt's famous definition: *Der Marrane ist Katholik ohne Glauben und Jude ohne Wissen, doch Jude im Willen* ('The Marrano is a Catholic without faith and a Jew without knowledge, yet a Jew by will')? He doesn't. Gebhardt's approach to Marranism is, to say the least, highly patronizing: in the manner reminiscent of the practices of Inquisition, it doubts *a priori* the authenticity of the Marranos' conversion, denies their access to Jewish tradition, and presents them as *Juden ohne Eigenschaften*, filled with nothing but a helpless will to remain Jewish: Carl Gebhardt, Introduction to *Die Schriften des Uriel da Costa*, ed. Carl Gebhardt (Amsterdam: M. Hertzberger, 1922), xix. Contrary to this, Derrida's Marranism is a conscious choice which involves modern questioning of *all* faith, be it Christian or Jewish, or, as Cixous subtly names it, all unreflected traditional *crude-credulity*: 'I don't believe. It fits him like a glove, fits the question of his Judaism, this circumprofession of faith . . . Such is his profession of faith in incredulity, always this quarrel looking to pick a fight with itself at the heart of all believing. You ask him: "Are you Jewish?" he responded: *I don't believe*' (PJD, 45).

from which the aforementioned quote derives. In her *Portrait of Jacques Derrida as a Young Jewish Saint*, Cixous approaches the Toledo passage slowly and carefully, starting from her own 'circoncession':

> I am not myself therefore, not Jewish-self at least so far as I know, or feel or live, Jewish if you insist, a Jew as if, but *concesso non dato* eh – *circoncesso* – I merely concede, for the time being. As Kafka circumceded, *Man kann doch nicht nicht juden* – 'Yet one cannot not Jew [*juivre*].' In the end he is so fed up with this saw, I am tired, tired sick of it [*marre*]. And that's when the figure of the Marrano comes to him – like an unheralded *messiah* – not so long ago – perhaps ten or twelve years ago. Coming from a book – coming as a present from a son – the Marrano is the coming, his coming-right away he takes to it. Lost, he finds himself again in this figure, it's him without a doubt, that's me, face to face with myself suddenly. Unfindable, even in dictionaries. (PJD, 85–6)[10]

To be *marrane* is to be *marre*: tired sick of being-non-being Jewish, which always comes as a concession after a long and exhausting battle of denial and then only as the Kafkan double negation that refuses to mature into an affirmatory statement. But to be able to name this ordeal – this 'tortured Judaism' (Americo Castro's *semitismo atormentado*) – has an immediate healing, even messianic, effect. 'Ten or twelve years ago', which would be around 1992, by a lucky chance Derrida receives a gift of a book by his son, Pierre, which treats about the *conversos*, and he seems overjoyed to be found again. The unfindable word, absent from the dictionaries, rescues Derrida from feeling lost. Whatever joy he experienced in being hidden for so many years gives in to despair: he wants to be found, named, summoned, called. For him, 'Marrano' is not just a name: it is a calling, now fusing with the vague sense of election which derives from his secret

---

[10] Could it be that the gift from Derrida's son – most likely Frédérick Brenner's 1992 photographic book called *Marranes*, later on mentioned in *Archive Fever* – was a trigger that activated his Marranism? Yosef Hayim Yerushalmi notices a certain rule among the Iberian *conversos*: 'even before he began to Judaize, every New Christian was a potential Marrano, whom any of a variety of circumstances could transform into an active Marrano': Yosef Hayim Yerushalmi, *From Spanish Court to Italian Ghetto: Isaac Cardoso; A Study in Seventeenth-Century Marranism and Jewish Apologetics* (New York: Columbia University Press, 1971), 39–40. Marina Rusov comments: 'To go from 'potential' to 'active' status, one did not need the chance to embrace Judaism openly outside the peninsula; one needed only the right books, a chance encounter, a crisis of conscience, or some other turn of events': Marina Rusov, 'Yerushalmi and the Conversos', *Jewish History* 28, no. 1 (2014): 16 (the concept of the Marrano as a 'potential Jew' derives from Israël Salvador Révah, 'Les Marranes', *Revue des études juives* 118 (1959–60): 29–77, 55. Yet, in case of the Marranos, such activation of the potential Jewishness proved to be highly problematic. In his monograph on Alonso de Cartagena and Juan de Torquemada – the two defenders of the *conversos* in fifteenth-century Spain – Bruce Rosenstock argues against the idea of 'potential Jew', who can always return to Judaism given proper circumstances, and claims that the cases of *conversos*' relapse to Jewish religion should be described as a merely *quasi-conversion*: 'I use quotation marks because when such *conversos* redefine themselves as Jews, their religious self-understanding is obviously unlike that of Jews who had never lived as Christians [...] I would suggest that it perhaps makes more sense to treat crypto-Judaism in relation to converso Christianity than in relation to traditional rabbinic Judaism': Bruce Rosenstock, *New Men: Conversos, Christian Theology, and Society in Fifteenth-Century Castile*, Papers of the Medieval Hispanic Research Seminar nr 39 (London: University of London, 2002), 93.

Jewish nickname, *Elie/élu*. He thus takes to it, takes faith in it, even before he knows what it means – in the Augustinian manner of *dato non concesso*, 'accepted without conceiving', while before, his Jewishness was the matter of the reverse *concesso non dato*: a somewhat reluctant 'circoncession' without acceptance. The personal *eureka* of the Marrano calling comes with the exhilarating hindsight of *Nachträglichkeit*: Monsieur Jourdain discovers that all this time he was speaking a Marrano prose.

> When he declared himself the last of the Jews, he didn't know how apt it was, the last of the last, and after, the worst and most precious. The last talks to himself. Who else remains to remind of your presence? So it was the Marrano he was calling, the Marrano that he already was although he didn't know it. One of those Jews without knowing it and without knowledge, Jew without having it, without being it, a Jew whose ancestors are gone, cut off, as little Jewish as possible, the disinheritor, guardian of the book he doesn't know how to read, half buried and all the more tenacious for that. He who dreams of tunneling under the ground of the circle, of the house of the circular temple and escaping, or who'd dream of being lifted up from the host and hostage scene as Elijah was removed from the persecution of the faithful Elisha, from above, all in flames, he who would like to escape the cruel circus of inheritance, he's tired of inheriting and leaving legacies. *But it was only a dream.* (PJD, 86; emphasis added)[11]

It is in the nature of a 'true Marrano' not to know that one is a Marrano: this lack of reflexive dimension of self-introspection, which remains the *forte* of the Augustinian 'certain Christianity' (FK, 55), will be the theme of the last part of *Foi et Savoir*, locating the Marranos on the side of faith 'without knowledge'. While carrying the buried Jewishness in themselves, without an aid of introspection, Marranos are, therefore, *cryptophores*: the carriers of crypts which they guard tenaciously, accepting it without conceiving, *dato non concesso*, the fatalistic past once given and never understood. As Nicolas Abraham and Maria Torok explain in their definition of the psychic condition of cryptophoria: 'this past is present in the subject as a *block of reality*; it is referred to as such in denials and disavowals. This

---

[11] In her very aptly titled essay – 'Derrida's Marrano Dream' – Martine Leibovici makes a similar point about the therapeutic value of the Marrano *rêverie* for Derrida, which allows him to ease the traumatic pressure of his Jewish aporia ('I am a Jew/I am not a Jew'). When commenting on Derrida's confession in Safaa Fathy's movie, staged in Toledo's former synagogue – 'If I fell in love with the word "Marrano," which became a kind of obsession and which reappears in all my texts for the last few years...' – she writes: 'Like all the words, "Jew" comes [to him] from the outside, and it is charged with a threat, comparable to a "hurting mark" (*flèche blessante*). Contrary to this, the word "Marrano," encountered much later, far away from the childhood traumas, inspires love. It contains a seductive force, an evocative power, for it sends him back to the supposed origins of his maternal line, Judeo-Spanish or Portuguese: the splendid world annihilated by the Inquisition': Martine Leibovici, 'Le rêverie marrane de Jacques Derrida', in *Les marranismes: De la religiosité cachée à la société ouverte*, ed. Jacques Ehrenfreud and Jean-Philippe Schreiber (Paris: Demopolis, 2014), 270. This *rêverie* should also remind us of Calderon's censored dream which forbids itself to divulge the secret.

reality cannot quite die, nor can it hope to revive'.[12] Hence Derrida's stake which comes to the fore already in *Fors*, his preface to Abraham's and Torok's *Wolf Man's Magic Word*: to transform the Marrano tragic cryptophoria, which carries the dead weight of the departed, long-gone Judaism as a terrible *Ate* – 'fate of an entire family line'[13] – into a 'paradoxical opportunity' (MO, 53): a kind of an enabling trauma which will allow the 'necrotic bone' of the Jewish ancestry to turn into a spectral inner presence, not fully alive but not completely dead either, carrying the message of the 'messianicity shorn of everything' (MO, 68).[14]

The Marrano cryptophores cannot think – conceive, fathom, understand – but they nonetheless can dream, and their dreams are, in fact, never *just* dreams: they articulate an extimate, deeply uncanny hyperreality. What do Marranos dream about? Most often about being like Houdini, the great escapist, who could break any circle of chains, the *shalshelet ha-kabbalah*, the 'chain-of-tradition' included: they dream about 'the acquittance of a debt, or of a crime' (F, xx). The Marranos, forming 'the going-awayness alliance', have intense *rêveries* about 'the departure, the detachment, the way-making' (PJD, 85). Or about being like Elijah, shooting into air, above the 'circus of inheritance', the first man to ascend into heaven and be-like-God. These dreams of the seemingly impossible strangely come true, so the dreamer wakes up and

> suddenly here's someone who got away, he surges up blinking his eyes, it's a mole – the blessed disinheriting it's him, the remainder guardian of what remains. The Celant, the self-concealed, still a little maroon, fugitive I mean. (PJD, 86)

Once Derrida decides to imagine himself as a Marrano – the Celan/*Celantus*, the hidden one, as well as a maroon, the West India fugitive[15] – his relation to Judaism acquires clarity; no longer solely 'tormented', its 'lastness' begins to make positive sense of guardianship and protection. Derrida thus becomes a *defensor fidei*, all the more tenacious for the secrecy of his messianic mission:

> Here's one who, if there's such a thing as faith, has got it. He prays and does not know what he says. To think he was a Marrano all along and didn't know it. A true Marrano. Don't tell a soul. It's a secret. (PJD, 86)

---

[12] Abraham and Torok, *The Shell and the Kernel*, 159.
[13] Ibid., 140.
[14] In *Monoligualism of the Other*, Derrida describes his Marrano milieu: 'the greater majority of these young 'indigenous Jews' remained, in addition, strangers to Jewish culture: a strangely bottomless alienation of the soul: a *catastrophe*; others will also say a *paradoxical opportunity*' (MO, 53; emphasis added). Derrida also uses here a cryptophoric metaphor in order to describe his Jewish 'negative heritage' based on the 'handicapped memory' that forms in him a kind of the 'necrotic bone': 'This incapacity, this handicapped memory, is the subject of my lament here. That is my grievance. For as I thought I perceived it during my adolescent years, when I was beginning to understand a little what was happening, *this heritage was already ossified, even necrotized*, into ritual comportment, whose meaning was no longer legible even to the majority of the Jews of Algeria. I used to think then that I was dealing with a Judaism of "external signs"' (MO, 54; emphasis).
[15] In Chapter 5, we shall see that the Haitian 'maroons' indeed bear affinity to the Marranos.

But it is not a dirty secret. Derrida receives the Marrano calling as a gift, not as a curse: when he 'marranates himself',[16] it is not because it corresponds to his bad conscience of a 'tormented Jew' – a filthy traitor, but because it saves him from his earlier *semitismo atormentado*. By including Derrida into the Augustinian tradition of *felix culpa*, Cixous states: 'Luckily there was a fault, so there could be redemption. Everything is owed to a fault.'[17] For Derrida, Marranism is precisely such a happy fault: the *conversos* were paradigmatically 'faulted' Jews, so for them, the issue of redemption became all the more pressing and for that reason they produced an enormous variety of messianic scenarios. In this regard, Derrida, with his highly innovative project of the 'messianicity shorn of everything' (MO, 68), is indeed a typical Marrano. But for him, Marranism is even more fortunate than a *felix culpa*. While the historical figure of the Marrano refers to those disoriented Jews in pain, hopelessly stuck between the two traditions, for Derrida it begins to mean something else: not a morass, but a way out; not an impasse, but a solution. Because it comes late, after his tortured 'prayers and tears' which he didn't yet know were so typical of the *'conversos* style', this 'afterwardness'/*Nachträglichkeit* arrives with a strike of revelation and relief. It is precisely for the reason that 'he was a Marrano all along and didn't know it' – a Marrano not marred by the knowledge of Marranism – he can be a *true*, unblemished and unprejudiced, Marrano. A Marrano of faith without knowledge, who can suddenly see a new affirmative – even sublime – dimension of his predicament:

> Marrano, the sublime figure of Oblivion in which memory keeps watch, dozes off, more Marrano than ever, about the wide earth he goes, running away. From himself. He attends to safeguarding the unknown, the stranger he is. Alone. Almost. (PJD, 87)

It goes to Cixous's credit to have noticed that, in Derrida's elaboration, the Marrano is most of all the figure of Oblivion and, precisely for that reason, sublime. In *Geneses*, the late essay devoted in large part to Cixous's literature, Derrida links the secret to the memory deposited and deactivated in the crypt: the memory thus no longer remembered, rather lingering in a latent limbo, between life and death, *hypomnesiac*.

> Giving a secret away may mean telling it, revealing it, publishing it, divulging it, as well as keeping it so deeply in the crypt of a memory that we forget it is there or even cease to understand and have access to it. In one sense a secret kept is always a secret lost. (GGG, 20)

---

[16] This witty phrase comes from Cixous too (TSB, 56). According to Derrida's friend, complicit in the Marrano affair, such active *self-marranation* expresses his solidarity with the nameless race of 'di-Jews and dys-Jews [*dijuifs et dejuifs*]': 'Recently we have seen the most nameless the most defiant the most obstinate of these peoples rise in his memory to the surface. He finds himself, finds himself anew, in feint and truth, a marrano. An adoption that sits well with his essential way of assenting to the secret, of giving to secrets their incalculable share. To let himself be overtaken, exceeded' (TSB, 55).

[17] Hélène Cixous, *Readings: The Poetics of Blanchot, Joyce, Kafka, Kleist, Lispector, and Tsvetayeva*, ed. and trans. Verena Andermatt Conley (Minneapolis: Minnesota University Press, 1991), 6.

The *power* of forgetting – meant as power, that is, not as privation but as creative excess – constitutes the main characteristic of the Derridean Marrano turned into a positive figure. It is this power – simultaneously opposed to the sovereign notion of power – which allows Marranos to 'disperse, multiply' (FK, 100) and, in Rosenzweig's words, 'pace the whole orbit of creation' (SR, 235). *Alone, almost* – the Marranos nonetheless form a paradoxical community based on the 'the going-awayness alliance' (PJD, 85) of universal strangers. This vision is, as I will argue, Derrida's high argument which is staked on the messianic inversion, this time applied to the Marrano 'rejected stones': a vision of a new universal community and a new universal religion, dictated not by the jealous God who sets his unforgettable law in stone, but by a generous 'God who made me forget', imagined as a Greco-Abrahamic version of *Khôra*. As usual with Derrida, bestowed with a strong sense of exemplarity, what suggests itself as his own private saving solution becomes a redemptive model for the whole humanity. While his *semitismo attormentado* falls into a vertiginous 'spiral of overbidding', the Marrano calling – accepting the name 'Marrano' as a new profession, *dato et professo* – leads out, in the act of Derrida's own private Exodus, of the aporetic self-cancelling declarations of 'the less one is Jewish, the more Jewish one is':

> insofar as the Jew's identity to himself or to Judaism would consist in this exemplariness, that is in a certain non-identity with oneself, 'I am this' meaning 'I am this and universal,' well, the more one dislocates one's self-identity, the more one says 'my own identity consists in not being identical to myself, in being a foreigner, the non-coinciding with the self,' etc. the more Jewish one is! And at that point, the word, the attribute 'Jewish,' the quality of 'Jewish' or of 'Judaism' are locked in a spiral of overbidding. It allows one to say that the less one is what one is, the more Jewish one is, and, consequently, the less one is Jewish, the more Jewish one is [. . .] The logical proposition 'I am Jewish' thus loses any kind of assurance, it gets carried away in ambition, a kind of pretension, a spiral of overbidding! (PJD, 83; see also TG, 41, in different translation)

While referring to this fragment from Derrida's conversation with Elisabeth Weber, Cixous says that, thanks to the Marrano 'strategicomic profession of faith', he can state, 'I am the last of the Jews, *without boasting*' (PJD, 77; emphasis added). The vertiginous aporetic – 'Am I Jewish or do I flee from Jewish? *Suis-je juif ou fuis-je juif?*' (PJD, 8) – can for a moment take less fretting form of the Marrano two-in-one, where declaring Jewish identity and escaping Jewish identity converge into an almost homophonic fusion. Derrida, man-child weary, he had travelled, he can rest – this is how Cixous, constantly having in mind their, hers and Derrida's, favourite topic of conversations, James Joyce's *Ulysses*, tends to see his paradoxical homecoming to the 'home which is not exactly home': the French Bloom's discovery of his for ever *unheimlich* Marranism. The Marrano take on exemplarity allows thus to escape the pretensions of identitarian overbidding, yet without diminishing the ambition of Derrida's project which is nothing less than the issue of Jewish survival: 'After the last of the Jews what or who can one be waiting for, what follow up, succession, coming or extinction? *What ashes or phoenix?* . . . Perhaps he meant to say I am the last de-Jew? He who announces a generation of re-Jews?' (PJD, 77). There is an obvious risk involved in this procedure of renewal, where 'de-Judaizing' can but does not have to lead to a new 're-Judaizing': as we shall see in a moment, the 'theology of hazard' is the characteristic antinomian feature of the Marrano doctrine which Derrida also embraces ('Watchfulness is always embattled. All can still be saved. All can still yet be lost. All may still be lost', TSB, 65). It will be one of my aims in this book to demonstrate that, by choosing to be a Marrano, Derrida takes on board all elements of the historical Marranism, whether he knows it or not (but, as I will also claim, rather the former: he knows more about the 'Marrano figure' than he wishes to reveal). The antinomian messianicity of the most rejected stones, the secret desire to renew the 'sickened tradition', the bold venturing into 'theology of hazard', the investment in survival as the core teaching of Abrahamic religion, and – last but not least – the sublime figure of Oblivion as the right way to follow the hidden/ hiding God: all these motives, which can be found throughout the ages in modern thinkers close to the Marrano line, can also be found in Derrida, especially in his late period.

Also the Derridean attachment to the secret realm of *d'ailleurs*, the always elusive 'elsewhere', is of a Marrano origin. In 1982, Michel de Certeau publishes his *Mystic Fable* (*La fable mystique*): a book on the sixteenth and the seventeenth transformations on modern mysticism, which designated the 'Marrano experience' as crucial for the development of a new inward-bent type of mystical contemplation. In de Certeau's approach, the 'new Christians' such as John of the Cross and Teresa of Avila inaugurate a distinctly modern 'mystic fable' which speaks from an *elsewhere/ l'ailleurs*: a 'no-place' of radical inwardness that welcomes the refugees from the outside world of distinct identities. They are all misfits, banned from the world by social and religious exclusions and relegated to their own inner castles/crypts:

> In sixteenth-century Spain, Teresa of Avila belonged to a *hidalguia* deprived of functions and of goods; John of the Cross, ministering to the sick in the hospital of Salamanca, belonged to a bankrupt and *declasse* aristocracy, and so on. But more important than social ranking were the ethnic discriminations based on the *raza*. Now, close to the marrano tradition – that is, the *gespaltete Seelen* (J. A. Van Praag), divided souls, lives split in two by the necessity of a hidden inner self – the *nuevos cristianos*, whose 'converted' face was, for their contemporaries, the mask of the excluded Jew, were extremely numerous among the 'illuminated' devotees, or *alumbrados*; they were the most eminent figures among them: Melchior, the Cazallas, the Ortizes, Bernardino Tovar, Pedro Ruiz de Alcaraz, San Pedro Regalado, and many *beatas*. They participated in this 'converso style' that, after the manner of the picaresque novel, of poetry, or of spirituality, disturbed the literature of the Golden Age with the critical irony or the insatiable lyricism that Americo Castro has associated with a 'tortured Semitism' [*semitismo atormentado*]. In Christianity, they articulated *the experience of an elsewhere*, but within the tradition they adopted. Neophytes, distant from the age-old way of thinking and acting of Spanish Catholicism, *often inclined to free themselves from the formalism of the Synagogue and unwilling to fall into that of the Church*, members of a *scriptural intelligentsia* that was seduced by the Erasmian conception of an Evangelical 'body' and repelled by the doctrinal racism subjacent to the ranking according to the

limpieza de sangre, readers of a Bible that they approached independently of its scholastic or established preambles – they introduced into the 'letter' the technical and/or mystical play of a different 'spirit.' Forbidden in certain orders (first the Hieronymites, the Benedictines, and others), suspect among the Dominicans, these 'scorned Ones' became the great Franciscans (Francisco de Osuna, Diego de Estella), Augustinian friars (Luis de León), Jesuits (Lainez, Polance, Ripalda, and others), Carmelite friars or nuns. Had not Teresa of Avila's grandfather, having gone back to the Judaism of his ancestors, been subjected, with his three sons (among them Alonso, Teresa's cherished father), to the humiliating public ceremony of abjuration required of the 'renegades' (1485)? *A family memory, decisive but 'unspeakable', as in many other cases.* From John of Avila (who makes the University of Baeza the asylum for the 'new Christians') to Molinos, *a strange alliance joins the 'mystic' spoken word to the 'impure' blood.* The meeting of the two religious traditions, one removed to an inner retreat, the other triumphant but 'corrupted,' allowed the new Christians to become, to a great extent, the creators of a new discourse, freed from dogmatic repetition, and, like a *spiritual Marranism*, structured by the opposition between the purity of the 'inside' and the lie of the 'outside.' Just as the massive adoption of German culture by the Jews in the nineteenth century made possible theoretic innovations and an exceptional intellectual productivity, the upsurge of mystics in the sixteenth and seventeenth centuries was often *the effect of the Jewish difference in the usage of a Catholic idiom.* (MF, 22–3; emphasis added)[18]

Having in mind that Derrida deeply admired the old Jesuit, whom he met on various occasions and who died in 1986 while preparing the second volume of *La fable mystique*, one should not hesitate to put Derrida's 'wish to be a Marrano' in the light of Michel de Certeau's *spiritual Marranism* which the former will eventually adopt with a slight revisionist twist.[19] In *Monoligualism of the Other*, published in 1996, where the Marrano theme already looms large, de Certeau's mystical 'elsewhere', already by him

---

[18] Indeed, Americo Castro confirms de Certeau's diagnosis of *conversos*' sense of absolute alienation as leading inwards and thus towards a new understanding of the self as most of all interiority: 'The Spanish convert of the fifteenth and sixteenth centuries expressed himself in somber modes because circumstances drove him back to the deepest roots of his own existence': Americo Castro, *The Structure of Spanish History*, trans. E. L. King (Princeton: Princeton University Press, 1954), 565.

[19] In the 1986 colloquy on the Derridean concept of alterity, in which Derrida participated, de Certeau's *Mystic Fable* gets mentioned few times in the context of the former's 'mysticism of departure and exodus, and not of a fusion with or return to the One': Jacques Derrida and Jean-François Labarrière, *Altérités* (Paris: Osiris, 1986), 28. In the series of questions Derrida replies: 'I can't say that I do not possess a mystical desire, but this necessity which governs my life is totally alien to the mysticism conceived in a trivial sense. Though I don't recall de Certeau's definition literally, when I hear it again, I must say: yes, why not! [...] I would indeed distinguish between two types of mysticism: the "henological" one (inspired by Neoplatonism and partly present in the Eckhartian spirituality) and the less "restive" and more "errant," more "diasporic" one. It is the latter which pervades de Certeau's *La Fable mystique*' (ibid., 38). And – we may add – it pervades also the whole of Derrida's ouevre, written under the auspices of 'departure and exodus'.

associated with the intervention of the *nuevos cristianos*, emerges as the *thema regium* of Derrida's *ouevre*:

> Certainly, everything that has, say, interested me for a long time – on account of writing, the trace, the deconstruction of phallogocentrism and 'the' Western metaphysics [. . .] – all of that could not not proceed from the strange reference to an 'elsewhere' of which the place and the language were unknown and prohibited even to myself, as if I were trying to translate into the only language and the only French Western culture that I have at my disposal, the culture into which I was thrown at birth, a possibility that is inaccessible to myself, as if I were trying to translate a speech I did not yet know into my 'monolanguage,' as if I were still weaving some veil from the wrong side (which many weavers do, I might add), and as if the necessary passage points of this weaving from the wrong side were *places of transcendence, of an absolute elsewhere*, therefore, in the eyes of Graeco-Latino-Christian Western philosophy, but yet inside it (*epekeina tes ousias*, and beyond – Khôra – negative theology, Meister Eckhart and beyond, Freud and beyond, a certain Heidegger, Artaud, Lévinas, Blanchot, and certain others) [. . .] The paths and strategies that I have had to follow in this work or passion also follow the dictates of some structures and therefore of some assignations that are internal to the Graeco-Latino-Christiano-Gallic culture to which my monolingualism forever confines me; it was necessary to reckon with this culture in order to translate, attract, and seduce into it the very thing, the 'elsewhere,' toward which I was myself ex-ported in advance, namely *the 'elsewhere' of this altogether other with which I have had to keep, in order to keep myself but also in order to keep myself from it*, as from a fearsome promise, *relationship without a relationship*, with one guarding itself from the other, in the waiting without horizon for a language that only knows how to keep people waiting. (MO, 71; emphasis added)

In Derrida's idiom, the *elsewhere* is deliberately overdetermined: it designates 'places of transcendence' which he obsessively seeks in the Graeco-Latino-Christian Western philosophy, but also *his own private transcendence* which refers him to 'this altogether other' which/who he simultaneously keeps and keeps himself from in a strange, Blanchotian-Lévinasian, cryptophoric and apotropaic 'relationship without a relationship'. He compares himself to a weaver who weaves a veil from the wrong side: not from the *bereshit*/origin which remains 'prohibited' but simultaneously towards and away from it. His 'tormented Judaism' which remains 'inaccessible', laid down in the windowless crypt without keys, points to a 'no-place' (F, xx) that makes him particularly sensitive to the occurrences of 'elsewhere' in every other language, where he hopes to find the impossible translation of 'a speech I did not yet know'. He wants to find himself in *l'ailleurs/ d'ailleurs* – his 'elsewhere' and his always protesting 'still' – but then also use it as an alibi for not belonging unconditionally to here and now: 'One has to go elsewhere to find oneself here. The here-now does not appear as such, in experience, except by differing from itself. And one trace always refers to another trace. It thus *secretes*, it produces, it cannot not produce some alibi. Ubiquity of the alibi'

(WA, xvii; emphasis added). He deliberately clings to the void, dreaming of a Marrano imagined 'community out of step with the times'.[20]

'In the beginning was the fable', says Valery and Derrida confirms: 'In the beginning was not [...] the Logos, but the Fable' (BS1, 190).[21] We can safely assume that by the word 'fable' Derrida does not mean a 'myth' in general, but also – if not predominantly – Michel de Certeau's *La fable mystique*, the Marrano fiction of the secret, which, as *fiction*, binds mystical religion to literature as the surviving modern remnant of the former. When Derrida states: *La littérature reste un reste de religion*,[22] 'the literature remains the remains of religion', he clearly indicates that his experimental Marrano theology is a literary enterprise. Derrida's Marrano thinking is thus as much philosophy as it is literature: a new genre of a philosophical storytelling which centres on Derrida's Marrano 'auto-fable'. In order to elucidate his *marranismo*, Derrida not only constantly draws on the literary works – Kafka, Celan, Joyce, Cixous – but also forms his philosophy on the model of a literary narrative. My book attempts to reconstruct Derrida's unique metaphysical vision on the basis of those 'surviving remnants' of old religions and theologies, which, as he claims, can still be found in modern *littérature au secret*: the Wittgensteinian spirit still hovering over the ashes. In Derrida's interpretation, the Marrano secret of literature consists precisely in hiding, but also carrying forth the revelatory message of the 'messianicity shorn of everything', that is, no longer supported by the traditional overt forms of cult, but – precisely because of that – truer to the unnameable messianic vocation.

Politics of non-identity: Marrano *votum separatum*

The metaphysics of non-identity, which will be my main focus in this book, is a less known sister of Derrida's politics of non-identity. We saw that, for Derrida, the name 'Marrano' is always associated with being *une sorte*, 'a sort of': the same formula will also appear in Derrida's most famous – as well as enigmatic – allusion to 'a sort of Spanish Marranos' (*une sorte de marrane espagnol*) in the 1996 text of *Faith and Knowledge* (FK, 100). To be a Marrano can never aspire to fully 'authenticated' identity; to be 'a

---

[20] Compare Hélène Cixous's Kafkan description of her Oran Marranism: 'The Jewish trapezists cling to the void. A community out of step with the times. One often spoke a rather elegant French, the language of the denied and oft-flattered enemy. Hebrew? So suppressed. At best one was at the Marrano stage but unaware of it [...] Imagine the enormous weight of the word Jew, the swelling, the erection of the word, sole survivor of an extinct verbal population' (PJD, 115) – as well as Derrida's matching comment in *Monolingualism*: 'What was, for me, such an epiphany of the word jew in my Algerian childhood? [...] These two appellations, these two words that are neither common nor proper, are not "Daddy" and "Mommy," but God – and Jew' (AO, 10).

[21] 'In the beginning was the Fable': Paul Valery, *Selected Writings* (New York: New Directions Books, 1950), 201. Derrida often commented on this passage: the list of all those places is given in Peggy Kamuf, *To Follow: The Wake of Jacques Derrida* (Edinburgh: Edinburgh University Press, 2010), 48.

[22] Jacques Derrida, 'Littérature au secret : une filiation impossible', in Jacques Derrida, *Donner la mort* (Paris: Galilée 1999), 208.

sort of' signifies an avoidance of any identification and assumes instead an *identity without identity* which doubts and subverts the politics of official 'authentications'. Hesitant, shadowy, the *une sorte* nomination evades the light and 'the monstrous law of an impossible face-to-face' (C, 171): it fades out the moment it is called.

Yet, there is nothing hesitant in the very strategy of calling oneself a sort of Marrano and its political implications. Pace the current identitarian trends, which enhance increasingly more incommunicable differences between identities formed in disparate historical conditions and power relations, Derrida announces that the 'Marrano experience' not only can but also must be generalized: there is a universal message contained in this first modern process of *losing identity* where the 'Marrano experience' constitutes a paradigmatic case. If I use the term 'Marrano experience', deriving from Yirmiyahu Yovel, and not a 'Marrano identity', it is precisely because the Marrano experience questions the very idea of a fixed identity as such. What the generalized 'Marrano experience' targets is precisely what identity politics cannot conceptualize: the non-participatory remnant of otherness which is not just the other of this or that particular tradition, but becomes a bearer of a new universalism, based not on the abstract notion of human nature but on the non-identity, a distance-from-identity or what Yovel calls the 'identitarian concession' (OW, 363), or 'non-integral identity'.

> Whether synchronically or over time, a human self is capable – and should be allowed – to operate on several planes at once without fully coherent unification, and to balance different choices and allegiances without allowing any one to take over as the completing identity or 'true self.' Therefore, the non-integral identity that the Marranos throw into sharp relief, and that many others – from the Inquisition to modern nationalism and other ideologies, as well as fundamentalist communities – view as devious, illicit, illogical, or immoral, should rather be recognized as a *basic human freedom*. (OW, 348; emphasis added)[23]

It is precisely this *new universalism* of the non-integral (non)identity, which concerns me here: not the traditional universalism of a unified human nature, which treats all particular features as mere accidents, but a 'Marrano universalism' in which all human beings can be addressed as *remnants*, ultimately non-identifiable in terms

---

[23] The view that the Marrano constitutes the paradigmatic modern subjectivity and that she tests the modern transformation in the individual's approach to her own tradition is also confirmed by Paweł Maciejko and Theodor Dunkelgrün, the editors of *Bastards and Believers*, the collection of essays devoted to the Jewish converts to Christianity throughout the ages: 'Modern liberalism [...] endorses the view that our origin does not determine our destiny, and that while we cannot choose the former, our individuality and freedom are defined in large part by our agency concerning the latter. The ability (true, at least subjectively) to choose and therefore to change who we are turns the *Schicksalsverwandtschaft* into a *Wahlverwandtschaft*, an elective affinity, to our religion or community. We might suggest that the successes and failures of premodern and modern converts to choose their destinies speak to the breadth of our own anthropologies. In their testing of the possibilities and limitations of human freedom, the converts stand for us': *Bastards and Believers*, 25.

of any politics of identity, always transcending any fixed belonging.²⁴ The Marrano process of self-alienation or self-othering can thus be regarded as the precursorial canvas for the emergence of the modern self which cannot be captured in terms of a Western-Christian hegemony and precisely because of that can still be defended: *die freischwebende Subjektivität*, free-floating and oscillating between identities and thus gaining a space of existential and intellectual freedom which, according to Karl Mannheim, fostered the most vivid milieu of Western intelligentsia.²⁵ To individuate beyond the scope of identity, whether hegemonic or particular, or, as Harold Bloom calls it, deviating from the Party of Belonging, is originally – and historically – an experience of those Marranos who ventured into the uncharted territories of 'neither/nor'.²⁶ Derrida is thus an exemplary '*universal Marrano* [. . .] beyond what may nowadays be the finished forms of Marrano culture' (A, 74).²⁷

---

[24] Yovel begins his *Other Within* by declaring that he wants to tell the story of the Marranos, but also 'use it as a vehicle for a wider philosophical reflection' (OW, ix). He thus presents the Marranos the Spanish and Portuguese *conversos*, who nonetheless preserved (or were assumed to preserve) the elements of their hidden Jewish tradition, as the first modern subjects who lost solid footing in their traditions and thus became 'ineradicably other', not only to those who still enjoyed pre-modern fixed identities but also to themselves (OW, 58). Split in their identities and loyalties, the Marranos either 'confused the two rival religions' or 'became equally indifferent to both' (OW, 61), thus giving way to the two typically modern tendencies: the pursuit of idiosyncratic forms of religiosity mediating between Judaism and Christianity on the one hand, and the 'free-oscillating subjectivity' or a 'type that lives beyond the spheres of conventional belief and mentality' (OW, 61), which does not identify with any tradition, on the other. It is not surprising, therefore, that for Yovel, the most interesting contemporary representative of Marranism is Derrida, whose 'non-Jewish Jewishness', consciously turned into a universal condition, offers the split, non-integral, and unfinished identity as a paradigm of the modern subject which, precisely because of that, can only be described in terms of a meta-identitarian remnant: 'A modern Jewishness was created, one that is concerned with its new meaning and will not renounce it, even when incapable of defining it unequivocally. What could be more Marrano?' (OW, 366).

[25] See Karl Mannheim, *Ideology and Utopia: An Introduction into Sociology of Knowledge*, trans. Louis Wirth and Edward Shils (London: Routledge, 1936), 272. Yovel also uses the term 'free oscillation' in reference to the paradigmatic modern Marrano phenomenon, namely the 'free thinking'.

[26] See Harold Bloom, *Anxiety of Influence: A Theory of Poetry* (Oxford: Oxford University Press, 1997), 23.

[27] As I will try to prove in this book, Derrida's Marrano universalism constitutes a strongly polemical variant of the 'Converso Paulinism': simultaneously a continuation and a departure from the teachings of Saul/ Paul, the paradigmatic Jewish convert, with whom Derrida had been wrestling all his life, starting from a ready embrace during his Algerian childhood, when Paul would represent for him a fierce critic of Pharisaism: 'I used to think then that I was dealing with a Judaism of 'external signs' [. . .] I could not lose my temper, except from what was already an insidious Christian contamination: the respectful belief in inwardness, the preference for intention, the heart, the mind, mistrust with respect to literalness or to an objective action given to the mechanicity of the body, in short, a denunciation, so conventional, of Pharisaism [. . .] I was not the only one to be affected by this Christian "contamination." Social and religious behavior, even Jewish rituals themselves were tainted by them, in their tangible objectivity. The churches were being mimicked, the rabbi would wear a black cassock, and the verger [*chemasch*] a Napoleonic cocked hat; the "bar mitzvah" was called "communion," and circumcision was named "baptism"' (MO, 54). As Claude Stuczynski convincingly shows in his studies on 'Converso Paulinism', such penchant for internalization, which Derrida confesses to have felt in his early years, was typical for many generations of the Iberian Marranos who 'turned to Paul the Jew and the Apostle to the Gentiles for inspiration and legitimacy': Claude B. Stuczynski, 'Converso Paulinism and Residual Jewishness. Conversion from Judaism to Christianity as a Theologico-Political Problem', in *Bastards and Believers*, 133.

Perhaps, there is time for a little parallel 'confession' of the author: why does Derrida's project of Marrano universalism speak to me so strongly that I decided to write a whole book about it? I do not have Sephardic roots, but I am, paraphrasing Derrida, 'a sort of a *marrane* of the Polish Catholic culture', descending from the once-Jewish families, on both sides deeply assimilated into the lore of Central European intelligentsia. Michael Löwy created a beautiful portrait-tribute to the complex Judeity of this region – 'the Jewish cultural universe of *Mitteleuropa*' – in which Haskalah and Kabbalah coexisted in the one 'house of the tradition' whose walls were often shaken by an 'apocalyptic breeze', giving rise to messianic dreams of radical justice.[28] This unique mixture of Kabbalistic mystery, mediated by East-European Hassidism, on the one hand, and Western haskalic Enlightenment, on the other, produced within the most progressive branch of rabbinic Judaism, remained in the later generations of Jews who would assimilate to their host cultures, often after the conversion – usually Catholic, but also, even within Catholic cultures, Protestant (till today, the Evangelical cemetery in Warsaw holds a special section for the converted Varsovian Jews). My family was officially Catholic, but they would never go to church. Confessionally speaking, we were *nothing*: in the pre-war Poland, we passed for assimilated Jews who broke with Judaism, while in the post-war Communist Poland, we passed for atheists. But in fact, we all clang to this *void* – precisely as in Hélène Cixous's description of her Oran Marranism, where the members of her once-Jewish milieu get compared to Kafka's 'trapeze artist': 'The Jewish trapezists cling to the void. A community out of step with the times. One often spoke a rather elegant French, the language of the denied and oft-flattered enemy. Hebrew? So suppressed. At best one was at the Marrano stage but unaware of it' (PJD, 115). Just change the languages – French to Polish, spoken in my family with pristine elegance despite a complex *Hass-Liebe* relation to Poland herself, and Hebrew to Yiddish, occasionally surging in my grandparents' talk – and the portrait will be uncannily true. Yes, we were at the Marrano stage and even unaware of it. Yes, we were desperately clinging to the void – the precious *neither-nor* of *l'ailleurs* – while remembering without remembering our lost roots. And when she says, 'Imagine the enormous weight of the word Jew, the swelling, the erection of the word, sole survivor of an extinct verbal population' (PJD, 115), it is also a dead-ringer to the innumerable situations when the word 'Jew' would fall amidst the family conversation and immediately kill it, indeed as if there suddenly appeared among us a survivor, *homo sacer*, a taboo envoy from another, quite scary dimension, and a bit filthy to that. Just as Derrida, therefore, I can say that I have *always* regarded myself as a Marrano even if I could not name it – precisely because disorientation belongs to Marranism, this limbo of identities. Just as Derrida, I grew very tired – *marre* – of constantly feeling apologetic about my own Jewishness, even to the point of self-doubt; of convincing myself that I nonetheless *am* Jewish or, rather, *nonetheless-Jewish, after-all-Jewish*: the last and the least in the hierarchy of all the Jews in the world, who do not have to cling to the void and live happily outside the limbo. I grew *marre* of my

---

[28] Michael Löwy, *Redemption and Utopia: Jewish Libertarian Thought in Central Europe: A Study in Elective Affinity*, trans. Hope Heaney (London: Verso, 2017), 3.

semitismo atormentado and its trapezist schtücks of hanging in the empty air between the two pair of hands that tried to catch me from the two opposite ends: Judaism, which came back to Poland after 1989 and, by faithfully repeating the story of the Sephardic *conversos* who, once in Amsterdam, were offered a chance of *tshuva*, attracted many of my 'Marrano' friends – and Catholicism, the religion which I joined against my parents' wish and without their knowledge, at the tender age of seven, when holidaying in the Polish Highland. So, just as Derrida, I decided to treat the Marrano figure not as an affliction but as a redemption, not as a problem but as a solution: a promise of a *messianic reversal*, which always initially attaches itself to misery, tragedy, and unease. A hidden gem or a glowing cinder in the midst of ashes and ruins: commonly regarded as 'devious, illicit, illogical, immoral' (OW, 348) or, in Derrida's words, *voyou*, 'rogue', shady, and suspect. The historical Sephardic Marranos attempted such reversal few times, particularly within the Sabbatian movement, and the Polish Marranos can also call upon the antinomian doctrine of the Frankists, which advocated a 'secret mission' of the Jews converted to Catholicism. If there ever was a true *voyou*: a tragico-comical messianic hooligan calling himself 'a sort of Marrano of the Polish Catholic culture', it was definitely Jacob Frank to whom, as I will try to show, Derrida shows some resemblance as, in David Farrell Krell felicitous coinage, 'the purest of bastards'. Would it be possible, then, to retrieve such reversal in order to defend the diasporic Marrano culture as a separate Jewish non-identity, no to be immediately compared – and dwarfed in comparison – to the more 'legitimate' forms of Jewishness? Could Derrida be our new Marrano Moses, who one day will get us out of the Egypt of our inferiority complex? A prophet of a *Marrano Exodus*?

The messianic reversal is not a Marrano invention. It is a jewel in the crown of the long series of 'normative inversions' which constituted Judaism as the site of radical transvaluation of the so-called pagan world: from nature to history, from immanence to transcendence, from tragedy, which always repeats the same cycle of daring and defeat, to messianic hope which promises a future.[29] The mechanism of these reversals closely resembles Freud's *Durcharbeiten*: working through the trauma – of exclusion, failure, tragic loss – in such a way that the initially banned 'rejected stone' becomes a founding moment of a new narrative. 'To turn' in Hebrew is *shuv* (שוב) and the word usually connotating conversion/return to Judaism – *tshuva* – is based on this verb. And although Derrida would never call himself *baal tshuva* – the one who returns to Judaism – he nonetheless uses the figure of 'turning around': a complex, partly apotropaic, operation of return to his Jewish origins with resistance. In conversation

---

[29] In *Moses the Egyptian*, Jan Assmann describes the originis of Judaism as the most spectacular case of 'the principle of normative inversion, prescribing all that is forbidden in Egypt and forbidding all that is prescribed there [...] *The principle of normative inversion consists in inverting the abominations of the other culture into obligations and vice versa* [. . .] The principle of normative inversion or the construction of cultural otherness is obviously working retroactively too. Starting from a given order, it imagines a culture based upon the inverted mirror image of that order and, by this very procedure of retrospective inversion, turns the past into "a foreign country"': Jan Assmann, *Moses the Egyptian: The Memory of Egypt in Western Monotheism* (Cambridge, MA: Harvard University Press, 1997), 31; 67; emphasis added.

with Elisabeth Weber, Derrida, while alluding to the wound of circumcision, describes his variant of *tshuva* as a paradox signifying 'obsession but also avoidance':

> As if you couldn't detach yourself from what obsesses and, at the same time, as if you were avoiding getting too close; there is thus a contradiction in turning around, in the two senses of this expression; and above all in turning around something that remains a wound: that has taken place, that has already taken place inside the body. And how can you turn around a wound which in one way is your own? From a topological point of view, this already resembles the logical game of an impossible geometry: you can't turn around your wound. A wound has already taken place that marks an incision in the body; it forbids you this distance or this play which consists in turning around. The game is no longer possible. And yet this hopeless challenge – that's what it is, in fact – which takes the form of an unbelievable topology or phoronomy, of an impossible displacement, perhaps engages precisely what is going on, at any rate what describes the figure, very difficult to represent, for me as much as anyone, of my experience or the experience of my relationship to [. . .] I don't venture to say Judaism – let's say, to circumcision. (TG, 40)

'This hopeless challenge' is met by Derrida's Marrano 'serious play' which introduces distance and a potentiality of reversal where the game no longer seemed possible. While nothing can 'turn around' the very fact of circumcision, the play of *shuv* can nonetheless displace the idea of the wound into a centre of Derrida's imaginative auto-fiction of the last and the first of Jews, which turns the *blessure* into a *blessing*.[30] The inversion of the Marrano attribution – from the tragic indictment to the potentially messianic chance – is, therefore, the paradigmatic case of the inversion which Derrida sees as the necessary moment of deconstruction: 'deconstruction includes an indispensable phase of reversal' (DIS, 5–6). While it may be seen, in Catherine Malabou words, as a catastrophe in the sense of 'upset, the tragic and unforeseeable event that brings about the ruin of the established order', it can also be treated as a 'surprise [that] interrupts the teleological trajectory' (CP-M, 4). The deconstructive turn, deriving from the Greek *strephein*, aims at the inner transformation of the catastrophic event, conceived as a tragic downfall, into a messianic *Umkehr*: 'Derrida's whole work produces the catastrophe, that is to say, the reversal, of this [tragic] catastrophe' (CP-M, 8). Perhaps it would be even more apt to name this particular reversal a *Marrano trope*, where *tropos* means precisely a 'turn' but also implies a distance in which the new meaning travels away from its origins. 'Tropes are tours, changes of place, from somewhere to somewhere else: displacement, voyage, transfer or transposition', says Derrida in

---

[30] In the foreword to Hélène Cixous's collection of stories, called *Stigmata*, Derrida praises it as a 'sublimity of a book in twelve songs on the wound [*blessure*]. I hear it as a *blessing of the blessure*, a great poetic treatise on the scar at the origin of literary writing – and no doubt of all writing': Jacques Derrida, 'Foreword to Helene Cixous's *Stigmata*', in Hélène Cixous, *Stigmata*, trans. Eric Prenowitz (London: Routledge, 1998), ix; emphasis added.

'Faxitexture',[31] and this 'rhetoric of travel' (CP-M, 193) fits the Marrano condition perfectly well. Malabou calls it rightly a 'metaphoric catastrophe' – a drift of meaning which cannot be 'driven back to the garage of literal sense, for it to be moored to the shore of a circular Odyssey' (CP-M, 210). This 'failure of any anchor' (CP-M, 210), most tangible in the Marrano case, turns the metaphoric catastrophe into a *catachresis*: a trope that can never go back to its for ever-lost origins. The 'impossible displacement' Derrida is looking for is thus to be found in the Marrano *tropos* which is simultaneously apotropaic and catachrestic towards his lost Judaism.[32]

Quite a lot has been said on Derrida's Jewishness, but very little on this specific variant of Jewishness – or rather no-longer-Jewishness – which he himself identified as *marrane*. Alluding to the catastrophic fate of those Spanish and Portuguese Jews who were forced to convert to Christianity but nonetheless kept some elements of their old faith undercover, Derrida's *circumfession* joins the Marranos in their troubled relationship with Judaism. Those who wrote on Derrida's Jewishness tend to present it indeed as a *trouble*: Susan Handelman as a trouble for the orthodox rabbinic Judaism, at whose fringe she locates his semi-religious heresy;[33] John D. Caputo as a trouble for Derrida's interpreters, lost in his aporetic 'being Jewish without being Jewish';[34] and Gideon Ofrat as a trouble mostly for Derrida himself with which he had to tarry all his life.

Especially to the latter, Derrida appears to be encumbered by an unresolved nostalgic burden which he himself captured in the pun of *nostalgeria*. According to Ofrat, he is 'bearing the bundle of a different Judaism' (JD, 21) as if it were a cross; he is a 'Jew whose crucifixion is relentless and lifelong', entailing no 'redemptive intellectual elevation', but instead 'condemned to ashes, to absence, to memory, to mourning, to death, without the Hegelian phoenix of intellect to rise reborn from its debris' (JD, 3). Cut off from the origin to which he cannot return, Derrida perceives his Jewishness as a dead remnant, a necrotic bone, a lethal wound, and a curtailing 'injury' (*coupure*). His 'dead Judaism' is the one of 'relics' (JD, 12), which underwrites his project of deconstruction with dark nostalgic tones of eternal *galut*, exile. When Derrida exclaims, 'Of course, I am Jewish!' and immediately, 'Of course, I am not

---

[31] Jacques Derrida, 'Faxitexture', trans. Laura Bourland, in *Anywhere*, ed. Cynthia Davidson (New York: Rizzoli International Publications, 2015).

[32] Derrida's Marrano non/identification must thus be read as *simultaneously* tropic and apotropaic, as much a circumfession as a denial of any confessional form of Judaism – a warning very aptly formulated by Geoffrey Bennington who cautions against analysing the Marrano trope as something that 'might seem to add weight to the arguments of those who have always striven to *identify the Jew in Derrida* (to the point of claiming improbably that *Glas* looks like the Talmud), and even to add an infinite weight, given that the logic of the marrano [...] is such that it makes of the truest Jew the most secret Jew, and thus turns the inaccessible secret itself into an *infallible mark of identification and belonging*' (MARS, 154; emphasis added). While I do not find anything too improbable in seeing *Glas* as a modernist variant of the Talmudic hypertext, I indeed agree with Bennington that the Marrano trope in Derrida is not about a secret 'Jewish identification': it is rather about a secret non-identification which, paradoxically, lies at the core of being Jewish.

[33] See Susan A. Handelman, *The Slayers of Moses: The Emergence of Rabbinic Interpretation in Modern Literary Theory* (Albany: SUNY Press, 1982).

[34] John D. Caputo, *The Prayers and Tears of Jacques Derrida: Religion without Religion* (Bloomington: Indiana University Press, 1997), xvii.

Jewish!' (TG, 42), it thus spells an inevitable 'rupture': a blockage of an insoluble aporia and its purely negative imagery of something deadening, paralyzing, and life-draining. For Ofrat, Derrida's theo-biographical contradiction is lived through one unending mourning day of *Yom Coupure* in which he darkly celebrates his being for ever cut off from the life-giving roots and withers away *bamidbar*, in the desert of eternal errance.

But would it be possible to look at Derrida's Marrano declaration in a different way, without presupposing all these negative connotations? Such an attempt has been undertaken by Sarah Hammerschlag in *The Figural Jew*, who claims that Derrida 'uses his own problematic relationship to Judaism to cultivate a discourse of being Jewish that capitalizes on its ambiguities and contradictions in the service of a political end' and then defines this end as the deconstruction which 'calls into question both a particularist politics of identity and a discourse of political universalism or humanism.'[35] In what follows, I would like to expand this more affirmative approach and offer a reading of Derrida's Marranism as a formula which allows to transcend the initial aporia of the two apparently contrary self-diagnoses – being and simultaneously not being a Jew – and establish a new quality of non/identification. I intend to prove that Derrida's Marranism, far from being a nostalgic variation on the 'deadness of tradition', demonstrates a peculiar *hidden* form of life: restless, capricious, mercurial, and precisely because of that – *life*.[36] For Derrida, Marranism is not the last resort option or an expression of helplessness in face of his 'nostalgerian' aporia: it is a desired, deliberately chosen, secret name. As he himself admits, he represents the 'death of Judaism, but also its *one* chance of survival' (TG, 42). Perhaps, just one of many and not the only one possible, but, still, a chance which cannot be overlooked. The diasporic mixed identity, which accepts the Marrano as a 'paradoxical opportunity' (MO, 53), takes this chance to turn itself into a last – but not necessarily least – variant of modern Jewishness.[37]

---

[35] Sarah Hammerschlag, *The Figural Jew: Politics and Identity in the Postwar French Thought* (Chicago: Chicago University Press, 2010), 205. Hammerschlag rightly notices that Derrida 'sees being Jewish as a key site and the source for deconstruction itself' (ibid.), a diagnosis fully confirmed by Derrida himself: 'Being-Jewish would be more than and other than the simple strategic or methodological lever of a general deconstruction, it would be the experience of deconstruction itself, its chance, its menace, its destiny, its earthquake' (AO, 29).

[36] Derrida's interest in the hidden life of the seemingly lost God has been well spotted by Caputo in his recent eulogy, where he praises Derrida for his 'deferred and deferential "atheism"', or atheism-with-a-*différance*: 'His devilish intervention upon theology occurs at a strategic point, conjuring up the specter of God, the peculiar, spectral and powerful way God lives on after the death of God. *Nothing is ever simply dead.* He feels about in the dark for the traces of an almost atheistic, almost Augustinian, almost Jewish covenant with the impossible, poking about like a blind man with a stick, or like a devilish knight of faith strolling the streets of Laguna Beach, the Left Bank or Greenwich Village': John D. Caputo, 'Like a Devilish Knight of Faith', *Oxford Literary Review* 36, no. 2 (2014): 189, emphasis added.

[37] Only Hélène Cixous goes as far as to attribute to Derrida an open and strong '*desire* to be a Marrano' which she, in 'This Stranjew Body', compares to the Kafkan desire to be an Indian, a dream-wish of unconstrained freedom and a happy, liberated life. According to Cixous, Derrida 'marranates himself' in his 'Jewfeint' mode: 'norcatholic norjew midjew midsame midindian midhorse' (TSB, 55). On Derrida's Marranism, apart from Sarah Hammerschlag's already cited *The Figural Jew*, see also the two essays: Yvonne Sherwood, 'Specters of Abraham', and Urszula Idziak-Smoczyńska, 'Deconstruction between Judaism and Christianity', in *Judaism in Contemporary Thought: Traces and Influence*, ed. Agata Bielik-Robson and Adam Lipszyc (London: Routledge, 2014), as well as my *Jewish Cryptotheologies of Late Modernity: Philosophical Marranos* (London: Routledge, 2014), especially the introduction.

The whole point here is to see the possibility of the affirmative reversal within the Marrano predicament which prima facie appears only tragic: the forced conversion (which Derrida obviously would never endorse) contains nonetheless a fruitful paradox that, according to Derrida, reveals a universal claim to otherness and non-belonging as the essential feature of being a Jew. In the late speech, 'Another Abraham', Derrida states that 'what one calls the Jew' is

> the exemplary figure of a universal structure of the living human, to wit, this being originally indebted, responsible, guilty. As if election or counter-election consisted in having been chosen as guardian of a truth, a law, an essence, in truth here, of a *universal responsibility*. The more jewish the Jew [*plus le Juif est juif*], the more he would represent the universality of human responsibility for man, and the more he would have to respond to it, to answer for it. (AO, 12)[38]

For Derrida, the particularity of election – the chosenness of Jewish people – can only mean one thing: the exemplarity which makes the Jewish calling even more universal, that is, representing the 'universal responsibility' of *any* 'living human'. In his commentary on Derrida's conjunction of election and exemplarity, Elliot Wolfson writes:

> Derrida promptly notes the paradoxical logic that proceeds from arguing that the particularity of Jewish election entails the universal: self-identity 'consists in not being identical to myself, in being foreign,' and hence 'the less you are Jewish, the more you are Jewish.' The Jew, in a word, personifies the 'identity as non-self-identity'. This leads Derrida to draw the following startling, and counterintuitive, conclusion: 'Jews who base their Jewishness on an actual circumcision, a Jewish name, a Jewish birth, a land, a Jewish soil, etc. – they would by definition be no better placed than others for speaking in the name of Judaism' (TG, 41). Jews are coerced to affirm simultaneously that they are Jewish and not Jewish, for the otherness of the Jew perforce must comprise its own other, the universal that exceeds the particular in which it is contained. It is in this spirit that Derrida recalls the statement from *Circonfession* that he is the 'last of the Jews' ... inasmuch as he discerns that his identity as a Jew entails not knowing exactly what it is to be authentically Jewish, that he belongs to Jewish culture by essentially 'not belonging.'[39]

For Wolfson, who summarizes Derrida's reflections on exemplarity with absolute precision, their conclusion seems nonetheless 'startling and counterintuitive'; it somehow does not ring right. Thus, when Derrida once again insists on the essentially

---

[38] See also: 'I am testifying to the humanity of human beings, to universality, to responsibility for universality' (TG, 41).
[39] Elliot Wolfson, *Giving Beyond the Gift: Apophasis and Overcoming Theomania* (New York: Fordham University Press, 2014), 164.

split nature of Jewish exemplarity, which paradoxically joins the particular and the universal – 'The Jew is also the other, myself and the other; I am Jewish in saying: the Jew is the other who has no essence, who has nothing of his own or whose own essence is not to have one' (SQ, 54)⁴⁰ – Wolfson comments with some degree of sarcasm: 'that is, he can remain within Judaism only by abandoning it. In this sense, Christ could be considered prototypically the last of the Jews [. . .] the effort to emancipate himself from the dogma of revelation and of election can be interpreted as the very content of these dogma.'⁴¹ But, why not? What if *betrayal* – the emancipation from the identitarian dogma of the 'chosen people' – indeed belongs to the very heart of the aporetic Jewish (non)identity? And what if the diasporic situation, which enhances 'the otherness of the Jew', makes her better aware of 'her own other, the universal that exceeds the particular in which it is contained'?⁴² If so, then the 'universal Marrano' or 'Marrano's Marrano', with whom Derrida (non)-identifies according to the logic of the remnant, would be the uncanny secret mirror of all of us. He wants to keep this mirror

---

⁴⁰ Comp. also 'Edmond Jabes and The Question of the Book': 'The Jew is but a suffering allegory [. . .] Jew's identification within himself does not exist. The Jew is split, and split first of all between the two dimensions of the letter: allegory and literality. His history would be but one empirical history among others if he established or nationalized himself within difference and literality. He would have not history at all if he let himself be attenuated within the algebra of an abstract universalism' (WD, 92). According to Steven Jaron, 'Jabès sensed himself outside the Jewish tradition yet, in a strange and undefined way, profoundly attached to it. Again, Derrida was among the first to write about the problem', but it took him more than three decades to formulate the dilemma of *non-appartenance* in the Marrano terms: Steven Jaron, *Edmond Jabès: The Hazard of Exile* (Oxford: Oxford University Press, 2003), 10. Indeed, the dilemma of the split self comes to the fore very strongly in Derrida's penultimate seminar, where it is represented by Montaigne: 'I no longer know where Montaigne said the following or what it concerned, but I know it by heart: "We are, I know not how, double within ourselves, with the result that we do not believe what we believe"' (DP 2, 68). For Derrida, Michel de Montaigne is a paradigmatic Marrano: 'Montaigne [. . .] whose wily and enigmatic hand-to-hand combat with Christianity, or even with the Marrano Judaism that haunted his filiation on the side of his mother' (DP1, 276).

⁴¹ Ibid., 165.

⁴² Ibid., 164. See Hammerschlag's comment: 'This possibility is best represented for Derrida by the figure of the Marrano, for the Marrano represents the possibility of responding to election in such a way that the claim to election is undone by its disavowal. To be a Marrano is, for Derrida, an *intensification of what it is to be a Jew*, or at least it is as an intensification of the dynamic of deracination, appearing as a form of betrayal or breach of contract *parjure*': Hammerschlag, *The Figural Jew*, 245; emphasis added. This once again brings associations with Derrida's complex relationship with Paul who can also be seen as a borderline figure who intensifies Judaism by breaking with Judaism: 'the last of the Jews' and not-yet-Christian – precisely the way he is presented by Daniel Boyarin: 'Paul lived and died convinced that he was a Jew living out Judaism [. . .] The very tension in his discourse, indeed in his life, between powerful self-identification as a Jew [. . .] and an equally powerful, or even more powerful, identification of self as everyman is emblematic of Jewish selfhood': *A Radical Jew: Paul and the Politics of Identity* (Berkeley: University of California Press, 1994), 4. The affinity with Paul comes to the fore also in Colby Dickinson's commentary on Derrida's Marrano declaration, which he calls an *as-if-Judaism* – a variation on the Pauline motif of *hos me* as seen via Agambenian lenses: 'And perhaps this is to live 'as if' he were not jewish in order to become *more* jewish [. . .] In this sense, living 'as if' he were not jewish would certainly seem to be a most faithful approximation to the Abrahamic core of Judaism. It would also, perhaps, bear a certain affinity with those readings of Paul and the nature of the "as not" which seemed to condition his decisions to live as a Jew to the Jew and as a Gentile to the Gentile, "as if" he were both, or neither': Colby Dickinson, 'The Logic of the 'As If' and the Existence of God: An Inquiry into the Nature of Belief in the Work of Jacques Derrida', *Derrida Today* 4, no. 1 (2011): 12.

constantly before our eyes, so that we do not fall again and again into the dogmatic slumber of identitarian closures.

The metaphysics of non-identity

Despite Derrida's claim to be a 'lay Marrano', his circonfession harbours a deeper, cryptotheological, dimension. Just as 'the desire to be Marrano', which Cixous attributes to Derrida (TSB, 56), indicates a liberty to jump fences of particular identities, it also expresses a desire to engage in religious thinking which would not be bound by the dogmas of any orthodoxy. More than that, as a truly liberated, or, as Löwy would have called it, *libertarian* theological speculation, it goes against the rigid law of the tradition – and becomes *antinomian*. The link between Marranism and antinomianism is not gratuitous. The scholar who demonstrated with a mathematical precision the deep connection between the two was Gershom Scholem: the fascination with which so many twentieth-century diasporic Jews approached the 'Marrano theology' as a living hypothesis is mostly indebted to his *not* purely historical work devoted to present it as a still actual phenomenon within the Jewish world. Thanks to Scholem, the Marrano idea acquired a rich symbolic potential, linked to the messianic ferment of the Sabbatians who, as Scholem has shown, were in large number Marranos. The most famous of them, Abraham Miguel Cardoso, wrote an entire treatise, *Magen Abraham* (*The Shield of Abraham*), devoted to the messianic significance of Marranism, in which the seeming vice of secrecy cunningly turned into a virtue of deeper truth. For, says Cardoso, the true faith can *only* be hidden – and Scholem repeats the same esoteric truth with full conviction few centuries later.

Derrida's Marrano intuition that the spectral 'truth of the tradition' may lie deeper and even at odds with the 'chain of the tradition', transmitted from generation to generation through the overt Teaching, was indeed first articulated by Scholem who, in his *Ten Unhistorical Aphorisms on Kabbalah*, composed in the 1940s, plays on the ambivalence of the Latin verb *tradere* (meaning 'to pass on', but also 'to betray') and insists on the difference between *Tradition* in its 'truth' and *Tradierbarkeit* as that which can be transmitted (*tradendum*):

> The kabbalist claims that there is a tradition (*Tradition*) of truth which can be handed over (*tradierbar*). This is a very ironic claim since the truth, of which it speaks, is anything but capable of being handed over (*tradierbar*). The truth can become known but not passed on, *for precisely in what can be passed on, the truth is no longer*. The authentic tradition remains hidden; the falling tradition stumbles upon an object and shows its greatness only in the fact that it falls.[43]

---

[43] Gershom Scholem, 'Zehn Unhistorische Sätze über Kabbalah', in Gershom Scholem, *Judaica 3: Studien zur jüdischen Mystik* (Frankfurt am Main: Suhrkamp Verlag, 1973), 264; emphasis added.

This is not as heterodox as it might seem *prima facie*. The potential contrast between the tradition as transmissibility and the tradition as the hidden truth comes to the fore already in the opening sentence of *Pirke Avoth*, the wisdom of the founding fathers of Talmud: 'Moses received the Torah from Sinai and transmitted it to Joshua. Joshua transmitted it to the Elders, the Elders to the Prophets, and the Prophets transmitted it to the Men of the Great Assembly. They said three things: *Be deliberate in judgment, raise many students, and make a protective fence for the Torah.*' Scholem makes this contrast explicit, by charging the chain of tradition, conceived as *Tradierbarkeit*-transmissibility, with the role of building a 'shell' that would guard the 'kernel' as *das Wahre* of the tradition and simultaneously guard its disciples from the overexposure to the hidden truth. 'The truth can become known but not passed on', because it cannot be communicated. The revelation establishes a unique, each time singular relation between the radical divine transcendence and the equally radical inwardness of the self, which mirrors the former in a sort of a concave *tselem*/likeness – and, as such, cannot be translated into the horizontal message handed over by the 'chain of tradition' (*shalshelet ka-kabbalah*) in which every singular *tselem* becomes merely a ring sustaining the strength of cultural identity. Yet, at the same time, one cannot rest for ever in the eternal 'elsewhere' (*l'ailleurs*) of the revelatory relation which bypasses the world and endangers the self with mystical annihilation: even if *Tradierbarkeit* distorts the singular truth, one is not allowed to desist from the dialectical work of lessening the betrayal, nonetheless always present in the very act of *tradere*. The truth is most precious, but it is also most dangerous: this is a necessary double bind of every 'authentic tradition'. The tradition shows its greatness precisely when it falls, that is, reveals its inner aporia: it stumbles upon the 'object' which is the hidden truth and in this manner shows that it exists precisely as limping, hindered by the antinomian 'kernel' that cannot be fully assimilated by the 'shell' of the Teaching-*tradendum*. The word 'object', seemingly strange in the context of the mystical singular encounter between the *Ehad* and its *tselem*, is, in fact, well chosen. As we shall yet see, the Scholemian 'object' stands for the Derridean 'inhabitant of the crypt': the secret spark surrounded by the shards of the worldly discourse which can never capture 'the Thing' in its categories. The resisting 'object' is thus carried by the tradition which inevitably betrays its 'object': already Judaism is cryptophoric and *marranismo* even more so.

But if the authentic tradition must remain hidden, then the only way to keep it that way is *silence*. Not any 'uncharacteristic silence', as Harold Bloom perceptively notices in his essay on the Scholem Non-Historian,[44] but a very specific one which has only one equivalent-precursor: the Marrano *silenzio*. Scholem's silence is indeed anything but 'uncharacteristic': for him, it is a *via negativa* through which tradition must pass in order to renew itself. The silence, which points to the 'hidden truth,' designates a crisis in the Höderlinian antinomian understanding of the term, that is, the point of risky intersection between *das Gefährlichste* and *das Rettende*, the highest

---

[44] Harold Bloom, 'Scholem: Unhistorical or Jewish Gnosticism', in Harold Bloom, *The Strong Light of the Canonical: Kafka, Freud and Scholem as Revisionists of Jewish Culture and Thought* (New York: The City College Papers, No. 20, 1987), 55.

danger, in which the tradition 'falls,' by approaching destruction in a total oblivion, and the chance of salvation when it rises again as a Phoenix from the ashes: a 'fine line between religion and nihilism'.[45] Himself a 'product of the purgatory of assimilation and secularization',[46] Scholem, via his highly characteristic 'Hebrew silence', attempts to purge and thus renew the tradition by putting it to the same ordeal: he will try to find the 'hidden truth' which resists the transmission chain of 'what can be handed over' in the near-death experience of the disappearing *tradendum* of traditional Judaism. For, if the relation between the truth and the transmission is as aporetic as he suggests in his Kabbalistic thesis, then the 'sickening of the tradition' conceived as *Tradierbarkeit* makes it possible to reveal 'what cannot be passed on', but what this tradition still contains as its non-transmittable kernel.[47]

Already in his diaries from 1918, when he is only 21, Scholem obliquely refers to the 'Marrano experience' in which he himself participates as a member of the half-assimilated 'tormented Jewry'. While sketching an imaginary portrait of an ideal adept of the Jewish tradition as the one 'who could be silent in Hebrew', *wer Hebräisch schweigen kann*, he writes:

> Hebrew must be the superlative of the Teaching's silence. The person able to be silent in Hebrew surely partakes in the quiet life of youth. There is no one among us who can do this. We cannot use our existence as an argument precisely because silence, or more accurately stillness *die Stille*, is the step in which *a life can become an argument*.[48]

If one were to interpret this fragment as a Marrano allusion, the silence and the stillness would address the famous *silenzio* of the Iberian *conversos*, which designates the Marrano secret, but also an *amidah*: a silent prayer preserved and transformed in the new-Christian context as 'being silent in Hebrew' that contemplates the divine mysteries without mediation of treacherous words, precisely as in the case of the Marrano mystics, John of the Cross and Teresa of Avila, so well described by Michel

---

[45] Scholem, 'Zehn Unhistorische Sätze', 271.
[46] As Paul Mendes-Flohr characterizes both Scholem and Benjamin in 'The Spiritual Quest of the Philologist', in *Gershom Scholem: The Man and His Work* (Albany, NY: SUNY Press, 1997), 14.
[47] The secret hope for the renewal of the Jewish tradition *ex nihilo* of its 'sickened' exilic form, harboured by young Scholem, was also noticed by Amir Engel who, while commenting on Scholem's diary entries dating as early as 1914, writes that he 'yearned for the transformation of exilic culture into a source from which social harmony, spiritual renewal, and political autonomy might spring': Amir Engel, *Gershom Scholem: An Intellectual Biography* (Chicago: University of Chicago Press, 2017), 54. The term 'sickened tradition' derives from Benjamin's interpretation of Franz Kafka, as well as the division between the truth and the *tradendum*/doctrine: 'Kafka's work represents a sickening of tradition': Walter Benjamin, *Selected Writings*, vol. 3, ed. Michael W. Jennings (Cambridge, MA: Harvard University Press, 2006), 326.
[48] Entry from 1 April 1918: Gershom Scholem, *Lamentations of Youth: The Diaries of Gershom Scholem, 1913–1919*, ed. and trans., Anthony David Skinner (Cambridge, MA: Belknap Press of Harvard University Press, 2008), 219.

de Certeau in *La fable mystique*.⁴⁹ This heavy eloquent silence wandered also into the teachings of the Polish Frankists who spoke about the 'burden of silence' (*m'as duma*). But what makes Scholem's remark truly intriguing is the link between *silenzio* and *life*: a mysterious connection in which 'life can become an argument.' This line is a polemical cryptoquote from Nietzsche's *Gay Science*, where he says: 'That lies should be necessary to life is part and parcel of the terrible and questionable character of life [. . .] Life is no argument.'⁵⁰ According to Nietzsche, the fact that we live and want to live on does not magically transform all the lies we applied to make the world liveable into a truth. But, really – doesn't it? On Scholem's account, the Zionist youngster as the perfect adept of Judaism should be able to do precisely that: turn life into an argument which would speak for the *verification* of all the ruses used by life in order to secure a further survival. Life made into argument would thus be a positive result of an implication which has a power to *verify* – literally, make-true – even the falsest of premises: whatever cunning, evasion, ruse life resorts to would become true if it results in the 'blessing of more life'. Would it be far-fetched to treat it as an oblique hint to the Marrano condition of someone forced to lie, perjure, and betray in order to survive? Perhaps not at all. Perhaps, young Scholem, who very early on senses the affinity between the 17ᵗʰ century *converso* experience of the Iberian Penninsula and the 19ᵗʰ century assimilation of German Jewry, secretly identifies with a metaphorical Marrano: he lives, he survived, he has broken with the tradition which he preserves only in *silenzio*, 'being-silent-in-Hebrew', yet he refuses to feel guilty and 'tormented' about it, even if he also immediately admits that no one he knows is actually capable of such daring act of liberation. In his dream, his life becomes an argument – and this 'step' inaugurates an *inversion*: from the tragic predicament of the victims of coercion to the messianic hope of the 'rejected stones', promising a radical and innovative reversal of the perspective. Perhaps, Scholem suggests here that the Marranos, for whom life as such indeed became a serious argument, broke with the overt tradition in order to survive – yet did not break with the 'truth of the tradition' and its promise of more life, which can only stay 'hidden', *verborgen*, and thus kept in silence. For, 'Life can become an argument' chimes here with the divine imperative, *ubaharta bahayim* – 'Choose life!' (Deut. 30.18) – the only open articulation that alludes to the secret truth and trumps every choice of death, including the glorious martyrological death

---

49 '... the silent inner prayer of the *Alumbrados dexados* also reflects a common attitude among crypto-Jewish conversos. In Judaism the *Amidah* prayer is of precisely this silent, contemplative type; but silence had more special meanings for conversos. Once Jews converted, they no longer had the freedom to express out loud Jewish views they might still have held': Matt Goldish, 'Patterns in Converso Messianism', in *Millenarianism and Messianism in Early Modern European Culture: Jewish Messianism in the Early Modern World*, eds. M. Goldish and R. H. Popkin (The Haague: Kluwer Academic Publishers, 2001), 51.

50 See the aphorism no 121 of *Gay Science*, titled 'Life no Argument', where Nietzsche dismisses the livable arrangement of the world as nothing but a necessary vital lie: 'We have arranged for ourselves a world in which we can live – by positing bodies, lines, planes, causes and effects, motion and rest, form and content; without these articles of faith nobody now could endure life. But that does not prove them. Life is no argument. The conditions of life might include error': Friedrich Nietzsche, *Gay Science*, trans. Josefine Nauckhoff (Cambridge: Cambridge University Press, 2001), 180.

as an expression of faithfulness to the tradition. *Silenzio*, therefore, marks the break with tradition as *Tradierbarkeit*, but keeps faithful to the tradition as its hidden truth, *Wahrheit*. Marranos, choosing to live on, merely broke free from the 'chain of tradition' (*shalshelet ha-kabbalah*), unfettered themselves from the obligation to trasmit the Teaching overtly – but did not break with the secret core of this Teaching, which they continue in 'the superlative of the Teaching's silence'. Against Nietzsche's debunking of life as a web of lies, Scholem would thus claim that the authentic hidden Jewish tradition chooses life as the strongest possible argument: stronger than death, either inflicted or honourable. Life as survival, finding expression in the *Hebräisches Schweigen* – a silent prayer worshipping God in the desert of exile[51] – would be the secret treasure as well as the kernel of Judaism as a messianic revelation. And yet, Scholem insists that 'there is no one among us who can do this': the sense of guilt prevails, by preventing life from becoming an argument and thus enabling a messianic inversion. Survival – the 'quiet life of the youth' which takes life for granted and does not feel guilty about being alive – this most despised 'rejected stone' should – can – become a foundation of the tradition once again renewed in the repeated revelation of its hidden truth.

But Scholem's true adventure with the Marrano theology begins only in 1927, when he incidentally discovers Abraham Miguel Cardoso's treaties dealing with what he would interpret as *die Theologie des Hasards*, the risky messianic theology walking a 'thin line between religion and nihilism'; as David Biale suggests, this will trigger his lifelong interest in the Sabbatian movement.[52] It is indeed in the Marrano-Kabbalistic-Sabbatian syncretism of Cardoso that Scholem will have found the confirmation of his choice 'to keep silent in Hebrew': only what is concealed can be an authentic faith; what becomes positively revealed is nothing but an official religion of 'what can merely be handed over'. Hence, the real faith needs to protect its subversive-antinomian character by avoiding open pronouncement and articulation. Cardoso, having already

---

[51] Comp. Exodus 7.16: 'Then say to him, "The Lord, the God of the Hebrews, has sent me to say to you: Let my people go, so that they may worship me in the wilderness."'

[52] In Biale's opinion, young Scholem begins working on Sabbatianism in 1927, when he finds in the Oxford library a manuscript of Cardoso's authorship: David Biale, *Gershom Scholem: Master of Kabbalah* (New Haven: Yale University Press, 2018), 78. The Cardoso trigger is far from accidental. While Scholem had read about Sabbatai Tsevi before, it was only Abraham Cardoso who awakened in him a sense of historical analogy between the mass conversion of first, the Iberian, and then Turkish Jews to their respective hegemonic religions, Catholicism and Islam, and the situation of assimilated German Jewry: 'the new inner-outer dichotomy led to the splitting of identity into the private and public compartments characteristic of modern Judaism' (ibid., 84). Scholem himself confirms this analogy while commenting on Cardoso's 'hazard theology' (*Theologie des Hasards*), which openly plays with the risks caused by the crisis of tradition: 'Before the powers of the world history led to the massive uprooting of Judaism in the 19th century, its reality became questioned from the inside before. Already at the time of the Sabbatians, the whole "reality of the Hebrews" was threatened to become an illusion': Gershom Scholem, 'Die Theologie des Sabbatianismus im Lichte Abraham Cardosos', in *Judaica 1* (Suhrkamp: Frankfurt am Main, 1997), 142. According to Biale, the Marrano cataclysmic experience, the consequences of which he saw for the first time in Cardoso's system, influenced Scholem's thinking about the whole *kitvei Ari*: 'The Lurianic Kabbalah taught that the cosmos started with the self-expulsion of God; the world could only be created in the empty space from which God was absent. Luria's myth of creation thus involved a catastrophe of divine exile. God not only reveals himself; he also hides himself. This paradoxical theology could not have arisen, in Scholem's view, without the catastrophe of 1492': Biale, *Gershom Scholem*, 114.

experienced the Marrano apostasy, is far from being shocked when it is committed by Sabbatai Tsevi, who, under the duress, converts to Islam. He is already prepared to interpret the Messiah's apostasy as an act of free will, demonstrating that only a 'hidden faith' can be genuine: inner, unconcerned, and unhindered by official norms and religious institutions which can be exchanged like garments, with no concern for the secret kernel of the messianic faith. Scholem writes: 'For Cardoso the apostasy of the Messiah represented a kind of highest justification of the apostasy of the Spanish Marranos in 1391 and 1492'[53] – and vice versa: the Marrano theology had grown 'in silence' for the two centuries in order to deliver the scheme of the antinomian reversal according to which only a *converso* could become a Messiah.

According to Cardoso, Marranos are the true chosen people – 'the band of survivors' constituting 'the righteous remnant of the true Israel' (Isa. 37.32) – destined to save the world and spread the divine message of *u-baharta ba-hayim* (choose to live) through all the nations, by subverting their pagan institutions from within. Sabbatai, therefore, not only followed the way of those reflexive Marranos but also justified it and showed its deeper spiritual meaning; now, to convert to Christianity or Islam meant to be able to expand the messianic practice of 'lifting the sparks' from the realm of *kelipot*, the 'broken vessels', and to penetrate the darkest regions of the created world (such as Islam or the Roman-Catholic 'Edom', as it will be the case with the Polish Frankists[54]). To choose faith in a hidden way meant a deliberate effort to keep the antinomian impulse opposed to all the oppressive laws of this world, both secular and religious, from contamination with a fallen reality; to maintain it in the Derridean form of a hovering 'spectre', distanced from any direct positive realization or 'what can be handed over'. It is precisely here, in Cardoso's Marrano theology, that the 'hidden tradition' undergoes a messianic inversion: it loses persecutory and negative aspects of deficiency and becomes a new and hopeful mode of living, believing, and thinking.

> Two years ago it was revealed to me that the king messiah is destined to dress in the clothes of a converso [*anus*], and because of them the Jews will not recognize him; in short, he is destined to be a converso like me [. . .] It is not enough that the messiah the son of Joseph will be desecrated for our sins, but he must rather bear the transgressions of Israel on his shoulders, to be killed by the gentiles as atonement for us. And because they [the Jews] abandoned the Torah, desecration was decreed on the messiah son of David, that he become a converso against his will, in a manner which prevents him from keeping the Torah [. . .] And God

---

[53] Gershom Scholem, 'The Crisis of Tradition in Jewish Messianism' (MIJ, 64).
[54] The belief that conversion is the right choice confirmed by the prophets of the Hebrew Bible appears very strongly in the so-called *Red Letter* which was issued to his followers by Jacob Frank: 'But none of the wicked will understand, only those of real understanding will know that anyone who has a spark of the seed of Abraham, Isaac, and Jacob must enter into the holy faith of Edom, and whoever will accept this creed with love will be saved from all of them [the persecutions] and will merit all of the consolations promised in Isaiah and in all the Prophets': Jacob Frank, 'The Red Letter', in *Sabbatian Heresy: Writings on Mysticism, Messianism, and the Origins of Jewish Modernity*, ed. Paweł Maciejko (Waltham, MA: Brandeis University Press, 2017), 162.

inflicted on him the sins of us all, because we were all required to become converts [...] This is similar to what occurred to Esther.⁵⁵

Just as Esther/*Hastara*, whose name means *I will hide myself*, conceals her Jewishness for the sake of her people, so will the *converso* Messiah bring redemption to the Jews and all other nations plunged into the condition of universal exile. By referring to Esther, the Marrano 'saint', Cardoso articulates the foundations of the Sabbatian doctrine of the 'redemption through sin' or the 'mitsva in reverse' (*mitsva ha'ba'averah*): while *avoda zara* (the idol cult) still remains a transgression, not only it is not condemned but paradoxically *commanded* by the Torah whose Teaching secretly insists on its own betrayal. The hidden Torah, therefore, contradicts the overt Torah. Hence the Marrano paradox: if the tradition is to continue in its hidden messianic truth, it must be constantly betrayed on the level of its overt articulation. Scholem comments on this paradox with both surprise and fascination:

> The psychology of the 'radical' Sabbatians was utterly paradoxical and 'Marranic'. Essentially its guiding principle was: Whoever is as he appears to be cannot be a true 'believer'. In practice this means the following: The 'true faith' cannot be a faith which men publicly profess. On the contrary, the 'true faith' must always be concealed. In fact, it is one's duty to deny it outwardly, for it is like a seed that has been planted in the bed of the soul and it cannot grown unless it is first covered over. *For this reason every Jew is obliged to become a Marrano.* (MIJ, 109; emphasis added)

In this essay, characteristically titled 'Redemption through Sin', Scholem-the-Historian demonstrates the link between Cardoso's Marrano theology and the later radical development of the Sabbatian movement in which 'messianism was transformed into nihilism' – but this is not a damning comment. We saw that in his *Theses*, *not* written from the perspective of the historian, he tends to identify with those who daringly walk 'the fine line between religion and nihilism' in order to reinvigorate – breath in a new life, or simply, *life* – into the 'sickening tradition'. To what extent does he identify with Abraham Cardoso and his 'shield' (*magen*) protecting the hidden truth of the messianic good news? After all, we know that in his private jokes on the Kabbalistic theory of the transmigration of souls (*gilgul*), he imagined himself as the incarnation of Johannes Reuchlin, the seventeenth-century Christian Kabbalist, who created a Judeo-Christian amalgam analogous to the ones produced by the Marrano theologians (while his older friend, Walter Benjamin, was supposed to host the soul of Isaac Luria himself).⁵⁶

---

[55] Quot. In Goldish, 'Patterns of Converso Messianism', 48.
[56] According to Moshe Idel, the significance of Reuchlin's influence on Scholem goes far beyond the private joke for it is responsible for the latter's symbolic – rather than mystical and theurgic – interpretation of the whole Kabbalistic lore, which appears more characteristic of the Schellingian *erzählende Philosophie* than of the original intention of the Kabbalists: 'He once remarked that if he believed in metempsychosis, he would perhaps see Reuchlin's soul as having transmigrated into himself. Certainly, Reuchlin's influence is conspicuous in Scholem's and his followers' overemphasis on the paramount importance of symbolic language and thought as representative of and essential of the entire Kabbalah': Moshe Idel, *Old Worlds, New Mirrors: On Jewish Mysticism and Twentieth-Century Thought* (Philadelphia: University of Pennsylvania Press, 2010), 87.

But is the hypothesis that the Marranos – Cardoso's true people of exile – represent the 'authentic tradition' as opposed to the Jews recentred around the sacred space of the Synagogue, really so shocking in its audacity? According to Jan Assmann, Mosaism originated precisely on the basis of 'the principle of normative inversion [which] consists in inverting the abominations of the other culture into obligations and vice versa'.[57] For the traditional Jews, therefore, the Marranos, especially those with such bold religious claims, are indeed abomination – but for the Marranos, who took the former abomination as a new obligation, already at the other shore of the Red Sea, the Jews are now a new Egypt, a 'foreign country'. This split within Judaism itself – a new dynamic religion based on the ever-repeating narrative of Exodus – is also the theme of Benjamin D. Sommer, who, in the essay called in a perfectly Derridean manner: 'Expulsion as Initiation', contrasts the two authors of the Hebrew Bible, the priestly P and the more original J. While the former represents 'an ideology of the center, according to which God and Israel belong in a particular sacred space',[58] J writes in favour of the exile/exodus:

> JE texts that describe origins exhibit a striking pattern: *all beginnings entail exile.* This pattern presents itself in the JE texts dealing with the origins of humanity (Genesis 2-4), with the introduction of Israel's first ancestor (Genesis 12), and with the early life of Israel's liberator and lawgiver (Exodus 2). Note how often, for example, the words *geirash* (expel) and *shillaf* (send away) appear in these three, very brief, texts (Gen 3.23, 3.24, 4.14, 12.20, Exod 2.17, and cf. the name *Gershom* in 2.22). Moreover, while the theme of exile is unambiguously present in all three of these narratives, the identification of the nature and location of exile in each is indeterminate. *The exile into which characters move is always in some way a nonexile, and the home from which they come is always less than a home.*[59]

On Sommer's reading, the paradigmatically Derridean deconstruction of the home-exile binary – particularly striking in the case of the Marranos who got arrested in the aporia between departing and arriving – would thus be the very message of the Torah itself, precisely as predicted by Cardoso. Exile – out of the Garden of Eden into the world, as well as out of Egypt into the desert (these two stories overlap, by sharing the same words and phrases) – is not a negative concept; it rather naturally interferes with Exodus: *yetziat* as *shillaf*, 'getting out' chiming in harmony with 'sending away'. For Derrida, *sending away* – a posting or an envoy, which 'disperses and multiplies' (FK, 100) – is the central figure of the tradition whose God always 'sends away': from himself and into the world, deeper and further into the adventure of worldliness. It is thus a paradoxical tradition in which, in a precise opposition to Yeat's vision, *the centre does not hold and is not supposed to hold*; on the contrary, the things are to fall apart, in the constant Schellingian *Abfall* from God, far and away, in the centrifugal movement

---

[57] Assmann, *Moses the Egyptian*, 31.
[58] Benjamin D. Sommer, 'Expulsion as Initiation', in *Beginning/ Again: Towards a Hermeneutics of Jewish Texts*, ed. Aryeh Cohen and Shaul Magid (New York: Seven Bridges Press, 2002), 24.
[59] Sommer, 'Expulsion as Initiation', 26; emphasis added.

of a 'widening gyre', of which the Marrano ring forms the most distant periphery.[60] For Scholem, on the other hand, more ambivalent in this respect, it is rather the word *geirash*, 'to expel', which rings in his chosen Hebrew name, *Gershom*: to be in the exile may constitute a universal condition, but it is still a tragedy of alienation.

For both, however, Scholem and Derrida, the Jewish 'authentic tradition' *moves* in the opposite direction to the gentile traditions of the sacred centre, nostalgically pictured by W. B. Yeats in his famous poem. This is why it can also be called a *counter-tradition*, since it completely subverts the pattern of binaries between home and the outside, cosmos and chaos, the sacred and the profane, the centre and the exile – which the phenomenologists of religion, such as Mircea Eliade, saw as absolutely defining for *any* tradition *as such*. To say that 'the exile into which characters move is always in some way a nonexile, and the home from which they come is always less than a home' means to find oneself in a completely different, radically non-traditionalist universe of the original *uncanny*, *das Unheimliche*, which does not have a positive counterpart: there is no 'canniness' or 'homeliness' of the origin from which we were allegedly expelled. All that is, is Movement – precisely as in Moses Hess's dynamic *u-topia* of the Party of Movement, which can never find a place of rest, against the immobile Party of Stillness, guarding the 'centre that holds'[61] – always pressing forward, restlessly proleptic, and messianic, where the messianic promise does not consist in offering a new *topia* of the 'promised land', but in deconstructing all *topias* as wrong traditions which try to present the home as *more* than just a 'home where we start from'. This felicitous phrase of D. W. Winnicott, a British psychoanalyst of the Kleinian school, gives the most succinct definition of home: it is where we start *from*, it is nothing more than a place of departure, to be left once we mature, and never to be looked back in a retrogressive nostalgia. In the same vein, Gustav Landauer, seconding Moses, criticized all existing religious and philosophical utopias as complete misnomers which, in fact, are nothing but *topias*: partly inspired by the messianic dream of creating a new social place 'without ills and injustices', and partly led by the misguided desire to *domesticate* the exilic, for ever *unheimlich*, world.[62]

---

[60] The concept of *der Abfall* – the falling-away precursorial to the Yeatsian image of 'things falling apart' – appears in Schelling's 1804 essay called *Philosophie und Religion*. Here Schelling reveals himself as an infinitist absolutist who denies any reality to the finite world, viewed by him as a merely negative by-product of extreme ontological privation: 'there is no continuous transition from the Absolute to the actual; the origin [*Ursprung*] of the phenomenal world is conceivable only as a complete breaking-away [*Abbrechen*] from absoluteness by means of a leap [*Sprung*] [...] There is no positive effect coming out of the Absolute that creates a conduit or bridge between the infinite and the finite [...] The Absolute is the only actual; the finite world, by contrast, is not real. Its cause, therefore, cannot lie in an impartation of reality from the Absolute to the finite world or its substrate; it can only lie in a remove [*Entfernung*], in a falling-away [*Abfall*] from the Absolute': Friedrich Wilhelm Joseph Schelling, *Philosophy and Religion*, trans. Klaus Ottmann (Putnam: Spring Publications, 2010), 26; emphasis added. As we shall yet see, Derrida will completely reject the absolutist moment of Schelling's reasoning, but will affirm the description of the world's emergence in terms of the 'complete breaking-away'.

[61] See Moses Hess, *The Holy History of Mankind and Other Writings*, trans. Shlomo Avineri (Cambridge: Cambridge University Press, 2004), 23; 40.

[62] See Gustav Landauer, 'Revolution', in *Revolution and Other Writings: A Political Reader*, ed. and trans. Gabriel Kuhn (Pontypool: The Merlin Press Ltd, 2010), 113.

In that sense, the Marrano would be *das Unheimliche* of the Jewish tradition: the extimate truth of a Jew who defends himself against the existential difficulty of his counter-tradition, by creating a recentering shelter of *Tradierbarkeit*: the *tradendum*, the teachable and transmissible doctrine of home, sacred spaces, and identity. Sommer does not even have to mention the Marrano experience in order to capture the sense of the Jewish *Unheimlichkeit*. Already the language of the Torah itself is both troubled and troubling, because it is a 'rhetoric of displacement': 'Home is displaced, or supplemented by exile. Divine presence itself is displaced [and this] effects a radical displacement of the priesthood and of the orderly universe to which they aspire.'[63] This unsettling counter-tradition of displacement, which subverts homeliness and supplements it by exile, is dictated by the originary act of the exile of God from Himself, 'for insofar as the deity comes into contact with creation (indeed, insofar as the deity creates, which is to say, begins), the divinity expels itself from the divine realm'.[64] The *lekh lekha* line, therefore – *les deux mots pour Juif*, 'the two words for Jew', summing up the imperative of deracination – does not start with God demanding from Abraham to 'get out of here' but with God who exiles himself from his quiet kingdom of infinity in order to let be the messy world. Before God will 'send away' – first Adam and Eve from the Garden of Eden, then Abraham from the place of his natural birth, and finally the whole Israel out of Egypt – He himself becomes an *envoy*: posted, turned into a sign of himself, exposed to the hazard of writing, no longer a living presence capable to inform believers about his true intentions. The original *shillaf* is thus also the beginning of writing – the wandering of signs – which, in the Marrano manner, is for ever cut from its living origin of the voice. Everything, beginning with God, is in the condition of universal exile, diaspora, *écriture*. Yet, at the same time, since there is no homely condition with which to contrast the exilic one – for, even God fails to represent the absolute repose – 'the exile [. . .] is always in some way a nonexile': it determines a mode of being which, as Derrida will argue, is the only possible one. In this manner, 'the ontotheological Marrano' – a character appearing in the crucial section of *Faith and Knowledge* (FK, 100) – becomes a cryptonym of the universal *modus essendi*, which, in accordance with the strictest logic of univocity, is also shared by God:

> Let us figuratively call Marrano *anyone* who remains faithful to a secret that he has not chosen, in the very place where he lives, in the home of the inhabitant or of the occupant, in the home of the first or the second arrivant, *in the very place where he stays without saying no but without identifying himself as belonging to*. (A, 81; emphasis added)

Exactly the same logic leads to the deconstruction of the false binary between the host and the guest: the one who owns his place and welcomes the other – and the one without place and roots, who comes from the outside. By referring to the original ambivalence of the French word *hôté*, meaning both 'host' and 'guest', Derrida states in

---

[63] Sommer, 'Expulsion as Initiation', 37.
[64] Ibid.

'Hostipitality': 'Laughter and tears, then – through the tears, the welcoming smile, the *hôte* as ghost (spirit or revenant, holy spirit, holy ghost or revenant), here is what awaits us' (AR, 359). This description of the holy *hôté*, being neither host nor guest – and both at the same time – fits perfectly the concept of the Marrano God who is neither exiled nor at home in the world, and both simultaneously. The divine spectre/revenant smiles with a welcoming smile, but this is not an invitation to join him in the house of creation, of which he would be a designer and an owner. Once the World emerges – a place to wander through – everything becomes *uncanny*. Neither host nor guest, the Marrano God errs through the worldly domain, while the Marranos, his secret believers, faithfully follow him in his errance.

In my reading, therefore, Derrida will emerge as the most radical thinker of *tsimtsum*, the Kabbalistic self-negation of God, understood in the Scholemian manner as the *release* or 'liberation of creation', which can only happen when beings partly *forget* where they came from and become all universal Marrano-a/theists (or, as it will be explained later, *almost-atheists*). The issue of forgetting, crucial for Derrida's metaphysical intrigue of the gift, constitutes the most controversial and sensitive part of the Marrano project. Even if dialecticized by the Blanchotian *sans* as 'forgetting without forgetting', it still flies in the face of the central imperative of Jewish tradition: *zakhor*, 'remember'. As Baal Shem Tov put it succinctly and as Yad Vashem portal inscription warns those who enter: 'Forgetfulness leads to exile, while remembrance is the secret of redemption.' Derrida would not contest the first part of the sentence, but he would beg to take issues with its second half, if only to remind us – also those who still participate in the hypermnesiac enterprise of Jewish tradition as *Tradierbarkeit* – that forgetting also has a place in the redemptive plan, perhaps even more legitimate: that *forgetting* is the secret of redemption. Yet, not as a 'psychological forgetting', which may or may not be advantageous for the singular living, but forgetting in the metaphysical sense of the word as the absolutely *sine qua non* of the gift of being, which has its carrier in the 'ontotheological Marrano' – the new chosen one of Derrida's 'religion without religion'. Indeed, if the Blanchotian figure of *X sans X* finds its embodiment in Derrida's writings, it is precisely in the Marrano flesh and bone: 'So this is a permanent *Stimmung*: I am a prophet without a prophecy, a prophet without being a prophet', Derrida says about himself.[65] Judaism without Judaism, forgetting without forgetting, religion without religion, fidelity without fidelity, belonging without belonging, prophecy without prophecy, and so on – all these abstract aporias, so often wrongly perceived as Derridean dead-ends, become a lived reality of the Marrano existence. They no longer 'block the way' but rather pave the way towards a new form of life and freedom: individual, social, political, religious. As Derrida puts it in *Demeure*, 'in this way the witness translates the untranslatable': the Marrano witness, who survived 'the instant of

---

[65] Jacques Derrida, 'The Becoming Possible of the Impossible: An Interview with Jacques Derrida', in *Passion for the Impossible: John D. Caputo in Focus*, ed. Mark Dooley (Albany: SUNY Press, 2003), 27.

his death' as a traditional Jew, translates the abstract impossibility of the aporia – surviving despite the death of his identity – into a difficult, yet liveable, condition of permanent survival.[66]

I will thus attempt to prove that the Marrano Derrida is a yet another Derrida and a whole Derrida at the same time: not just a peripheral potentiality in the abyssal *apeiron* of his *ouevre*, but *whole another Derrida*, akin to his favourite late hero, 'another Abraham'. The Marrano thread runs through all his works, also the earliest ones, and when carefully pursued reveals a completely new *Gestalt*: the 'serious play' of Derrida's Marrano comedy, where ultimately everything turns out to be a matter of the hazardous *jeux/jest/gesten* ('game', 'joke', 'telling a tale' in Middle English) or the Lurianic-Mallarmean 'throw of the dice' (where the verb *iacere* – as in *allea iacta est* – is also related to *iocari*, 'to joke') that inaugurated a truly 'unprejudiced becoming' of the world.[67] In the dialogue with Elisabeth Roudinesco, Derrida admits: 'I often see myself as a mad figure (comical and tragic at the same time) committed to a deadly difficult task to be unfaithful for the sake of the spirit of fidelity' (FWT, 156), and this confession comprises his metaphysical project in a microcosmic nutshell: the madness of the 'chrematistic vertigo' (GT, 159) which accompanies the 'unprejudiced becoming' of the world without safety-nets, alibis, and in eternal exile; the tragico-comic oscillation of the *récit* reverberating simultaneously with the fear of catastrophe and joyful 'yes-laughter', and – last, but certainly not least – the self-assumed Marrano condition of 'betrayal without betrayal', a deadly difficult task of walking the Scholemian 'thin line between religion and nihilism'. All this has been very aptly captured in Hélène Cixous's portrait of Derrida as a *Marrano saint* playing his picaresque tragico-comical role to perfection:

'Was I Jewish?' the fugitive muses [. . .] A poet born-condemned, condemned to be if-not-Jewish – hence *the greatest philosophical player* one can ever read. Read, un-read [*delire*], forget-read [*oub-lire*] and all that, let us recall it to the ear and not just to the eye. No one has performed more learned yet more innocent pirouettes

---

[66] John D. Caputo immediately understood that Derrida's Marranism must be interpreted not as an assumption of the identity but as an evasion of identity according to the logic of the Blanchotian *sans*: 'Derrida, whose family came to Algeria in the nineteenth century from Spain, describes himself as a Marrano, inwardly a Jew but outwardly sucked into the French Catholic culture of Algeria, speaking Christian Latin French, but with this twist, that he is a Marrano who is not quite secretly Jewish on the inside either, who is not exactly Jewish or not Jewish, who is not Christian and not quite free of Christianity, who is neither Algerian nor not, neither European nor not, neither American nor not. In the logic of Blanchot, Derrida is a Jew *sans* Judaism, Christianized *sans* Christianity, an Arab *sans* Islam, a French citizen *sans* being French, an American "phenomenon" *sans* being American, a religious man *sans* theism – Derrida *sans l'être*. This atheist Arab Jew who speaks French and lives in France, whose greatest recognition is in the United States, suffers from the "illness of Proteus"': Caputo, *The Prayers and Tears*, 304. See also C, 198.

[67] See Hans Jonas's version of the Lurianic myth: 'In such self-forfeiture of divine integrity for the sake of unprejudiced becoming, no other knowledge can be admitted than that of *possibilities*, which cosmic being offers in its own terms: to these, God committed his cause in effacing himself from the world': Hans Jonas, *Mortality and Morality: A Search for the Good after Auschwitz*, trans. Lawrence Vogel (Evanston: Northwestern University Press, 1996), 134.

around words, no one has ever managed to get French stodginess more joyously drunk, giving philosophy the full measure of its greatness once and for all, which is both its tragic and its comic dimension. He makes writing laugh [*ec-rire*]. One cannot read him without being appalled at the urge to laugh with enchantment. (PJD, ix; emphasis added)

We shall yet go back to Cixous's congenial reading of Derrida's Marranism, partly inspired by her intervention, in Chapter 4: his powers of undoing and re-doing, made possible by the Marrano dialectics of attachment-detachment-re-attachment, which results in a 'delirious reading' (*de-lire*) bringing outrageous joy (*ec-rire*) and a 'forget-reading' (*oub-lire*), faithful and unfaithful at the same time. For, 'Marranism' is a particularly useful category when it comes to mediation between the idiom and the institution, private idiosyncrasy and the body of tradition, innovation, and betrayal. In one of his letters, Walter Benjamin – himself a 'philosophical Marrano' – compares tradition to the sea and the individual to a single wave, but, contrary to the expectations, this is not a conservative harmonious image: each wave becomes, even if for a short moment, a separate *apex* that breaks from the ocean, stands up and foams in its own inimitable way:

> The teachings are like a surging sea, but for the wave (if we take it as an image of man) all that matters is to surrender itself to its motion in such a way that it crests and breaks with foam.[68]

Such is also Derrida's attitude towards Judaism: while emerging from the sea of ancestral teachings, he breaks with it in the Marrano *clinamen*, and finally crests with his own religious doctrine which uses the nourishing waters of tradition in order to turn them into a singular, delicate, lace-like, foamy structure of a unique *haggadah*, a picaresque story of everything, designed to carry the Scholemian secret 'truth of the tradition'. According to John D. Caputo, the Derridean 'religion without religion' is mostly idiosyncratic: 'Jacques Derrida has religion, a certain religion, *his* religion, and he speaks of God all the time. The point of view of Derrida's work as an author is religious – but without religion and without religion's God.'[69] True, but not quite. The Benjaminian metaphor works not only in explaining Derrida's attitude towards Judaism, but also to Marranism. Derrida's religion is indeed *his* religion and a *Marrano* religion which has already grown its own archive of more or less idiosyncratic strayings into non-normative regions. Marranism, therefore, is also an institution, however paradoxical – another vast sea making its own waves – and my goal here is to inscribe Derrida's idiom into its still unexplored archives.[70]

---

[68] Walter Benjamin, *The Correspondence of Walter Benjamin, 1910–1940*, trans. Manfred R. Jacobson and Evelyn M. Jacobson (Chicago: University of Chicago Press, 1994), 94.
[69] Caputo, *The Prayers and Tears*, xviii; emphasis added.
[70] Derrida's Marranism should thus be interpreted alongside the general description offered by Yosef Hayim Yerushalmi, who sees the 'Marrano religion' as a new tradition fostering individual deviations and idiosyncrasies: Yerushalmi, *From Spanish Court*, 35; emphasis added.

The secret: How *not* to avoid speaking

Derrida never emphasizes his Jewishness but also never silences it either; he expresses it and performs it most efficiently precisely in a Marrano way, that is, through the tropes of concealment, evasion, and avoidance. Derrida's most masterful Marrano performance takes place in his 1987 essay: *Of Spirit. Heidegger and the Question*. By commenting on Heidegger's art of *vermeiden* (avoidance) in the Blanchotian mode of *X sans X* – 'I'm thinking in particular of all those modalities of 'avoiding' which come down to saying without saying, writing without writing, using words without using them' (OS, 2) – Derrida once again secretly alludes to his own secret, of which 'almost nothing will ever be said' but which will be performed in the manner of repetition, usually assumed by the 'body language' of symptoms: yet another 'language under the sun', particularly fit for the 'oblique offering' of secrets (OS, 2).

Yet there is nothing involuntary about this symptom which Derrida cunningly turns into an intentional manoeuvre, by staking on the 'saying without saying' through the language of the body, with its seal of circumcision and the memory impressed into flesh itself, deeper than any form of conscious remembering: more archival, physical, real. The circumcised body remembers and confesses, by cutting into the signifying chains with their own encumbered stammering rhythm, by creating its own field of speech disturbance, which, according to Lacan, allows the Real to come to the fore. But unlike Lacan, who in his model of therapy advocates coming back to the place 'where it was' (*wo es war*), the site of the Real and the Truth, Derrida, who always professed his 'resistance to psychoanalysis', does not believe in any lessons of good return/*nostos*. He does not intend to go back to any place of some real, pure, true Jewishness; he does not go anywhere, remains *here*, in the Edom of his French culture and language, which he transposes into one vast field of speech disturbance: the *différance* that always runs forward to the future and never looks back.[71]

---

[71] There is no doubt that, for Derrida, circumcision constitutes his central trauma which may be seen as the particular case of what Lacan describes as the state of the mutilated body. It emerges in the so-called mirror stage, when the child contemplates his image as an integral whole being, simultaneously corresponding and not-corresponding to its inner experience of *le corps morcelé*, a body overwhelmed by the mortal fear of dispersion. In the order of the Real, therefore, 'the subject is no one. It is decomposed, in pieces': Jacques Lacan, *The Ego in Freud's Theory and in Technique of Psychoanalysis: The Seminar of Jacques Lacan 1954–1955: Book 2*, ed. Jacques Alain-Miller, trans. Sylvana Tomaselli (New York: Norton, 1991), 54. The *image* of the autonomous ego is thus nothing but a fiction of the imaginary, proving totally helpless in light of the 'truth', *wo es war*, where the traumatic encounter with *das Ding*, the Real, and the castrating presence of the Other occurred, and with it the experience of one's own death. Yet, Derrida's solution to his traumatic predicament is radically different. In his critical reading of Lacan's 'Seminar on The Purloined Letter', called 'Le facteur de la verité' ('The Purveyor of Truth'), Derrida questions the Freudian-Lacanian paradigm of return to the place of the traumatic truth, which forces the letter/envoy to arrive at its destination: 'the phallus has to be kept [*gardé*], has to return to its point of departure, has not to be disseminated en route' (P, 464). By breaking with the psychoanalytic law of return – the *nostos* to the truth of the origin – Derrida deliberately invests in the subjective *auto-fiction* as 'an unverifiable non-truth' which continues to weave its texture in the 'irreducible dis-regard' to its origin/ destination, thus rebelling against 'the passion of unveiling which has one object: the truth' (P, 469). The subjective auto-fiction can only develop in the secretive shadows, hiding from the apocalyptic passion of truth-seeking – or what Nietzsche calls the 'murky shop of the soul' (more on this in Chapter 4).

'No one has ever managed to get French stodginess more joyously drunk', Cixous writes about Derrida (PJD, ix), meaning precisely his stammering speech disturbance turned into a mastery of linguistic innovation in which he had only one equal: James Joyce.

Yet, at the same time, this very gesture – to oppose any return and restlessly press forward – appears to Derrida more faithful to the 'origin' than any open act of homecoming or conversion (*tshuva*). For, if at the origin God says to Abraham – *lekh lekha*, 'leave your place of origin' – then the simple return to the origin negates the very meaning of the original message. To be truthful to the origin would thus indicate, seemingly paradoxically, not to be able to return: to cultivate in oneself the opposite capability to leave, to 'get out', to engage in permanent Exodus (*yetziat mitzraiim*, 'getting out of Egypt') which forever invalidates the very act of return. In his stubborn refusal of any return-conversion, therefore, Derrida proves to be a more truthful reader of the Abraham story than Emmanuel Lévinas who, in 'The Trace of the Other', famously contrasts the Abrahamic nomadism with the Greek ideal of *nostos*, the homecoming of Odysseus, in order to distil a pure Jewish idiom which can be neatly set against to the *nostos*-dominated discourse of Western philosophy, from Plato to Hegel. While Lévinas wants us to return to the place defined by the very impossibility of any return in order to oppose the prevailing discourse based on the idea of return – Derrida, always critical of Lévinas's illusion of Jewish 'purism' (mostly in 'Violence and Metaphysics', but not only), turns out to be a more authentic follower of Abraham, literally *following* him in his nomadic stepping into the element of contamination. In Derrida, the Babelian element of dissemination and mongrelization of languages, where the impure Babel becomes a place of a more privileged revelation than the arche-pure Sinai, is the very beginning of *différance*: the messianic rhythm of differing and disseminating every sameness, as well as deferring any final closure. 'I am not going *anywhere*', says Derrida, and with this refusal to go back to the Jewish roots declares his participation in the 'French-Catholic culture', but it does mean breaking with his Jewish origin. To the contrary: it means to be *in* this culture, both his and other at the same time, marked by a slight differing *clinamen*, which secretly subverts any identitarian participation, by undermining the very idea of origin, return, or identity. Cutting into the opposition of rootedness and a free-floating subjectivity, his Marrano strategy of non/identification follows the path of being truthful to the origin which is never truthful to itself. A difficult path of secrecy, ellipsis, and *apophasis*, which manifests itself only indirectly, in a spectral halo surrounding everything openly revealed, said, or 'handed over'.

But, if Marranism were indeed so important to Derrida, why doesn't he mention it more often? It's a fair point, raised by many Derridean scholars, most notably Geoffrey Bennington. Yet, in case of the interpretations involving *littérature au secret*, the frequency analysis simply does not hold the key. The whole point of the hermetic discourse is to drop hints occasionally, obliquely evoking a secret bond of *hamevin yavin*: 'those who know, know', a Jewish version of *sapienti satis*. Does Derrida's secret participate in such hermetic Marrano communication of 'those-who-know'? Yes and no. Yes, because Derrida indeed reduces his Marrano expression to minimal clues, very rarely allowing himself to admit his Marrano allegiance. And no – because Derrida truly wants to be found out. 'It is joy to be hidden, but disaster not to be found', says Winnicott, and this beautiful aphorism perfectly depicts Derrida's position on his

Marranism.⁷² Derrida finds unique joy in being hidden: his *veil* (*le voile*) is his *sail* (*la voile*], and he travels far on his secret fuel. He hides from all forms of external identity and belonging, like a Marrano Augustine – filtered through Teresa of Avila, the Marrano mystic-saint – always bent inward, towards his *morada*, 'inner castle' or the 'inner *fors*'. But he also hates not to be found out, ignored in his idiosyncrasy, overlooked by the systems of signifiers, not subtle enough to catch his meandering tropes and drifts. In *Paper Machine*, he clearly states: 'I would not want to let myself be *imprisoned in a culture of the secret*, which however I do rather like, as I like that figure of the Marrano, which keeps popping up in *all* my texts' (PM, 162; emphasis added). So, secret – yes, but only insofar as it does not stop the reader from an inquiry: the Marrano secret – as Derrida himself admits, ubiquitous in all his works – is not to be surrounded by a halo of impenetrable mystery, but only inspire to dig deeper: until we hit the subterranean crypt and peep into Derrida's 'deep self' which lies there, waiting to be unearthed.

It is no secret that most of Derrida's writings are about secrets. *It's no secret*: in this way one could, in fact, summarize his teaching on the nature of the secret, which deals with its clandestine message so intensely and suggestively that, in the end, reveals everything, though never directly. Derrida gives the lesson on how not to say anything and nonetheless say it all in his essay, 'Comment ne pas parler: Dénégations', which appeared in the volume *Psyche: inventions de l'autre*, in 1987. Freely associating the themes from negative theology and psychoanalysis, Derrida approaches the secret in terms of the Freudian denegation, *Verneinung*: the disavowal which avows, that is, indirectly asserts the content which the patient vehemently negates. Denegation, therefore, sublates the negativity of the secret because already in the very paradoxical nature of the secret there lies the inherent tendency to come out:

> There is a secret of denial and a denial of a secret. The secret as such, as secret, separates and already institutes a negativity: it is a negation that denies itself. It de-negates itself. This denial does not happen by accident; it is essential and originary [. . .] There is no secret as such; I deny it. And this is what I confide in secret to whomever allies himself to me. *This is the secret of the alliance.* (HAS, 95)

Is this alliance a secret bond of *hamevin yavin*? It is certainly not an accident that the lecture, which became the canvas for the essay on de-negations, was given by Derrida in Jerusalem: 'I knew that I would have to do it in Jerusalem. But what does such an obligation mean here?' (HAS, 73). This question receives an oblique answer in the course of the lecture in which Derrida describes *all* apophatic theologies *except* the Jewish and the Islamic, and then exposes this omission as deliberate:

> In other words, what of Jewish and Islamic thought in this regard? By example, and in everything that I will say, a certain void, the place of an *internal desert*, will perhaps allow this question to resonate. The three paradigms [Platonic,

---

⁷² Donald Woods Winnicott, *Playing and Reality* (London: Routledge, 1971), 95.

Neoplatonic, and Heideggerian – A.B.-R.] [. . .] will surround a resonant space of which nothing, *almost* nothing will *ever* be said. (HAS, 100; emphasis added)

A few pages earlier Derrida quotes Wittgenstein's sentence: 'what cannot be talked about, must be kept silent', which, despite its seemingly prohibitive verdict, nonetheless allows the possibility of *showing*. Indeed, what cannot be talked about can be demonstrated and performed, even though *almost* nothing will *ever* be said about it. The whole lecture – and not just this lecture – amounts to such a performance in which Derrida simultaneously negates and de-negates, hides and imparts, conceals and reveals his secret which is never to be spoken about but merely to *resonate* with all other words or be merely *spectrally* present as the 'true', truly ineffable core of all apophatic traditions, more anterior, more 'deserted', and more 'nothing-like' than their holy objects, still tinged with kataphatic positivity. In the footnote to the aforementioned fragment, also containing the allusion to the 'internal desert', Derrida avows that the lecture on de-negations is 'the most "autobiographical" speech I have ever risked' whose underlying question is 'how not to speak of oneself'; how to avoid mentioning what he at the same time designates 'the closest thing to me: the Jew, the Arab' (HAS, 135). The Jerusalem lecture, therefore, constitutes a significant prelude to the *Circonfessions* where this double identification, so far denied and avoided, becomes finally revealed, and then immediately topped by the third one, in which Derrida decides to call himself a Marrano: a sort of *marrane* of the French Catholic culture, who practices his contaminated and impure Jewishness (Jew-Arab, Jew-Catholic, Jew-Philosopher) *undercover*, secretly, using *other* languages – marrying the speeches of strangers – to convey the apophatic call coming from the 'internal desert':

> This small piece of autobiography confirms it obliquely. It is *performed* in all my foreign languages: French, English, German, Greek, Latin, the philosophic, metaphilosophic, Christian etc. (HAS, 135)

But which language then would *not* be foreign? Does it exist at all? Would it be – according to the ultimate Marrano metaphor created by Charles Reznikoff – the Hebrew spoken either in silence/*silenzio* or in all languages under the sun?[73] Derrida's declaration from *Monoligualism of the Other* – 'It is possible to be monolingual (I thoroughly am, aren't I?) and speak a language that is not one's own' (MO, 5) – points to the linguistic Marrano strategy which combines Scholem's *Schweigen auf Hebräisch* with Reznikoff's 'ventriloquism': a metaphor used by Derrida himself in 'Marx & Sons' (MS, 263). What he represents is the unspeakable Marrano *différance* which does not have a language of one's own, but splits and disturbs every monolingual tradition.

There are two ways in which to approach Derrida's Marranism. One is to dwell into the Sephardic lore of the *conversos* culture in which Derrida's Maghrebian family was immersed, as it has been superbly done by Erin Graff Zivin in her *Marrano Specter*.

---

[73] Reznikoff's great poem, *Joshua at Shechem*, can indeed serve as a motto for all the Marranos of the world: 'And God scattered them – / Through the cities of Medes, beside the waters of Babylon . . . / And God looked and saw the Hebrews, / Citizens of the great cities, / Talking Hebrew in every language under the sun': *The Poems of Charles Reznikoff*, 113.

Another one, chosen by me, is to loosen a bit the idea of the historical Marrano and treat it as a trope/figure in the Scholemian manner, applying also to those from the outside of the Hispanic context, but going through the analogical 'Marrano experience' of exile and cultural-religious contamination. Hence a slightly different constellation of thinkers and writers whom I propose in this book as glosses to Derrida's 'desire to be a Marrano': Scholem, Benjamin, Rosenzweig, Adorno, Celan, and Cixous.[74] I say 'slightly', because such names as Celan or Cixous appear very often in the works on Derrida but rarely in reference to Derrida's Marrano self-(non)-identification. To paraphrase Vivian Liska's recent title,[75] I wish to see Derrida as a part of 'German Jewish thought', as its legitimate 'afterlife' and not so a 'tenuous legacy'. My aim is to put Derrida within the 'secret company' of thinkers who wrestled with the Marrano condition in which, as Sommer has put it, 'the exile [. . .] is always in some way a nonexile, and the home [. . .] is always less than a home' and who, because of that, always already practiced deconstruction *avant la lettre*.[76]

---

[74] Catherine Malabou calls this Marrano constellation nicely 'the other shore': 'This other shore is not that of a country; it is not Israel. It skirts the coast of a symbolic archipelago formed by a family of linguistic travellers: Kafka, Lévinas, Scholem, Benjamin, Celan, Arendt, Rosenweig. All of them exiles or foreigners who write in order to invent their citizenship, a citizenship that has, in a sense, been lost since or from its origin' (CP-M, 90). The idea that exile is not to be denied but worked-through towards the acceptance of *Un-heimlichkeit* as a permanent condition found its great expression in Adorno's *Minima Moralia*: 'it is part of morality not to be at home in one's home' (MM, 39). This is one more reason to put Derrida's thought in the constellation of, in Martin Jay's phrasing, 'permanent exiles' who, similarly to the Derridean universal Marranos, constantly wander through the infinite spaces of the cosmic *galut*, always far from home, but at the same time strangely at home with *das Unheimliche*: Martin Jay, *Permanent Exiles: Essays on the Intellectual Migration from Germany to America* (New York: Columbia University Press, 1985).

[75] Vivian Liska, *German Jewish Thought and Its Afterlife: A Tenuous Legacy* (Bloomington: Indiana University Press, 2017).

[76] In his conversation with Elisabeth Weber, Derrida puts himself in the German-Jewish constellation of thinkers, while calling it a 'knot': a traumatic tangle comparable to the Freudian *Traumnabel*, to which he feels drawn in an ambivalent manner. While he admits affinity with those German-Jewish precursors in the Marrano-like experience of assimilation, he also wishes to deconstruct the toxic fascination which attaches itself to the 'specularity' (the mirror stage?) of the 'desire for alliance and appropriation, for an "I am more German than the German" in some Jews' (TG, 46), including Cohen, Benjamin, Adorno, and even Scholem: 'Each knot has a definite singularity of its own, but you have to pull the whole string! If we want this fascination to be interrupted – or, at any rate, no longer to give rise to murder as we have lived it in the most intolerable form – we must try to think that through! It is also a political duty' (TG, 47). Derrida's direction – as I will try to prove in this book – is to use the Marrano metaphor in the reverse: not as a specular attempt to become more German or French than the Germans or the French, but to de-assimilate without, at the same time, returning to the roots. In my approach, therefore, Derrida will be tied by an 'elective affinity' (whether he wants it or not) to 'the generation as well as a particular current within the Jewish cultural universe of *Mitteleuropa*: a generation of intellectuals born during the last quarter of the nineteenth century, whose writings were inspired by both German (romantic) and Jewish (messianic) sources': Löwy, *Redemption and Utopia*, 3. On the German-Jewish-Marrano elective affinity see also the superb book of Dana Hollander, *Exemplarity and Chosenness: Rosenzweig and Derrida on the Nation of Philosophy* (Stanford: Stanford University Press, 2008), which closely examines Derrida's seminar on Rosenzweig, conducted in the years 1984–8, and convincingly demonstrates the latter's influence on Derrida's constructs of chosenness, exemplarity, singularity, and universality that, as Hollander argues, can only be meaningful when coming from a particular angle, never to be sublated by the abstract language of philosophy.

Yet, creating even the most secret company for someone who preferred to live and think in the sole company of his secret is a highly problematic task which must take into account Derrida's will to separation. In his speech, delivered on 22 September 2001 in Frankfurt on the reception of *Adorno Preis*, Derrida admits:

> For decades I have been hearing voices, as they say, in my dreams. They are sometimes friendly voices, sometimes not. They are voices in me. All of them seem to be saying to me: why not recognize, clearly and publicly, once and for all, the affinities between your work and Adorno's, in truth your debt to Adorno? Aren't you an heir of the Frankfurt School? (PM, 176)

The first instinctual reaction would be: precisely, why not? Why not link Derrida to the legacy of the Frankfurt School, especially that, in *Fichus*, he very willingly joins the company of the Jewish dreamers and, at the same time, Philosophical Marranos who dared to infect late modern philosophy with the messianic fever? Yet, to be a Marrano is to be separate and thus inevitably betray those who seem the closest. When one grows up as a Marrano, one thinks he is the only Marrano in the world – and to get used to the idea that one is the only something in the world, the most idiosyncratic singularity possible, means not to elect affinities but – seemingly paradoxically – elect non-affinities: always attempt to penetrate and befriend the farthest removed regions of otherness and overlook those who toil in the same Marrano mill. The secret simply wants to stay a secret: a unique trauma-wound or a *Traumnabel* of incurable narcissism which refuses to be turned into a 'common unhappiness'.[77] There can be no doubt that Derrida was a great 'Jewish saint' as well as a Marrano narcissist, but in this 'unavowable community', formed by the disjointed 'we', a shade of narcissistic compulsion was necessary for survival.[78] The inner voice may thus call the Marrano to avow the affinity with those threading the same winding path, but something in him will always say *no*: despite all the promises to develop themes common to him and Adorno, which Derrida gives towards the end of *Fichus*, he never delivered a single

---

[77] Comp. Freud's letter to Breuer: 'much will be gained if we succeed in transforming your hysterical misery into common unhappiness': Sigmund Freud and Joseph Breuer, *Studies in Hysteria*, trans. James Strachey (London: Penguin, 2004), 306. One of Derrida's persistent resistances to psychoanalysis consists precisely in denying this gain.

[78] When, in *Fichus*, Derrida announces that he is speaking to the audience 'in the night' (PM, 167), he seems to be evoking what Blanchot a propos Bataille calls a 'nocturnal communication' of the *communaute acephale*: 'Nocturnal communication, that communication which does not avow itself [. . .] opens up upon community, when a small number of friends, each one singular, and with no forced relationships between them, form it in secret through the silent reading they share [. . .] No commentary could accompany it: *at best a code word* [. . .] that, communicated to each *as if he were the only one*, does not recreate the "sacred conjuration" that had once been dreamed, but which, without breaking the isolation, deepens it in a solitude lived in – common and bound to an unknown responsibility (in regard to the unknown)': Maurice Blanchot, *The Unavowable Community*, trans Pierre Joris (New York: Station Hill Press, 1988), 19–20; emphasis added. While the secret shared by the *acephales* was the sacrifice, which put them simultaneously together and for ever apart – the secret shared by the Marranos, which has exactly the same effect, is the betrayal: the shame of abandoning one's tradition, but also a shy hope in its revival and innovation.

one. One should, therefore, try to impersonify the 'friendly voice' and not to admonish the lonely Marrano for having forgotten his precursors. There is a logic inherent to his forgetfulness, which demands a 'respect for the secret'.

The antinomian vertigo: Between hubris and humbleness

And yet, not to find out Derrida's Marranism would be a disaster, both to Derrida himself and to those who continuously try to understand him. As Winnicott teaches – and I believe him – the joy of being hidden can only be experienced as such when matched by the joy of being found. Even if being a Marrano is only a part of Derrida's overdetermined secret, it nonetheless forms its crucial part: it is one of the central keys to the crypt buried at the bottom of Derrida's multifarious self as another, perhaps even more original, name for what has become known as the Derridean *différance*. For, what is hidden there is truly daring: so daring that it must be kept from sight, even – or rather, mostly – from Derrida's own eyes. There is nothing humble in Derrida's confession to be 'the last of Jews': the Marrano operation of secret reversals runs like a red tape–ribbon through '*all* his texts' (PM, 162) and the Marrano uncanny – the extimate truth of Judaism as the paradoxical counter-tradition of radical otherness, separation, and walking away from the origins – makes Derrida also 'the first of Jews'. If there ever was a thinker who, in the secret of his heart, dared to follow Scholem's oblique injunction that *every Jew is obliged to become a Marrano* (Scholem, MIJ, 109) and, in the spirit of 'normative inversion', turn abomination into obligation – it was definitely him.

The vertiginous oscillation between lastness and firstness characterizes all antinomian strands of the messianic thought, which always try to build new churches on the rejected stones and, once they complete their architectonic construction, immediately die under the weight of the newly accumulated archive; in order to be reborn – again and again – they must burn the archives and let the fiery *ruah* seek other outcasts who inevitably become new priests, and so on, *da capo al fine*. The Marrano messianism, which Derrida embraces, is aware of this incipient danger and, because of that, remains simultaneously *spectral* and *archiviolithic*. The Spirit must remain *secretive* and like Marrano in its clandestine operations; it should never establish a church of its own. The Spirit/Spectre, therefore, has no identity, has no fixed abode, and evades ontological classification of either being or non-being, because *ruah* is the call of justice so radical that it cannot ever be reconciled with the laws of this world. This, as we shall see in the following chapters, is the most difficult moment in Derrida's doctrine which tries to navigate, in the typically Marrano manner, between Lévinas and Heidegger: between the former's ideal of justice, which is literally too good to be and hence 'otherwise than being' – and the latter's concept of *Seinlassen*, letting-be as a pure gift of being (*es gibt*); or, between the antinomian haunting-hovering of the Spirit/Spectre, which secretly subverts all general laws of being for the sake of absolute singular justice, and the quiet generosity of *Khôra* as the source of letting-be. What, however, unites these two instances – of radical justice, on the one hand, and generous *Seinlassen*, on the other – is that they never enter the spectacle of being and remain absolutely transcendent. As such they can never function in the role of a law-founding *arche*; on the contrary, they challenge the very principle of *archiphilia* which lies at the ground of all non-antinomian traditions, based on the stability of their *tradendum*.

The defence of Spirit's antinomianism is the reason why, in the *Archive Fever*, Derrida engages in the critique of Yoseph Yerushalmi's *Zakhor*: a work which emphasizes the exceptional character of Judaism as the 'archive of memory', based on the unique imperative of *zakhor / remember!* Contrary to Yerushalmi's thesis, Derrida proclaims a necessity of the opposite, *archiviolitic*, gesture which will burn down the archive – yet not in the name of some empty *an-archy*, but precisely *in the name* of the Hebrew Spirit called *ruah*, that is, in the name of the spirit of the very tradition which has accumulated its own massive archive. For, if the spirit of this tradition is *messianicity* – the universal call for radical justice, which, precisely because of that, cannot be appropriated by any particular tradition – then it not only can but also must transgress the Law which organizes the house of Judaism, or the tradition understood as the archiphilic Scholemian *Tradierbarkeit*: 'what is handed over'. Thus, in the manner similar to Sabbatai Tsevi, who claimed that the ultimate goal of studying the Torah is the violation of the Torah, Derrida will maintain that the final destiny of the Jewish archive is to turn into a heap of ashes. The messianic futurity *cannot* be but universal and thus an-archive; even if it grows within a particular archive-tradition, it cannot but aim at the transcendence of such particularity. To turn the archive into ashes is thus the secret vocation of the archive: 'The secret is the very ash of the archive' (AF, 100).[79]

Yet, these ashes do not spell a 'deadness of tradition', but, to the contrary, its hidden messianic vitality: the embers keep glowing. Even if the history is full of the Marrano hooligans who, as Jacob Frank, advocated literal execution of the call to burn the archives, Derrida's insistence on bringing archives to ashes is purely virtual, even if riskily playing with the image of *auto da fé* which became a tragic part of the history of the Iberian *conversos*. The symbol of the burnt archive is to remind us of the antinomian relation hidden within the womb of Judaic tradition – the contrast between the fiery spark of its messianic truth and the highly flammable library of *Tradierbarkeit* – which needs to be constantly remembered: this is the true aim of *zakhor*. But for Derrida, what remains after the archive's fever/fire is not just a barren heap of ashes: the glowing

---

[79] It is not improbable that, while recommending to burn the archives in the *Archive Fever*, Derrida might have in mind the imperative – *il faut brûler les livres* – which was formulated by Marc-Alain Ouaknin in *Le Livre Brûlé: Lire le Talmud* (Paris: Lieu Commun, 1986), 389. In Quaknin's interpretation of Nachman of Bretslav, who famously – and in a precursorial gesture to Kafka – wished to burn all his works as totally inadequate to the ineffable mystery of the creation, this imperative acquires a deep antinomian significance: 'This seems to be a solution: "one must burn the books"; let the objects to pass into a stage of "almost-objects"; erase the *Tav* [symbolizing death, thus leaving only the aleph, the symbol of the divine spirit – A. B.-R.] and make apparent the lack, the void, the rupture; let the fire be seen, which won't allow these books to be consumed by the totality of the world' (ibid., 388).

cinders – *feu la cendre* – symbolize the Phoenix-like renewal of the tradition.[80] For Derrida, Marrano is precisely such a figure of a Jewish Phoenix: certainly less sublime, but nonetheless capable to walk through the virtual *auto da fe*, limping like Jacob on the desert, but still – living on.

In *Archive Fever*, Derrida playfully betrays his Marrano sympathies, while referring to Yerushalmi's essay on the photographs of the 'last Marranos' in Portugal made by Frederic Brenner. While watching the portraits of the Portuguese Marranos, Yerushalmi asks, 'But are they really the last?' – and this question receives an oblique reply from Derrida: no, they are not; this secret tradition will continue. Not only does he assert that he has 'always secretly identified' with the Marrano heritage (immediately adding in the joking parabasis: 'but don't tell anyone'), but also drags into this heritage of Jewish secrecy the father of psychoanalysis himself, by claiming that 'this crypto-Judaic history greatly resembles that of psychoanalysis after all' (AF, 69). Then, on the next few pages, Derrida gives us a brief prolegomena to any future Marrano strategy, which he identifies with messianicity 'radically distinguished from all messianism' (AF, 72): a universal form of Jewishness which, in distinction to the 'terminable Judaism' of the rabbinic formation of *tradendum*, remains the interminable, inextinguishable, indestructible, eternal 'truth of the tradition'.

> It can survive Judaism. It can survive it as a heritage, which is to say, in a sense, not without archive, even if this archive should remain without substrate and without actuality [. . .] This is what would be proper to the 'Jew' and to him alone: not only hope, not only a 'hope for the future,' but 'the anticipation of a specific hope for the future'. (AF, 72)

This is what 'constitutes Jewishness beyond all Judaism', or, in the Blanchotian manner, *judaisme sans judaisme*: an 'archive without archive' – a condition which Derrida attributes to the Marranos who survived the trial by fire. As we have already seen,

---

[80] See Jacques Derrida, 'Feu la cendre', *Anima* 5 (December 1982): 45–99. In this literary phantasy, Derrida imagines *la Cendre* as 'a feminine phantom tremble deep within the word, in the smoke, the proper name deep within the common noun', which most directly refers to *ruah* (the feminine Hebrew name of the Spirit/Spark) as the fiery truth and the invisible proper name concealed in the concept of God who reveals himself in the smoky column drawing through the desert, but, more obliquely, also evokes *Khôra*, another female name hidden within the common noun: Jacques Derrida, *Cinders*, trans. Ned Lukacher (Lincoln: Nebraska University Press, 1991), 33. As Ned Lukacher's introduction promptly reminds us, the antinomian reversal hidden in the metaphor of embers was first spotted by Shakespeare who makes his Anthony declare: 'Oh, and I shall show the cinders of my spirit through the ashes of my chance': William Shakespeare, *Anthony and Cleopatra*, w *The Works of Shakespeare: Collated with the Oldest Copies, and Corrected*, vol. 7 (London, 1723), 204. This could indeed be the motto to Derrida's Marrano dialectics in *Archive Fever*: Judaism's vitality lies precisely in the cinders of its Spirit burning against ashes of its so often disastrous historical chances – the inner fire of *ruah* against the outer fire of *auto da fé* and Shoah. On the Kabbalistic symbolic of the cinders, see also *Zohar*: 'he who cares to pierce into the mystery of the holy unity of God should consider the flame as it rises from a burning coal': Gershom Scholem and Moses de Leon, *The Book of Spendor: Basic Readings from the Kabbalah*, trans. Gershom Scholem (New York: Schocken, 1963), 14.

this aporetic *X sans X* is not a blockage, but an opening: 'To be open toward the future would be to be Jewish, and vice versa [. . .] In the future, remember to remember the future' (AF, 74; 76). And although Derrida quotes Yerushalmi's definitions of 'Judaism interminable' not without irony, he nonetheless confirms that what counts in this whole enormous archive, accumulated obsessively by the Jewish archons of memory, is the unique index of its imperative to remember: it is not past-oriented towards the acts of grounding and legitimating a supposedly distinct ' Jewish identity' (for which he gently reproaches Yerushalmi), but future-oriented, proleptic, and unprecedentedly open – to a *futurité*. This messianic index, although maintained only by the archive of tradition, is thus also something that destroys the archive in its function of preserving and guarding the chosen nation's particularity. So, when Yerushalmi says, 'Only in Israel and nowhere else is the injunction to remember felt as a religious imperative of an entire people' (AF, 76), Derrida will immediately twist this identificatory sentence with its pathos of distinction into a messianic formula of promised universalization which, in the future, will have abolished 'the alternative between the future and the past, or between "hope" and "hopelessness," the Jew and the non-Jew, the future and repetition' (AF, 79).

The hyper-formulaic power of *zakhor*, the incantation of the phrase that impresses with the force of 'the strong light of the canonical' emerges again in Derrida's late essay, 'Abraham, the Other'. Here once again it associates itself immediately with the motif of secrecy. Following the theme of the 'Freudian Impression' – the *Niederschrift* of the unconscious which keeps its inscriptions intact in their materiality as a force beyond siginification – Derrida talks about *zakhor* in terms of a deeply hidden code, heavy and material in its weight of a sheer impression, *Ein-druck*. It thus belongs to the bodily archive of circumcision – a kind of an inner circumcision, a 'circumcised heart', yet without the Pauline connotations of pure spirituality. It is still *material*, despite the fact of being secret and inward:

> Hence this law that comes upon me, a law that, *appearing antinomian*, dictated to me, in a precocious and obscure fashion, in a kind of light whose rays are unbending, the hyper-formalized formula of a destiny devoted to the secret – and that is why I play seriously, more and more, with the figure of the marrano: the less you show yourself as jewish, the more and better jew you will be. The more radically you break with the certain dogmatism of the place or of the bond, the more you will be faithful to the hyperbolic, excessive demand, to the hubris, perhaps, of a universal and disproportionate responsibility towards the singularity of every other. (AO, 13; emphasis added)

This hyper-ethical, hyper-political, hyper-philosophical responsibility 'burns at the most irredentist core of what calls itself *jew*' (AO, 13). Secret, spectral, remnant-like; refusing to be captured in any philosophical and theological idiom; antinomian in its law-like injunction to break every law and attend to singularity only; universal in its effervescent indefinability – this 'core of what calls itself a *jew*' will burn 'interminably' until, according the meaning of 'irredentism', it *recovers what had been lost*: the sense of the *messianic justice*, submerged under so many archives-pyramids and so many overt identifications of so many different Abrahamic denominations. What thus needs to be recovered-remembered (*zakhor*) is the lost – encrypted, hidden, buried – *messianicity* and its future-oriented index of universal promise and hope. This is the 'severe light of the canonical' (*das strenge Licht des Kanonischen*) that emanates from the crypt with its 'unbending rays'.[81] Everything else must bend to this Law of Laws, accept a merely relative status, while the Law itself – the antinomian Law of Justice – will remain indeconstructible.

' – Have we lost *it* then? – Almost' (PJD, 85–7). In what follows, I will try to prove that finding out Derrida's Marrano secret is the same as saving the universal messianic promise. The stake is high. It is not just the question of discovering yet another Derrida, however important this project may be for the ever-growing Derridologist archive (I leave for a moment a question of whether and how it should accommodate Derrida's archiviolithic desire). His own 'disaster' of not being found out as a Marrano translates into the disaster of much graver consequences: the loss of the messianic idiom, which does not have a language of its own and – just like the spiritual descendants of Iberian *conversos* – can only speak Hebrew through all other languages under the sun.

---

[81] Scholem, 'Zehn Unhistorische Sätze', 242.

1

Betray, betray again, betray better
Marrano theology of survival

From Jerusalem a remnant shall go out, from Mount Zion a band of survivors.
                                                                    Isa. 37.32

Everything that I say can be interpreted as arising from the best Jewish tradition and at the same time as an absolute betrayal. I have to confess: this is exactly what I feel.
                            Jacques Derrida, 'Confession et Circumfession', 83

As Derrida admits in his reply to the critics of *Specters of Marx*, he resorts to the Marrano metaphor often and seriously, although – as befits the true Marrano, the secret follower of Judaism undercover – rarely openly:

> we could, between us, use a coded language, like Marranos [. . .] For I found the allusion to the Marranos in 'The Specter's Smile' highly seductive. I know that Negri was thinking, as always, of Spinoza. But no matter. He probably does not know that I have often played, as seriously as can be imagined, at secretly presenting myself as a sort of Marrano. I have done so in particular, and openly, in *Aporias*, *Circonfessions* [sic] and *Archive Fever* – and, doubtless, elsewhere as well. And I have done so less only *everywhere* – for example, in *Le Monolinguisme de l'autre*. But I will not unveil all the other scenes of this simulacrum [. . .] Claims have also been advanced to the effect that the question of marranism was recently closed for good. I don't believe it for a second. There are still sons – and daughters – who, unbeknownst to themselves, incarnate or metempsychosize the ventriloquist specters of their ancestors. (MS, 262–3; emphasis added)

In those rare moments where the word 'Marrano' actually appears in Derrida's writings, it is often coupled with 'ontology' ('Marx & Sons') and 'ontotheology' (*Faith and Knowledge*): the sciences of being, of what things are *in* themselves, rather than sciences of knowledge, of what things are *for* themselves. The Marranos are marranic in themselves but not for themselves; the deepest secret of the *conversos* consists in being not recognizable even to their bearers: 'those who, though they are really, presently, currently, effectively, *ontologically* Marranos, no longer know it themselves' (MS, 263). A Marrano, 'unbeknownst to himself', is an object of the secret that chose him ('Let us figuratively call Marrano *anyone* who remains faithful to a secret that he has not chosen', A, 81), and not a subject which modern philosophy understands as being for itself, actively choosing and reflecting on its choices. By defining the Marranos as ontological, Derrida delegates *marranismo* to the realm of *sum*, more distinct and separate from the realm of *cogito* than even the deepest form of the unconscious. To be a Marrano is most of all *to be*: to possess a specific *modus essendi* which is non-accessible for the reflexive and conscious modes of existence – a way of being that cannot be captured by the subjective symbolic system of signs. In the Introduction, we saw that such non-symbolic way of being is characteristic of a 'remnant' which escapes any signifier. In this chapter, we will see that, for Derrida, this evasion characterizes the Marrano form of survival: the Marrano *sum* is *survie*, a stubborn living-on which survives the death of the tradition and goes on as a *bared life*: not a 'bare life' or 'mere life' – the Benjaminian *blosses Leben*, later on taken over by Giorgio Agamben as *nuda vita* – but a life denuded from the symbolic self-interpretation and constantly reaffirming itself in its remnant-like mode. I will try to prove that it is precisely the notion of the *bared life* and its survival that sits at the very centre of Derrida's Marrano-messianicity: by refusing to sacrifice for the sake of their God and religion, the Marranos realize the gist of the 'hidden' messianic vocation the goal of which is to take us out of the sacrificial logic, inherent to all cultic religions, and offer us a vision of a freer, happier way of living. The bared life, therefore, is not a reduced remainder of a once fully meaningful life, but an inkling of life liberated and no longer sacrificeable; not a '*mere* life' of a despised *survie*, but '*more* life' of the desired *sur-vie*. Paradoxically, the Marrano would be most faithful in his deepest betrayal: if, for Derrida, messianicity – the urge to go against and beyond sovereign structures of power and authority – is the most valuable core of the religious discourse, it is precisely the Marrano, the 'filthy traitor', who embodied the messianic possibility in the paradigmatic manner.[1]

A desire to be a Marrano: Into life

The specific feature of Derrida's Marrano self-diagnosis is that it actively *wishes* to embrace the Marrano condition as a chance and opportunity, not a curse. This, in fact, is far more enigmatic than his Marrano (non)identification: among those individuals scattered all over the world, who call themselves *marranes*, Derrida's affirmation forms

---

[1] At a Villanova conference on 'Forgiveness', in the roundtable discussion, Derrida admitted that he wrestled with the idea of sacrifice all his life, even while he saw it as sadly inevitable: 'I am constantly against the logic of sacrifice, especially in the question of forgiveness. I am trying to deconstruct the logic of sacrifice [. . .] So I try not to be simply sacrificialistic but at the same time I cannot deny that sacrifice is unavoidable': 'On Forgiveness: A Roundtable Discussion with Jacques Derrida', in *Questioning God*, ed. John D. Caputo, Mark Dooley, and Michael Scanlon (Bloomington: Indiana University Press, 2001), 67.

so far a 'party of one'. For, why would anybody want to identify with the Marranos? What could possibly be desirable in the condition of the forced *conversos* who were given a terrible choice: either death, if they were to stick to their Jewish faith – or life, but in a new, Christian, religion? For Alberto Moreiras, the expert of *marranismo* in Latin American culture, to be a Marrano is inescapably a form of a passively suffered affliction and to be called a Marrano an inevitable label:

> Starting from the fact that *marrano is not something one is but rather something that happens to one* – they call you a marrano, and *it is an insult, it is the stigma of double exclusion*. It is the consequence of a radical (indeed, lethal) exclusion from identity. *Whoever is called marrano must swallow it possibly in disagreement with the intentional tonality of the naming*. She or he will not be marrano in the sense of the accusation, a pig, a degenerate, but she or he understands that the other's perception performs or corroborates an exclusion from hegemony, an exclusion from the political game, in an abject (and abjected) situation from the game, *just an outsider, just an outcast that could be killed without murder or sacrifice*, to paraphrase Giorgio Agamben.[2]

A Marrano, therefore, would be an incurable abject in Julia Kristeva's *bestiarium* of the powers of horror, as well as the most despicable *homo sacer*, banned from the cultured *bios* of humanity proper and carrying only the worthless, *unlebeswertig*, 'bare life' which can be put down with impunity by anybody belonging to the higher, symbolic, forms of life. Yet, Derrida still insists on calling *himself* a *marrane*, a creature 'lower than dust'. As usual, it is Hélène Cixous who can help us with an answer. According to Cixous, just as Kafka expresses 'a wish to be an Indian' – a wish to ride a bucket like a child and enjoy the freedom of the prairy – Derrida articulates a similar *Wunsch*: to say *yes, yes* to his Marrano predicament and, by affirming it, turn it into his liberating advantage. He thus wants to find the 'all-speed' thanks to which he will no longer be bothered by any stationary identification which fixates, slows down, roots, and grounds; he wants to be an outsider and an outcast, excluded from the political games of naming, not in order to be killed with impunity, but in order to find '*more life*'. In Cixous' account, the desire to be a Marrano seizes Derrida quite suddenly, in a vivid dream of running blithely ahead with no sense of identity or purpose, without even remembering that there was ever a question/imperative of 'finding oneself'. From the perspective of the fixed ones – men and women bound to the territories of their names, belongings, and origins – this speedy run may appear as nothing but a flight in panic. But for Derrida – as well as for Kafka – it is not just an escape: it is a pure run, a new way of living without belonging; not a passive evasion, but an active 'becoming, being, doing'.

> *If one could be a marrano* – which is like the desire to become an Indian – this seizes hold of him one morning, a foreign seizure like the one that takes hold of

---

[2] Alberto Moreiras, *Against Abstraction: Notes from an Ex-Latin Americanist* (Austin: University of Texas Press, 2020), 41; emphasis added.

Kafka, that *Wunsch, Indianer zu werden*, but what is this being-Indian, is it flight feint or word, like that horse's desire, the becoming, the being, the doing, all that is interchangeable, *what is a marrano, how can one be one, one must first want*, and immediately, astride the stream that feigns being the Jordan, the body quivering with a shudder as though one were astride a real horse, *to the point of crossing from one side to the other* this stream that seems to be a sea all red, *to run faster than desire*, faster than possibility up to the moment where one throws off the reins for there are no more reins, to the moment of letting go the bit [*mors*], the dead [*le mort*], yet there never was a bit, death, only the word, the fugue or fury of the body of the soul, bodily seized, enchanted, more and more foreign more and more secret, and *one ends by no longer remembering that one has forgotten where one believed one would find oneself*, thanks to this all-speed it happens that he substitutes himself, that I substitute itself. Thus it is on the withers of a dream that *he marranates himself*. Jewfeint. The dream: *to believe oneself the child of a people northis northat in the time of a dream*. Norcatholic norjew midjew midsame midindian midhorse. For the dream like the Mishnah plays on the force of words. (TSB, 65; emphasis added)[3]

Just as in Scholem's dream-desire, which I discussed in the Introduction – to be someone capable to embrace life and survival as the winning argument in the game of tradition – Derrida's *Marrano rêverie* is also about living-on that trumps all traditional fixed forms of life. For Cixous, Derrida's Marrano auto-fiction – 'the imaginary marrano who strives to imagine or to imagine himself' – defines his 'strange ways: a demand for imagination (intimation or supplication?) which is a way to take up the counterpoint of the philosophical tradition' (TSB, 69). By siding with the despised survival which all traditions, both religious and philosophical, unanimously see as 'lower than dust', Derrida imagines himself as a Marrano Messiah who would pick up this rejected stone and throw it against the traditional systems of sublimation that leave no room for *survie*. In that sense, he indeed sees himself as 'elected' within the messianic line

---

[3] In *Fichus*, a speech given at the reception of Adorno Award, Derrida praises the Frankfurt precursor for challenging the 'philosophical sect' (APO, 25) with his serious approach to dreams, which chimes well with his own 'Marrano rêverie': 'What does Adorno suggest to us? The difference between the dream and reality, this truth to which the philosopher recalls us with an inflexible severity, would be that which injures, hurts, or damages *beschädigt* the most beautiful dreams and deposits the signature of a stain, a dirtying *Makel*. The *no*, what one might call in another sense the *negativity* that philosophy sets against the dream, would be a wound of which the most beautiful dreams forever bear the scar [. . .] Now the word that Adorno uses for this wound, *beschädigt*, is the very one that appears in the subtitle to *Minima Moralia: Reflexionem aus dem beschädigten Leben [Reflections from Damaged Life]*. Not "reflections *on*" a wounded, injured, damaged, mutilated life, but "reflections *from or starting from*" such a life, *aus dem beschädigten Leben*: reflections marked by pain, signed by a wounding' (PM, 166). The speech itself is a Marrano meisterschtück, implicating a secret society of dream-lovers – Benjamin, Adorno, and Derrida himself – which has its distant, never explicitly evoked, roots in the Talmudic dream hermeneutics: 'A dream that is not interpreted is like a letter that is unread' (Babylonian Talmud, *Berachot*, 55a). For Derrida, his 'Marrano rêverie' – starting from the dream told by Cixous – is precisely such a letter that cannot be ignored: a beautiful message of freedom, which gets damaged the moment it confronts the harsh light of reality and which then must be recovered in reflection 'marked by pain, signed by a wounding'.

foretold by Kafka and Benjamin. According to the latter, *The Castle* should be read as a grotesque portrayal of the situation of the assimilated German Jewry, which, as we already know, Scholem compared to the one of the Marranos: the Jews who lost the keys that could open the gate to the castle of the Holy of Hollies and now only survive at the foot of the hill. Yet, in contrast to Scholem, who would like to refind the key and revive the divine spectre haunting the castle, Benjamin stakes on life itself. Life emerges here as the true secret of the Scripture that should be reinterpreted anew, away from the sublime connotations of the tradition and closer to the message of survival (*u-baharta ba-hayim*), demanding to be properly heard for the first time in history and thus carefully 'studied'. From the old point of view of the Jewish *tradendum*, the keys may indeed seem lost, yet, when we shift the perspective towards *das Wahre*, life-survival suddenly offers itself as a new key:

> Whether the pupils have lost it [the Scripture] or whether they are unable to decipher it comes down to the same thing, because, without the key that belongs to it, the Scripture is not Scripture, but life. Life as it is lived in the village at the foot of the hill on which the castle is built. *It is in the attempt to metaphorize life into Scripture that I perceive the meaning of 'reversal'* [*Umkehr*], *which so many of Kafka's parables endeavour to bring about* [. . .] *Kafka's messianic category is 'the reversal' or the 'studying.'*[4]

We could, in fact, sum up Derrida's Marrano project in terms of the Kafkan reversal. It is a study of life as survival – *learning to live, finally* – at the foot of every hill that represents the lofty edifice of tradition, abstracted – absolved, detached – from the filth of the village life. The aim of this new study is *to metaphorize life into Scripture*: reverse the meaning of the Holy Message, desublimate it, and turn it, once again, into a religion of the living ('The religion of the living – is this not a tautology?' FK, 85). In *Faith and Knowledge*, Derrida claims that the key to the understanding of 'religion' is the process of abstraction: hence the word itself so often appears in Derrida's writings in inverted commas. Derrida's *abstraction of religion* constitutes an inversion of what he perceives as the common mechanism of the religious sublimation, that is, the *religion of abstraction*: a detachment from the ordinary life and world, which creates the idea of an eternal *ab-solutus*, the Supreme Being untouched – 'unscathed' – by anything finite, beyond change or harm. By opposing religion's flight into the icy regions of the absolute, the reverse manoeuvre abstracts 'religion' from its traditional theological rooting in the discourse of the Absolute and *re-attaches* it to life – always scathed and finite – from which it originally came as the 'religion of the living'. What thus Derrida calls in the Blanchotian manner 'religion without religion' has its parallel in a 'life without life': an abstraction from the theological abstraction, which returns the notion of life to its earthly dimension, deprived of the immortal component – a simple

---

[4] *Benjamin-Scholem Correspondence*, Letter 63, 135.

survival, totally immersed in the 'time of life'.[5] In the essay 'Psychoanalysis Searches the States of Its Soul: The Impossible Beyond of a Sovereign Cruelty', Derrida explains that the *foi originaire* expresses itself in the originary affirmation of survival *before* and *beyond* any principles and categories that rule the symbolic sphere and in that sense constitutes also the originary transcendence: the *sur-vie*, over-life, affirming its finitude not as a privation, but as an indelible mark of life worthy of being lived.

> The affirmation I am advancing advances itself, in advance, already, without me, without alibi, as *the originary affirmation* from which, and thus beyond which the death drive and the power, cruelty, and sovereignty drives determine themselves as 'beyond' the principles [...] It is not a principle, a princedom, a sovereignty. It comes then from a beyond the beyond, and thus from beyond the economy of the possible. It is attached to a life, certainly, but to a life other than that of the economy of the possible, an im-possible life no doubt, *a sur-vival, not symbolizable,* but the only one that is worthy of being lived, without alibi, once and for all, the only one from which to depart [...] for a possible thinking of life. Of a life that is still worthy of being lived, once and for all [...] *This can only be done on the basis of a sur-vival that owes nothing to the alibi of some mytho-theological beyond.* (WA, 276; emphasis added)

Careful not to recreate a sublime transcendence, Derrida will nonetheless meet the challenge of 'a sur-vival, not symbolizable' and attempt to articulate it in the symbolic sphere – a new Scripture – which will have to adapt to the discovery of a life-without-alibi, best represented by a Marrano.

Messianic ambivalence

The 'desire to be a Marrano' and to appropriate, at least partially, the powerful charge of accusation contained in this name, is thus not a fancy or a whim: its energy can indeed explode the philosophico-theological system of the West – *la grenade entamée* (FK-F, 100), a launched grenade thrown into the mist of the Capri seminar on religion – and bring something completely new, a new 'serious play' of messianic proportions. The transition – from the label attributed from the third-person perspective to the affirmative first-person auto-declaration – is a frequent move in Derrida's deconstructive practice. This particular conversion, however, concerning the Marrano nomination, is far from unproblematic. We already saw that it always involves a certain hesitance and deliberate imprecision of *une sorte*: one can never see 'a sort of Marrano' face to face (C, 171), but also the one who calls himself by the name 'Marrano' can never simply assume this nomination in the first person, grounded in the Cartesian certainty of '*therefore I am* [*donc je le suis*]' (AO, 5). The name 'Marrano' is indeed a 'grenade' which shatters the integrity of the reflexive subject and leaves it in the state of dissociation. In 'Abraham, the Other', Derrida addresses the issue directly, by describing

---

[5] On the Blanchotian construct of the Derridean survie as 'life without life', see King-Ho Leung, 'The Religion (without religion) of the Living (without life): Re-reading Derrida's *Faith and Knowledge*', *Eidos: Journal for the Philosophy of Culture* 3 (2021): 35–49.

the experience of a *dissociation that is at once possible, necessary, and impossible*. An alternative at once promised and denied [. . .] First, a dissociation between persons, the grammatical marks of the person [. . .] I designate in this way the dissociation between the first, second, and third persons, singular and plural [. . .] How do these persons translate into each other and is it possible? Can one authorize oneself to move from 'you are Jewish' [*tu es juif ou juive*] to a "therefore I am" [*donc je le suis*]? (AO, 5; emphasis added)

And although Derrida claims that 'this reciprocating conversion of the "you" into an "I" or a "we" is problematical, even impossible' (AO, 18), he nonetheless engages precisely in that very impossibility: the brazen audacious appropriation of a label, a gesture which goes beyond the Sartrean external interpellation, keeping the nominated as a hostage of the hostile gaze, towards a full-fledged messianic reversal where the most despised 'pig' becomes a new object of desire. We saw that, for Alberto Moreiras, who refuses any appropriating tinkering with the word 'Marrano', such transformation of the Marrano curse into messianic blessing is blatantly impossible and certainly non-necessary. A slightly more dialectical position was assumed by Gil Anidjar who follows Derrida in his experiment of the Marrano nomination, accepting the challenge of the impossible as the true task of deconstruction, but also to a certain point. While I would like to push it to the extreme of a total inversion, Anidjar pauses at the aporia of the possible/impossible 'scene of translation that allows – but how? – to pass from the second or third person to the first'.[6] According to Anidjar, there is no answer to this 'how': the translation gets necessarily arrested in the regions of the unconscious as a 'secret' – the third person within the first person – because to be named 'Marrano' involves a traumatic wound (*blessure*) that cannot be accommodated by the 'I':

> The Marrano names himself by the inscription of the wound in the secret of a destiny without destination [. . .] If he names himself, it is always in response to a nomination, an address and an apellation which destine him for a secret. He names himself by being named by the law which calls and destines him who will never know or even be able to tell if it is *him* called by the law by the name he calls himself.[7]

The secrecy, therefore, is *structural*: it is determined not by a mysterious content of the call, deposited in the *Niederschrift* of the unconscious, but a position of indeterminacy between the third and the first person or the gap in subjectivity which cannot close upon itself in the gesture of appropriating affirmation. Thus, when Derrida says, 'I am a sort of a Marrano', the hesitance of this declaration is inscribed into the very name 'Marrano' which is 'illegitimate and, without doubt, a misnomer'.[8] In naming himself a

---

[6] Gil Anidjar, 'Je te suis vrai (ce qui du marrane m'arrive)', in *L'Herne: Jacques Derrida* (Paris: Éditions de l'Herne, 2004), 251.
[7] Ibid., 252.
[8] Ibid., 253.

'Marrano', Derrida cannot arrive at any destination because the name 'Marrano' does not mean anything – apart from signifying a 'Jew' in a particularly offensive manner: 'The Marrano names a truncated Jew [*Juif de souche*]. The name of the Marrano remains a *Jew*'.[9] The name itself, therefore, does not create any surplus of significance: it merely adds to the meaning 'Jew' an abjectual halo of monstrosity, abomination, and horror, which – as Kristeva explains – can only be expelled outside, but never invited inside the conscious self. The *ab-ject* is 'something to be scared of'[10], projected out, removed from sight, but never a welcome guest to be received by the psyche with open arms. It may fascinate the desire, susceptible to its 'summons', but the self prefers to hold on to its Cartesian certainty and resist seduction:

> There looms, within abjection, one of those violent, dark revolts of being [. . .] ejected beyond the scope of the possible, the tolerable, the thinkable. *It lies there, quite close, but it cannot be assimilated.* It beseeches, worries, and fascinates desire, which, nevertheless, does not let itself be seduced. Apprehensive, desire turns aside; sickened, it rejects. *A certainty protects it from the shameful* – a certainty of which it is proud holds on to it. But simultaneously, just the same, that impetus, that spasm, that leap is drawn toward an *elsewhere* as tempting as it is condemned. Unflaggingly, like an inescapable boomerang, a vortex of summons and repulsion places the one haunted by it literally beside himself.[11]

The abjectual powers of horror also belong to the house of the messianic: to the *elsewhere* from which the Messiah comes in the Yeatsian form of 'some beast slouching towards Jerusalem to be born'. Hence the characteristic reserve of the Talmudic sage who accepts the inevitability of the messianic advent, but with apprehension, perhaps even revulsion: 'May he come, but I do not want to see him.'[12] This sentence articulates perfectly the ambivalence of the messianic desire: while 'may he come' responds to the 'summon' of the messianic call, the refusal to confront the Messiah face to face reverts to the lawful certainty of the here and now, of which the Talmud is so rightly proud. Derrida does not differ in this respect: his 'wish to be a Marrano', expressing his messianic desire, is equally ambivalent – apprehensive, often sickened, but also incurably fascinated, attracted to the severe 'unbending rays' (AO, 13) of the call which he, similarly the Kafkan 'another Abraham', would want to avoid and follow at the same time.

Anidjar does not mention Kristeva, but her definition of abjectuality aptly enhances the aura of insurmountable ambivalence which surrounds the Marrano 'appellation'. The name 'Marrano', invented by hostile others and forever 'traced with hatred',[13] names as a 'Jew' someone who no longer sees himself as a 'Jew' because his act of conversion

---

[9] Ibid., 250.
[10] Julia Kristeva, *Powers of Horror: An Essay on Abjection*, trans. Leon S. Roudiez (New York: Columbia University Press, 1982), 32.
[11] Ibid., 1; emphasis added.
[12] *Sanhedrin 98a*.
[13] Anidjar, '*Je te suis vrai*', 250.

proved, in fact, to be quite 'successful'.¹⁴ Derrida's conversion to the 'French Catholic culture' was certainly not a fiasco, having built in him a strong shield of 'certainty protecting him from the shameful'. The Marrano secret, therefore, once again shows a structural aspect of de-propriation (or the Heideggerian *Ent-eignis*, always hidden behind the call of *Er-eignis*¹⁵) which hinders the arrival of the name to the first person:

> The difficulty inscribed in the very name 'Marrano' consists in the fact that when it arrives, it immediately disappears, as if – by adding insult to injury – its existence were nothing but the invention of the other [...] How to affirm a situation in which a Marrano, if he calls himself that, cannot but do it through the act constitutive to a hostile law (even if what it reveals is love that sublates the Law) which interpellates him against his will, or, even better (or worse), against a will that is not his, merely imposed on him by the circumstances of his birth?¹⁶

Again, for Anidjar there is no answer to the 'how' of affirmation: no smooth passage from the offensive calling names to the inspiring Call of the Name. And yet, despite all apprehensions and worries, Derrida insists on calling *himself* a Marrano and in finding in it a new vocation; even better (or worse), he likes it, it grows on him like a new tallith, a second skin, perhaps even an 'alibi', though without a 'mytho-theological beyond' (WA, 276). At the same time, however, Anidjar is right: Derrida does not appropriate the name 'Marrano' in the first person in a Cartesian manner. He rather keeps it *in himself* – on the dialectical borderline/translation between introjection and incorporation, the first and the third person, the shell and the kernel, the self and the crypt, subject and object, abomination and obligation – as a 'silkworm of his own', that is, a secret worm that *secretes* all his writings which spin a protective cocoon-alibi and, at the same time, are the product-*imago* hutching out of the inchoate larve, the vague and broken name 'Marrano': 'a secret that perhaps keeps from judaism, but keeps as well a certain jewishness *in oneself* – here *in me*' (AO, 6; emphasis added). The en-crypted 'here-now [of the secret] does not appear as such, in experience, except by differing from itself. And one trace always refers to another trace. It thus *secretes*, it produces, it cannot not produce some alibi. Ubiquity of the alibi' (WA, xvii; emphasis added). The Marrano is thus never *for himself*: he is an 'ontological Marrano' *in himself*, always stumbling upon the Scholemian 'object'/Kristevan 'abject' that inhabits his inner crypt.

This experience of a dissociation between the 'I' and the 'It *in me*', therefore, is 'at once possible, necessary, and impossible' (AO, 5). Derrida is well aware of 'evil and risk' implied by it, but he simply cannot miss the 'opportunity' (AO, 5) which the Marrano nomination opens: the chance of a full messianic reversal in which this seemingly

---

¹⁴ Ibid., 247.
¹⁵ '*Ereignis*, a difficult word to translate (event or propriation that is inseparable from a movement of dis-propriation, *Enteignen*). This word *Ereignis*, which commonly signifies event, signals toward a thinking of appropriation or of *de-propriation* that cannot be unrelated to that of the gift' (GT, 19).
¹⁶ Ibid., 250.

modest 'certain jewishness' will have shaken the traumatic 'traces of hatred'[17] and turn the exception into a new rule according to which 'the less you show yourself as jewish, the more and better jew you will be' (AO, 13). It is precisely the hope for such a radical inversion that governs Derrida's discourse of *as if*: 'a certain *perhaps* of the *as if*, the poetical or the literary' (AO, 13).

> *As if* the one who disavowed the most, and who appeared to betray the dogmas of belonging, be it a belonging to the community, the religion, even to the people, the nation and the state, and so on – *as if* this individual alone represented the last demand, the hyperbolic request of the very thing he appears to betray by perjuring himself. (AO, 13)

Hence the highest antinomy which I will address in this chapter in detail: a call of the tradition, which can be heard and followed only by the one who openly betrays the tradition. To maintain oneself in the antinomy is a difficult – perhaps indeed impossible – state of exception of the soul, which requires a dissociation between a 'person' that follows and is (*je suis juif*) and a 'person' that unfollows and is not (*je ne suis pas juif*): a dissociation that can bring a risk of schizophrenic self-hatred, but also an opportunity of revealing and renewing the messianic stakes of Jewish tradition, its Scholemian, hidden and antinomian, *das Wahre*. Just as in the Lacanian teaching about the Real which can only be approached in a dream, Derrida is thus ready to betray the whole reality of Judaism in order not to betray his dream, his *Marrano rêverie*, and to transform it into a thinking that watches over the precious *Traumnabel*:

> *Overcoming* the dream without *betraying* it *ohne ihn zu verraten* – that's the way, says Benjamin [. . .] to wake up, to cultivate awakeness and vigilance, while remaining attentive to meaning, faithful to the lessons and the lucidity of a dream, caring for what the dream lets us think about, especially when what it lets us think about is the *possibility of the impossible*. The possibility of the impossible can only be dreamed, but thinking, a quite different thinking of the relation between the possible and the impossible, this other thinking I have been panting after for so long [. . .] perhaps has more affinity than philosophy itself with this dream. Even as you wake up, you would have to go on watching out for the dream, watching over it. (PM, 168)

Rewriting the scripture

The 'desire to be a Marrano' may thus be problematic to the point of impossibility, but it is not a 'misnomer'. Pace Anidjar who suggests that the meaning of the name 'Marrano' is *nothing* but 'Jew', so, as such, it merely creates an empty secret – a structural derivative of the non-appropriable 'trace of hatred' – I claim that it actually names *something*: a promise of the messianic reversal or an operation which, in *Faith and Knowledge*, corresponds to the 'abstraction of the abstraction' that re-attaches the 'holy' back to life conceived as an ordinary survival with no immortal supplements.

---

[17] Anidjar, '*Je te suis vrai . . .*', 250.

Seen from the perspective of the traditions based on the cults of the Absolute, such simple *survie* is nothing but abomination: a horrifying abject that pushes the subject away from itself and towards self-purifying sublimation (in Lacan's theory, such ultimate abject is *lamella*: a shapeless *tohu va-vohu* of life, a shameful bared base of the living process, a vital *pudendum* which the subject must negate in order to lift itself above sheer survival[18]). Yet, in Derrida's inverted perspective, survival becomes the very kernel of 'the religion of the living' (FK, 85): a new obligation which only a Marrano, the master of survival, can assume.

There is no reason why we should not interpret these radical shifts/*shuvs* with the terms used by the philosophers of religion in order to describe the 'normative inversion': the reversals that once created Judaism as a 'counter-religion' are still a living possibility, hidden in its core as latent seeds – precisely as those 'thousand seeds' in the opened pomegranate which figures in the centre of Derrida's Marrano Passover. The works of the 'normative inversion' are present everywhere in Derrida's *ouevre*, from the beginning till the end: the attempt to focus on the margins of the Western philosophico-theological thought and shift them to the centre is the explicit topic already in the eponymous *Margines of Philosophy*, but it begins to mature only with Derrida's Marrano project, involving a full messianic inversion – not only a simple transposition of the high and the low but a complete demolition of the hierarchical discourse. In Derrida's late thought, the antinomies of the Marrano nomination pave the way towards other recuperations of the low and despised with a messianic turn in view.

A characteristic first-person interception of the third-person blame occurs at the end of *Rogues*, when Derrida suddenly announces: 'The Rogue That I Am.' And indeed, the *voyou*, the citizen of the democracy to come, defined as the '*Khôra* of the political' (R, 44) bears the features of a universal Marrano:

> For the word *voyou* is itself a suspect word and the *voyou* himself a suspect character. Shady, questionable, of dubious character [*mauvais aim*], which is to say of suspicious origin [*mauvai salliage*] (as is said of bad or counterfeit money, illegal money that passes for genuine). It is always a question of a suspicious or mixed origin, of *alliage* and alliance, of, this time, some 'alligation' [*alligare*]. (R, 32)

Mixture, impurity, contamination, counterfaction, contrabande, secrecy, illegality, shadow: all that 'healthy society' deems suspect and criminal here becomes revindicated. Just as Marrano is a rogue believer – the *voyou* is a Marrano of social belonging. Marranos are thus rogue beings; dirty and impure from the start, they live and survive in the element of 'original heterogenity', contamination, exile, perhaps even catastrophe. And yet, or precisely because of that – Derrida desires to be a Marrano. What appears the lowest, basest, and good-for-nothing – 'northis northat', the *tohu-va-vohu* of the social universe, the nameless scum of the earth – becomes the centre

---

[18] Slavoj Žižek defines *lamella* as 'damp, unwholesome, and permeated with the decay of death', typically represented by the 'flayed, skinned body, the palpitation of raw, skinless red flesh': Slavoj Žižek, 'The Lamella of David Lynch', in *Reading Seminar XI: Lacan's Four Fundamental Concepts of Psychoanalysis*, ed. Richard Feldstein, Bruce Fink, and Maire Jaanus (Albany: State University of New York Press, 1995), 206, 208.

of a new paradoxical formation without formation. The denominated Marrano, who departed from his origins, but never arrived to a new promised land, is not a victim of a passive stuckness in the nameless limbo of universal exclusion. On the contrary, he is the Abrahamic imperative of *lekh lekha* embodied: like Kafka's Odradek, of 'no fixed abode' and nomadic to the extreme (not just 'walking away from the origins', running!), living his picaresque life at the foot of every Hill of Tradition. Marrano thus turns into what Agamben aptly calls a 'messianic *aphorismos*': the indivisible remainder of the 'band of survivors' – an early-modern prototype of the individual (*in-dividuus*) conceived as absolute remnant-like singularity.[19]

But for Derrida, Marrano is not just the *ontological différance* incarnate: *différance*, which disseminates and singularizes, and not difference, as in Heidegger's *ontologische Differenz* between Being and beings. In *Faith and Knowledge*, Derrida associates Marrano with ontotheology which forgets about the ontological difference and buries Being in a 'crypt'. Pace Heidegger, who always insists on the return to and pious remembrance of Being as the origin of all beings, Derrida takes the side of ontotheology and its incipient *Ursprungsvergessenheit*, the 'forgetfullness of the origin': just as ontotheology forgets the 'true' divinity, by misrepresenting it as *das Seiende* – so does Marrano forget about his 'true' God, by walking away from his origin, as well as *any* origin, also in the metaphysical sense. Thus, at the very end of his essay, Derrida says about ontotheology that it

> encrypts faith and destines it to the condition of a sort of Spanish Marrano who would have lost – in truth, dispersed, multiplied – everything up to and including the memory of his unique secret. Emblem of a still life: an opened pomegranate, one Passover evening, on a tray. (FK, 100; emphasis added)[20]

This is not a negative remark about loss; *in truth* (Scholemian *das Wahre*), it is an appreciation of the Marrano *conversos* who, only on the surface, would have lost the secret of their Jewishness. Because, *in truth*, they hadn't lost it, or rather: lost it *for* themselves, but not *in* themselves. The secret, fused with their mode of being, disperses and multiplies with them in the manner which the biblical topos affirms as the right thing to do, that is, as a mark of successful survival ('disperse and multiply!').

---

[19] See Giorgio Agamben, *The Time That Remains: A Commentary on the Letter to the Romans*, trans. Patricia Dailey (Stanford: Stanford University Press, 2005), 6, where he discusses Paul's self-attribution as *aphorismenos*, 'separated'.

[20] 'L'ontothéologie encrypte la foi et la destine à la condition d'une sorte de marrane espagnol qui aurait perdu, en vérité dispersé, multiplié, jusqu'à la mémoire de son unique secret. Emblème d'une nature morte: la grenade entamée, un soir de Pâques, sur un plateau' (FK-F, 100). When we discussed the idea of the book, Annabel Herzog pointed to me that there is no way a pomegranate would appear on a Passover plate, because not only is the fruit not ripe at the time of Passover but it is ripe at the time of Yom Kippur and Rosh Hashana, and it appears on the Rosh Hashana plate as a part of the Jewish New Year ritual. So, was this misplacement of the fruit deliberate or is it just a Marrano lack of knowledge? Or – yet another possibility – an expression of some unconscious wish to push the symbol of a new beginning away from Yom Kippur (Day of Atonement) and closer to the Passover celebration of the story of the Exodus, which, for Derrida, constitutes the paradigmatic narrative of messianicity?

The *marrano* (in Spanish, a 'pig') is the impure one, a person of the 'mixed blood', who lost the *memory* of her uniqueness and betrayed loyalty to her tradition, but the tradition still lives on, yet no longer as One: the Marranos carry it as multiplied and dispersed also internally, *plus d'Un* (FK, 100), contaminated to the point where it is no longer possible to tell the ownmost proper from the alien, the old Jewish faith from the new Christian one. Marrano is thus an emblem of a *still life* (*nature morte*): seemingly dead, but – *still/d'ailleurs* – a life that challenged the death of the old tradition; *still*, quiet, unassuming, restrained, mutilated, and yet – *still* – a life. A paradoxical emblem of a 'dead nature': yet un-dead and somehow *still* living-on, against all odds. A 'bared life' deprived of the grace of the symbolic, left to its own devices, and yet – *still there*, as if surprised by its own enigma of a simple survival.[21]

But the emblem of a 'dead nature' – if we understand it as the scholastic *natura pura* which signifies natural state of the world abandoned by the divine grace – suggests also something else: an association with the written letter as opposed to the Pauline living spirit, yet another 'rejected stone' of the Western philosophical tradition. And indeed, already in *Dissemination*, the *voyou* makes its first appearance as nothing else but *écriture* which had lost touch with its phonetic origins and wanders off into uncharted heterodoxy:

> It [writing] rolls this way and that like someone who has lost his way, who doesn't know where he is going, having strayed from the correct path, the right direction, the rule of rectitude, the norm; but also like someone who has lost his rights, an outlaw, a pervert, a bad seed, a vagrant, an adventurer, a bum. Wandering in the streets, he doesn't even know who he is, what his identity – if he has one – might be, what his name is, what his father's name is. (DIS, 143)

Writing, therefore – Derrida's favourite element – is like a vagrant-Marrano without identity, a restlessly Wandering Jew, and vice versa: the 'Spanish Marrano' also 'disperses, multiplies' (FK, 100) like the writing which is always in the process of a further and further dissemination. David Farrell Krell's comment makes this connection even stronger:

> Writing is forever an affair that *secretes itself again and again* as (impossible) legitimation, (inevitable) contamination of all domesticities, (invariable) confusion

---

[21] The concept of the enigma of survival was coined by Cathy Caruth who famously claimed that what truly traumatizes the subject is not so much the prospect of its death as that it somehow, mysteriously, is capable of surviving the instance of its death: 'Trauma is not simply an effect of destruction but also, fundamentally, an *enigma of survival* [. . .] The trauma consists not only in having confronted death but in having survived, precisely, without knowing it. What one returns to in the flashback is not the incomprehensibility of one's near death, but the very *incomprehensibility of one's own survival*. Repetition, in other words, is not simply the attempt to grasp that one has almost died but, more fundamentally and enigmatically, the very attempt to claim one's own survival. If history is to be understood as the history of a trauma, it is a history that is experienced as the *endless attempt to assume one's survival as one's own*': Cathy Caruth, *Unclaimed Experience. Trauma, Narrative, and History* (Baltimore: The Johns Hopkins University Press, 1996), 58 64; emphasis added.

and interweaving of lines and alignments, and (unstoppable) proliferation of genealogies. Writing is the orphan-bastard in distress [. . .] writing is both a wandering phantom abandoned by the father and a subversive parricide living off the fruits of his deferred crime. (PB, 206; emphasis added)

The Marrano, the *voyou*, and the writing are the three names of Derrida's 'serious play' which aims at the unheard of reversal of all metaphysical categories of the West – all based on sublimatory abstraction – which will be able to revert them to the forgotten 'religion of the living' and *rewrite the Scripture*.

Marrano Judaism, therefore, contracts into an encrypted secret – a *Niederschrift* of the unconscious writing – but this contraction, this radical *tsimtsum* of the tradition, does not spell its total demise; crippled, reduced, limping, it still survives, together with its impure carriers, the 'last of Jews' representing 'the death of Judaism, but also its one chance of survival' (TG, 42). In Derrida's account, the Marranos are the paradigmatic *masters of survival*: they choose to live on rather than die for the sake of their religious identity. From the point of Jewish orthodoxy, they are not masters of anything. Sometimes they are perceived as traitors and sinners, sometimes as unheroic cowards, sometimes as victims of historical misfortune, but despite the varying degrees of compassion, the accusation remains the same: instead of choosing *kiddush ha-shem*, a glorious death which sanctifies the Name, they chose life – life as living-on, the sheer *survie*. Judaism may, in fact, be more lenient towards life than other religions exalting in martyrdom, but still, to betray one's own kind for a purely pragmatic reason of staying alive and carrying on one's business/livelihood is certainly not a model of a good life that could be recommended by any, even most tolerant and compassionate, tradition. And yet, Derrida dares precisely that: he recommends nothing short of betrayal, deliberately choosing the antinomian path against the sanctioned and sanctified straight paths of all orthodoxies.[22]

---

[22] On the emergence of martyrdom as the new form of proving fidelity to the Jewish God, see Hans Jonas: 'In the long ages of faithfulness thereafter, guilt and retribution no longer furnished the explanation, but the idea of "witness" did instead, this creation of the Maccabean age, which bequeathed to posterity the concept of the martyr. It is of its very meaning that precisely the innocent and the just suffer the worst. In deference to the idea of witness, whole communities in the Middle Ages met their death by sword and fire with the *Sh'ma Jisrael*, the avowal of God's Oneness on their lips. The Hebrew name for this is *Kiddush-hashem*, "sanctification of the Name," and the slaughtered were called "saints." Through their sacrifice shone the light of promise, of the final redemption by the Messiah to come': Jonas, *Morality and Mortality*, 132–3. Which is not to say that either Judaism or Catholic Christianity of the fourteenth to sixteenth centuries can be easily reduced to such thanatic cultic structures: religion and cult are often at odds, especially in Derrida's account, where Judaism emerges as potentially most 'life-friendly'. Thus, although there were rabbis who, in the newly arisen Zealot mode, would demand from the Jews facing conversion a full readiness to martyrological sacrifice, the prevalent, less demanding and compassionate, position was set by Maimonides: 'Applying his logical mind to this burning (and perhaps personal) question, Maimonides discerned several modalities and degrees of conversion, and ruled that a forced convert must "abandon everything he possesses and walk day and night until he finds a place where he can reconstitute his [Jewish] religion"; *meanwhile*, he should keep a maximum of Jewish laws in secret' (OW, 43; emphasis added). See also: Moses Maimonides, 'Epistle on Conversion or a Treatise on Martyrdom', (Heb.) in *Epistles*, ed. M. D. Rabinowitz (Jerusalem: Rav Cook Institute,

This is the crucial moment in Derrida's meditation on the Marrano choice of living-on: to keep the antinomian path and *not* to allow for its orthodox correction, the way it was done by Emil Fackenheim who decided to rewrite the Jewish codex around the new term – *kiddush ha-hayim*, the sanctification of life. In *Jewish Return into History*, in the chapter called 'The 614th Commandment', Fackenheim famously explains the proposal of a new addition to the Maimonidean codification of Halakhah:

> we are, first, commanded to survive as Jews, lest the Jewish people perish. We are commanded, secondly, to remember in our very guts and bones the martyrs of the Holocaust, lest their memory perish. We are forbidden, thirdly, to deny or despair of God, however much we may have to contend with him or with belief in him, lest Judaism perish. We are forbidden, finally, to despair of the world as the place which is to become the kingdom of God, lest we help make it a meaningless place in which God is dead or irrelevant and everything is permitted. To abandon any of these imperatives, in response to Hitler's victory at Auschwitz, would be to hand him yet other, posthumous victories.[23]

After the Holocaust, claims Fackenheim, the Jews *must* learn to cherish their life – 'lest Judaism perish': *kiddush ha-hayim*, as opposed to the traditional *kiddush ha-shem*, which meant martyrdom for the sake of keeping the Jewish faith, is Judaism's sole chance of survival. Fackenheim locates this historical reversal in the writings of Issac Nissenbaum, the chief rabbi of Warsaw Ghetto, who saw in it a new hope, resurrecting for Jewish people after the *Shoah*:

> A statement of his spread like wildfire, inspiring believers and nonbelievers alike. This, he taught, was not a time for *kiddush ha-shem*, the sanctification of the divine Name through Jewish martyrdom. It was a time for *kiddush ha-hayim*, the sanctification of life. Formerly, he explained, the enemy wanted the Jewish soul,

---

1981), 64–5, as well as Isadore Twersky, 'Maimonides', in *Understanding Rabbinic Judaism: From Talmudic to Modern Times*, ed. Jacob Neusner (Eugene, OR: Wipf and Stock, 2003), 194, which contains a concise summary of Maimonides's *Letter on Conversion (Iggeret ha-Shemad)*. Indeed, the humane solution proposed by Maimonides has a good standing in the Talmud which, as Daniel Boyarin convincingly shows, does not advocate a heroic and possibly lethal confrontation, but essentially 'unheroic' art of evasion that puts as first the value of survival: 'The appropriate form of resistance that the Talmud recommends for Jews in this place is *evasion* [...] The central Babylonian talmudic myth of the foundation of rabbinic Judaism involves such an act of evasion and trickery, the "grotesque" escape in a coffin of Rabbi Yohanan ben Zakkai from besieged Jerusalem, which the Rabbis portray as the very antithesis of the military resistance of the Zealots who wanted to fight to the very last man and preserve their honor. Here we find the same political theory – *Get out of there!*': Daniel Boyarin, *Unheroic Conduct: The Rise of Heterosexuality and the Invention of the Jewish Man* (Berkeley: University of California Press, 1997), 94. According to Boyarin, the Rabbis do not really recommend martyrdom, but even if it occurs, the Jewish variant of martyrology appears different, somewhat 'sweeter' than the Roman-Christian model of a bloody painful death as continuation of the ascetic mortification of the body (ibid., 115).

[23] Emil L. Fackenheim, *Jewish Return into History: Reflections in the Age of Auschwitz and a New Jerusalem* (New York: Schocken, 1980), 23–4.

and Jews gave their lives. But now that the enemy wanted Jewish lives, it was a Jewish duty to defend them.[24]

Prima facie it would seem that Derrida and Fackenheim speak in the same voice: by questioning the martyrological imperative, they both lean towards survival as a higher value which can be identified as such also within the Jewish tradition. And while Fackenheim makes it a role of the Holocaust witness/survivor to spread Nissenbaum's message, Derrida projects it back into the past and sees the first Marranos, the seventh-century 'Hebrew citizen of Toledo', who first chose life instead of death, as already playing it.[25] But there is also an obvious difference. While for Fackenheim, the choice of life as the 614th Commandment constitutes an *addition* to the traditional codex of Halakhah – for Derrida, the Marrano gesture of opting for survival constitutes a *subversion* of the life spent under the surveillance of the Jewish Law. While for Fackenheim, the life chosen instead of death is the *Jewish* life, conceived as a 'miracle' capable of resurrecting Judaism – Derrida stakes on the messianic logic of a more radical reversal which disturbs the dualism of the sacred and the profane and thus no longer allows for a gesture of sanctification. In Derrida's take on the Marrano as a witness – the ambivalent figure oscillating between *marturion* and *testis*: the one who survived one's own death and testifies to his further living-on – the survival cannot be a *sacrosanctum* which inescapably links itself to the sacrificial logic. The Marrano witness must thus resist the fetishization of survival which turns it into the next Big Thing: a new *sacrum* demanding new sacrifices and commanding life according to a new law. While Fackenheim's *kiddush ha-hayim* requires that every new Jewish life, sanctified as life, should nonetheless sacrifice itself to the prolongation of Judaism – 'lest it perish' – Derrida's choice of life wishes to go beyond the sacrificial logic of obedience to any absolute, be it death or life. Survival simply cannot be object of any cult; to 'affirm survival' means to go beyond any form of cultic behaviour.[26] Instead of deciding for martyrology and the ultimate sacrifice in the name of the Jewish God, the Marranos do not invent a symmetrical gesture of *kiddush ha-hayim*: they rather prefer to indulge in their *conatus*, their drive-to-life in which life, as Derrida describes it in

---

[24] Emil L. Fackenheim, *To Mend the World: Foundations of Post-Holocaust Jewish Thought* (Bloomington: Indiana University Press, 1994), xliii.

[25] The triple association of the Marrano, the witness, and the survivor is confirmed by Derrida himself. In the letter from Istanbul, when visiting the local old Sephardic community, he confesses: 'I feel, a little like them perhaps, like a survivor, more Marrano than ever' (CP, 14). In *Demeure, Athenes*, the Marrano identification is missing, yet the phrase – 'doubly surviving witness' – seems to refer to Derrida's double survival and thus a double guilt: as the one who still lives after the Holocaust and the one who still lives after he lost his Jewish origins: 'This book bears the signature of one who keeps a vigil, involved in more than one mourning, a doubly surviving witness': Jacques Derrida, *Athens, Still Remains*, trans. Pascale-Anne Brault and Michael Naas (New York: Fordham University Press, 2010), 42.

[26] The last words of Derrida, which he scribbled right before his death, were: 'Always prefer life and constantly affirm survival' (*Préférez toujours la vie et affirmez sans cesse la survie*): Jacques Derrida, 'Final Words', trans. Gila Walker, in *The Late Derrida*, ed. W. J. T. Mitchell and Arnold I. Davidson (Chicago: The University of Chicago Press, 2007), 244.

Force de loi, always simply 'prefers itself' (AR, 289): it has no higher goal than itself, it is autopreferential and autoteleological, it just wants more of what it already is.[27]

For Derrida, however, this choice is not a simple betrayal: it is an antinomian treason which reveals the hidden – repressed – dimension of the Jewish religion. For, if religion is indeed the 'religion of the living', which only due to life's aporecity transforms into a cult of the deadened and deadening Absolute – 'Religion of the living: is this not a tautology?' (AR, 85) – then the Marrano gesture of betrayal and forgetting of *this* God, the absolute Sovereign demanding sacrifices, paradoxically reminds religion of its other secret source, which is life itself. Life that already *prefers itself* and thus needs no additional sanctification. Marranos, therefore, would *choose life* precisely the way it is prescribed by God himself who says: 'I put in front of you life and death – choose life!' (Deut. 30.18): they choose life against any absolutist sacrificial logic and thus recollect the lost life-affirming aspect of the messianic faith and hope, which became overshadowed by the thanato-sacrificial symbolic structures of religious cults.

Derrida describes the antinomian betrayal of the witness-survivor as opposed to the witness-martyr in his essay on Paul Celan, 'Poetics and Politics of Witnessing', where the Marrano treason lends an implicit background to Celan's wrestling with his own guilt of having survived the Shoah.[28] Although the term 'Marrano' does not appear here, the whole fragment on the perjury, in which the witness renounces his sacramental oath of belonging to his tradition in order *not* to become a martyr, can only be understood in the context of the *conversos* lying about their Jewishness in order to survive. For, what could be more aporetic than a situation in which a Jew forced to embrace Christianity swears that he is no longer Jewish, by laying his fingers on the Christian Holy Bible which may or may not, precisely at this very moment, be a sacred document for him? If he is (already) Christian, he does not lie and does not commit a sacrilege – but if he is (still) Jewish, he lies but does not profanate the sacred text which, for him, would (still) be the Tanakh. But who *really* knows if he is *still* Jewish or *already* Christian? Only himself in his secret heart, or not even that: for there is no witness to the witness. The path of enquiry ends here, just like in the case of Schrödinger's box: it is for ever undecidable whether the cat is dead or alive or whether the Marrano under oath is Christian or Jewish. Perhaps – and this is what Derrida wants to imply – in this secret moment of undecidability, the Marrano is *neither Christian nor Jewish*, but

---

[27] The autopreference of life looms large in Derrida's penultimate seminar, *The Death Penalty*: '*Loving-living: Loving: living* [. . .] This love is its relation to itself, its self-intimacy, its ineluctable self-intimacy, before any other supposed interiority' (DP 2, 83: emphasis added). The figure of the self-satisfied living-loving appears also in Derrida's Marrano pun on the name of his father Hayim Aime: '*Aime* being merely the French or Christian transliteration of Haim, that is to say, as you know, life. My father was therefore called Life – he was called 'Life' all his life, for life. Life: *aimé*, loved' (HC, 57).

[28] The guilt of survival also plagues Derrida as a non-martyred and thus not-fully-legitimate-witness who remained *sauf*: safe and sound despite the catastrophe. Cixous, as usual incredibly perceptive, notices: 'the Save, the *Sauf* haunts him. (*Sauf*: what a word, with its countless resources, anagram palindrome.) The one who is still living, who just escaped. He could have "leaped" ['*sauter*']. He leaps otherwise, a sidewise leap. Save to the side. He lives under imminence. In Reality-under-imminence. He lives like a safe-by-mistake, a fake safe [*un faux sauf*], a debtor who is going to have to pay in a little while. Time hurries him' (IJD, 15).

transports himself beyond the fences of all traditions into another dimension of the messianic promise (*l'ailleurs*). There and then, in this vertiginous instant, the Marrano is promised 'more life' in his act of betrayal, which, paradoxically, has the power to renew the oath as the most original *sacramentum* of faith, more 'inaugural' than the Torah or the New Testament:

> Perjury itself implies this sacralization in sacrilege. The perjurer commits perjury as such only insofar as he keeps in mind the sacredness of the oath. Perjury, the lie, the mask, only appear as such ('the role of revealing the mask as mask') where they confirm their belonging to this zone of sacral experience. To this extent, at least, the perjurer remains faithful to what he betrays; he pays the homage of sacrilege and perjury to the sworn word; in betrayal, he sacrifices to the very thing he is betraying; he does it on the altar of the very thing he is thereby profaning. Whence at the same time the wiliness and the desperate innocence of the who would say: 'in betraying, in betraying you, I renew the oath, I bring it back to life, and I am more faithful to it than ever, I am even more faithful than if I were behaving in an objectively faithful and irreproachable way, but was all the while forgetting the inaugural *sacramentum*.' For the unshareable secret of the oath or perjury, for this secret that cannot even be shared with the partner in the oath, with the ally of the alliance, there is consequently only bearing witness and belief. An act of faith without possible proof. The hypothesis of proof does not even make sense any more. But because it remains alone and without proof, this bearing witness cannot be authorized through a third party or through another bearing witness. For this witness there is no other witness: there is no witness for the witness. There is never a witness for the witness. (SQ, 83)

Understood that way, the Marranos are indeed *conversos*: when they turn away from their 'true' religion (conceived as *Tradierbarkeit*) in order to become nominally Christian, they, in fact, convert to the *true* religion (conceived as *Wahrheit der Tradition*), which is the messianic religion of life and which can come to the fore *only* in the perjury of the former. Both Cardoso's and Scholem's antinomian doctrines are comprised here in the imaginary witness's speech. By betraying his 'true' God, by not being true to his 'true' God, he actually proves to be more faithful to the secret *true* core of his tradition than all the martyrs who died with *Sh'ma* on their lips. Despised or, at best, commiserated by both 'true' Jews and 'genuine' Christians, the Marranos thus become the bearers of the *scathed life*: the finite, non-phantasmatic, ordinary life which always takes the form of *survie*, still-life or life-death (*la vie la mort*); the life which had traversed all religious fantasies and all symbolic identifications, but is *still* a life, in the form of the remnant – literally – *life-after-all*. Poised in between the Jewish covenant and the Christian authenticity, the Marranos are neither 'true' nor 'genuine', yet they live: the moment they choose life, they are left only with their minimal *conatus*, 'a survival, not symbolizable' (WA, 276). Abandoned by God(s), stuck in between the two institutional religions, 'northis northat', the Marranos have nothing but their bared life on their hands, the sole content of which is the task of survival. But this, says Derrida, is not a bad thing at all: by betraying the cultic *tradendum*, Marranos only prove to be faithful to the secret *truth* of the 'religion of the living' (FK, 85). What thus initially appears as a curse can and will turn into a blessing. The Marranos – who seemingly have lost themselves, yet *in truth* 'dispersed, multiplied' – take modern earth into their possession; they survive. By steering away from sacrificial demands, they challenge religions in their cultic forms and force them to change. In Chapter 2, we shall see that this change goes far beyond the stereotypical view of modernity as secularization: the Marranos may not be theists in the eyes of the traditional absolutist theology, but they do have a faith (as well as reason) of their own.

From survivor's guilt to better betrayal: A faithful perjury

And yet, all this should not exonerate the Marrano survivors from feeling guilty. Derrida strongly insists on guilt – in the right dose of a *pharmakon* – as an ethical treasure which cannot be squandered for the sake of the Nietzschean 'innocence of becoming'. While critical of the nostalgic dimension of the Marrano guilt, longing for the restoration of the lost traditional *Lebensform*, Derrida nonetheless affirms the form of guilt which accompanies living-on as a necessary compromise: life as an inevitable departure from a dead ideal; life as an inescapable contamination of non-existent purity; or, in short, *life as a betrayal of death*. The dilemma of the survivor's guilt – openly discussed in regard to Shoah survivors, but with the constant implicit reference to Marranos – emerges very strongly in Derrida's polemic with the author of *Totality and Infinity*, which Sarah Hammerschlag very aptly called his 'betrayal of Lévinas': not just a simple departure from the latter's ethical absolutism but a very deliberate betrayal that, moreover, issues in a full antinomian apology of betrayal.[29] In this modern philosophical version of the debate between the Marrano and the Rabbi, Derrida focuses on the relation between law and life: the law not only must be biophilic and choose life, it must also be *liveable*. It is thus in the name of life – 'life turned into an argument' and insisting on the *liveability of the law* – that Derrida opposes Lévinas, and with him *pars pro toto*, the religious traditions which choose 'icy abstraction' (ND, 4) of ethical ideals against the messy world of life, concerned mostly about survival. On the one hand, therefore, Derrida accepts the absolutely demanding call of the other as the ideal of justice forming the 'heavenly Jerusalem' – on the other, however, he also wants to speak in favour of the 'earthly Jerusalem' and the political need of the 'impossible translation'. The 'distressing aporia' between the two consists in the contrast between justice as 'yielding to this other, heteronymous curvature that relates us to the completely other' (A, 10) – and the very life of the subject who, in order to become a host/hostage to the other, must first of all *be*, that is, *not yield*, abide.

---

[29] See Sarah Hammerschlag, 'The Last Jewish Intellectual: Derrida and His Literary Betrayal of Lévinas', in *Jews and the Ends of Theory*, ed. Shai Ginsburg, Martin Land, and Jonathan Boyarin (New York: Fordham University Press, 2019), 88–107.

But, is *host* and *hostage* really the same thing? In 'Word of Welcome', an opening speech at the conference devoted to Lévinas on the first anniversary of his death, Derrida remarks on a possible difference between the early Lévinasian 'subject as a host', where every intentionality is quite literally hospitality, a 'welcome' addressed to the other – and the later 'subject as a hostage', where the hyperbole of originary accusation and persecution becomes the foundational act of ethical guilt.[30] Seemingly, he does not endorse this difference, yet, in fact, he works on it constantly as demonstrating the crucial difference between life and death – or, more precisely, between survival which grants the subject the right to be, on the one hand, and radical substitution in which the subject, taken hostage by the other, becomes indifferent to her own self-preservation, on the other. Having conceded to Lévinas that radicalization of the host into hostage is legitimate as a philosophical move, Derrida nonetheless points to a certain aporia in Lévinas's praise of ethical traumatism: a yet another form of an apocalyptic violence of the face-to-face relation that would institute eternal peace, but at the expense of life – a 'peace of a cemetery'. 'For Lévinas – he says – *eternal peace must remain a peace of the living*' (ADL, 94; emphasis added), but it is easier said than done in case of the subject yielding to the annihilating persecution. Without rejecting Lévinas's hyperbole, therefore, he subjects it to contamination and betrayal, here personified by 'the third' interrupting the directness of the face-to-face encounter, as the necessary condition of staying alive of the *living* moral agent. Moreover, he detects this implicit – silenced – betrayal in the very centre of Lévinas's reasoning: 'Is he not trying to take into account this hypothesis of a violence in the pure and immediate ethics of the face to face? A violence potentially unleashed in the experience of the neighbor and of absolute unicity? [. . .] *The third would thus protect against the vertigo of ethical violence itself* (ADL, 32–3; emphasis added).

The focus on the implicit interruption and betrayal signified by the third party marks Derrida's Marrano *clinamen* from Lévinas's rhetoric of pure fidelity to the Other. On Derrida's reading, to be *truly* faithful to the Other entails a betrayal for the sake of the third – that is, also for the sake of law and life, here marching hand in hand, in a deliberately non-Pauline conjunction. For, the third not only disturbs the face-to-face relation, by introducing the distant figure of a neighbour's neighbour, who must be taken into account while not faced directly. It also stops and bounds the accusatory process of *me* turning into a hostage of the other in a non-symmetrical relation, by reinstating *me* as an object of the universal law which protects my right to be – and this immediate reinstation constitutes a major betrayal that stops *me* from retreating all the way in the act of ethical *tsimtsum*. The law protects my *being* and in doing so it deviates from 'complete justice' which disregards ontological laws of self-preservation and for which the Rosenzweigian 'wish to remain' (SR, 4) or the Scholemian 'life as an argument' does not form a sufficient extenuating circumstance. For Derrida, however,

---

[30] *Adieu* was a speech given by Derrida during the burial of Emmanuel Lévinas, at the cemetery in Pantin on December 27, 1995. 'A Word of Welcome' was delivered one year later, on the 7th of December 1996, as the opening of the conference organized by Danielle Cohen-Lévinas, *Homage to Emmanuel Lévinas*.

the 'complete justice' may indeed be *complete* in its uncompromised integrity, but it is not yet *justice* which can begin only with the effort of *translating* this radical demand into the language of *inter-esse*, that is, the language of beings which have an interest and investment in the business of existence here and now. There is thus indeed a scandalous 'ContraDiction in the Saying (or Sinai)': *you must and you musn't sacrifice yourself*. The law cannot but protect the third as *being* with its *conatus*, which is a 'natural perseverance of each being in his or her own being'[31] – whereas the radical demand is the one of the substitutional self-offering. What a 'distressing aporia'!

This distress is precisely what constitutes the survivor's guilt. When commenting on Lévinas's fragment from *Dieu, la mort et le temps* – 'This is how I am affected by the death of the Other, this is my relation to his death. It is, in my-relation, my deference toward someone who no longer responds, already a guilt of the survivor'[32] – Derrida affirms the positive aspect of this 'guilt without fault and without debt' as, indeed, the very origin of ethics: 'it is, in truth, an entrusted responsibility, entrusted in a moment of unparalleled emotion, at the moment when death remains the absolute exception' (ADL, 6). The survivor's guilt is not an abstract issue for Derrida. In the February session of the 1997 seminar 'Hostipitality', Derrida avows:

> A Jew, a Jew of any time but, above all, in this century, is also someone who undergoes the test and the ordeal of the impossibility of forgiveness, of its radical impossibility. Besides, who would give this right to forgive? Who would give – and to whom – the right to forgive for the dead, and to forgive the infinite violence done to them, depriving them of burial and of name, everywhere in the world and not only in Auschwitz? And thus everywhere the unforgivable would have occurred? Besides, regarding everything for which Auschwitz remains both the proper name and the metonymy, we would have to speak of this painful but essential experience which consists in *reproaching oneself as well, in front of the dead, as it were, with having survived, with being a survivor*. There would be, there sometimes is, a feeling of guilt, muted or acute, for living, for surviving, and therefore an injunction to ask for forgiveness, to ask the dead or one knows not who, for *the simple fact of being there [être la]*, alive, that is to say, for surviving, for being here, still here, always here, here where the other is no longer – and therefore to ask for forgiveness for one's being-there *[être-la]*, a being there originally guilty. *Being-there: this would be asking for forgiveness; this would be to be inscribed in a scene of forgiveness, and of impossible forgiveness*. (AR, 382; emphasis added)

Once again, the reference point is Lévinas whom Derrida invokes polemically (imploringly?) when 'regarding the guilt of the survivor, which is not only that of the concentration camp survivor, *but, first of all, of any survivor*, of anyone who

---

[31] Emmanuel Lévinas, *In the Time of the Nations*, trans. Michael B. Smith (Bloomington: Indiana University Press, 1994), 61.
[32] Emmanuel Lévinas, *God, Death, and Time*, trans. Bettina Bergo (Stanford: Stanford University Press, 2001), 21.

is mourning, of all work of mourning – and the work of mourning is always an "I survive" and is therefore of the living in general' (AR, 383; emphasis added). But Lévinas remains adamant in his ethical fundamentalism and leaves no room for a pardon. On the contrary, he deliberately deepens the survivor's guilt, by turning it into an imaginary *causa efficiens* of the inflicted evil: 'This would be a responsibility for another in bearing his misfortune or his end *as if one were guilty of causing it*. This is the ultimate proximity. To survive as a guilty one [. . .] In the guiltiness of the survivor, the death of the other [*l'autre*] concerns me [*est mon affaire*].'[33]

While the Lévinasian ethics refuses forgiveness to the 'guilty survivor', Derrida insists on granting it. Yes, by surviving, we inevitably betray those who died and who, according to Lévinas's anti-ontological logic, returned to the realm of absolute justice *sans être* and its 'peace of the cemetery': but it is precisely this betrayal which becomes a necessary mediation between the heavenly and the earthly Jerusalem, the transcendent realm of the ideal of justice 'without being', which does not care for the self-preservatory *inter-esse* of life and the immanent realm of the living who care. There is, then, indeed a 'ContraDiction in the Saying': a non-dialectizable message of the 'non-existent' divine justice addressed to the 'existent' human recipient who, from this time on, remains forever torn between the 'complete justice', on the one hand, and the 'ontological law' of the Spinozist *conatus*, on the other. Thus, where dialectical mediation in the Hegelian conciliatory mode is impossible (both Lévinas and Derrida agree on that), it is only in the betrayal – *the perjury of justice* – where we can hope for a passage from pure ethics to mundane morals and politics. This is how, for Derrida, the law is born: in the contradiction and betrayal of pure justice done for the sake of the living and the law that protects the living as the third, absent from the absolutely demanding apocalyptic face-to-face (*panim el panim*) relation.

> When Lévinas says 'justice', we are also authorized to hear 'law', it seems to me. *Law [droit] would begin with such a perjury; it would betray ethical uprightness [droiture]* [. . .] An intolerable scandal: even if Lévinas never puts it this way, *justice commits perjury as easily as it breathes; it betrays the 'primordial word of honor'* and swears [*jurer*] only to perjure, to swear falsely [*parjurer*], swear off [*abjurer*] or swear at [*injurier*] [. . .] Henceforth, in the operation of justice one can no longer distinguish between fidelity to oath and the perjury of false witness, and even before this, *between betrayal and betrayal, always more than one betrayal* [. . .] Like the third who does not wait, the proceedings that open both ethics and justice are in the process of committing *quasi-transcendental or originary*, indeed, *pre-originary, perjury*. One might even call it ontological, once ethics is joined to everything that exceeds and betrays it (ontology, precisely, synchrony, totality, the State, the political, etc.). One might even see here an irrepressible evil or a radical perversion, were it not that bad intentions or bad will might be absent here, and were its possibility, at least the haunting of its possibility, a sort

---

[33] Lévinas, *God, Death, and Time*, 39; emphasis added.

of pervertibility, not also the condition of the Good, of Justice, Love, Faith, etc. (ADL, 33–4; emphasis added)

The only question for Derrida here is how to rethink this necessary originary betrayal in the properly antinomian way, so it does not deteriorate into a simple negation of the primary hostage relation, determined by the idea of pure justice; how to negotiate ethical and political 'liveability' of the infinite justice without negating it altogether. This is a paradigmatically Marrano dilemma: to ponder on the 'better' form of betrayal in the situation where 'affirmation of survival' necessarily entails a treason. The liveability of earthly – 'ontological' – Jerusalem leaves no choice as to the sheer necessity of perjury: to live and to live on is to betray the ideal of justice which belongs to the dead and 'otherwise than being'. If one wishes to survive, therefore, one can only follow a Marrano version of the famous imperative of Samuel Beckett: *betray, betray again, betray better*. 'Better' – obviously in the inverted commas where survival gives us only so many shades of the non-ideal:

> Nothing counts more, nothing weighs more heavily, than the quotation marks around the word 'better' [*meilleur*] here, the best [*meilleur*] word. Political civilization, says Lévinas, is 'better' than barbarism, but it is only 'better,' that is, less bad. It is not good, it is only a stopgap, but one that it is necessary to seek, that it is necessary not to stop seeking. (ADL, 112–3)

Yet, a 'better' betrayal is indeed better than a bad one, consisting in a simple defensive denial. A 'better' betrayal does not reject the unfeasible ideal with scorn and does not throw itself, with a nihilistic abandon, into the stream of life: this is not a choice of life that would prefer survival at the expense of everything of value, or would give up on all ethical commitments for the sake of living-on. The 'better' betrayal is always guilty, which means that it nonetheless preserves what it betrayed. Its choice of life is not a jump into abyss of anarchy but, on the contrary, an attempt to create a law that would protect the living: the right to live of the third. It is, therefore, not just a question of *abandoning* the radical justice, but of shifting it – *translating* via the act of treason – to the earthly level where survival itself becomes charged with ethical expectation. The 'truth' of *survie*, therefore, inflects the tradition in the new sense of the Scholemian *Tradierbarkeit*: transmissibility the role of which is to transmit the unliveable transcendent ideal into the midst of the liveable immanent life, the '*beyond-in*'.

> *Beyond-in*: transcendence in immanence, *beyond* the political, but *in* the political. Inclusion opened onto the transcendence that it bears, incorporation of a door [*porte*] that bears [*porte*] and opens onto the beyond of the walls and partitions framing it. At the risk of causing the identity of the place as well as the stability of the concept to implode. This lesson assigns to the transcendence included the space of a 'messianic politics,' an 'acceptable political order that can come to the human only from the Torah, from its justice, its judges and its master savants'. (ADL, 77)

'Justice begins *here*' – only at the Kafkan door to the Law, which is not *there* to be protected in its absolute purity by the fences, but to be transmitted into the messy living world; it begins at the aporetic threshold between transcendence and immanence. 'Justice *begins* here': it can truly begin only with this treason that enables transmission; the true *bereshit* is not in the *aleph*, the first letter of the Hebrew alphabet representing God and justice in themselves, but in *beth*, the second letter which symbolizes the house of being. 'Justice begins here': the simple fidelity to the good *autrement qu'être* is not yet ethics, not yet tradition; in its purity, it remains inoperative, ineffective, dead. Thus, only a 'contamination with being' – another name for betrayal – can make this heavenly ideal work in the conditions of earthly, 'ontological', Jerusalem.

The gist of Derrida's deconstruction of Lévinas's ethics consists in moving the contradiction from the external confrontation between the ideal and the real, which always leads to the accusation of the latter, into the internal dimension of the Sinai Saying, which itself calls for a necessary betrayal. While defending the world's right to be, despite all its weakness and moral fallibility, over against the too-good-to-be ideal of absolute justice, Derrida comes closer to the tolerant spirit of rabbinic *midrashim* than Lévinas. In the commentary on *Genesis*, dealing with the destruction of Sodoma and Gomorrha, rabbis imagine Abraham engaging in a lively polemic with God: 'You desire the world and you desire absolute justice. Take one or the other. You cannot hold the cord at both ends at once.'[34] For the rabbis, the divine justice is indeed caught in the internal contradiction, so the *real* justice begins only with the law which, as Derrida brilliantly demonstrates, constitutes the first perjury/injury of the ideal one: the first paradigmatic harm done to the no longer unscathed godhead (*l'indemne*) which should be pleromatic, absolute, and complete in itself, but instead appears as shot through with internal negativity. The Marrano betrayal, which nonetheless contains the guilt-driven imperative to *betray better*, once again reveals the hidden core of the Judaic tradition: the extimate truth of Judaism as the first ever religion to deviate from the cults of the indemnified and untouchable absolutes. There is a 'ContraDiction in the Saying' which tells to 'choose life', on the one hand, and to follow 'the justice of the Torah' on the other: one cannot – and yet must – hold the cord at both ends at once. The Marrano who chooses life and yet does not give up on *betraying better*, that is, leading a more just life, is the uncanny embodiment of this 'distressing aporia'. In that sense, Judaism – in its secret heart – would indeed appear more 'Marrano' than other traditions based on the severe cults of the Absolute, which allow no contaminating betrayals, only purifying sacrifices.

The antinomian relation between absolute justice and historical laws comes to the fore particularly strongly in Derrida's response to Anne Defourmantelle in the 1997

---

[34] *Genesis Rabbah*, 'Lekh Lekha' 39:6. See also Hegel, in his not so unusual 'rabbinic' mode, directed against Kant's moral intransigence: '*Fiat justitia* ought not to have *pereat mundus* as a consequence': G. W. F. Hegel, *Philosophy of Right*, trans. S. W. Dyde (Kitchener: Batoche Books, 2001), 130. Derrida is to Lévinas what Hegel was to Kant.

text, *Of Hospitality*, which openly claims that the perversibility of *the* Law by the laws is simultaneously a *sine qua non* of their historical perfectibility. The Marrano 'better betrayal' offers thus a necessary mediation between the unconditional and the conditioned, defending the former from remaining 'illusory':

> The law [of absolute hospitality] is above the laws. It is thus illegal, transgressive, outside the law, like a lawless law, *nomos anomos*, law above the laws and law outside the law [. . .] But even while keeping itself above the laws of hospitality, the unconditional law of hospitality needs the laws, it requires them. This demand is constitutive. It wouldn't be effectively unconditional, the law, if it didn't have to become effective, concrete, determined, if that were not its being as having-to-be. It would risk being abstract, utopian, illusory, and so turning over into its opposite. In order to be what it is, the law thus needs the laws, which, however, deny it, or at any rate threaten it, sometimes corrupt or pervert it. And must always be able to do this. For this pervertibility is essential, irreducible, necessary too. The perfectibility of laws is at this cost. And therefore their historicity. And vice versa, conditional laws would cease to be laws of hospitality if they were not guided, given inspiration, given aspiration, required, even, by the law of unconditional hospitality. These two regimes of the law, *the* law and the laws, are thus both contradictory, antinomic, and inseparable. They both imply and exclude each other, simultaneously. (OH, 79–80)

This passage derives from the seminar on hospitality, held in January 1996, the year of the French publication of *Foi et savoir* which concludes with the paragraph on the secret source of all religions that is always destined to 'disperse, multiply' in a Marrano manner: 'One + n', thus engendering infinite supplements (FK, 100). The same formula appears here in reference to the antinomy between the Law and the laws, which we can interpret as the Scholemian aporia between the secret 'truth of the tradition' and the tradition as *Tradierbarkeit*, that is, the transmissibility as a mechanism allowing for the transmission of the truth with its 'unbending rays' (AO, 13) into 'effective, concrete, determined' (OH, 79) form: 'The plural is made up of One + a multiplicity' (OH, 81), where the latter multiplies, distributes and differentiates the *nomos anomos* in the process of *différance* as the always inevitably perverse realization of the ethical ideal. Just as the 'Spanish Marranos' disperse and multiply their unique secret, simultaneously betraying it and letting it survive in the worldly conditions, so do the earthly laws, always in plural, betray the one and unique Law of Laws – if only because their multiplicity is the first negation of the original oneness – but they are also 'guided, given inspiration, given aspiration' by it. This complex dialectics of treason-tradition explains the cryptic analogy between 'Spanish Marranos' and the modern ontotheology as the two figures of the inevitably betraying transmission. For Derrida, the term 'ontotheology' implies precisely such a transition/translation – *Tradierbarkeit* – of the transcendent ideal/Idea to the immanent realm of 'effectivity' or of the theological Law of the Laws to the domain of 'ontologism'. It is only with *ontotheology* which transmits spirit into the *ontos* that the antinomian hyper-Law can become operative here and now – though always at the cost of perjury.³⁵

The Marrano *conatus*: Against sacrifice

By siding with the Marranos – but not against Judaism – Derrida daringly opposes the whole sublimatory tradition, indelibly marked with the contempt for sheer *conatus*, the simple drive of life to preserve itself, which, non-incidentally, became elevated into a philosophical concept for the first time by Spinoza, the paradigmatic 'Marrano of reason'. This reflexive elevation of *survie* constitutes the gist of Derrida's Marrano politics which subverts the fundamental tendency of the Western thought, both religious and philosophical, to denigrate finitude and thus also denigrate survival as a merely biological – lowest – process unworthy of any symbolic investment. Survival, understood as a sheer self-preservation, would simply go without saying, being nothing but a 'stupid self-contended life-rhythm' and an 'imbecilic particularity of one's immediate existence', which shows its repulsive nature in the abjectual *lamella*.³⁶ Slavoj Žižek's succinct definition of human subjectivity – 'I am precisely *not* my body: the Self can only arise against the background of the death of its substantial being'³⁷ – could thus serve as an epitomy of the sublimatory sacrificial logic – used by both, the Schmittian

---

³⁵ My argument here is a Marrano variant of the interpretation of Derrida's 'adieu to Lévinas', offered by Hent de Vries who argues that 'Derrida's single most wide-ranging insight' consists in proving that 'the infinite responsibility, as Lévinas would have said' entails 'its necessary betrayal in repetition': Hent de Vries, *Religion and Violence: Philosophical Perspectives from Kant to Derrida* (Baltimore: Johns Hopkins University Press, 2002), 294. The passage from the ideal to the real, therefore, involves 'the necessary perversion of the universal', which, at the same time, does not lose the universal from view: Hent De Vries, *Philosophy and the Turn to Religion* (Baltimore: Johns Hopkins University Press, 1999), 92. The necessary betrayal, therefore, is a *better betrayal* when it understands itself as such. A similar point was raised by Martin Hägglund who also strongly prioritizes the trope of the double bind as a form of radically antithetical thinking where everything happens as if doubled by its shadow: the good always evokes the presence of evil, fidelity betrayal, promise menace, and so on. Once the Lévinasian ethical ideal enters the real sphere of happening, which also includes the stakes of survival, it becomes inevitably compromised; the passage from the Ideal to the Real is not a peaceful transition, but an antinomian violent clash: 'Arche-writing is the origin of morality as of immorality. The nonethical opening of ethics. A violent opening' (GRAM, 140). Hägglund comments: 'In *Adieu* the nonethical opening of ethics is described as an arche-perjury or arche-betrayal that makes us doubly exposed to violence: "exposed to undergo it but also to exercise it" (ADL, 33) [...] The struggle for justice can therefore not be a struggle for peace, but only for "lesser violence" [...] Absolute peace is thus inseparable from absolute violence [...] Anything that would finally put an end to violence (whether the end is a religious salvation, a universal justice, a harmonious intersubjectivity, or some other ideal) would end the possibility of life in general. The idea of absolute peace is the idea of eliminating the undecidable future that is the condition for anything to happen' (RA, 99; 82; 84).

³⁶ 'Every authentic revolutionary has to assume this attitude of thoroughly abstracting from, despising even, the imbecilic particularity of one's immediate existence': Slavoj Žižek, 'Introduction: Robespierre, or the "Divine Violence" of Terror', in Slavoj Žižek, *Maximilien Robespierre, Virtue and Terror* (London: Verso, 2007), xviii.

³⁷ Slavoj Žižek, *Less than Nothing: Hegel and the Shadow of Dialectical Materialism* (London: Verso, 2012), 905.

Right in its defence of the Sovereign, on the one hand, and the Hegelian Left in its apology of the Revolutionary, on the other – against which Derrida's Marrano politics protests the loudest. The whole of Derrida's late *ouevre*, especially the last seminars – the *Death Penalty* as well as *The Beast and the Sovereign* – is devoted to the thorough deconstruction of this 'thanatopolitical imagery' which may, on the surface, seem nobly subversive towards the hegemony of liberal democracy, while in fact it harbours an incurable infatuation with the sovereign power as the modern political remnant of the unscathed (*l'indemne*). This time, therefore, Derrida turns against Blanchot, whom he otherwise admired, by calling his idea of the 'right to death' reactionary and his writings done under the thanatic auspices a *literaterror* (DP1, 117).[38] And, not at all accidentally, the Derridean patron and precursor in this deconstructive enterprise is Montaigne, the first thinker to resist the denigration of sheer survival and made it a *thema regium* of his *Essays* as precisely the *attempts* to rethink the idea of *survie* anew not as a privative lesser life, but as a positive concept of *vita nuova*, which will eventually begin to dictate different politics, beyond the deadlock of sovereignty and martyrology: the Lord who demands sacrifice, on the one hand, paired with the Subject who subjects itself to it, on the other. Often alluding to the fatal choice offered to the Iberian Jews, Montaigne critically targets and diagnoses a 'Zealot' attitude which actively seeks glorious death as a way out from the Žižekian 'imbecilic particularity of one's immediate existence':

> I witnessed one of my friends energetically pursuing death with a real passion, rooted in his mind by many-faceted arguments which I could not make him renounce; quite irrationally, with a fierce, burning hunger, he seized upon the first death which presented itself with a radiant nimbus of honour.[39]

For Derrida, Montaigne is the beginning of a truly subversive politics: not anti-modern, but *hyper-modern*, demanding further advancements into modernity and pressing towards a true 'democracy to come' in which the vertical transport towards the 'beyond' of 'more-than-life' will have been blocked for good, both to the sovereign 'above' and to the *homo sacer*'s 'below'. The goal of this true – Marrano, non-reactionary subversion – would be to expel the last traces of the thanatic sovereignty to which 'anyone who

---

[38] While commenting on Blanchot's 'The Literature and the Right to Death' (in Maurice Blanchot, *The Work of Fire*, trans. Charlotte Mandell (Stanford: Stanford University Press, 1995), 300–44), Derrida clearly sides with those suspect secret-holders or the 'rogues' of his Marrano *voyoucracy*: 'No one has the right to a private life any longer, everything is public, and the most guilty man is the suspect, the one who has a secret, who keeps a thought, an intimacy to himself alone. And, finally, no one has a right to his life any longer, to his actually separate and physically distinct existence. This is the meaning of Terror. Every citizen has a right to death, so to speak: death is not a sentence passed on him, it is the essence of his right; he is not suppressed as guilty, but *he needs death so that he can proclaim himself a citizen*' (DP1, 115; emphasis mine). The whole political lesson of the alternative 'citizens of Toledo' is precisely the opposite: it is the right to live which should make us the members of the 'democracy to come'.
[39] Michel de Montaigne, *The Complete Essays*, trans. A. M. Screech (London: Penguin, 2003), 61.

wants to live, to survive, to cling to their animal existence, becomes suspect,[40] and turn those previously suspect, guilty, shadowy, and 'beastly' *voyous* into new citizens of the '*Khora* of the political' (R, 44). Thus, while Robespierre, extolled by Blanchot, states in his speech condemning Deputy Philippe Briez, a survivor of the Siege of Valenciennes, precisely because he dared to survive – 'I would have wanted to share the fate of those brave defenders who preferred an honourable death to a shameful capitulation'[41] – the Marrano Derrida replies after Montaigne: 'you, Robespierre and the likes of you, are just one of those "energetically pursuing death with a real passion [. . .] with a fierce, burning hunger to seize upon the first death which presented itself with a radiant nimbus of honour".' Whether in the case of a priest demanding sacrifice for the sake of the divine sovereign or a revolutionary who first sacrifices himself in order to impose the glorious 'right to death' on others, the model remains the same: the sublime pristine dead-already to this world of the Master versus the 'stupid life' of the denigrated biological process which keeps the Slave in its thrall. Orthodoxy and Revolution shake hands.

To make life and survival *less* guilty and *less* shameful is one of the most serious tasks of the Derridean deconstruction, directly inspired by the 'Marrano experience': not to dissolve the survivor's guilt completely, yet simultaneously relieve survival of the accusation of 'filthiness' and impurity and redefine it in non-privative affirmative manner. *Betray better and live* – the quasi-Beckettian imperative which Derrida detects at the secret heart of the rabbinic tradition – stands as the glaring opposite to the martyrological injunction, applied both by most traditional orthodoxies and the seemingly subversive revolutions: *stay pure and die*. In his last interview, *Learning to Live Finally*, Derrida dispels all the claims that deconstruction locates itself on the side of death – be it the Heideggerian *Sein-zum-Tode* or the glorious death of *pereat vita, sed fiat iustitia*, advocated by the Incorruptibles of all traditions – and in the spirit of the universal Marranism declares that

> We are structurally survivors [. . .] But, having said that, I would not want to encourage an interpretation that situates surviving on the side of death and the past rather than life and the future. No, deconstruction is always on the side of the *yes*, on the side of the affirmation of life. Everything I say – at least from *Pas* (in *Parages*) on – about survival as a complication of the opposition life/death proceeds in me from an *unconditional affirmation of life*. This surviving is life beyond life, life more than life, and my discourse is not a discourse of death, but, on the contrary, the affirmation of a living being who prefers living and thus surviving to death, because *survival is not simply that which remains but the most intense life possible*. (LLF, 51–2; emphasis added)

It is precisely this Marrano-Beckettian formula, which turns bare *survie* into a desired *sur-vie*, that lies at the core of the modern Marrano politics, from Spinoza to Derrida.

---

[40] Arthur Bradley, *Unbearable Life: A Genealogy of Erasure* (New York: Columbia University Press, 2019), 235.
[41] Quot. in Bradley, *Unbearable Life*, 240.

The Marrano mass introit into Western modernity filled it with its unique secretly religious content: the defence of survival as the 'inalienable right to live', beyond the traditional double bind of sancti-sacrification. We could thus say that this new *cryptotheology of survival*, fuelling modern reversal/conversion, was inaugurated by the Marrano *conversos*: the radical turn due to which the singular finite life is not to be sacrificed for the sake of the tradition, but the other way round – tradition is to serve the individual life and its inalienable right to exercise the inner *conatus* as the desire to survive, grow and crave 'more life'. In that sense, Marranos are indeed the first modern people, but also the reverse is true: modern people are also ontological/ontotheological Marranos, because they all participate in the Marrano *modus vivendi*, whether they know it or not. When they refuse – or, at least, find problematic – the call to the sacrifice of their 'stupid life' and follow instead a compromise path of *better betrayal*, they *nolens volens* join the limping way of Jacob (Derrida's namesake and second favourite Hebrew hero after Elijah), who betrayed his brother, survived the duel with the mighty Angel of Tradition, and settled in the desert. The 'memory of the Passover' (FK, 100) evokes this radical 'desert in the desert' as the place of Jacob's dwelling, as well as the Exodus out of the kingdom of the death-dealing sovereignty into a 'new life', *vita nuova* of liberation and promise. But it also memorizes the Marrano *desertion*: the brave moment in which the *conversos* left the cohorts of organized religion – the ever-self-renewing Egypts of orthodoxy – in order to claim their inalienable right 'to stay, to remain' (SR, 4). It was first in their choice to rather live than die – the choice at first surrounded by guilt, repression, *silenzio* – that the life has gradually 'become an argument'. In the beginning, it was just a *bared life* which could not find an expression, having fallen away from all symbolic system. Yet, it eventually found it: first in Montaigne's insistence on the value of survival and Spinoza's notion of *conatus* and then, in those most progressive tendencies of modern legislation, increasingly more biophilic and protective of the singular right to live.[42]

---

[42] On the centrality of Marrano survival for Spinoza's ethics based on the notion of *conatus*, see the great commentary of Edward Feld: 'Spinoza sees the effort to survive to be the fundamental energy pushing the universe through time. Surely this view – seeing survival itself as the essential motivating force of all activity and especially descriptive of human behavior – represents a translation of the Marrano experience to universal dimensions. Life under the Inquisition meant that one's daily concern as a Marrano centered on the question of survival. One had given up one's religious practice, and outward manifestation of Judaism in order to continue to live in the land of one's birth. Spinoza understands the instinct for survival as the central principle around which we construct even our ethics, and it is clear that this principle is derived from the central experience of Marrano life': Edward Feld, 'Spinoza the Jew', *Modern Judaism* 9, no. 1 (Feb., 1989): 101–19, 115. According to Feld, the *auto da fé* of Jewish 'faithfuls' constituted for Spinoza a traumatic event which he attempted to counteract by creating an ethics grounded in the value of survival. In his letter to Albert Burgh, who had just converted to Catholicism, Spinoza, displeased with this fact, reminds him of a Jewish martyr who died at the hands of the Spanish Inquisition: 'I myself, know, among others, of a certain Judah, whom they call the Faithful [Don Lope de Vera y Alarcon, burnt at Valladolid, June 25, 1644], who in the midst of the flames, when he was believed to be dead already, began to sing the hymn which begins *To thee, O God, I commit my soul* [Ps. 31.4], and died in the middle of the hymn': Baruch Spinoza, 'Letter LXXVI', in *The Correspondence of Spinoza*, trans. and ed. A. Wolf (London: Routledge, 2019), 354.

Yirmiyahu Yovel would have most certainly identified Derrida's aspiration – 'to learn to live, finally' (LLF, 1) – as well as his hope for a *better law* that would take singular life into protection as highly characteristic of the early-modern Marranos. While the forced conversion to Christian religion removed the *conversos* from the Jewish ritual and imposed on them Pauline emphasis on individual salvation, they nonetheless expressed it in Judaic terms. By claiming that 'salvation lies not in Christ, but in the Law of Moses',[43] the Marranos proved to be neither Jewish, since they could no longer practice the halakhic law, nor Christian, since they refused to follow Paul's full sublation of law into love. Yet, they were also both: what they took from Christianity was a model of the Pauline *kathargein*, which would abrogate and internalize the Mosaic Law, by distilling from it a messianic promise of redemption, here and now, in the conditions of the worldly immanence. The Marrano constellation, therefore, was centred on the two major stars, sometimes colliding and sometimes pulling apart from one another: *this life*, which escaped all Procrustean beds of roles and identities, on the one hand – and the *new law* which would take 'this life' in protection and foster its aspirations towards the immanent salvation, on the other. For these two reasons, for Yovel, the most accomplished Marrano was precisely Baruch Spinoza: the first ever modern thinker to lift the immanence from metaphysical neglect, elevate a singular *conatus* of every living thing to an object of theologico-philosophical reflection, and bestow it with redemptive qualities, where salvation may be a matter of love, but not only: Spinoza's *amor intellectualis* is less love in the Pauline sense than the 'third knowledge' which gains ultimate understanding of the logical eternal laws governing the matrix of *natura naturans*. In this way, the Marrano rule – 'The salvation lies not in Jesus, but in the Law of Moses' – found its highly sophisticated revision in Spinoza's science of the natural law which was, at the same time, the divine wisdom and decree: not only not directed against the singular *conatus* but also drawing into the very centre of the cosmic legalistic system.

The Marrano redemption, therefore, was not oriented towards the Christian immortal after-life. Oscillating in the nowhereland between the two religions, the Marranos filled this in-between with a renewed interest in the worldly finite existence. Having been ejected from both transcendence-oriented religious systems, they discovered the realm of immanence – and the immanent life – as their new home. The orthodox Jews, therefore, could still cling to their *Leben in Aufschub*, life delayed in the expectation of the coming of the Messiah, while Christians could cherish their promise of personal immortality; the Marranos, however, found their own promised land in the *life finite*, lived in all its riches and to the full, which none of the premodern

---

[43] Yirmiyahu Yovel, *Spinoza and Other Heretics: The Marrano of Reason* (Princeton, NJ: Princeton University Press, 1989), 20–1: 'This formula was almost definitory of Judaizing Marranos; it was like a dogma of their hidden religion and a succinct description of their faith. This is, however, basically Jewish ingredients filling a Christian formula [...] In turning to salvation as their central religious concern, the Marranos displayed both their Catholic education and the needs of their situation [...] Educated in the Catholic milieu where salvation was a prime issue, they superimposed a Judaic interpretation over this Catholic concept: not Jesus Christ but the Law of Moses is the true way to salvation.'

institutional monotheisms wanted to claim. It was their Kingdom and the Glory, their promised land, the place to realize their messianic *esperanza*.⁴⁴

Hence, it would not be an exaggeration to say that the Marrano subjectivity – first unable, then deliberately refusing to assume a static identity – is the first modern *subject of life*: fluctuating in-between two (or more) rigid religious formations, turning belonging into a matter of decision, '*Schicksalsverwandtschaft* into a *Wahlverwandtschaft*', and finding home in no fixed abode. It is thus quite tempting to see Derrida's favourite human variety, the *voyou*, as a late avatar of the sixteenth-century Spanish *picaro* who, according to Yovel, was a Marrano invention that started the evolution of the modern novel.⁴⁵ The original 'Lazarillus of Tormes', the hero of the anonymous *Vida de Lazarillo de Tormes y de sus fortunas y adversidades*, written most probably by a Marrano author, leads an adventurous life which becomes a kind of an autotelic enterprise: the *picaro* infiltrates the hierarchical social structures and subverts them from within in order to liquefy all hierarchies and make them as fluid as life itself. His only interest is 'this life' which he – as befits his name, Lazarus – regains after he had died as a Jew and, having committed the sin of conversion, was removed out of the Book of Life. If he, however, resurrects as the original Lazarus in the Gospels, it is not for the Christian immortal life, but for the finite ordinary life writ small, which he now spends on the errance, turning the curse of the Wandering Jew into a way of life. By evading sublime destinies and having no clue as to what he should 'devote his life', Lazarillo does not wish to sacrifice it to anything: always escaping into 'adventures of the immanence', he simply lives it. As a 'shadowy character' and a citizen of the *demi-monde*, he invests in the picaresque 'more life', which he chooses against any vertical initiation into 'more-than-life' (FK, 88): a sublime trajectory which, according to Derrida, characterizes all official religions as 'ellipses of sacrifice', and which, according to Agamben, constitutes the very idea of *bios*, a cultured life raised above the level of *zoe* as 'mere life'. Hence the literary career of the title *vida* in the picaresque novel: for the first time, the concrete singular life becomes a topic of interest as a value and argument in itself; not a means to achieve a sublime form (as in the *hidalguya*, the Spanish noble tale, which the *picaro* novel mocks and attacks, e.g. in Cervantes's figure of Don Kichote), but an autotelic way of being *northis northat*, spent on the liminal margins of societal roles.⁴⁶

---

⁴⁴ This is why, according to Yovel: 'a philosophy of immanence is characteristically a philosophy of emancipation. It assumes that the recognition of immanence as the overall substance of life, when interiorized by the individual and impregnating the dominant culture and society, is likely to become a major liberating force': Yovel, *Spinoza and Other Heretics*, 184.

⁴⁵ See Yovel, *Spinoza*, vol. 1, 129: 'Some of the best-known picaresque novels have been written by conversos (among them *Guzman of Alfarache* and probably *Lazarillo de Tormes*, the first of the genre); [. . .] they abound with coded language, hints, and allusions to Marrano experience.'

⁴⁶ This new life is characteristically both nameless and lawless. While describing the strategy of anonymization in early picaro novels, Giancarlo Maiorino points also to its antinomian undertone: 'The title tells us that Lázaro cannot be severed from fortunes, adversities, and Tormes itself. They weigh him down and erode his *buena fortuna*. The narrator calls his book a *nonada* nobody [. . .] Lázaro can take pride neither in his own ancestry nor in his nation's heritage. Given the fact that so many *conversos* felt themselves outsiders in their own country, the picaro-turned-writer sketches a picture of a society in which *pride in names has been lost* [. . .] Giambattista Vico tells us that *nomen*

In the picaresque novel, therefore, life behaves like the meandering river in Freud's *Beyond the Pleasure Principle* or Benjamin's Haggadah, simultaneously evading and subverting the order of the Law. It is always in crisis, in close shave with death and danger, but always somehow escaping the judgement and preserving its *homo sacer* status of bared life: unfit for sanctification (as a 'pig', the unclean animal, he cannot serve as a sacrificial lamb), yet criminal enough to be removed from the society without much ado as *unlebenswertig*, 'not-worthy-of-living'. In this sense, it is also the first novel of the road: the hero leaves home never to arrive anywhere, precisely as in Malabou's commentary to *Counterpaths*, where she opposes Derrida as a travelling thinker to the paradigmatic dwelling one, Heidegger. While *picaro* gets out of one Egypt, he will not choose another one; he loses one identity never to embrace fully another identitarian closure. His life, therefore, becomes an *example* precisely because it has no identity; it turns into an *exemplary life* because it cannot be subsumed under any category, role, or title. Agamben's *examples*, showing the 'lives of infamous men', also belong to this *picaro* vein: *ecce vitae* – behold, here you'll see the *homo sacer*'s 'naked lives', risky and exposed, but nonetheless turned into a merit.[47] And just as this newly discovered *vida* can only be told, never captured by a rigid conceptual formula, or reduced to a general role, so is life in Derrida: always only a matter of a story, a *récit*, a living-on of words which turn around the events, adventures, meanders, peripetias, and vicissitudes of a singular life.

---

in Latin and *nomos* in Greek signify law': Giancarlo Maiorino, *At the Margins of the Renaissance: Lazarillo de Tormes and the Picaresque Art of Survival* (Philadelphia: The University of Pennsylvania Press, 2003), 102–3. The Marrano gesture of rejecting the name could thus also be read as an attempt at the subversion of the socio-economic law and order of hierarchical society, or – in Derrida's terms – going rogue. But, as we shall see in the last chapter, this antinomian lawlessness does not end the story: just as Spinoza is the first philosophical Marrano to codify the law of *conatus*, so is modern legislation constantly transformed by the demands of the rogue life.

[47] See Giorgio Agamben, *The Use of Bodies: Homo Sacer IV, 2*, trans. Adam Kotsko (Stanford: Stanford University Press, 2016), 227; emphasis added: 'It is striking that to find examples and materials of a life inseparable from its form in our society, one has to rummage through pathographic registers – or, as happened to Foucault for his *Lives of Infamous Men* – in police archives. In this sense, form-of-life is something that does not yet exist in its fullness and can be attested only in places that, under present circumstances, necessarily appear unedifying. In any case, it is a matter of an application of the Benjaminian principle according to which the elements of the final state are hidden in the present, not in the tendencies that appear progressive but *in the most insignificant and contemptible*.' Compare also the opening passage of *The Life of Lazarillo of Tormes, His Fortunes and Misfortunes as Told by Himself*, which promises to reveal things yet unheard, because they deviate from the traditional patterns of symbolic articulation and, for this reason, call for a new form of storytelling: 'I think it is good that such remarkable things as these, which may never have been heard of or seen before, should come to the attention of many people instead of being buried away in the tomb of oblivion.' The picaresque formula will then often serve as a canvas for the 'lives of infamous Marranos' who strayed into other cultures, but never meekly adopted their ways. It was naturally assumed by Jacob Frank who, himself a half-literate, wrote his autobiography in a rich seventeenth-century Polish vernacular full of irreverent vulgarities and graphic details; it was deliberately chosen by Ilya Ehrenburg in his *Eventful Life of Lasik Rotschwanz* (where 'Lasik' is a Russian version of the original 'Larazillo', but also means a 'vagabond'); and then reappeared, in a modernised form fit to the reality of-twentieth-century Chicago, in Saul Bellow's *Adventures of Augie March*.

Derrida's *yom coupure*: From tragic guilt to messianic hope

Would it be too far-fetched to apply Daniel Boyarin's phrase – the 'unheroic conduct' – to the Marrano choice of life instead of persecution and death? Even if Boyarin declares his mistrust towards Derrida and his 'modern rewriting of ancient Judaism', his rabbinic apology of a gentle and effeminate Jewish male as opposed to the Roman military model of virility chimes very well with Derrida's defence of *u-baharta ba-hayim* as closer to the core of the Judaic teaching than a heroic choice of martyrological death. According to Boyarin, it is precisely the emphasis on survival at the expense of more 'virile' virtues as honour, fidelity, and glorious death that had sealed the association of the Jewish 'unheroic conduct' with the feminine 'weapons of the weak'. For Boyarin, however, who locates the topos of the feminization of the Jews in the Roman Empire, there is absolutely nothing wrong with it, since 'it is this counterphobic rejection of the charge of effeminacy that produces the most toxic political (gender and sexual) effects within dominated male populations, as opposed to its alternative, *enjoyment of feminization*'.[48] Contrary to this forced and alien mode of, as Lacan would call it, 'male sexuation', Boyarin advocates 'the "female" mode of resistance, renunciation of the phallus, as being the highly honored option [. . .] What I am postulating is that within the culture the "weapons of the weak" were valued, not despised'.[49] And although there is no mention of the *conversos* in Boyarin's book, his analysis easily lends itself to such extrapolation: the Marranos represent the 'feminine arts of survival'[50] in a manner even more pronounced than the Jewish male population falling into the 'gender patterning' of its own tradition. Also, the conclusions concerning the shame and guilt, experienced by the Marranos – the most feminine among the already effeminate race – are very much in harmony with Derrida's intentions.[51] The shaming should not come from the core of Judaism since it traditionally values survival; if Marranos experience shame and guilt themselves, and if they are shamed and despised by Jewish orthodoxy, it is mostly due to the influence of the Christian host culture, deeply rooted in the Roman concepts of honourable virility and glorious death. It thus makes perfect sense to call this guilt an 'original sin' – as Yovel notices in his description of the Marrano Yom Kippur rites, where he stresses the 'Catholic' character of the way in which Marrano felt ashamed of their not at all happy 'fault':

> Yom Kippur was the most revered day of the year. Four centuries of Marranos have known it under such names as *día puro* (the Pure Day, or Day of

---

[48] Boyarin, *Unheroic Conduct*, 97; emphasis added.
[49] Ibid., 98.
[50] Ibid.
[51] This Jewish gender-bender, so emphatically affirmed by Boyarin, is also met with a big *yes, yes* by Derrida who often equates circumcision with effemination and is quite willing to accept Otto Weininger's diagnosis as a praise, not an accusation. This motif is nicely summed up by Gideon Ofrat: 'Women and Jews represent the simulacrum of emasculation, and what is emasculation if not circumcision? [. . .] Derrida sees this unity (woman = Judaism) and this contradiction (Judaism as against army, state, etc.) as challenge to all the nations of the world, Israel included' (JD, 50).

Purification) *ayuno mayor* (Great Fast) or simply *Quipur* (distorted into *equipur*, *antepur*, and *cinquepur*). Efforts were made to celebrate this day in great solemnity. Judaizing Marranos wore light clothes, fasted, and recited all the prayers they knew. As in rabbinical Judaism, the Marrano holiday was devoted to the theme of pardon, but with a special Marrano edge. The day of purity was a moment of truth. As layers of pretense and beguiling were shed, the *Marrano's soul stood as if naked before itself and its maker*; and, *conscious of the sin inherent in its dual mode of existence*, begged Adonay to extirpate it – all while *knowing that the sin must go on*, and would go on. Thus, to the more discerning Marranos, a certain beguiling of self and God was built into their very moment of purification, making it, too, a moment of duality. Seen from a different angle, *ayuno mayor* came to express a *Marrano variation of the Christian theme of original sin*. The Judaizing Marranos lived in a state of 'fallenness' caused by their fathers' betrayal of Judaism. The brunt of this guilt passed to the children, who failed to emigrate from the peninsula when they could, and whose form of life – the Marranesque mode of existence – was marred by ongoing idolatry, duplicity, and *failure to be Jews even when Judaizing*. Such a sense of fallenness and guilt, which adheres to one's very existence (the rudiments of the consciousness of original sin) is a Catholic sensibility basically; but it fitted the Judaizing Marranos' situation and penetrated into their self-feeling, where it was buried under the humdrum of daily life, but emerged to the surface on special occasions, in particular on Yom Kippur, the greatest Jewish moment of the year [. . .] those who kept the flame of their ancient religion were excluded from the essence they willed and imagined for themselves by those who embodied its seamless continuity – the Jews. (OW, 240–1; 61; emphasis added)

Would Yovel dismiss Derrida's Marrano attempt to reclaim the 'essence of Judaism' as merely a product of an idle *esperanza*, a *voeu pieux*? Probably so. According to Yovel, the Marrano 'hope' to be reunited with the core of the Jewish faith is an 'ideal, infinite dream', which, like the Messiah, always comes and never arrives: a dream that is doomed to stay *merely a dream*, an endless *marrano rêverie*.

Judaizing Marranos were still *Jews by aspiration* – by their persistent *esperanza*, much derided by Spanish playwrights – but they were not *Jews in fact* [. . .] Moreover, even their aspiration to Judaism acquired a *distinctly unreal nature*. As demonstrated by their failure to emigrate, most Judaizing Marranos no longer yearned for Judaism as a concrete reality, but as an *ideal, infinite dream*. (OW, 204–5; emphasis added)

For some, this depiction would indeed fit perfectly Derrida's messianism of a 'distinctly unreal nature', but I want to argue strongly against it. Derrida's messianism may indeed be dream-like, but it is also *painfully* real, constantly tested by the necessity of betrayal, which, for him, constitutes the permanent structural element of the Marrano condition of survival: not some past 'original sin', passed on the next generations in the manner of the tragic *hamartia*, but the daily, deliberately 'unheroic', commitment to *survie*, defending the 'weapons of the weak' against the sacrificial pressure of the sublime cults of the dead/ideal Absolute. In 'Abraham, the Other', Derrida once again confirms his Marrano choice of the 'better betrayal' as belonging to the 'unheroic conduct' of determined survival which both Derrida and Boyarin perceive as inherent to the deep truth of Judaism:

> Henceforth, one had to grant the terrifying consequence of this superlative antinomy: the least is the most, the least is the paradoxical condition of the most, a *certain experience of perjury is the painful and originary enduring of faithfulness* [...] the theme of perjury is among those to which I have stayed the most faithful. (AO, 12–13; emphasis added)

The theme of perjury is indeed ubiquitous in Derrida's late writings, but it is particularly poignant in his references to the Marrano Yom Kippur which, for the *conversos*, was the most important of all Jewish Holidays, because it involved a revocation of all oaths: a ritual allowing the 'strayed Jews' a momentary reunion with their betrayed God. Indeed, in Derrida's description of the Day of Purification in *Circumfession*, the presence of white dominates: 'the day of the Great Pardon, presence of white, my immaculate tallith, the only virgin tallith in the family, like the feathers of the cocks and hens that Haim Aime wants to be white for the sacrifice before Kippur' (C, 245–6). The whiteness – immaculate, virginal, light as a feather – calls symbolically for an absolute forgiveness: return to the innocence, the clean sheet of a free soul, no longer burdened by guilt. But also – a return to time no longer marked by the 'incision'/*coupure* left by the *milah*, the sign of the fated belonging, doomed from the start by the 'failure to be Jews even when Judaizing' (OW, 61): a subversive gesture overruling the reconciliatory spirit of at-one-ment (as it is often spelt instead of the simple 'atonement'). Gideon Ofrat, when interpreting Derrida's solemn parody of Saint Augustine, very rightly reads Derrida's experience of Yom Kippur as a *Yom Coupure*, the Day of Eternal Incision:

> Circumcision is the experience of the eternal scar that will never heal; eternal eschatology, eternal injury, a never-ending crucifixion, an ocean of blood and a mighty sponge, as in St. Augustine's *Confessions*. Yom Kippur and Yom Coupure mutually intermingled to become an *eternal Yom Kippur in Derrida's life*. (JD, 46; emphasis added)

But is *coupure* to be understood only as the circumcising 'incision'? The 'presence of white' on the Day of Pardon suggests that Derrida dreams also of another kind of *cut* that could invert the fatality of the former one: a break, perhaps even a *lucky break* from the burden of the fated belonging of the failed last Jews, which would allow them, precisely as in the therapeutic narrative devised by Jonathan Lear, to turn back on their incurable condition of 'lastness' – 'knowing that the sin must go on, and would go on'

– and exclaim in an outburst of liberating laughter: *this is all crap!*[52] I admit, it is hard to hear this laughter in *Circumfessions*, written behind the veil of tears in anticipation of the most painful mourning in Derrida's life, but it is nonetheless there, contained in the very genre of *picaro* comedy as the natural articulation of the 'Marrano experience'. In Chapter 4, we will hear it saying its light-hearted – light as a feather – YES in *Hear Say Yes in Joyce*, a parody of the Kabbalistic treatise, where the all-giving and all-pardoning *oui, oui* runs through the whole of the universe as divine signature: the signature of an author who abandons his creation either because it is a precious 'gift', or because it is a useless 'crap' (Schellingian *Abfall*) – and in this parodistic vertigo it is impossible to tell one from another, the benevolent from the slightly derisive laughter of Rabbi Derrisa. The same affective undecidability surrounds the Derridean *coupure* which is as much a lamented 'incision' as it is a 'lucky break' from the predestined condition of eternal failure. The Marranos *laugh* – from the picaresque novel with its scathing sense of humour to Derrida's and Cixous's laughter through tears – and this constitutes their unique strategy of survival.

For Derrida, therefore, the Marrano experience of Yom Kippur as *Yom Coupure* is an alchemic moment of the highest reversal, according to Hölderlin's antinomian rule: *wo aber Gefahr ist, wächst das Rettende auch*. Instead of reliving it in the 'Catholic' manner as described by Yovel, that is, with a crushing sense of irredeemable guilt akin to the tragic *hamartia*, Derrida turns it into an event of a potentially liberating crisis: a new *Marrano separation* which will renew the series of the original separations that constituted the religion of Israel. Israel, formerly Jacob, the 'heel-clutcher', had been rewarded by a new glorious name for his perjury, treachery, and, last but not least, his ability to be truly separate, not to *clutch*, resist belonging. *Coupure*, therefore, could be yet another cut, yet another Exodus, yet another leap into the unknown – the desert – where new revelations await; yet another renewal of the tradition of betrayal in its quest for the *true* God; yet another transformation of the most despised *homo sacer* into a new founding father: this is what the crisis of Yom Kippur secretly promises to Derrida. While, as Boyarin helpfully reminds, the rabbis often allude to Jacob in justification of their 'unheroic conduct', it is all the more proper in the case of the Marrano who sees himself as an even more faithful repetition of the holy traitor. Derrida – a new Jacob, 'seriously playing' with the Marrano non-identity, and 'recollecting forward'

---

[52] As Lear explains, the *lucky break* arrives when a person, so far encumbered by the heavy task of giving a symbolic rationale and justification to her every motivation, affect, word or behaviour, suddenly gains a distance to this compulsive obligation to present herself as at-oned and whole, and with deep sigh relief, exclaims – 'this is crap!': Jonathan Lear, *Happiness, Death, and the Remainder of Life* (Cambridge, MA: Harvard University Press, 2000), 117. This moment of crisis – a rapid *coupure* of her efforts of symbolic reconciliation – instead of darkening her misery, makes her, paradoxically, happy. For happiness, opened by such lucky break, means nothing more than an acceptance of life in its undistorted form, that is, as always excessive in regard to meaning – a 'too much' of sheer energetic quantity, disrupting the qualitative field of sense. We can find a lot of such *lucky breaks* in the picaro novels which always see *la vida* as precisely 'too much' to be ever understood.

the Jacobean pattern of ultimate survival, is indeed the 'structural survivor' (LLF, 51), so well described by Rosenzweig in his portrait of the messianic remnant:

> In Judaism man is always somehow a *survivor*, an inner something, whose exterior was seized by the current of the world and carried off while he himself, what is left of him, remains standing on the shore. Something within him is *waiting*. (SR, 404-5: emphasis added)

The Marrano as *homo sacer*? Derrida versus Agamben

Derrida always avoided open confrontation with Giorgio Agamben: only once, in *The Beast and the Sovereign*, he entered into a heated polemic with the author of *Homo Sacer* series, who, on his part, ignored Derrida almost completely.[53] Yet, as this chapter has proved already, it is impossible to think about the Marrano *survie*, which oscillates between mere living-on and a messianic promise of more life/*sur-vie*, without having in mind Agamben's construct of *homo sacer* – especially that both, Derrida and Agamben, draw on the same source: Benjamin's *Critique of Violence*, where the notion of *blosses Leben*, bare life or mere life, appears for the first time. Much ink has been spilled on describing the rivalry between Agamben and Derrida and, indeed, these two thinkers seem to race very closely head to head.[54] The question of how to (dis)solve the nexus that binds sacrificial logic, rationality, and violence of the sovereign subject, as well as how to revise the messianic tradition in order to venture 'beyond sovereignty' – constitutes *thema regium* of both. But the differences abound too: while for Derrida, the main focus in his treatment of the Marrano *homo sacer* is his survival – for Agamben, it is his death or a paradoxical *living death* which forms a crux of the messianic thanatopolitics. While, for Rosenzweig and Derrida, 'In Judaism [and in Marranism all the more so – A.B.-R.] man is always somehow a *survivor*' (SR, 405) – in Agamben's rendering, *homo sacer* 'enters into an intimate symbiosis with death without, nevertheless, belonging to the world of the deceased' (HS, 100) and finds in this limbo of undecidability between life and death, being and not-being, his ultimate liberation.

---

[53] In the twelfth session of the seminar, Derrida criticizes Agamben's opposition of bare life and life qualified as simply untenable: 'All of Agamben's demonstrative strategy, here and elsewhere, puts its money on a distinction or a radical, clear, univocal exclusion, among the Greeks and in Aristotle in particular, between bare life, common to all living beings (animals, men, and gods), and life qualified as individual or group life *bios*' (BS1, 316). While Derrida agrees that in modern times, the 'politics of life' acquired a new intensity, he contests the rigid division between life purely biological and life political. In case of human beings, even the barest life will still be a part of a political culture; there is thus no *bare life* as such, only a *bared life* of individuals stripped of their qualifications (like Marranos), which can never coincide with the animal *zoe*.

[54] To mention just one example, but the most interesting to our – partly also theological purposes: Adam Thurschwell, 'Cutting the Branches for Akiba: Agamben's Critique of Derrida', in *Politics, Metaphysics, and Death: Essays on Giorgio Agamben's 'Homo Sacer'*, ed. Andrew Norris and Thomas Carl Wall (Durham, NC: Duke University Press, 2005), 173–97.

For Agamben, this intimacy with death is a positive factor: it offers a resistance to the biopolitical system of life, which feeds on the instinctual will-to-live of the citizens inhabiting modern Hobbesian state. The modern life-maintaining sovereignty constitutes a Scholemian 'force without significance': a pure biopolitics, concerned merely with bare life and deprived of the meaningful content that used to legitimize power via revelation, religion, and tradition. Like the plural Leviathan in Hobbes's vision, the new sovereignty is made by the multitude of those who are driven by their sheer *conatus* – and because of their sole interest in *conservatio vitae*, hand over the sovereign power, including 'the right to kill', to the state. Agamben's description of modern state goes thus hand in hand with Yovel and Derrida, who see political modernity as a universalization of the 'Marrano experience' – individuals thrown out of joints of their traditional forms of *bios* and reduced to their bare life – but presents it more as a nihilistic horror than a chance. While for Derrida, Marrano modernity harbours a potential of 'messianic politics' as the *better betrayal*, which attaches itself to *bared life*, the new political subject being neither *bios* nor *zoe*, in order to protect it legally – for Agamben, modern age is a desert of meaninglessness, populated by universal Marranos as *homini sacri* who exited their traditions and are now only interested in securing their further survival: a senseless hanging on to life with pathetic mechanical tenacity. While referring to the famous letter on Kafka, written by Scholem to Benjamin, which describes the modern crisis of religious traditions in terms of Yom Kippur made permanent – the suspension of all law, covenant, and meaningful content – Agamben exposes the biopolitical mechanism of the modern form of sovereignty, dealing solely with the mere life of its surviving subjects:

> Being in force without significance [*Geltung ohne Bedeutung*]: nothing better describes the ban that our age cannot master than Scholem's formula for the status of law in Kafka's novel. What, after all, is the structure of the sovereign ban if not that of a law that *is in force* but does not *signify*? Everywhere on earth, men live today in the ban of a law and tradition that are maintained solely as the 'zero point' of their own content, and that include men within them in the form of a pure relation of abandonment. All societies and all cultures today (it does not matter whether they are democratic or totalitarian, conservative or progressive) have entered into a legitimation crisis in which law is in force as the pure 'Nothing of Revelation'. (HS, 51)

Scholem's formula appears in the same correspondence in which Benjamin addresses the issue of the 'zero point' of significance as *creating* a new form of life: 'without the key that belongs to it, the Scripture is not Scripture, but life. Life as it is lived in the village at the foot of the hill on which the castle is built'.[55] Against Scholem, who still insists on the creative power of *das Erscheinende*, hidden in the Castle behind the Cloud, Benjamin states that the only new revelation can come only from below, from

---

[55] *Benjamin-Scholem Correspondence*, Letter 63, 135.

the new form of life as survival: 'It is in the attempt to metaphorize life into Scripture that I perceive the meaning of "reversal" [*Umkehr*]'.⁵⁶ We have seen that Derrida follows closely Benjamin's intuition: the Marrano 'normative inversion' wants to rewrite Scripture and in this manner create new symbolic forms able to capture the new form of life 'at the foot of the hill'. Agamben, however, perceives survival as always and only a *mere-survival*, merely conforming to the Hobbesian pattern of *conservatio vitae*, which keeps *homo sacer* in the trap of the sovereign ban, simultaneously excluded (from all meaningful content of traditions) and included (into an abstract machine securing staying in life without qualities). This is the crux of difference between them: what for Agamben is a 'zero point' of tradition, nothing but its lowest ebb, for Derrida constitutes its hidden 'truth' – a promise addressed to a singular survival, bared and denuded of all symbolic forms, 'shorn of everything' (MO, 68). For Agamben, the 'Nothing of Revelation' truly means *nothing*, a contentless obsolete remainder of once meaningful tradition – for Derrida, this reduction to 'nothing' involves an antinomian reversal which aims at the recovery of the secret *Wahrheit*. For Agamben, the loss of signification of the tradition leads inevitably towards profanation – for Derrida, it offers a chance to renew the sense of the 'holy', made possible by the 'sickening' of all dogmatic *tradenda*.

Agamben's project is wholly staked on the profaning-disenchanting potentiality incipient to the modern Hobbesian notion of survival: a life that sacrifices itself in order to save itself. This aporetic condition engenders further aporias. The modern biopolitical form of *bios* – a civilized cultured life – has in fact no other content than self-preservation: the will to survive, driven by the fear of death, is so afraid to lose life that it relinquishes the use of it and deposits it in the hands of the sovereign who is supposed to defend it. This in turn results in the paradoxical situation of biopolitical sovereignty which always finds itself on the verge of self-impeachment; the 'zero content' of tradition signifies that this new form of *bios* has no other content than biological life itself – or, more paradoxically, that *bios* has no other object to care for and cultivate apart from *zoe* which it simultaneously bans and sacrifices. In its last modern variant, therefore, sovereignty produces a kind of *bios* which already coincides with *zoe* – but this coincidence is still 'hidden in the present'⁵⁷ as a non-actualized potentiality. It still demands foundational acts of sacrifice, without which the cultural *bios* could not come into existence, though now they are committed precisely for the sake of what has always been sacrificed in all traditions when they still had a 'content': *zoe*, the simple natural life. While before humans sacrificed their animal 'filthy life' for the sake of becoming initiated into 'meaning' – language and tradition, capable of turning them into proper human subjects – now they sacrifice their *cursed* part in

---

⁵⁶ Ibid.
⁵⁷ Giorgio Agamben, The Use of Bodies: Homo Sacer IV 2, trans. Adam Kotsko (Stanford: Stanford University Press, 2016), 227.

order to simultaneously save it as their most cherished *sacred*: hence the ambivalence of *homo sacer* as cursed and sacrosanct at the same time.[58]

Agamben's goal is to reveal this hidden 'coincidence' of *bios* and *zoe*, which is already operative in the biopolitical paradigm, and free it from the sacrificial logic of what, in *The Open*, he calls 'anthropological machinery': the device producing cultured human subjects, similar to the torture machine described by Kafka in *The Penal Colony*, which incises the letters of the law on the victim's body. As Derrida, Agamben too is against the sanctification of bare life, but only because he, faithful to his anarchic model of profanation, is also against *any* form of *bios* as a cultured/cultivated form of life and shaped externally by the law. While Derrida's *better betrayal* of the Marrano survivor is set to modify modern legislation 'little by little' (DP1, 201), demanding that 'a new table of the law', so far in service of religious cults, should now turn into a biophilic protection of individual *conatus*/survival – Agamben's hope in *homo sacer* relies on her potentiality to shed the Hobbesian form of legal sovereignty and inaugurate an anarchic mode of being *sponta sua et sine lege*, which will have destroyed the Scripture and the law 'from top to bottom'.[59]

Prima facie, many of Agamben's concepts seem to fit the Marrano experience perfectly well: most of all, the 'cut of Apelles' as the *coupure* so deep that it splits and explodes all categorial orders – of Jews and non-Jews, Christians and non-Christians, even humans and non-humans. After all, as Yovel claims, the strategy of dehumanization, which culminated in the Holocaust, began in the late medieval period when *conversos* were perceived as lacking the cultured form of *bios* and carrying their stigma of Jewishness directly in their blood as an animal element: '*Blood purity* in Iberia, like 'race purity' in modern Germany implies that Jewishness is not contingent on the individual beliefs, actions, consciousness, self-perception, or on any attribute or predicate; instead, it inheres in the person's *bare existence*, stripped of all qualities' (OW, 374). The Marranos, therefore, could indeed be regarded, after Alberto Moreiras, as the first modern *homini sacri*: reduced to their *vita nuda*, stripped of all cultured marks of proper *bios* and, because of that, sipping through the conceptual nets of social structures. If Marranos could be compared to the Cartesian wax – a 'featureless person' (OW 58) as a bearer of 'bare existence' – able to take in many forms and none simultaneously, then Agamben's *nuda vita*, making the substance of modern biopolitics, would indeed be rooted in the Marrano experience of the first modernization: not only the production of the modern subject, *der Mann ohne Eigenschaften* (man without qualities) – but also of the modern post-Cartesian body. *Nuda vita*, thrown out of the joints of the meaningful history of

---

[58] Agamben writes on the sacrificial logic of language acquisition, characteristic of Kojeve and Lacan, in many places, but most of all in *Language and Death: The Place of Negativity*, trans. Karen E. Pinkus and Michael Hardt (Minneapolis: Minnesota University Press, 1991), 104–6. Derrida also discussed it in *The Death Penalty* seminar, but much more critically and with an alternative – non-sacrificial and life-affirming – concept of language in view.

[59] See Agamben on the messianic function of Bartleby the Scrivener: 'And Bartleby comes not to bring a new table of the Law bur, as in the Cabalistic speculations on the messianic kingdom, to fulfill the Torah by destroying it from top to bottom': Giorgio Agamben, *Potentialities: Collected Essays in Philosophy*, trans. Daniel Heller-Roazen (Stanford: Stanford University Press, 1999), 270.

Being, a pure living substance 'without qualities' (*lamella*) and because of that always threatened to be banned as *unlebenswertig*, appears to be embodied by the Marrano/picaro *vida* in the paradigmatic way.

Yet, this conceptual match is not as tight as it seems – the bone of contention is the issue of survival which serves Agamben as a vehicle of profanation and Derrida as a vehicle of antinomian reversal. The best way to illustrate this fundamental disparity is to refer to Maurice Blanchot as their common precursor. What Agamben takes from Blanchot is the figure of *dying* as the most profane and meaningless form of death, constituting a saving counterpart to modern meaninglessness of bare life which, in order to rescue itself from all sovereign structures, now 'without significance' anyway, should abandon the fear of death and enter into an 'intimate symbiosis' with it: 'Life can only be light from the moment that it stays dead-living while being freed, that is to say, released from itself' (D, 88). Derrida, however, takes something else: the figure of *living-on* which survives the death of the tradition and, in this very act of 'sur-vival, the not symbolizable' (WA, 276) for the first time recognizes itself as *life* – released from the sacrificial duties of serving the Name, itself nameless, free to disperse and multiply (like the all-present effusive *lamella*, but with no horror attached to it). While reflecting on the hero of Blanchot's novella, 'The Instant of My Death', Derrida writes:

> He lives, but he is no longer living. Because he is already dead, it is a *life without life*. All of the phrases that Blanchot tirelessly forms according to the model 'X without X' ('to live without living [*vivre sans vivant*],' 'to die without death [*mourir sans mort*],' 'death without death,' 'name without name,' 'unhappiness without unhappiness,' 'being without being,' etc.) have their possibility, *which is not only a formal possibility but an event of possibilization in what happened there*, that day, at that actual instant, that is, that henceforth, starting from that stigmatic point, from the stigma of a verdict that condemned him to death without death being what ensued, there will be for him, for the young man, for his witness and for the author, a death without death and thus a life without life. *Life has freed itself from life; one might just as well say that life has been relieved of life*. A life that simply stops is neither weighty nor light. Nor is it a life that simply continues. Life can only be light from the moment that it stays dead-living while being freed, that is to say, released from itself. A life without life, an experience of lightness, an instance of 'without,' a logic without logic of the 'X without X,' or of the 'not' or of the 'except,' of the 'being without being,' etc. In 'A Primitive Scene,' we could read: 'To live without living, like dying without death: writing returns us to these enigmatic propositions' [. . .] *Neither nor: in this way the witness translates the untranslatable demourance*. (D, 88–9; emphasis added)

In Agamben, the same fragments from Blanchot support his redemptive vision of the limbo in *The Coming Community* the members of which 'live without living, like dying without death' in the undecidability of neither/nor that enjoys the ultimately profane 'zero point' of all symbolic traditions. It is in the limbo which nullifies the perspective of either salvation or damnation that the 'greatest punishment' – the 'Nothing of Revelation' – transforms into the greatest blessing, a simple 'natural joy':

> The greatest punishment, the lack of the vision of God, thus turns into a natural joy; irremediably lost, they persist without pain in divine abandon. God has not forgotten them, but rather *they have always already forgotten God* [...] Their nullity [...] is principally a neutrality with respect to salvation [...] The truly unsavable life is the one in which there is nothing to save.[60]

For Derrida, Blanchot gestures in another direction: an *intimate symbiosis with sur-vie*, also 'not symbolizable', but not because it is indifferent to meaning, but rather because it constitutes the antinomian Marrano truth of the Judaic tradition – not a *zero* but a *gist* of the messianic idea of redemption. It is not the point where 'a neutrality with respect to salvation' finds its completion, but rather the Hölderlinian point of simultaneously the highest risk/hazard and the greatest culmination of *das Rettende*. The Marranos are not innocent 'unbaptized children' who 'have always already forgotten God', immersed in the limbo of perfect oblivion. They rather forget without forgetting: when they gradually lose touch with the tradition as *tradendum* and lose sight of the Castle on the Hill, they nonetheless still carry the seed of the messianic promise, now hatching from below, from their new form of life as survival.

Derrida's gloss on Blanchot is also an oblique description of the Marrano condition. If we substituted 'Judaism' for 'life', we would obtain a Marrano 'Judaism *sans* Judaism' which is not simply privative but also transformative – while 'zeroing' the old given forms of life, death, religion, and so on, the 'without' produces a *remnant-survivor* who survives tradition and yet goes on, *il demeure*, where *de-mourance* does not announce a triumphant resurrection but rather *de-dying*, a kind of Lazarillo-like abiding that survives on the margins and defies all classifications. The Blanchotian 'belonging without belonging', as discussed by Derrida in *Le derniere Juif*, becomes here a space of freedom as a marginal indefinable non-identity. *Judaism has freed itself from Judaism; one might just as well say that Judaism has been relieved of Judaism*. The remnant-survivor is thus also a witness: his abiding translates the untranslatable demourance – the apparent impossibility of living-on after the death of tradition – which, in that manner, becomes a solid Scholemian *argument* not to be ignored. Its persistent survival *must* be taken into account, 'metaphorize itself into Scripture', transform the symbolic order so it can articulate 'the impossible', and lead to the establishment of a new table of law and thus a new form of 'tradition without tradition'. Every 'I'/eye-witness who survived, therefore, carries in himself a crypt for the martyr who died. What then lives on is a spectral *sur-vie*: 'life without life' – without *bios* as a qualified human life – yet not as a *bare life* that has fallen out completely and for good from the symbolic grip (as in the case of the Agambenian *Muselmann*, too indifferent to care about the difference between life and death), but only as a *bared life*, submitted to the 'baring' process of the

---

[60] Giorgio Agamben, *The Coming Community*, trans. Michael Hardt (Minneapolis: Minnesota University Press, 1993), 5; emphasis added.

sans, still insisting on being universal (as in the case of the Marrano, never indifferent to his life as an argument). The Blanchotian *sans* conveys thus the logic of persistent survival – beyond any belonging, form, qualified existence – which should not have happened, but nonetheless did, and now needs to be captured by a *new* symbolic form that would replace the traditional one, invalidated by the Marrano enigma – but also a miracle – of survival. The dialectic of the witness/martyr, therefore, has a distinctly Marrano dimension. Marrano *la vie la mort* carries on beyond the death of tradition, but instead of just giving in into the melancholy commemoration of the loss, it also opens to a new possibility: a renewal of the tradition, now, however, conceived as a 'tradition without tradition' – or, in Scholem's unpacking of this aporia, as the 'authentic Tradition' without the chains (*shalshelet*) of *Tradierbarkeit*. The Marrano *vivre sans vivre* leads not to the collapsive 'intimate symbiosis with death' but rather to the secret transformation of the tradition which is forced to renew itself after the demise of the transmittable symbolic form of life. The Marrano *sans*, therefore, is not privative: it is *revelatory*.[61] It is a first step of the 'normative inversion', leading towards a full messianic reversal.

It is precisely this enigma of survival – 'life without life': the living-on beyond reach of old Scriptures – which occupies Derrida in *Demeure*. By contrasting the enigmatic form of survival, which later on he will associate with the 'Spanish Marrano', with the Christian *concept* of resurrection and its Hegelian speculative avatars (I will look at Derrida's take on Hegel more closely in the next chapter), Derrida states:

> One can only survive it without surviving it. If one wanted to speak here of resurrection through the experience of a Christlike passion, there would be no Christology, no speculative Good Friday, no truth of religion in the absolute knowledge of Hegel [. . .] Already in the life without life of this *survivance*, henceforth, as it were, fictional, *all knowledge will tremble, and with it all testimonial statement in the form of knowledge*. (D, 64; emphasis added)

If knowledge fails and trembles, is it faith alone which can carry the Marrano 'testimonial statement'? In this chapter, we saw how the Marrano theology of survival manages to transform sheer *survie*, the daily and 'unheroic' toil of survival, into *sur-vie*, the 'most intense life possible' (LLF, 52) as the true 'object' of the Judaic tradition, despite all the betrayals and *yom coupures* it had to inflict on the Jewish chain of transmissibility. In the next chapter, which will be devoted to the close reading of Derrida's *Foi et savoir*, we shall see how the Marrano revelation of survival from below gathers momentum and gradually evolves into a wholly new faith which begins to write a new Scripture for itself. By subverting the traditional ideals of home, homecoming and at-one-ment, it affirms exile, errance, and dispersion.

---

[61] As Caputo nicely puts it: 'this *sans* is not the scene of a loss but of an opening that lets something new come', Caputo, *The Prayers and Tears*, 81.

2

Secret followers of the hiding god

Marrano a-theism

Like certain Marranos I would have begun by forgetting...
                                                                    Derrida, *Counterpaths*

Would the forgetting of a being (an umbrella, for example) be incommensurable with the forgetting of Being?
                                                                    Derrida, *Spurs*, 141

This chapter is a Marrano midrash on Derrida's seminal text from 1996, *Faith and Knowledge*, which, as I will attempt to show, constitutes a *crypto-credo* of his Marrano 'religion without religion' and simultaneously a bold *vista* opening a possibility of a new metaphysics: the one of exile, survival, and non-identity. Pace Martin Hägglund's thesis according to which Derrida's philosophy should be classified as 'radical atheism', I will claim that it is rather a *radical iconoclasm* which does not annul the idea of divinity, but merely *hides* it away from sight.

As Derrida often admits, radical apophatic iconoclasm often goes hand in hand with atheism, but it nonetheless should not be mistaken with the latter: it is rather an *a-theism* which mistrusts open theological discourse, but, at the same time, is not ready to give up on God completely. For Derrida, this seemingly very weak and merely half-negative not-giving-up-on-God, often attributed to the Marranos and their 'minimal theology',[1] does not indicate a condition of traumatic loss or enforced self-reduction: for him, the loss of faith, understood as traditional cultic piety, does not appear tragic. On the contrary, it rather harbours a saving potential for what Hegel, in his version of *Glauben und Wissen*, calls *die Religion der neuen Zeiten*, 'the religion of modern times'. Just as Marranism appears to Derrida 'Judaism's one

---

[1] Hent de Vries's phrase – 'minimal theology' – fits perfectly well, not only because it evokes the Benjaminian picture of the ugly dwarf of theology, who must be hidden from sight, but who nonetheless pulls the strings of all serious discourses of modern times: also because it points to the *iconoclastic contraction* which, as I will try to show here, is highly characteristic of the Marrano religion embraced by Derrida: Hent de Vries, *Minimal Theology: The Critique of Secular Reason in Adorno and Lévinas* (Baltimore: Johns Hopkins University Press, 2005).

chance of survival' (TG, 42), so, in its universalized variant, it also emerges as a saving mediation between faith and knowledge: between traditional theism, which openly declares its faith in God – and modern Enlightenment with its secular culture of *laïcité*. Derrida's universal Marranism, therefore, offers itself as a dialectical third between the two warring antitheses: neither theistic not atheistic, it inscribes itself in the yet uncharted territories of what Gershom Scholem tentatively called 'pious atheism' and 'non-secular secularism'.[2] The modern universal Marrano *lives* through these aporias and turns them into a new way of religious life in the time of the world/*saeculum*. Even if theological absolutism of old traditions seems gone for good, Abrahamic religions are not fated to die together with the 'death of God', conceived as the Absolute. They still can survive as the *religions of the world* – and, if they are indeed closer to the 'truth' hidden behind the orthodox facades of 'transmissibility', then, perhaps, fare even better than in their traditional form. In the end, the Marrano faith in God, who withdraws from sight and erases His image in order to let the world be, may indeed be the one (and only) chance of survival for 'the religion of modern times'.

Derrida's essay is a vast and many-faceted meditation on *die Religion der neuen Zeiten*, which Hegel identified with the deep sense of mourning: 'The feeling that God himself is dead is the sentiment on which the religion of modern times rests.'[3] For Hegel, the 'death of God' is an ambiguous condition: on the one hand, it reflects the melancholy essence of the reformed, Protestant-Lutheran, Christianity which Hegel embraces – on the other, however, dangerously opens the doors to the development of modern atheism. For Derrida, who, in his variation on *fides et ratio* theme, begins to experiment with a new concept of a non-normative Marrano religiosity, 'the feeling that God himself is dead' means something else: it does not announce a demise of God pure and simple, rather a complex operation of sending God to the crypt or his *en-cryption*. One of the main tenets of Derrida's essay is the analysis of – to paraphrase Benjamin – *the faith in the age of mechanical reproduction*. At the end of the second millennium, religions triumphantly return in the process of globalatinization (*mondialatinization*) as an ubiquitous presence of hyper-visibility, which spreads its 'good news' through all possible channels of television, forcing everybody, believers and infidels alike, to witness its 'miracles' through the medium of the globally operating 'machine'. But Derrida locates the true 'religion of modern times' in the opposite move: a *retreat from visibility*, an en-cryption so deep that makes even the name of God unmentionable, or – in other words – *radical iconoclasm*. Contrary to the tele-evangelist tendency of religion turned into a one big divine spectacle, Derrida champions the invisible self-withdrawing God who commits *tsimtsum* for the sake of the world, so far hidden in God's shadow: while the former premodern Absolute negates itself and retreats into nocturnal desert, the World, *le monde*, treats into the light and steals the whole show.

---

[2] Gershom Scholem, *On Jews and Judaism in Crisis: Selected Essays*, ed. Werner Dannhauser (New York: Schocken Books, 1976), 283.
[3] G. W. F. Hegel, *Faith and Knowledge*, trans. W. Cerf and H. S. Harris (Albany, NY: SUNY Press, 1977), 134.

This alternative *mondialization* constitutes a secret lining of the Latin/Christian version: the *tsimtsem* God belongs here to the less official and less visible modern 'hidden tradition' which Derrida associates explicitly with the heritage of 'Spanish Marranos' (FK, 100). While the former globalism invokes the phallic powers of Life Unscathed (*la vie indemne*), which use the machine of cult to produce the effect of a monstrous erection of God in his triumphant hyper-spectacular glory, the latter is staked on a different notion of life as *survie* – the earthly life without life immortal – which prefers to stay in the shadow. Thus, while the traditional religious imaginary routinely opposes Life to Machine, Derrida states that

> instead of opposing them, as is almost always done, they ought to be thought together, as one and the same possibility: the machine-like and faith, and the same holds for the machinal and all the values entailed in the sacrosanct (*heilig*, holy, safe and sound, unscathed, intact, immune, free, vital, fecund, fertile, strong, and above all, as we will soon see, 'swollen') – more precisely in the *sacrosanctity of the phallic effect* [. . .] Is it not the phenomenon, the *phainesthai*, the day of the phallus? [. . .] *Light takes place*. And the day [. . .] Let us not forget: even when it did not dispose of any common term to 'designate,' as Benveniste notes, 'religion itself, the cult, or the priest, or even any of the personal gods,' the Indo-European language already concurred in 'the very notion of god' (*deiwos*), of which the 'proper meaning' is 'luminous' and 'celestial'. (FK, 83; 46; emphasis added)

While objecting to the religion returning to conquer the world on the Day of the Erected Phallus, Derrida chooses another option: a nocturnal religion of God who stays buried in the crypt. He will thus attempt to get beyond the blinding light of all Indo-European *deiwos* and reach another source: where light can indeed *take place* because place was already *given* by the more inaugural origin which, because it only *gives place*, can never step into the light of the day. Everything that merely *takes place* – like Blake's Tyger 'burning bright in the forests of the night': the poetic emblem of those celestial light-beings – is secondary: it derives from the primordial 'forest of the night' which, in the first place, *gives way* and *gives place*. First things first: 'since what is at stake is *the truth of the night*, that which is *not to be retained when day breaks*'.[4] Derrida's essay can thus also be seen as an exercise in the technique of *contre-jour*, blacklighting or obfuscation, which he discusses with Safaa Fathy in their 1999 commentary on *D'ailleurs, Derrida*: the diminution of light so radical that eventually all that remains are the 'memoirs of the blind'.

This is why, in the symphony of voices, which Derrida orchestrates in his extremely rich essay, there is one particularly significant: Hegel. Hegel was the first thinker to question the *phosocentric* essence of God as *Lichtwesen* (light-being), and it is also in the polemic with his concept of the 'death of God' and the melancholy 'memory of the Passion' (FK, 50) that Derrida develops an alternative, Jewish-Marrano, idea of the

---

[4] Maurice Blanchot, *The Infinite Conversation*, trans. S. Hanson (Minneapolis: University of Minnesotta Press, 1993), 126; emphasis added. This could be yet another variation on the Scholemian antinomian ratio between the 'truth' and the 'transmissibility' of tradition.

'memory of Passover' (FK, 100): partly overlapping with the Christian Easter rites, but also very distinct from the 'speculative Good Friday', commemorating not the tragedy of the cross, but the Exodus from Egypt, not the mourning of a departed God, but a liberation of the world. Hegel and Derrida are thus two modern Jacobs who wrestle with God in the middle of the night and earn two very different blessings: Hegel his guilt which he will redefine as the speculative essence of Christian faith, and Derrida his hope which he will champion as the gist of his Marrano *messianicité*.[5]

The Christian Hegel: *God is dead and we have killed him*

Unlike Nietzsche, from whom the above phrasing derives,[6] Hegel sees the 'death of God' motif not as an attack on Christianity, but as the very essence of Christian faith, which is *kenosis*. The Hegelian God who dies as the sovereign ruler and creator – eternally safe and sound Absolute – in order to get contaminated by the creaturely element and work within this condition of impurity as the Spirit, is the kenotic God at his extreme. One cannot imagine a greater 'self-humbling' than the original death, retreat, self-restraint, self-withdrawal, and radical self-negation in which the Infinite gives up its absolute sovereignty for the sake of the adventure of becoming. This '*kenosis* in creation', which Hegel smuggled surreptitiously under the heading of *Entäußerung* – the word meaning 'exteriorization' in the Hegelian vocabulary, but before that used by Martin Luther in his translation of Paul's term *kenosis*[7] – is the divine self-humbling

---

[5] I will apply a similar rule in regard to the symphony of Derrida's commentators and choose one reader, Michael Naas, who devoted the whole book to Derrida's *Faith and Knowledge: Miracle and Machine*. Nass, however, makes little of Hegel's presence in Derrida's essay on religion, despite the borrowing of the title. In his 'Observation on Hegel', Naas admits that it is always possible that Derrida is hiding his major influence, but 'a lot of interpretive work would need to be done to make this case, and even more would need to be done to show that Derrida was trying, in "Faith and Knowledge," to intervene in the debate between Kant and Hegel. In his attempt to understand the nature of religion today, Derrida had other things in view. For instead of ending his text with a reference to the speculative Good Friday, he concludes with an equally dramatic reference to violence, to ashes, to the massacre at Chatila, and to "an open pomegranate, one Passover evening, on a tray"' (MM, 310). While not disagreeing with Naas, I would like to challenge his dismissal of Hegel and demonstrate that Derrida constantly refers to Hegel in order to subvert, but also supplement his 'memory of the Passion' with a different memory of a different mourning, violence, and ashes: a Marrano testimony of the forced loss of God, which created a different kind of memory and commemoration.

[6] In the 125th paragraph of *Gay Science*, tha Madman famously exclaims: 'Gods, too, decompose! God is dead! God remains dead! And we have killed him! How can we console ourselves, the murderers of all murderers! The holiest and the mightiest thing the world has ever possessed has bled to death under our knives: who will wipe this blood from us?': Friedrich Nietzsche, *Gay Science*, 120.

[7] On the importance of Luther's translation of *kenosis* for Hegel, see Catherine Malabou, *The Future of Hegel: Plasticity, Temporality, and Dialectics* (London: Routledge, 2005), 82: 'This injury is made clear in the Hegelian concept of a divine alienation, central to the dialectical conception of *kenosis* and its principle. "Kenosis" means the lowering or humbling of God in his Incarnation and the Passion [. . .] Luther translates κενωσις as *Entäußerung*, literally "the separation from the self through an externalisation." Now from this *Entäußerung* or "alienation", Hegel forges a logical movement which becomes constitutive of the development of the divine essence. God necessarily departs from himself in His self-determination.'

to the point of self-erasure, from which there begins the 'Golgotha of the Absolute Spirit'. It commences with the self-emptying of the First Idea, which gives itself over to the world and loses in the alien being in order to resurrect in the future, prophesied by Hegel as the dawn of Absolute Knowledge. In the meantime, however, the Spirit's sacrifice is remembered in the form of the 'infinite grief': the 'religion of modern times' is the religion of mourning. But religion is not enough: the next necessary step on the way towards Absolute Knowledge consists in transforming the religion of mourning into an abstract philosophical position which Hegel, also in the same essay, calls famously a 'speculative Good Friday'. Derrida names this position in Heideggerian terms as ontotheology: a philosophical account of the 'death of God' which sublates the living imagery of *Vorstellungsdenken* (picture-thinking) into an iconoclastic – deadened, abstract, but also paradoxically saving – concept of God.

Hegel would return to the idea of 'the infinite grief in the finite' many times, always accentuating the tragic clash between infinity and finitude, which inevitably demands the sacrifice of the latter. If, as Kant had already argued, Christianity is the only 'moral religion', it is because it focuses solely on the act of ethical compensation, in which the believer, following the law of the talion, pays with his 'sensuous life' for the loss of the infinite vitality God had sustained in the kenotic process of incarnation. Unlike the 'pagan' cults, therefore, which praise God's infinite vitality, Christian religion consists in a mournful cultivation of the sense of guilt and debt (*Schuld*) which must be duly repaid. The prospect of reconciliation between man and God becomes thus possible only if man agrees to engage in the *imitatio Christi* as the repetition of the 'tragedy of the cross'. For Hegel, faith is most of all a *faithful mimesis* of the suffering God, which occurs in the inner shrine of the soul and serves the *absolute satisfaction* of the Spirit:

> For the reconciliation of the individual person with God does not enter as a harmony directly, but as a *harmony proceeding only from the infinite grief, from surrender, sacrifice, and the death of what is finite, sensuous, and subjective*. Here finite and infinite are bound together into one, and the reconciliation in its true profundity, depth of feeling, and force of mediation is exhibited only through the magnitude of harshness of the opposition which is to be resolved. It follows that even the whole sharpness and dissonance of the suffering, torture, and agony involved in such an opposition, belong to the nature of the spirit itself, whose *absolute satisfaction* is the subject-matter here.[8]

By referring to Freud's 1917 essay on *Mourning and Melancholia*, we can phrase the main question of Hegel's philosophy as: can the 'infinite grief' ever be finished? Can it realize itself in a complete work of mourning, or must it perpetuate into infinity as an unworkable burden of melancholy? Hegel is visibly torn between the idea of the infinite process of mourning, which sustains itself in the image of the God dying on the cross and thus keeps the sacrificial scheme of the 'death of God religion' for ever

---

[8] G. W. F Hegel, *Aesthetics: Lectures on Fine Art*, trans. T. M. Knox (Oxford: Oxford University Press, 1975), 537; emphasis added.

valid – and the prospect of the sublation of religion into philosophical knowledge, which simultaneously ends religion/faith with its picture-thinking and its call for sacrifice, and then keeps it going in a higher, abstractly ontotheological, and iconoclastic form. In his own take on *fides et ratio* theme, Derrida points to this aporetic tension in Hegel's logic which makes 'grief' infinite (non-sublatable) and temporal (sublatable) at the same time:

> Infinite pain is still only a *moment*, and *the moral sacrifice of empirical existence* only dates the absolute Passion or the speculative Good Friday. Dogmatic philosophies and natural religions should disappear and, out of the greatest 'asperity', *the harshest impiety*, out of *kenosis* and the void of the most serious privation of God [*Gottlosigkeit*], ought to resuscitate the *most serene liberty* in its highest totality. Distinct from faith, from prayer or from sacrifice, ontotheology destroys religion, but, *yet another paradox*, it is also what perhaps informs, on the contrary, the theological and ecclesiastical, even religious, *development of faith*. (FK, 53; emphasis added)

And although Derrida does not identify with Hegel's 'sacrificial' position, he nonetheless is willing to pick up the Hegelian thread of the *iconoclastic ontotheological abstraction* – and then play it out differently, with his own Marrano *clinamen*. While for Hegel, the concept can only be reached through the sacrifice of the sensuous content, Derrida decisively rejects the sacrificial logic hidden behind the process of conceptualization, as well as any sacrificial logic *tout court*.[9] Derrida will thus attempt to abstract and detach 'the most serious privation of God' from the tragic remnants of the sacrificial scheme, which linger in the notion of the 'infinite grief' and hinder the Hegelian abstraction on its way to become properly iconoclastic and thus enter the realm of the 'most serene liberty'. On Derrida's account, it is precisely the stubborn 'picture-thinking' of the Christian 'tragedy of the cross' that infects Hegel's effort of sublation with an unwished-for and unreflected regressive iconophilia. Or, perhaps, *philia* is not the right word here: the abiding image of the crucified God, preserved in the persistent 'memory of the Passion' (FK, 50), suggests rather a traumatic *iconic fixation*. While all other Hegelian concepts pass through the purifying 'sacrifice of the sensuous', it is only this one – the concept of God – which cannot free itself from the terrible image of the dying body. While all other concepts become 'impersonal presences' which are nothing but 'tombstones weighing on the void' – the concept of God stubbornly refers to the corpse painfully

---

[9] Adorno calls the Hegelian condition of passing to conceptual thinking 'the sacrifice of the empirical' (MCP, 95), but the best description of the murderous/sacrificial nature of language can be found in the Hegelian variations of Blanchot: 'I say my name, and it is as though I were chanting my own dirge: I separate myself from myself, I am no longer either my presence or my reality, but an objective, impersonal presence, the presence of my name, which goes beyond me and whose stonelike immobility performs exactly the same function for me as a tombstone weighing on the void. When I speak, I deny the existence of what I am saying, but I also deny the existence of the person who is saying it': Blanchot, *The Work of Fire*, 324.

rotting in the tomb's crypt. All other thoughts may thus become 'serene' and 'free' in their abstract sublimation, but not this one: *the frightful thought that God himself is dead*. If it remains so 'frightful', it is because it is fixated on the traumatizing, unspeakably scandalous horror-image: the Icon of all Icons, the *vera icona* of Christ in Passion. Hegel's note on the 'death of God' from the 1831 lectures leaves no doubt that, when it comes to the killing-negating essence of conceptual language, God constitutes a sovereign exception:

> *God has died, God is dead* – this is the most frightful of all thoughts, that everything eternal and true *is not*, that negation itself is found in God. The deepest anguish, the feeling of complete irretrievability, the annulling of everything that is elevated, are *bound up* with this thought.[10]

Thus, everything can be sacrificed, but not the God on the cross; or rather, everything else should be sacrificed precisely because He was (or, as Joyce would have said: *He war*). The frightful monstrosity of Christ's Passion constitutes an Image which binds and fixates the thought that can never sublate it. The abstract edifice of Hegel's conceptuality is thus founded on the non-sublatable Icon of God's *kenosis* issuing in the tragedy of the cross: the dark trauma that can never be worked through and make its way into language.

For Derrida, therefore, Hegel heads in the right direction, but is not iconoclastic, not ontotheological enough: the obstinate icon-fixated thought of the divine *kenosis* as the sacrifice ending in frightful death prevents him from fully embracing what he himself advocates, 'the serene liberty' of thinking. Thus, by simultaneously continuing and correcting the Hegelian analysis of *die Religion der neuen Zeiten*, Derrida will claim that the current return of the religious 'proclaimed in every newspaper' (FK, 43) or this 'machine-like return of religion' (FK, 53), which becomes all-too-visible and spectacular, should indeed be challenged by the 'feeling that God himself is dead' resulting in the Hegelian 'harshest impiety', taken to its extreme that was not yet fully realized by Hegel himself. Derrida – after all, a 'Marrano of the French *Catholic* culture' – must have been aware of the Catholic practice of 'Calvaries' which put the Christ's Passion onto a stage as a cathartic spectacle that mesmerized its viewers and easily turned them into a vengeful mob ready to persecute the Jewish neighbours for the unforgivable sin of killing their Lord. These 'Calvaries', which faithfully reproduced Christ's torment at the twelve Stations of the Cross (Mel Gibson's *Passion* is just a modern televised version of this old ritual), were the first religious theatres that staged the tragedy of the cross fully in accordance with Aristotle's prescription of the perfect tragic drama. They aimed at the violent carnivalesque *katharsis* of negative emotions which, by blithely circumventing Hegel's idea of the 'serene' sublation of religion into reflexive thought, often issued in pogroms: all over the Catholic Europe, the Jews usually dreaded the

---

[10] G. W. F. Hegel, *Lectures on the Philosophy of Religion (The Lectures of 1827 – One Volume Edition)*, trans. R. F. Brown (Oxford: Oxford University Press, 2006), 465; emphasis added.

advent of Easter, when Christianity was regularly turned into a *spectacle* (and they still do). Something of this ancient fear still pervades Derrida's take on religion in the age of mechanical reproduction, when the 'Calvary' can always become an everyday spectacle, watched by the millions of viewers – and with a similar effect.

Far from dismissing the religious as the bygone madness of dark ages, scorched by the modern 'light of the day' (FK, 46), Derrida throws himself straight into the Hölderlinian messianic paradox: the coincidence of the highest danger and the growing possibility of redemption, or the aporetic oscillation between 'the most radical evil' and the 'promise of salvation' (FK, 43). If 'radical abstraction', by which religion travels today all over the globe thanks to the machine of telecommunication, spells the evil of 'deracination, delocalization, disincarnation, formalization, universalizing schematization, objectification' (FK, 43), the *other abstraction* harbours a possibility of a 'new reflecting faith' (FK, 49) which breaks with dogmatic cults and spectacles, always rooted in particular sacred spaces, and becomes global, by opening itself to a universal moral appeal. And if the 'harshest impiety' brought by the Enlightenment can indeed lead to the war on religion waged for the sake of killing God, it may also suggest a different outcome: a *retreat* to 'the void of the most serious privation of God', the very 'desert in the desert' in which there is no telling 'what is yet to come' (FK, 47) – what God, living or dying (or, perhaps, 'northis northat'), might appear on the radically emptied (or as Nietzsche says, 'wiped-out') horizon. The proper abstraction of ontotheology could thus still overcome the false one, while a new form of a reflecting faith could form the ground '*in whose name* one would protest against' the existing form of religiosity which 'only *resembles* the void' (FK, 55; emphasis added). This protest against the distorted forms of the modern faith, therefore, is not ventured on the grounds of knowledge, but rather on the grounds of another – withdrawn, invisible, 'harsher', iconoclastic, yet at the same time 'serene' – *foi originaire* which Derrida wants to reveal (as much as it is possible) and defend:

> *The abstraction of the desert can thereby open the way to everything from which it withdraws.* Whence the ambiguity or the duplicity of the religious trait or retreat, of its abstraction or of its subtraction. This deserted *re-treat* [*re-trait desertique*] thus makes way for the repetition of that which will have given way precisely for that in whose name one would protest against it, against *that which only resembles the void* and the *indeterminacy of mere abstraction*. (FK, 55; emphasis added)

In Derrida's harshest possible ontotheological abstraction, the origin is conceived as a *place-maker* whose role is only to *give way*: withdraw and make something else possible *in-stead*. But that also means that, by giving space to everything and anything, the origin can also possibilitate a religion of the fully visible – monstrously large-looming – gods-idols who overshadow and cover up the modest source in retreat. Religion returns thus with the vengeance – as indeed in Gilles Kepel's famous analysis of the fundamentalist renaissance as *revanche de Dieu* – in the name of the living, present, and palpable gods who loudly protest against the modern claim that 'God is dead'.[11] But Derrida, being the master of dialectics, is far from dismissing this protest. He is ready to protest together with the fundamentalists against the false voiding of the 'death of God' theology inaugurated by Hegel, as well as against the indeterminate abstraction of the *mondialatinized* God who, Christian in origin, became falsely universal by losing its roots and entering the global stage as 'God without qualities': falsely abstracted/absolved from the world as *ab-solutus*, the Absolute Abstraction, icy and deadened. To this Derrida opposes *another abstraction*: the other source of religion as 'the unconditional without sovereignty', which abstracts itself from the world not because it is a sovereign Absolute, but because it 'opens the way to everything from which it withdraws' (FK, 55). So, he is also ready to protest against the fundamentalists in the name of what he perceives as the *determinate abstraction*: a particular process of the iconoclastic purification of faith which has not lost its Jewish specificity and remains determined by the Second Commandment. Thus while today's religious integrists reject the diluted, ontotheological, and 'liberal' concept of God in the name of His commanding living presence – Derrida cuts into this global-Christian dispute with his Marrano *votum separatum*: keeping an equidistance from both, theological absolutism turned into a seemingly universal philosophical discourse, on the one hand, and the resurrected God-Idol of the 'returning religion', on the other. Neither is the post-Christian ontotheology so universal as it claims – nor is the Living Presence of the fundamentalists cults free of the 'indeterminate abstraction', which, as Kepel argues, makes them all more similar to one another than they would ever be ready to admit. Derrida will thus champion his third way meandering between the 'death of God/God of death' and God's unscathed Life. Neither dead nor alive, neither simply particular nor simply universal, Derrida's godhead will *survive* in the properly iconoclastic 'Marrano' variant of ontotheology: 'distinct from faith, from prayer or from sacrifice', but, at the same time, advancing modern, no longer sacrificial and icon-fixated, 'development of faith' (FK, 53). In order to understand this development, we must look closer at its most significant ingredient: the concept of God's retreat/*retrait* which should *not* be conflated with the divine *kenosis* or any forms of the 'speculative Good Friday'.

The 'deserted re-treat', or the hidden truth of abstraction

What does it mean that the God of the Christian-derived globalatinized religion 'only *resembles* the void' (FK, 55)? And what would be the real void, the true *kenoma* –

---

[11] See Gilles Kepel, *The Revenge of God: The Resurgence of Islam, Christianity and Judaism in the Modern World* (London: Polity Press, 1994). The original title, *La revanche de dieu*, however, suggests something else: not so much a 'revenge', as the 're-vista' which is used in the game of bridge in the process of counter-bidding. In that sense, God returns to the gaming table with new cards in hand – and this metaphor is quite close to Derrida's intention to spot also unexpected *vistas* that open new chances in the phenomenon of the 'returning religion'. In Chapter 4, the metaphor of the divine gamble will once again appear a propos Derrida's interpretation of James Joyce's *Ulysses*.

and not the one which only pretends to be *kenotic*: humble and empty? What would be the *mechanism* of such pretence? The discussion with globalitinizing Christianity, in which Derrida engages in *Faith and Knowledge* in the first section, written in the Roman Italic as the privileged font of the Global Christian Latin, is organized around these questions. Derrida's thesis seems to be the following: the merely apparent desert that only 'resembles the void' (FK, 55) derives from the false pretence of Christian *kenosis* which overtly presents itself as an act of self-humbling – the God plunging into the scathed dimension of the finite life – but secretly harbours the inversion where all the pride of the unscathed – the *perfect* self-sacrifice, preserved by memory in the *icona vera* of Christ's Passion – is still maintained. According to Derrida, the 'death of God religion' is indeed a Christian monopoly – but not for the reasons for which it is usually extolled. The Hegelian thinkers associated with the 'death of God theology' and sympathetic to its iconoclastic leanings – Thomas Altizer, Jean-Luc Nancy, Slavoj Žižek – insist on the absolute uniqueness of Christianity as the only religion that contains atheism structurally within itself and as such paves the way to the modern process of secularization. Yet, Derrida begs to differ precisely on that point: in his subtle deconstruction of the Christian triumphant hegemony, best articulated in the famous claim that 'only an atheist can be a good Christian; only a Christian can be a good atheist',[12] Derrida demonstrates that it is precisely the Hegelian image-fixated 'memory of the Passion' (FK, 50), which blocks the advances of modern ontotheology on its way towards a-theization or a-theologization:

> Fundamentally, this theme of the death of God is first of all Christian, which reactivates in the nineteenth century with Hegel. *Khôra* is foreign to the death of God, and thus it is a desert which even the Judeo-Christian figure of the desert cannot capture. (CS, 145)[13]

> Everything begins with the presence of that absence. The 'deaths of God,' before Christianity, in it and beyond it, are only figures and episodes. *The unengenderable thus reengendered is the empty place.* (FK, 65; emphasis added)

As we have seen, Derrida challenges Hegel, by putting in doubt his thesis according to which it is necessary to think the salvation as 'the redemption, before or after evil, fault or sin' (FK, 43), that is, as paying back the debt: life for life, *kenosis* for *kenosis*. The real void, beyond any pretence and bargain – properly *kenomatic*, icon-free – is named by him *Khôra* or 'empty place'. This true *kenoma* comes to be thanks to the

---

[12] This sentence whose first part derives from Ernst Bloch and the second from Jürgen Moltmann, appeared on the cover of the first 1968 German edition of Bloch's *Atheismus im Christentum: Zur Religion des Exodus und des Reichs*, the reprinted as the epigraph to the English translation: Ernst Bloch, *Atheism in Christianity: The Religion of the Exodus and the Kingdom*, trans. J. T. Swann (London: Verso, 2009).

[13] The term *atheology* derives from George Bataille, who meant by it a 'science of destruction and death of God', which would not result in a simple atheism, but would attempt, in the Nietzschean fashion, to uncover the true wild *sacrum* beneath the Judeo-Christian pseudo-religion of morals: Georges Bataille, 'Sacrifices', in *Œuvres complètes*, vol. 1 (Paris: Gallimard, 1970), 92.

act of *tsimtsum*, the non-sacrificial re-treat of God, which does not leave creation in the state of the 'infinite grief' and the necessity to repeat the gesture of self-offering. While Christianity follows to the tee the logic of 'religion as the ellipsis of sacrifice' (FK, 88), this other possibility – which Derrida attaches to the modern Marrano experience of an even more radical *Gottlosigkeit* – allows the exodus out of the sacrificial paradigm, which constitutes the first source of religion, and open it to the second, equally original, source: the future-oriented messianicity propelled by a single imperative – *no more sacrifices!*

The very concept of withdrawal/re-treat (*re-trait*), which plays such a fundamental role in *Faith and Knowledge*, derives from the Lurianic Kabbalah which for the first time put the talmudic term *tsimtsum* (contraction) to metaphysical use, by turning it into a primary creative act: the Infinite receding – withdrawing, retreating – for the sake of the alterity of the finite world.[14] And although Derrida almost never mentions *tsimtsum* explicitly and even distances himself from the anthropo-theological appropriations of the 'deserted *re-treat*', which he wants to guard in its cold iconoclastic abstraction, it is nonetheless Luria's intervention that is precursorial to all subsequent notions of the self-negating and self-erasing Absolute: Hegel's '*kenosis* in creation', Heidegger's *Entzug des Seins* (withdrawal of Being), as well as Derrida's self-effacing spatiality of *Khôra*, which, though Platonic in origin, is never really described as 'withdrawing' by Plato himself.[15] In *Timaeus*, Plato talks about *Khôra* in strictly apophatic terms as a passive, indifferent and infinitely susceptible 'receiving vessel' capable to accommodate all forms (*hypodokhe*), and, by calling her a 'nurse of generation', he denies her/it even the slightest activity which is implied by such Derridean terms as 're-treat', 'withdrawal', or 'making-place'. As Derrida himself notes, '*Khôra* comes to signify *this enigma of a place* that Plato himself cannot think from the perspective of Platonism' (CS, 145; emphasis added). This residual activity inscribed into *Khôra*, in which *khorein* consists in receding for the sake of all things to appear, derives from a different tradition: the one of *tsimtsum* which radically questions God's revealability. The purpose of Derrida's Marrano – that is, mixed, Greco-Abrahamic – take on *Khôra-in-tsimtsum* is

---

[14] This version of *tsimtsum*, in which God 'takes in his breath' and restricts his glory – the spectacular show of *kavod* blinding with the light – for the sake of something else to emerge *instead*, derives already from Isaiah, as described by Elliot Wolfson in his interpretation of one of the bahiric texts: 'The notion of withdrawal, itself withdrawn and thus not stated overtly, is a secret exegetically derived from the verse *lema'an shemi a'arikh appi u-tehillati ehetam lakh le-vilti hakhritekha*, "For the sake of my name I will postpone my wrath and my glory I will hold in for you so that I will not destroy you" (Isa. 48.9). The plain sense of the prophetic dictum relates to divine mercy expressed as God's long-suffering, the capacity to restrain his rage. The expression *tehillati ehetam*, literally "my glory I will hold in," is parallel to *a'arikh appi*, "I will postpone my wrath." One may surmise that at some point in ancient Israel the notion of a vengeful god yielded its opposite, the compassionate god who holds in his fury': Elliot Wolfson, *Alef, Mem, Tau: Kabbalistic Musings on Time, Truth, and Death* (Berkeley: University of California Press, 2006), 132–3.

[15] There is only one explicit mention of *tsimtsum* as 'linked to the mythology of Louria' in Derrida's oeuvre: 'Dissemination', devoted to Philippe Soller's novel *Nombres* (DIS, 344). On the significance of the Lurianic heritage especially for German Idealism, see my: 'God of Luria, Hegel, Schelling: The Divine Contraction and the Modern Metaphysics of Finitude', in *Mystical Theology & Continental Philosophy: Interchange in the Wake of God*, ed. David Levin, Simon Podmore, and Duane Wiliams (London: Routledge, 2017), 32–50.

to demonstrate that the iconoclasm, which forbids any image of God, is deeply rooted in the very nature of God who *himself* withdraws from glory, visibility, and sight. His is, as Blanchot put it poetically, 'the truth of the night, that which is not to be retained when day breaks'.

Indeed, Derrida's Marrano idiom of practicing thinking in the Joycean 'greekjew-jewgreek' style – to which he admits as early as in the essay devoted to Lévinas, 'Violence and Metaphysics' (WD, 192) – culminates in his treatment of *Khôra* which is being secretly reinscribed as *makom* according to 'a deep affinity with a certain nomination of the God of the Jews, [where] He is also The Place' (AO, 33).[16] The Talmudic tradition of naming God *makom*/place gave a canvas to Luria's metaphysical speculation on *tsimtsum* as precisely the act of *place-making*, where the mystery of creation centres precisely around the 'enigma of the place' (CS, 145). *Makom* is also the other secret name of the Derridean *Khôra* which patiently gives room to everything that emerges as a 'pure singularity'. As such she/it provides a 'link to the other in general': a 'fiduciary link' which 'precedes all determinate community, all positive religion, every onto-anthropo-theological horizon' and which Derrida calls the 'original faith', *la foi originaire* (FK, 55). This emphasis on what Derrida also names elsewhere (in *Psyche*) the 'invention of the difference' – creating a possibility for the emergence of 'the other in general', the alterity as such – may indeed be used as a proof that Derrida shares his main metaphysical concern with Isaac Luria who was one of the first thinkers to break with the Greco-Christian hegemony of Platonism, unable to contemplate the 'enigma of the place'.

If, for the Neoplatonic thinkers, the fundamental question is: how the One can create the Many, or the passage from unity to manifold, for Luria, it is: how the Same can create the Other, or the passage from homogeneity to alterity. As such, these questions form two parallel versions of the passage *from the infinite to the finite*. The Neoplatonic system makes no room for the real finitude: the finite manifold is merely an epiphenomenon of the Infinite which never gives up on its eternal oneness and integrity. Contrary to this, in Luria's system the Infinite truly recedes in order to make a separate free room for the things finite which are given their own autonomous reality. Thus, while the Neoplatonic One makes no room for anything else in its *hyper-pleroma* – the Lurianic Infinite (*Ein-Sof*) does nothing else, but makes room, by creating *kenoma/tehiru* out of itself. This parallel can also be explained in reference to the Lacanian difference between the Big Other (*A* as in *Absolute*) and the small other (*a* as in *autrui*): while the former gathers everything under His sovereign jealous control, himself remaining abstracted/absolved from the world – the latter represents the horizontal alterity of the 'scattered existence', into whom we trust as always wholly other and do not wish to subject to any pre-established unity. While the former is the

---

[16] Michael Naas also notices Derrida's 'jewgreek-greekjew' tendency to produce a dense interference of the two idioms, for instance, in the description of his tallith in 'A Silkworm of One's Own' which brings it close to *Khôra*: 'and, finally, the tallith, the white tallith, as what belongs to the 'night, the absolute night' also resembles *Khôra* as "the place of absolute exteriority," the "nocturnal source" of both religion and science. The tallith is thus, in some sense, another name for *Khôra*, the place that gives place and has no name that is absolutely proper to it' (MM, 231–2).

'wrong abstraction' of the castrating Absolute whose unscathed full-of-light vitality must be nourished by the sacrifice of the finite lives (from the pagan cults to Hegel's Christianity) – the latter is simply our neighbour, the Rosenzweigian *Platzhalter*/place-keeper who just happened to *take place* next to us in the space of *Khôra*: the 'good abstraction' of the self-detaching and self-withdrawing nocturnal source.[17] Religion thus bifurcates from the very beginning: it either takes the form of the faith in the Big Other as the One, Whole, and Holy, who jealously keeps all being and life to itself, or the faith in the small others, always plural, *plus d'Un*, given right to take place and then freely 'disperse, multiply' (FK, 100).

But why does not Derrida mention Luria directly? There is a good reason why he should conceal the Lurianic source: his Marrano reluctance to be associated with any particular messianic traditions, the Jewish-Kabbalist included, which all grow *out* of the kenomatic abstraction of the 'desert in the desert', and thus lose the radical iconoclasm of the 'hidden tradition' in the process. In the light of his 'harshest' abstracted messianicity, which relates to the Lurianic messianism in the same manner as the general structure of revealability (the Heideggerian *Veroffenbarkeit*) relates to any concrete revelation (*Veroffenbarung*), *Khôra* emerges as a better candidate for the *kenomatic* source of religion, because it is free of any secondary anthropo-theo-sophic associations. While it gives place for each and every thing, there is no place for it in any official discourse, beginning with Platonism. Thus, if it gives room/place/space, it does it abstractedly, indifferently, anonymously, and, as if, *mechanically*: not out of love, kindness, or generosity, which motivates the Lurianic *Ein-Sof* in his *miraculous* act of self-retreat. Even those affective images are forbidden to express the originary, strictly iconoclastic, 'giving beyond the gift': as Derrida will try to prove in the course of his essay, it is precisely the most abstract ontotheology which comes closest to the 'truth' of the 'hidden tradition', carried by the 'Spanish Marranos' (FK, 100). In Derrida's vision, it is precisely the Marrano secret – almost forgotten, bordering on a/theology or even atheism, yet at the same time, not without its own paradoxical form of piety and memory – that offers the aptest model for the 'religion of modern times'. Just as the Marrano encrypts the Jewish *deus absconditus* in the inner crypt of his seemingly impious self, so does the modern faith hide behind the façade of ontotheological knowledge and develops further, undercover and in secrecy, without overt expression in religious imagination. Knowledge, therefore, not only represses faith in the (once) Living God, but it also protects faith as *foi originaire* in the place-making origin-in-retreat: *Khôra/Makom/kenoma/empty place*. This alternative *fides abscondita* is *not* to be dragged out from the shadow of the crypt into the light of presence: if it develops and becomes a new 'religion of the modern times', it is only thanks to the empty darkness of the 'desert in the desert', which is its proper hiding place. The extreme iconoclastic

---

[17] Comp. Rosenzweig on what Derrida would call the *khorein*/choreography of the neighbourly love: 'The neighbor is only a representative; he is not loved for himself, he is not loved for his beautiful eyes, but only because he is just there, because he is just my neighbor. In his place – in this place that is for me the one neighboring on me – there could just as well be another person [...] The neighbor is [...] only a place-keeper' (SR, 234).

hiddenness, which the crypt provides, is not a tomb of faith's death; on the contrary, it is the necessary condition of its survival.

What I, therefore, following Derrida's logic, propose here to call the Marrano *kenomatic* God is the further radicalization of the already radical motif of the divine 'ordeal' (*epreuve*) or the Hegelian 'Golgotha of the Absolute Spirit': God who not only humbles himself in the act of *kenosis*, but truly 'empties himself out', *entäussert sich*, by transforming into the 'desert in the desert' which the Jewish-Gnostic tradition calls *tehiru*: 'the void of the most serious privation of God (*Gottlosigkeit*)' (FK, 53). Thus, if Hegel describes 'modern religious sentiment' in terms of the 'abandonment by God', it also – or rather, most of all – means that God had abandoned *himself*; that he *verliess*, let go and gave up his sovereign Godhead, or, in Derrida's idiom, resigned from his unscathed, indemnified purity and oneness for the sake of contamination with the alien element of the world and its 'unprejudiced becoming'. It is not God who got *hidden*, as in the proto-atheistic conceptions of *deus absconditus* – but God actively *hiding*. And, further on, not the *disappeared* God of *atheism* – but the *disappearing* God of *a-theism* which protects divine concealment and defends it against iconophilic 'theomania'.[18] Thus, while simple atheism can be defined as the *non-belief in God's presence* – the Marrano a-theism can be defined as the *belief in God's absence*: 'Everything begins with the presence of that absence' (FK, 65). Although both positions refer to the same state of the visible world – the non-presence of God here and now – the connotation of this reference is totally different. For atheism, God no longer enters the present picture of the world as it is. For *a-theism*, it is precisely the continuous withdrawal from the visible immanence, which protects the transcendent, image-less and unimaginable, 'otherwise than being' that, precisely due to its *autrement qu'être*, lets everything else be and take place.

Religion of the finite life?

In *Faith and Knowledge*, Derrida distinguishes two sources of religion. The first source is absolutely *pleromatic*: it is life always 'safe and sound', infinite and beyond harm (*indemne*), in which there is no room for anything else apart from the self-delighting sameness. The second source is *kenomatic*. It 'exists' only in erasing itself from existence, in the act of radical withdrawal/retreat which negates sameness and makes room for the Other – the alterity of everything else. Derrida does not call it that way, but, as we

---

[18] This great term – *theomania* – was coined by Elliot Wolfson who, among all Derrida's commentators, truly saw into the heart of his apophatic *via negativa*: 'Jacques Derrida [was] able to carry the project of *dénégation* one step further [...] [He] embarked on a path that culminated in the aporetic suspension of belief [...] He well understood that the removal of all images from God, if maintained unfailingly, seriously compromises the viability of devotional piety [...] Indeed, the horizon established by this eventuality – as vividly as it may present itself to human imagination – is best depicted as a territory that is peculiarly not a territory, a *territory beyond all territorialization*, the margin to which we are propelled by attunement to the surpassing of language through language': Wolfson, *Giving Beyond the Gift*, xvii–viii; emphasis added. The 'territory beyond all territorialization' is also a great formula for *Khôra/makom* and its 'eventuality': a placeless place giving place beyond the gift.

have seen, it is essential not to misrecognize it as *kenotic*: although self-emptying, it constitutes an ultimate openness to the 'wound' which is no longer conceived as a sickness-to-be-healed or a crisis-to-be-overcome. No longer a negative concept, it does not denote a *skandalon* or catastrophe. The *kenoma* which God willingly assumes in order to make room for the otherness of the other – the surprise of alterity, the 'real' product of dissemination beyond any control and mastery – presents the 'death of God' in far less sacrificial manner, and therefore also no longer inducing sin, guilt, debt, and – last but least – the icon-fixated 'memory of the Passion' (FK, 50). While the 'living God' of the first source demands to be constantly present in the light of the memory – the 'disappearing God' of the second source retreats into the night of oblivion.

The critique of *life unscathed/la vie indemne* is the most crucial moment of the whole reasoning, first announced in *Faith and Knowledge*, and then endlessly elaborated in Derrida's last seminars, all devoted – in the most passionate and religious sense of the phrase: *l'hayim* – to life. Yet not Life with the capital L, modelling itself after the Hegelian *unverletztes Leben* of the self-healing Trinity (on which in a moment), but life of the singular living: finite, precarious and thus always inescapably 'scathed', yet not at all, for that reason, 'pseudo-real'.[19] In the previous chapter, I have already suggested that Derrida's deconstruction of religion aims at arresting the transition from life finite to life infinite, and then, from life infinite to absolute death. All religions start as 'religions of the living' (FK, 85), in which finite life celebrates itself as a gift, then pass into the cults of *la vie indemne*, imagined as the pleromatic source capable of giving life, and finally – seemingly paradoxically – give up on life altogether and invest in the image of the eternal Absolute as 'more than life'. This mysterious leap from the love of the life immortal and unharmed, in which our finite life wishes to augment itself as 'more life', into a cult of something beyond life, which turns against the finite life as unworthy of living, is, according to Derrida, the most dangerous mechanism of all religions, not just the Christian one. The seemingly spontaneous, purely mechanical logic of the first pleromatic source, which gives and takes life in order to keep its living plenitude intact, must, therefore, be *arrested*, that is, made at least 'reflective':

> This mechanical principle is apparently very simple: life has absolute value only if it is worth *more than life*. And hence only in so far as it mourns, becoming itself in the labour of infinite mourning, in the indemnification of a spectrality without limit. It is sacred, holy, infinitely respectable only in the name of what is worth more than

---

[19] Needless to say, Derrida's critique of the unscathed pleroma of all-powerful vitality goes against the understanding of the sacred among the so-called phenomenologists of religion, such as Rudolf Otto or Mircea Eliade. Compare the latter's praise of the ontophanic fullness present in the religious cults of the premodern traditions: 'The man of the archaic societies tends to live as much as possible in the sacred or in close proximity to consecrated objects. The tendency is perfectly understandable, because, for primitives as for the man of all premodern societies, *the sacred is equivalent to a power, and, in the last analysis, to reality: The sacred is saturated with being*. Sacred power means reality and at the same time enduringness and efficacy. The polarity sacred- profane is often expressed as an *opposition between real and unreal or pseudoreal* [...] Thus it is easy to understand that religious man deeply desires to be, to participate in reality, *to be saturated with power*': Mircea Eliade, 'Introduction' to *The Sacred and the Profane*, 12–13; emphasis added.

it and what is not restricted to the naturalness of the bio-zoological (sacrificeable) – although true sacrifice ought to sacrifice not only 'natural' life, called 'animal' or 'biological,' but also that which is worth more than so-called natural life. The price of human life, which is to say, of anthropo-theological life, the price of what to remain safe (*heilig*, sacred, safe and sound, unscathed, immune), as the absolute price, the price of what ought to inspire respect, modesty, reticence, this price is priceless. It corresponds to what Kant calls the dignity [*Würdigkeit*] of the end in itself [. . .] This dignity of life can only subsist beyond the present living being. Whence, transcendence, fetishism and spectrality; whence, the religiosity of religion. This excess above and beyond the living, whose life only has absolute value by being worth more than life, more than itself – this, in short, is what opens the space of death that is linked to the automaton (exemplarily 'phallic'), to technics, the machine, the prosthesis: in a word, to the dimensions of auto-immune and self-sacrificial supplementarity, to this death-drive that is silently at work in every community, every *auto-co-immunity*, constituting it as such in its iterability, its heritage, its spectral tradition [. . .] Religion, as a response that is both ambiguous and ambivalent is thus an ellipsis: *the ellipsis of sacrifice*. (FK, 87–8; emphasis added)

Yet, Derrida's aim is not just to arrest the sacrificial logic of the first source which is the cult of the unscathed pleromatic Life turned against life. Having in mind the second – kenomatic – source, he also immediately asks: 'Is a religion imaginable without sacrifice and without prayer?' (FK, 88). This is not a rhetorical question with an implied answer in the negative. Just few pages before Derrida told us that it is ontotheology which is 'without sacrifice and without prayer' (FK, 53): a properly modern philosophical doctrine which, in a semi-Hegelian fashion, sublates/devours the religious content not in order to destroy it, but to preserve it in the abstracted, immaculately iconoclastic, form. The relation between *fides et ratio*, the religious faith and the philosophical knowledge is thus formal, precisely as in Hegel's succinct definition: 'Faith already has the true content. What is still lacking in it is the form of thought.'[20] Derrida's purpose is analogical, while venturing beyond the scope of Christianity: he is looking for a better form to articulate the 'truth of the tradition' than can be found in the openly religious/theological forms of *Tradierbarkeit*. Hence the reference to the fate of the 'Spanish Marranos' who were forced to break the chain of tradition and bury the Jewish God in their inner crypts long before the 'murder of God' announced by Nietzsche. They had experienced it first, so they also pioneer a characteristically modern form of defence – a *crypto-religious cryptophoria* – which preserves hidden *fides* under the façade of worldly *ratio*.[21]

---

[20] G. W. F Hegel, *Lectures on the Philosophy of Religion*, vol. 3 (*The Consummate Religion*) (Oxford: Oxford University Press, 2008), 148.
[21] The classical locus which discusses the 'murder of God' is Erich Voegelin's critique of modernity as taking 'the order of being [. . .] under man's control. And taking control of being further requires that the transcendent origin of being be obliterated: it requires the decapitation of being – the murder of God. The murder of God is committed speculatively by explaining divine being as the work of man': Eric Voegelin, *Science, Politics and Gnosticism: Two Essays* (Washington: Regnery Publishing, 1997), 53.

It is, therefore, quite justifiable to read *Faith and Knowledge* as the deconstructive critique of all religions understood as the cults of the unscathed – and Martin Hägglund's *Radical Atheism* is the best example of such interpretation. According to Hägglund, Derrida, who defends the 'time of life' against eternalizing hypostases, is the most radical type of atheist. His investment in the ever-disseminating temporality, which can only leave a transient trace of its presence, makes Derrida a staunch enemy of any form of the Absolute conceived as a timeless *nunc stans*. By insisting on the inherent connection between transience and life, Derrida dismisses all religious attempts to think in terms of life infinite and immortal as leading out of the domain of life and into the realm of death: the unchanging and untouchable Absolute can never be alive; it is death pure and simple. For, as long as there is life, there is exposure to time, scathedness, and vulnerability: the idea of an Absolute Life, essential to *all* religions, is thus a *contradictio in adjecto*. Life can only affirm itself as a constant effort of survival, which, according to Hägglund, is the defining feature of radical atheism. It is merely the desire for survival which dissimulates itself as the desire for immortality. But while it precedes the latter, it also contradicts it from within: 'There is thus an internal contradiction in the so-called desire for immortality. If one were not attached to mortal life, there would be no fear of death and no desire to live on' (RA, 2). In *Dying for Time*, Hägglund calls this contradiction a double bind characteristic of the human 'chronolibido':

> Desire is chronophobic since whatever we are bound to or aspire for can be lost: it can be taken away from or be rejected by us. Yet, by the same token, desire is chronophilic, since it is because we are bound to or aspire for something that can be lost that we care about it, that we care about what happens.[22]

Hägglund's interpretation aims at re-reading the whole of Derrida's work, from his earliest deconstruction of Husserl in *Speech and Phenomena* up to his latest seminars on death penalty and sovereignty, in terms of the determined attempt to reformulate our attitude to survival as ultimately positive: 'The radical finitude of survival is not a lack of being that is desirable to overcome. Rather, the finitude of survival opens the chance for everything that is desired and the threat of everything that is feared' (RA, 2). Because of that, the very concept of God who is 'beyond everything that can be predicated by a finite being' (RA, 7) and who cannot die ('If God were not immortal, he would not be God', RA, 8) – must be abandoned. To say, therefore, that 'God is dead' is not enough. According to Hägglund, Derrida radicalizes the atheist thesis by implying that 'God is death', that is, that he is the direct opposite, as well as negation, of all things alive and finite:

> If to be alive is to be mortal, it follows that to *not* be mortal – to be immortal – is to be dead. If one cannot die, one is dead. Hence, Derrida does not limit himself to

---

[22] Martin Hägglund, *Dying for Time: Proust, Woolf, Nabokov* (Cambridge, MA: Harvard University Press, 2012), 14.

the atheist claim that God is dead; he repeatedly makes the radically atheist claim that *God is death*. That God is death does not mean that we reach God through death or that God rules over death. On the contrary, it means that the idea of immortality – which according to Marion is 'the idea that we cannot not form of God' – is inseparable from the idea of absolute death. (RA, 8)[23]

This is all very true: if Hägglund treats Jean-Luc Marion – Derrida's famous adversary in many discussions – as the paradigmatic exponent of the religious belief which, following the long tradition of Anselm's ontological argument, imputes the incapability to sustain any 'wound' to the very essence of the pleromatic godhead – then Derrida, indeed, is the radical denier of such faith. But is this tendency to conceive God as the ultimate realization of the 'chronophobic desire' the only possible one? Derrida's critical treatment of the Hegelian-Kantian model of God's demise complicates the dualistic picture painted by Hägglund, based on the simple opposition of God who by definition cannot die, on the one hand, and the radical atheism which accepts the premise that whatever is alive must be mortal, on the other. Despite Hägglund's atheistic interpretation, Derrida does not reject *all* possible religion. Although historically *almost* all actual religions tended to define themselves as deeply 'chronophobic' cults of the unscathed, understood either in the immanentist terms of the invulnerable life ('pagan' religions) or in the transcendent terms of the otherworldly Infinite (Abrahamic religions), he is nonetheless mostly interested in the self-deconstructive tendency of the 'modern religious sentiment' which attaches itself to the motif of the divine 'scathedness', and which the Hegelian Christianity defined – partly rightly, but also partly confusedly – as the 'religion of the death of God'. The question, therefore, is: can there be a chronophilic religion of the scathed – the vulnerable, finite, exposed – without any recourse to the Absolute? Again, it is Hegel who delivers here main categories: just as his 'death of God religion' cuts into the neat dualism of traditional religiosity, sporting the image of the divine sovereign, on the one hand, and atheism resulting from 'Nietzsche's two words', on the other – so does his early concept of *unverletztes Leben*, 'unscathed life', serves to depict the inner mechanism of religious cults. But what if this very *mechanism* broke? What if it got jammed, became 'reflective', and began to self-deconstruct, more and more aware of the double bind permeating the depths of human desire? What if God himself, so to say, stepped down from the

---

[23] The paradox of the deadening idemnification is a frequent subject of Abraham and Torok's reflections on the en-cryption, cryptonymy, and cryptophoria, also commented on by Derrida in his preface to their *Wolf Man's Magic Word*: 'A crypt, people believe, always hides something dead. But to guard it from what? Against what does one keep a corpse intact, safe both from life and from death, which could both come in from the outside to touch it? And to allow death to take no place in life?' (F, xxi). Indeed, 'day in day out, *the crypt itself remains unscathed*': Abraham and Torok, *The Shell and the Kernel*, 152; emphasis added. The 'shell', therefore, that is, the wall which creates the crypt, not only deadens/ oppresses the 'kernel', which lies there deposited, but also protects it and guards in its hiddenness – which, for Derrida, is precisely the dialectical model for the relation between Knowledge (shell) and Faith (kernel).

pedestal of undamaged vitality (or dead immortality) and let the second – kenomatic/chronophilic – source come more strongly to the fore?[24]

The change which occurs in Hegel's thought between his early theological writings and the inception of *Phenomenology* – the shift from the traditional Christian image of religious community as mirroring perfect, unscathed, and timeless life of the godhead to the heterodox Christian-Gnostic notion of God depleting himself and emptying out into creation in order to participate in the adventure of temporality – can also be seen as the canvas for Derrida's own deconstructive manoeuvre. Far from refuting all 'religious sentiments' as inevitably gravitating towards the 'safe and sound', he, just like Hegel before, aims to distil – abstract – the streak of the other, self-deconstructive religiosity which affirmatively welcomes the finite and scathed. *Faith and Knowledge*, therefore, does not deconstruct religion from the outside – the radical atheist position Hägglund attributes to Derrida – but from the inside, following and enhancing the internal self-deconstructive moment of religion itself, which he – after Hegel (but also, as I insist here, implicitly, Isaac Luria) – identifies with the 'death of God' as the Lord and Master: a self-willed demise of sovereignty.

The experiment of *Faith and Knowledge*, precursorial to Derrida's last seminars, is thus to test out for the first time the possibility of a 'modern religious sentiment' which will ultimately free itself from the infatuation with sovereign power: the 'more than life' image of the unscathed Absolute to which no harm can be done. Derrida's double portrayal of the second source – the Abrahamic messianicity on the one hand, and Platonic *Khôra* on the other – deliberately emphasizes their weakness and vulnerability, uncharacteristic for the foundational *arche*: *Khôra* is an 'open wound' itself, but also the messianic principle is *an-archic*, swerving away from the royal image of the *melekh ha-olam*, the King of the World. This rhetoric of weakening aims at presenting these two visions of the second source as equally *kenomatic*: self-emptying, self-humbling, self-offering, self-disseminating.

The Marrano Hegel: Between *kenosis* and *tsimtsum*

The gist of Derrida's Marrano reading of Hegel, which he inaugurates already in *Glas*, consists in the secret implicit lining of his main notion, *Entäußerung*, with the

---

[24] In the fictional dialogue staged by Catherine Malabou between differing voices at the end of *Counterpaths*, one of them asks if Derrida's 'metaphysics of travel' and its 'path of separation' implies 'leaving out God'. The other answers: 'No, *not if by God one means the real leap of chance or the throw of the dice*. Yes, if by God one means an origin excepted from the way that it still manages to open up, a non-vehicular or non-conveyed instance, still alive to the extent that it never exposes itself to the possibility of accident, to catastrophe in general' (CP-M, 283; emphasis added). She thus confirms that Derrida's views on metaphysics can indeed be inscribed into Cardoso's and Jonas's legacy of the Marrano 'theology of risk'. Thus, while Malabou understands that the risk of self-erasure of the origin does not have to indicate 'leaving out God', Hägglund has a tendency to identify every trace of the divine as the 'positive infinity' (RA, 85) and every theological discourse as referring to the immutable Absolute.

Lurianic idea of *tsimtsum*. In Hegel the Christian, it is God himself who consents to die, but his kenotic self-sacrifice encumbers the world with the guilt which must be bought off/redeemed at the end of history. In Luria's thought, on the other hand, the world emerges in the act of pure liberating *gift* which is also to be remembered, but in a different way than the remorseful 'memory of the Passion' (FK, 50). Derrida is well aware that, despite some surface affinities, the Lurianic *tsimtsum* is *not* the same as the Christian *kenosis*: it is not God's self-sacrifice and self-offering which burdens the world with the sense of a terrible and scandalous loss. It is a 'death of God' for sure, if we mean by it a demise of the sovereign highest being, but it is also *God's self-estranged afterlife*: his only mode of a non-sovereign 'living-on' in and with the world which he simultaneously made his own creation and let go as a free other-being, and as such his 'one chance of survival' (TG, 42). The *tsimtsem*/contracted God does not die *for us* (and we didn't kill him), because he does not simply *die*: he limits his primordial infiniteness and becomes finite not in order to make creation eternally guilty, dependent, and obliged, but in order to pour himself into and affirm finitude as the right and only way to be. He himself, therefore, is the most powerful spokesman for the principle of the radical univocity of being as universally *finite*.

It is precisely by having in mind *tsimtsum* as the other, that is, *non-sacrificial* gift that Derrida writes his commentary on Hegel whose account of the beginnings contains both moments – the gift and the sacrifice, the play and the fire – aporetically intertwined:

> This perhaps: *the gift, the sacrifice, the putting in play or to fire of all*, the holocaust, are under the powers of ontology [. . .] Without the holocaust the dialectical movement and the history of Being could not open themselves [. . .] could not annul themselves in producing the solar course from Orient to Occident. Before, if one could count here with time, there is, there will have been the *irruptive event of the gift*. (G, 241; emphasis added)

Yet, which gift? For Hegel, who understands creation in terms of the Christian *kenosis*, it simply must take on the form of self-offering: hence the simple enumeration in the first quote: 'the gift, the sacrifice. . .' But, is it possible to think the gift *without* the sacrifice? For Hegel, it is obvious that the primordial *Lichtwesen*, the 'light-being' of the most archaic Oriental religions (into which Hegel includes not only the old Indo-European *deiwos* but also the Kabbalistic *Ein-Sof*), must have offered itself to the fire which it was in the first place, commit an auto-holocaust or a burnt self-offering in order to 'set down' and produce the 'solar course from Orient to Occident': the 'irruptive event of the gift', without which there would be no world of beings, *must* be thought within the sacrificial logic. The first reflective movement of dialectics, in which the fiery substance of the 'light-being' transforms into subject, occurs when it turns *against* itself, in an act of violent self-negation. But Derrida questions precisely this very logic and asks: is it possible to think about the gift *without* the sacrifice? For, once gift becomes 'gifted'/poisoned with the sacrifice, it begins to guard itself as something precious that immediately creates a space of debt – debt to be necessarily returned and paid back – and thus stops being a gift. This is what Derrida, already pressing towards a non-sacrificial logic of the gift, calls the 'constraint': the dogmatic axiom in Hegel's reconstruction of the 'first movement' from which everything begins.

> From the moment of this constraint, this constriction of the 'must' comes to press the *mad energy of a gift*, what this constriction provokes is perforce a countergift, an exchange, in the space of the debt. I give you – a pure gift, without exchange, without return – but whether I want this or not, the gift guards itself, keeps itself, and from then on you must-owe, *tu dois* [. . .] I give you without expecting anything in exchange, but this every renunciation, as soon as it *appears*, forms the most powerful and most interior ligament [. . .] *The gift can be only a sacrifice*, that is the axiom of speculative reason. (G, 242; emphasis added)

This is precisely the dogma which Derrida wishes to deconstruct as the last ditch of sovereignty that reinstates itself the very moment it allegedly gives up on itself. God who 'dies for us' may have relinquished his master-vitality of the 'terrible living God', but he immediately recreates it in the newly opened 'space of death' (FK, 88), in which he becomes the sovereign paradigm of the perfect self-sacrifice: as we already know, the Hegelian 'infinite grief' manifests itself primarily in 'the moral sacrifice of empirical existence [which] only dates the absolute Passion or the speculative Good Friday' (FK, 53). Hence *kenosis*, even the most radical and seemingly self-humbling, is still God's self-offering, and because of that a toxic gift – indeed, the German *Gift* – which does not liberate its recipients but enslaves them by the perverse gesture of sovereignty.[25] This is also the reason why, pace Nancy's official thesis that Christianity is already a deconstruction *avant la lettre*, Christian religion can never fully deconstruct itself into atheism, because it will always be kept on the leash of indebtedness and obligation: a 'bad conscience' which keeps returning – explicitly in Hegel, but implicitly also in Nietzsche, Heidegger, and Nancy, despite their explicit allegiance to the 'innocence of becoming'. The Christian dead God, says Derrida, can never let his people go, the way

---

[25] In *Derridabase*, Geoffrey Bennington very rightly reduces Derrida's deconstruction of Hegel to the motif of the gift as an extra-logical – *miraculous* – element which cannot be incorporated into the Hegelian dialectical *machine*: 'in Hegel's own text, the tracks of what withdraws from the speculative dialectic, this gift can, for example, be the light of the sun [. . .] We cannot prevent dialectical thinking from drawing on this, but the fact remains that the dialectico-ontological circle must open onto this preontological gift that it cannot receive as such but must constantly presuppose. If one cannot receive this gift as such, no more can one refuse it - the gift is thus always poisoned (gift, *Gift*, as Derrida reminds us, playing on English and German)': Jacques Derrida and Geoffrey Bennington, *Jacques Derrida* (Chicago: The University of Chicago Press, 1993), 191. The Joycean play across languages, which Bennington invokes, takes place in 'Tours de Babel', where Derrida speculates on the gift of tongues, poisoned from the start by 'Confusion' which is one of God's proper names: 'And the name of God the father would be the name of that origin of tongues. But it is also that God who, in the action of his anger (like the God of Jakob Böhme or of Hegel, he who goes out of himself, determines himself in his finitude and thus produces history), annuls the gift of tongues, or at least embroils it, sows confusion among his sons, and poisons the present (*Gift*-gift)' (PS1, 193). In another essay from *Psyche*, Derrida states: 'Nothing is more difficult than to accept a gift' (PS1, 147).

it is expressed by the Jewish God of Exodus, recollected in the alternative 'memory of Passover': he would for ever make them *schuldig*, bound by guilt, subjugated not by force, but by moral obligation. Thus, in modern thinking about God-becoming-finite, we must pass beyond the traps of *kenosis*, which smuggles under its *skandalon* the idea of a cosmic catastrophe and thus prevents from imagining this *finitization* as a truly free opening, beyond the economy of debt and redemption.[26] This is precisely where *tsimtsum* enters the scene as the non-sacrificial and non-catastrophic gesture of God's self-limitation: the *gift without sacrifice*. In Derrida's rendering, therefore, the Hegelian account of the 'beginnings' is Lurianic – the 'first movement' is indeed the self-exteriorization of the divine light which reflexively turns on/against itself and contracts/sets down – but the way in which he insinuates into it the toxic motif of *kenosis* is Christian. It is indeed a 'poisoned present' – a '*Gift*-gift' (PS1, 193).[27]

But what is this 'first movement' which creates all: the world of beings, as well as time, difference, and history? In the beginning, there is nothing and everything simultaneously: the undifferentiated All manifesting as the light of *Lichtwesen*, the all-consuming fire or the *Or Ein-Sof*, the light of the primordial 'Without Limits'. This fiery light is engaged in the ceaseless 'holocaust' which immediately reduces whatever emerged from the flames back to ashes. It is the Hegelian apocalyptic 'fury of destruction' (*die Furie des Zerstörung*) embodied or – to use a more contemporary psychoanalytic idiom – the pure death drive which leaves no traces while it also leaves no room for anything else, by annihilating all being as well as itself. Whatever the light brings into being/visibility, the fire at once destroys by annulling all the difference: the

---

[26] In the book devoted to Nancy, *On Touching*, Derrida fiercely attacks what he calls the Christian *delectatio morosa*, unable to stop revelling in the 'tragedy of the cross': '*For a certain Christianity will always take charge of the most exacting, the most exact, and the most eschatological hyperbole of deconstruction, the overbid of "Hoc est enim corpus meum." It will still make sacrifice of its own self-deconstruction. Hey, Sade – go for it!*': Jacques Derrida, *On Touching – Jean-Luc Nancy*, trans. Christine Irizarry (Stanford: Stanford University Press, 2005), 60; emphasis added. Alluding to Lacan's 'Kant avec Sade', which found a sadistic component of *jouissance* in a seemingly purely formal Kantian ethics, Derrida points to the libidinal surplus of enjoyment in the paradoxical pride taken in the absolute uniqueness of Christianity as the religion of the God which it killed.

[27] Derrida's dissatisfaction with the Hegelian axiom of *kenosis* comes to the fore very visibly in his preface to Catherine Malabou's *Future of Hegel*, where God's self-emptying figures very largely as the axiomatic canvas of the whole phenomenological process of the divine self-recuperation: 'The Death of God thereby appears for Hegel as a moment in the divine being in the form of a first negation, logically destined to be reduplicated and reversed: "Rather, a reversal takes place: God, that is to say, maintains himself in this process, and the latter is only the death of death *der Tod des Todes*." The expression *mors mortis* is found many times in Luther's writing, but the singularity of the Hegelian version shows itself in the way he interprets this death of death as a "negation of negation." Supported by such an interpretation we can already predict the transition from the theological signification of *kenosis* to its philosophical meaning': Malabou, *The Future of Hegel*, 107. Agreeing with Malabou's emphasis on the importance of *kenosis* for Hegel, Derrida, worried by the past-oriented retributive character of the redemptive process, comments: '[Such] God would have no future, he would not even be able to promise or give himself both because he leaves and impoverishes himself (he says farewell to himself) and because, while leaving himself, he still does not leave himself, he does not abandon himself [...] Too much emptiness, too much fullness [...] *We should then accomplish one more step, add a supplement of farewell to this Hegelian farewell, and say farewell to this farewell of God to God*': Jacques Derrida, 'Preface' to Malabou, *The Future of Hegel*, xlii; emphasis added. In my interpretation, this 'one more step' supplementing the 'Hegelian farewell' is the idea of *tsimtsum*.

other cannot come into a lasting existence (*Dauer*) and separate itself from the burning Sameness. Thus, even if the primordial *Lichtwesen* contains all *in nuce*, the particular beings cannot yet assert themselves in their distinct being; they 'burn' to the ashes of de-differentiation, the cyclically self-renewing *Indifferenz*.

> Pure and figureless, this light burns all. It burns itself in the all-burning it is, leaves, of itself or anything, no trace, no mark, *no sign of passage* [...] The all-burning is 'an essenceless by-play' [*Beiherspielen*], pure accessory of the substances that *rises* without ever *setting*, without becoming a subject. And without consolidating through the self its differences [...] *this play does not yet work*. (G, 238; emphasis added)

It is only in the next – totally inexplicable – move that the substance *gibt sich dem Fürsichsein zum Opfer* (G, 240): instead of remaining for ever a playful substance projecting 'torrents of fire destructive of figuration' (G, 240), it suddenly 'decides' to 'set down' and thus become a subject through self-sacrifice of its own substance. And although later, in the *Science of Logic*, Hegel will call this move by the purely philosophical name of 'negation of negation', in which the first light retreats from destruction and thus *annihilates the annihilation* in order to let beings be, Derrida insists on presenting it in the more archaic series of theosophic images which are to remind us about its unsettled – 'miraculous' – origin. Just as in *Faith and Knowledge*, already here, in *Glas*, Hegel is suspected of the iconophilic residue of *Vorstellungsdenken*, lurking behind his seemingly fully sublated philosophical abstraction. For, it is not an abstract and neutrally philosophical 'negation of negation' which is mechanically inscribed into the nature of the First Idea, but the miraculous 'irruptive event of the gift': on the one hand, the *tsimtsum*-like 'setting of the sun' that no longer blinds and burns to ashes particular beings, but also, on the other a kenotic self-offering which 'insures its guarding' and in this manner transforms gift into debt. And yet, at the same time, the picture-thinking indeed recedes in Hegel's speculation and paves the way to philosophical ontotheology. The Hegelian religion of the dead God repeats thus the self-sacrificial gesture of the great departed One: just as God dies in order to let beings be, so religion must die in order to be sublated by philosophy.

> This explains how Hegelian philosophy – through and through a philosophy *of* religion – could be read as an effect of Christianity as well as an implacable atheism. Religion accomplishes itself and dies in the philosophy that is its truth, as the truth of past religion, of the essence as thought past [*Gewesenheit*] of the Christian religion. Truth – the past-thought – is always the death (relieved, erected, buried, unveiled, unbandaged) of what it is the truth of [...] History is the process of a murder. *But this murder is a sacrifice*: the victim offers himself. (G, 33; 32; emphasis added)

As we just saw in the previous section, Derrida is not at all against Hegel's definition of the truth as the death of *what* it is the truth: after all, this is a possible interpretation of Scholem's antinomian distinction between the *tradendum* and the 'truth of the tradition', which Derrida will associate *both* with the abstraction of ontotheology and 'Spanish Marranos'. Yet, just as the kenotic sacrifice of the divine light does not allow to be forgotten and turns the Hegelian 'through and through philosophy *of* religion' into an incessant 'speculative Good Friday', so does the religious 'picture-thinking', which Hegel promises to dissolve into a pure philosophical argument, insist on returning to the unexplained 'irruptive event of the gift' that inaugurates the history of being. Derrida's reading of Hegel is thus an *Erinnerung*, the recollection of what *refuses to die* in the Hegelian speculation: the persistent 'memory of the Passion' (FK, 50) transposed into the 'first movement' which *should* allow the dialectical history to begin, thus securing the passage from the play of pure light into the serious work of real differences.

But – does it? This refusal to die – the paradox of *kenosis* as simultaneously (or rather timelessly) the death and the resurrection of God – is the ultimate obstacle which hinders the desired passage from the playful infinite into the serious finite. The Trinitarian doctrine, as perceived by Hegel and then read by Derrida, does not really let God die: by dividing the second person of the Trinity, the Son, into the dying-finite and the immortal-infinite, the doctrine immediately *undoes* the 'tragedy of the cross' and turns into 'God's play with himself', that is, merely a *dokos* or a mere 'appearance', which, despite all its orthodoxy, makes it dangerously close to the heretic teachings of the docetists. Having in mind Marx's malicious remark about German Idealism as a hermetic *Spiel* resembling masturbation, Derrida accuses Hegelian use of the Trinitarian scheme as precluding any true otherness for the sake of oneness kept by never severed 'familial bonds'. Instead of producing a truly alienated alterity – 'inventing the other' – the merely apparent 'death of God', who in fact refuses to die, dissolves into a familiar play of the Same which steps out of itself only for a moment and then immediately returns to its mono-fold. Everything thus stays in the family:

> God knows and recognizes himself in his son. He assists (in) his death, burial, his magnification, his resurrection. The knowledge relation that organizes this whole scene in a third, a third term, the element of the infinite's relation to self: it is the holy spirit. This medium obtains the element of *familiarity*: God's familiarity with his very own seed, the element of *God's play with himself*. The (infinite) exemplar gives itself and makes the (finite) exemplar return to it. The infinite father gives himself, by self-fellation, self-insemination, and self-conception, a finite son who, in order to posit himself there and incarnate himself as the son of God, becomes infinite, dies as the finite son, lets himself be buried, clasped in bandages he will soon *undo* for the infinite son to be reborn. (G 31, emphasis added)

'The whole system repeats itself in the family' (G, 20) and Spirit, the third person in the familial Trinity, is envisaged as most of all a filial bond of instantaneous reconciliation and *restitutio in integrum*.²⁸ While Judaism represents for Hegel an abstract *Moralität* of a separated individual ('Kantianism is, in this respect, structurally a Judaism', G, 34), Christianity represents communal *Sittlichkeit*, based on the familial 'bonds of love' ('there is no love before Christianity', G, 34). And while Judaism favours violent separation, diremption, and antithesis leading to irreconcilable otherness, Christianity attempts to bind and repair the broken whole with filial *Liebesbande*. Yet, this attempt of reparation, occurring alongside the divide which affects the passage from the infinite to the finite, does not even give either time or space to the finite otherness; the immediate 'undoing' of the fatal results of God plunging into the condition of finitude does not give a chance for the latter to assert itself in its finite way of being.²⁹

The crucial step, therefore, is to abstract the highly vulnerable, non-immune, and self-atheologizing deity, which Hegel puts in the centre of *die Religion der neuen Zeiten*, from the Christian context of *kenosis* that still keeps Hegel in its thrall, by arresting him in the blind spot of the aporia which he cannot (or will not) solve dialectically. This aporia is a typical 'double bind': on the one hand, *kenosis* implies the highest possible sacrifice on God's part, ending in the Hegelian 'feeling that God himself is dead' – on the other, however, *kenosis* appears always within the Trinitarian 'machine', in which God can simultaneously plunge into the depths of creation as the incarnated Son, and somehow – miraculously and paradoxically – remain unscathed as the first person of the Trinity, God the Father. This Trinitarian trick of God dying and resurrecting at the same time; this 'play' (*Spiel*) in which the 'harm' (*Verletzung*) can be done and undone simultaneously, maintains the kenotic abandonment of the life unscathed still within

---

[28] Derrida will often return to the idea of family bond as the symbol of what Geoffrey Bennington rightly calls the 'dialectico-ontological circle': *Derridabase*, 191. It will reappear in *The Counterfeit Money*, as well as in *Ulysses Gramophone: Two Words for Joyce*, which also – via Joyce – attacks the logic of indemnity implied by the Triune God who manages to circumvent the birth of the finite vulnerable deity by the finite earthly mother, by 'sending Himself' directly to the Son: 'It is thus a question of sending oneself [. . .] The 'sending oneself' barely allows itself a detour via the virgin mother when the father imagines that he sends himself the seed of a consubstantial son: "a mystical estate, an apostolic succession, from only begetter to only begotten. . ." This is one of the passages on '*Amor matris*, subjective and objective genitive, may be the only true thing in life. Paternity may be a legal fiction [. . .] He Who Himself begot middler the Holy Ghost and Himself sent Himself, Agenbuyer, between Himself and others, Who' (DJ, 78).

[29] On the Trinitarian dialectics of emptiness and fullness, *kenosis* versus *Eucharist*, dying on the cross versus coming alive again in the act of communion, see also: Werner Hamacher, *Pleroma – Reading in Hegel*, trans. Nicholas Walker and Simon Jarvis (Stanford: Stanford University Press, 1998), as well as Stuart Barnett, 'Eating My God', in *Hegel after Derrida*, ed. Stuart Barnett (London: Routledge, 1998), 131–44, which ingeniously supplements the Hegelian definition of philosophy as a 'speculative Good Friday', where God permanently dies, with a new definition of speculative idealism as a 'permanent Last Supper' which 'reads the history of the Absolute on the basis of the signs of its disappearance [. . .] In this Last Supper signs are eaten, disgorged, and then readied to be eaten again [. . .] Hegel can only accept the notion of the finitization of God if it follows the model of the Last Supper' (ibid., 144; 142). As such, the Last Supper puts together the dispersed pieces of the disappeared God and thus, as Hegel himself formulates it, 'resurrects him daily' (PS, 299): by staging the ritual of *restitutio in integrum*, it makes God whole again.

the traditional scheme which demands an instant restoration of God's infinite vitality.[30] This means, however, that while Christianity, especially in its modern version, makes a move towards the acceptance of finitude, it is immediately counteracted by the traditional structure of the Trinitarian compensation, which brings the 'harmed' God back to his untouchable indemnity in – literally – no time.

But, as I have already indicated, Derrida detects in Hegel something else, a different aspect of the 'first movement', which goes beyond the logic of *kenosis* and its surreptitious undoing in the Trinitarian scheme. If history can truly begin, it is only because this alternative manner of contraction and self-limitation does not demand to be 'undone'; once God 'declines', he no longer refuses to die. He erases himself out of existence in order to become a spectral Subject which had released all that once belonged to his substance into the free open of absolutely non-familiar and non-familial alterity (*freilassen*), precisely the way in which Scholem describes the Lurianic act of *tsimtsum*: 'By positing a negative factor in Himself, *God liberates creation.*'[31] By obliquely invoking the opening scene of *Zohar*, in which the primordial light of *Ein-Sof* occludes itself in the cloud of darkness, Derrida comments:

> The light envelops itself in darkness even before becoming subject. In order to become subject, in effect the sun must go down [decline]. Subjectivity always produces itself in a movement of occidentalization [. . .] That is the origin of history, the beginning of the going down, the setting of the sun, the passage to occidental subjectivity. Fire becomes for (it)self and is lost. (G, 239)

Hegel connects the birth of the Occident, *der Abendland*, with the 'setting down of the sun'. Religion travels from the East to the West, which coincides with the crucial passage: *from Substance to Subject*, where God stops being the all-consuming light-fire and, by negating himself – 'setting down' – becomes reborn as subjectivity: the spectre hovering and spectating over the spectacle of being, with its substance now emptied out [*entäußert*] completely into the finite world. God the Absolute dies, so the World can enter the metaphysical stage and step into the light: by travelling from the East to the West, religion shifts its object from *deus absolutus* (Hegel bears in mind that the most integral form of 'theological absolutism' was born within the 'Oriental' Islamic *kalam*) to the World. God, therefore, withdraws – and paves way to the Occidental *religion of the world*, in which the

---

[30] As Hegel himself observed in *Phenomenology of Spirit*, calling the 'facile' Trinitarian synthesis *ein eitles Spiel*: 'Thus the life of God and divine cognition may well be spoken of as disporting of Love with itself; but this idea sinks into mere edification, and even insipidity, if it lacks the seriousness, the suffering, the patience, and the labour of the negative. *In itself*, that life is indeed one untroubled equality and unity with itself, for which otherness and alienation, and the overcoming of alienation, are not serious matters' (PS, 11). This objection, uttered mostly against Schelling's notion of the self-healing Absolute, marks a significant change in Hegel's theological views. Before, that is, at the stage of *Early Theological Writings*, he would still maintain the idea of the holy as *das unverletzte Leben*, 'life unharmed' – the obvious prototype for Derrida's *vie indemne* – which excludes by definition any moment of negativity: lack, suffering, or death. It is only in the mature middle phase, when he composes *Phenomenology*, that he opens himself to another possibility: of fully and seriously admitting 'the frightful thought that God himself is dead' and that negativity is not just an attribute of the profane, but also the most holy affair.

[31] Scholem, *On Jews and Judaism in Crisis*, 283; emphasis added.

sacred will have wandered into the profane and begin to work through it from within.[32] And as Hegel quite surprisingly announces, the first religion of the West – the land of the setting sun whose delicate evening light no longer burns, but puts the details of the differentiated world into a strong relief – is the 'religion of flowers': the first blooming (*eclat*) of the divine subject as the 'finite spirit' within the worldly reality:

> Then in place of burning all, one begins to love flowers. The religion of flowers follows the religion of the sun. (G, 239–40)

And just as before Derrida was critical towards the familial aspect of Hegel's Christianity, now he fully endorses the *real* passage from the all-consuming infinite to the truly other fragile finite, symbolized by a delicate bloom of Isaiah's fading 'flower of the field' (Isa. 40. 6-8). But in order to ensure that the spectre does not stop smiling while watching over the liberated – and still very precarious – creation,[33] Derrida must be prepared to detect and then deconstruct every recurrence of *kenosis*: the self-sacrificial death of God, who, by stubbornly refusing to die, does not let beings be.

But why should the new religion of the World begin with the 'religion of flowers'? Could it be that Hegel, an avid reader of esoteric literature, who admired the main symbol of the Rosicrucians – 'the rose on the cross of the present'[34] – conflated it with yet another rose, also of a mystical origin, famously portrayed by Angelus Silesius? Silesius's mysticism is rightly seen as prophetic in regard to the developments of modernity. It is, in fact, a mystico-poetic variation on Duns Scotus's scholastic thesis on the *univocatio entis*, vividly transformed into an intense vision of all things existing on the same plane with God, equally strongly and *causa sui*: 'without why' (*ohne warum*) – autotelically and beyond the need of justification:

> *Die Rose ist ohne warum; sie blühet, weil sie blühet*
> *Sie achtet nicht ihrer selbs, fragt nicht ob man sie siehet.*[35]

---

[32] Adorno's epigram: 'No theological content will last untransformed; every single one will have to face the test and enter the sphere of the profane' is the best summary of the Hegelian transformation of the 'Oriental' theology of the Absolute into the 'Occidental' theology of the world: Theodor W. Adorno, 'Vernunft und Offenbarung', in Theodor W. Adorno, *Stichworte: Kritische Modelle 2* (Frankfurt am Main: Suhrkamp, 1969), 608.

[33] The 'smiling spectre' is a figure conceived by Antonio Negri in his commentary to Derrida's *Specters of Marx*: 'The Specter's Smile', where he also – non-incidentally – alludes to Derrida's Marranism: in *Ghostly Demarcations: A Symposium on Jacques Derrida's 'Specters of Marx'*, ed. Michael Sprinker (London: Verso, 2008), 5–16.

[34] Hegel resorts to this esoteric metaphor – *die Rose auf dem Kreuz der Gegenwart* – few times: 'To recognize reason as the rose in the cross of the present, and to find delight in it, is a rational insight which implies reconciliation with reality': Hegel, *Philosophy of Right*, 19; and later on, in 1824: 'in order to pluck reason, the rose in the cross of the present, one must take up the cross itself': G. W. F. Hegel, *Lectures on the Philosophy of Religion*, vol. 2, 248. On the hermetic meaning of this Hegelian phrase see: Alexander Glenn Magee, *Hegel and the Hermetic Tradition* (Ithaca, NY: Cornell University Press, 2008), 248.

[35] In Mortimer's translation: 'It blooms because it blooms, the rose that has no Why,/ Forgets itself and cares not for any gazing eye'; Angelus Silesius, *Sacred Epigrams from the 'Cherubinic Pilgrim'*, trans. Anthony Mortimer (New York: AMS Press Inc., 2013). Compare Lk. 12.27: 'Consider the lilies in the field, how they grow: they toil not, they spin not; and yet I say unto you, that Solomon in all his glory was not arrayed like one of these.'

This one epigram of Angelus Silesius can easily explain the Hegelian idiosyncrasy of declaring the mysterious 'religion of flowers' as the first truly Occidental form of cult: the mystical promise of blossoming and its 'spontaneous production of the chromatic light' (G, 246) sheds a new visibility on the finite beings in the world, no longer occluded by the 'all-burning' hyper-luminescence of the Absolute.[36] The *eclosion*, the blooming shine of the 'chromatic light' represents for Hegel his favourite dialectical manoeuvre which also chimes close with the Derridean *différance*: the deferment/delay/diffusion of the primordial light now refracted in the 'many-coloured dome' (Shelley) of worldly differences, no longer forced to return to the abyssal *Indifferenz*.

> The introjection of the sun, the sublime digestion of the luminous essence, will end 'in the heart of the occidental': it begins in the flower. (G, 246)

In his lectures on aesthetics, Hegel himself openly praises Angelus Silesius for the 'greatest audacity and depth of intuition and feeling which has expressed in a wonderful mystical power or representation the substantial existence of God in things and the unification of the self with God'.[37] Hegel's interpretation of Silesius goes even further than the idea of singular beings merely engaging in *imitatio Dei*; what he implies is the most 'audacious' transformation in God who now is in a restless search for his own being, while singular creatures enjoy the divine 'substantial existence' *causa sui*. Infinity is denied access to being which is now reserved solely for the innocent, self-justifying finite: the traditional ontological hierarchy of God's stronger being dominating the weaker and dependent existence of creatures undergoes a dramatic reversal. This is also the reason why Leibniz, while extolling wild beauty of Angelus's poetry, nonetheless accused it of 'inclining almost to godlessness' (*beinahe zur Gottlosigkeit hinneigend*) (ON, 36).

Almost – but not quite. Not to be confused with a simple atheism, this *presque-athéisme* (as Derrida translates Leibniz's formulation: *inclinant presque à l'athéisme*) still contains an element of piety which takes the form of gratitude for the perfect gift: the possibility of the creature to revel in its own glory, *as if* God, the donor himself, no longer existed. The almost-atheism of Silesius is thus synonymical with the *almost-oblivion*: the creature enjoys most the perfect gift of creation the very moment it forgets

---

[36] For Adorno, this is the very beginning of a new metaphysics which, from that moment on, will relinquish the asymmetry between the perfect Absolute and the deficient world and focus on the co-validity of the ideal form and the material concrete: 'If we start from an awareness that, for us, the equation of the immutable with the good, the true and the beautiful has been simply refuted, then the content of metaphysics is changed [. . .] There are isolated motifs scattered in the history of ideas which hint at this. And, curiously enough, they are to be found less in the history of philosophy, if you leave aside certain elements in Hegel, than in *heretical theology* – that is to say, in mystical speculation, which has always been essentially heretical and has always occupied a precarious position within institutional religions. I am thinking here of the mystical doctrine – which is common to the Cabbala and to Christian mysticism such as that of Angelus Silesius – of *the infinite relevance of the intra-mundane, and thus the historical, to transcendence, and to any possible conception of transcendence*' (MCP, 100; emphasis added).

[37] Hegel, *Aesthetics*, vol. 1, 371.

that it had ever been created. But the moment in which the creature sees itself as *ohne warum*, 'without why', and forgets God as the creator, the hidden deity only triumphs in its withdrawal. As Derrida says in *Shibboleth* on the paradox of the trace, which strictly parallels the paradox of creation: 'one can only recall it to oneself in forgetting it (*on ne peut se la rappeler qu'en l'oubliant*)' (SQ, 49). This unique almost-forgetting-without-forgetting constitutes *sine qua non* of creation as *Seinlassen*: letting beings be. Hence the idea of *oublier sans oublier*: a different form of *memory betrayed*, which Derrida links to the Marrano variant of *Gelassenheit*.

In *Sauf le nom*, the essay wholly devoted to Angelus Silesius, Derrida elaborates on God's *Gelassenheit*/abandonment in the magnanimous context of *tsimtsum* which truly lets beings be, by releasing them into the open – which Hegel calls *Freilassen*. The secret word that, for Derrida, combines 'to let' and 'to leave' is *laisser*. Derrida chooses it as the best French equivalent of Angelus's *Gelassenheit* which he, in a visible *clinamen* from Heidegger ('whether Heidegger likes it or not' ON, 82), understands as a 'serenity of abandonement' (ON, 84) relaxing in 'all the withouts' – without reason, without purpose, without guilt and debt, without justification. The true *Gelassenheit*, therefore, is the highest art of 'abandoning God who abandons himself' (2: 92): not clinging to him, not trying to grasp him, not even feeling obliged to do so. The duty of redemption as repayment is annulled for the sake of a new imperative: 'not give back *anything* to God, not even Adieu, not even to his name' (ON, 84). *Oubliez Dieu* – yes, but this oblivion will not be as unproblematic as the simple Nietzschean injunction to forget God, imposed from the outside of the theological realm. This movement of releasement occurs inside, following the unique logic of *tsimtsum*:

> This is how I sometimes understand the tradition of *Gelazenheit*, the serenity that allows being without indifference, lets go without abandoning, unless it abandons without forgetting or *forgets without forgetting*. (ON, 73; emphasis added)

In the slightly earlier text, *Given Time*, Derrida renders this paradoxical 'forgetting without forgetting' and the *gelassen* 'without why' the very condition of the gift: 'The gift would be that which does not obey the principle of reason: It is, it ought to be, it owes itself to be without reason, without wherefore, and without foundation' (GT, 23). Derrida's intention, therefore, is to let us see that the true challenge facing our reflection on modern religion consists in rethinking the idea of abandonment/*Verlassenheit* (of God as well as Being) as a *cryptotheological manoeuvre*: not as a secular gesture of aggressive atheization and rupture with all theological discourse, but as a move occurring within the 'modern religious sentiment' itself and its peculiar 'religion(s) of the death of God'. The Eckhartian serene *Gelazenheit* is here the prototype of the Hegelian ideal of the 'serene liberty of thinking' (FK, 53) which, as we have seen, Hegel failed to realize, because of his hindering attachment to the 'axiom of *kenosis*'.

The nod of *Verlassen/Freilassen/Seinlassen*, on which Derrida meditates in *Sauf le nom*, points to a new metaphysics of finitude, implicitly endorsed by the Lurianic Hegel, where the Marrano *oublier sans oublier* plays a crucial role – a 'lighter', more 'relaxed' form of memory which allows to carry on the trace of the withdrawn origin, but, at the same time, does not allow the gift of being to overburden the recipient and implicate her into the 'net of guilt'. The 'forgetting without forgetting' becomes thus Derrida's favourite apophatic instrument, closest to his intuition of negative theology as radically iconoclastic: nothing better ensures the *Bilderverbot* than this state of half-oblivion into which God himself withdraws, evading all immanent representations. To the question, therefore, 'How to avoid speaking?' – Derrida gives a typically Marrano answer: by keeping in memory only the trace of erasure, a spectral halo of the 'disappearing God'. This is a yet another variant of Derrida's persistent motif which we discussed in the previous chapter: *the faithfulness in perjury*. If forgetting is a part of the Marrano 'betrayal' of Jewish God, then in Derrida's logic of the messianic reversal, it becomes an affirmative mode of being faithful to 'God who abandons himself' – who does not wish to be represented, talked about, even remembered. A God of pure generosity, who lets be and lets go – even the very memory of himself.[38]

Heidegger, mon frère... the brotherhood of ruah

The critique of *hypermemory* or *hypermnesia* in the name of the Marrano 'forgetting without forgetting' appears often in Derrida's later work and not only in reference to Hegel (it will resurface in Chapter 4, devoted to Derrida's reading of Joyce as Hegel among writers): it is also a guiding theme of his critical reading of Heidegger. We already know Derrida's objection against the Hegelian *hypermnesia* of Absolute Knowledge: the more the subject submerges itself in the 'memory of the Passion' – be it the 'infinite grief' of Lutheran piety or the 'speculative Good Friday' of philosophy – the less it is able to receive the gift of being. But this is also Derrida's constant concern with Heidegger and his stubborn insistence on rescuing Being from oblivion. Yet, just as in the case of Hegel, where Derrida finds a way to insinuate into his system of

---

[38] The Jewish angle of Derrida's interpretation of Hegel has been also accentuated by Edith Wyschogrod's *Spirit in Ashes: Hegel, Heidegger and the Man-Made Mass Death* (New Haven: Yale University Press, 1985), which discusses the destructive aspect of the Hegelian progress of the spirit, and Elliot Wolfson, who praises her approach in *Beyond the Gift*: 'Wyschogrod is to be given credit for connecting the kabbalistic account of God contracting the infinite essence into a dot with the Hegelian idea of the extension of space into the punctiformity of time. The Sabbath, in her reading, "expresses the turning of space into time, the respite from creation as the temporal self-articulation of identity-in-difference"': Wolfson, *Giving Beyond the Gift*, 224–5; Edith Wyschogrod, 'Crossover Dreams', *Journal of the American Academy of Religion* 54 (1986): 546. But while Wolfson links Derrida and Wyschogrod as the two Jewish Kabbalah influenced thinkers who ventured into a properly iconoclastic speculation on the nature of God, I wish to stress a difference between them, which derives precisely from the latter's vision of the cosmic Sabbath. While for Wyschogrod, at the end of times the time will triumph and the *tikkun* will occur as a Hegelian repetition of the original *tsimtsum*, in which the alienation of space will have been sublated into a respite of time – for Derrida, the spatialization, which constantly produces new finite beings in the process of dissemination, is *to no end*: it neither serves any redemptive goal, nor can it be stopped. The *tsimtsum* which paves the way towards alienation/ spatialization/ dissemination is irreversible – and this is the main reason why Derrida attacks the Hegelian axiom of *kenosis* in creation as the remnant of the mythic system of retribution, which demands the cosmic sacrifice to be repaid and thus undone.

knowledge some saving elements of faith – the Lurianic *tsimtsum* tacitly substituting for *kenosis* – he does the same to Heidegger whom he reads, despite all the explicit evidence against, as a brother in spirit – or, more precisely, a brother in *ruah*.

The apophatic spectral non/presence of *ruah ha-kodesh*, the Hebrew Holy Spirit in feminine, hovers over the few great essays from 1987, but the most significant among them is *Of Spirit. Heidegger and the Question* (*De l'esprit: Heidegger et la question*). In Derrida's intellectual biography, the year 87 stands more than ever under the Heideggerian auspices: the *Comment ne pas parler* concludes with the long treatise on the apophatic evasions of the 'master from Germany'; also *Khôra*, published in the same year, focuses on the Heideggerian interpretation of Plato. Again, there is no accident here: Derrida's secret Jewish theme comes to the fore most distinctly precisely apropos Heidegger and *the* (Jewish) question: Heidegger and his infamous rectorate speech which for years lay secretly buried in the archives and saw the light only in 1987, thanks to Victor Farias's demascatory book.[39] This is the moment when Derrida talks Heidegger even more intensely than usual, by letting him speak out his unavowed and evaded (*vermeidet*) secret: and not just the secret of his true involvement in the NSDAP, but also another one, perhaps even more embarrassing, concerning his indebtedness to the tradition fighting against which he so eagerly joined in the 1930s, namely the 'whole tradition of Jewish thought as an inexhaustible thinking about fire' (OS, 101): the fiery legacy of the *ruah* whose secret burns in them both, Heidegger and Derrida. Instead of opposition, therefore, Derrida obliquely suggests the 'secret of the alliance'.

This secret alliance, spitefully signalled by Derrida despite the indignant climate of Heidegger's universal condemnation, consists in the affinity – even *brotherhood* – at the level of philosophical strategy. So, at the time when Farias's discoveries haunt philosophical Europe like a vengeful spectre, Derrida praises Heidegger in his Jerusalem lecture for 'the most audacious and most liberated repetition of the traditions' (HAS, 122) in which he attempted to reach beyond them all in order to touch the virginal land of absolute originality (or, as Scholem would say, the very 'truth of the tradition'). The fact that he failed only speaks to his advantage: by trying to penetrate to the very bottom of the pure and philosophical Germanness, Heidegger found himself not on a hard ground, but in the abyss of *Abgrund*. This route, though unintended by Heidegger himself, suits Derrida, because, for him, the true origin is the bottomless secret that can never be taken into possession, either by a mystic or by a philosopher. For, *das Geistliche*, the flame of free spirit Heidegger mentions apropos Georg Trakl's poetry, is in its very structure undistinguishable from the secret: it is an enigma also to itself and as such 'heterogeneous from the origin' (OS, 108), never resting in its identity, always outside of itself, in the act of withdrawal and self-denegation, always giving way to inflaming the other. Derrida's Marrano secret, bottomless and immemorial, leads him thus to the hypothesis that the *Spirit itself is a Marrano*: has no identity and no fixed abode. It is a non-original origin, from the outset contaminated and contagious,

---

[39] The French translation of Farias's *Heidegger and Nazism* appeared in Paris in 1987, but Derrida knew its content earlier.

being itself only in being *outside itself* – and in burning its own archives which then only leave a trace in the form of cinders. The Spirit/*ruah* knows no fixed identities and boundaries, but is *die Unruhe*, the original 'rousedness' that needs no other external cause of movement towards the Other than itself: 'what is proper to spirit is this auto-affective spontaneity which has no need of no exteriority to catch fire or set fire, to pass ecstatically outside itself' (OS, 98). The *ruah*, therefore, is the origin which has no home and is everywhere in 'exile which is [. . .] in some way a nonexile';[40] while it always 'invents the other', it can never rest in sameness. Just as *Khôra* cannot but give way to the other – *Ruah* cannot but self-transcend towards the other (as we shall yet see, these two feminine instances will be related in more than one way).

Can one go back to the origin like that? With and pace Heidegger simultaneously, Derrida will say that it is now *too late* to instigate 'wars of etymology' (OS, 99) the goal of which would be to get to the most virginal, arch-pure, and homogenous origins. This ambition of absolute 'earliness' (*das Frühste*), which motivated Heidegger in his attempts to reach the pure 'early-Greekness' and establish the 'new beginning' (and which, on the other side of the fence, could also be attributed to Lévinas with his analogical programme of rediscovery of the original Hebraism), today appears, as Nietzsche would have called it, *unzurzeitig*, untimely. *Too late*: this is also a characteristic declaration of a more 'timely' Marrano who already knows that he will never disentangle himself from the neo-Alexandrian 'Jew-Greek, Greek-Jew confusion' (WD, 153) but does not want to do so either. On the contrary, he is more than ready to endure the difficult predicament of overdetermination where all the words – and 'spirit' most of all – mean more than they can bear and shine with all possible, multihued specters. The Babelian 'contamination is everywhere' (V-D, 77) – but it does not announce a danger. The Marrano, contamination embodied, knows that the origin itself was no different: *ruah* is anything but the pristine virginal beginning which could be traced back in its integrity. Rather, as in Benjamin's speculation from the preface to *The Origins of the German Tragic Drama*, is it an *Ur-Sprung*: an arche-leap into the element of alterity, a fiery contagion. Heidegger's effort to go back to *das Früheste*, the earliest beginning – beyond the rules set up by the Platonic metaphysics and the resulting Christian ontotheology – could thus be used for a different purpose than the one presupposed by Heidegger himself: to recover not so much the archaic Greekness, which allegedly resonates in Georg Trakl's poems, as to remind us of yet another, less palpable and visible source which from the very beginning burnt all its archives, unwilling to be captured by any particular identitarian testament.

The absolute deconstructive *meistershtück* of *De l'esprit* consists thus in the Marrano interception of Heidegger's strategy of avoidance/*vermeiden*. While, at the first glance, Heidegger's attempt to avoid/forget speaking of *ruah*, the Hebrew name of the Spirit, might seem as a malevolent evasion of the Jewish tradition, it actually *turns* into the most effective apophatic strategy of 'how to avoid speaking' which Derrida himself

---

[40] Sommer, 'Expulsion as Initiation', 26.

applies in regard to the secret of the Spirit's Marrano non-identity: the self-erasing trace of *ruah* which has no fixed abode in any official religious archive, but constitutes their 'hidden tradition'. In the conclusion of the essay, Derrida stages a confrontation between two imaginary figures: a Radical Theologian and the imagined Heidegger, if he ever cared to break his silence and respond to *the* question, on the other. The former approaches Heidegger in a 'brotherly' manner and says:

> What is most matutinal in the *Frühe*, in its best promise, would in truth be of an other birth and an other essence, origin-heterogeneous [*heterogene à l'origine*] to *all the testaments, all the promises, all the events, all the laws and assignments which are our very memory* [. . .] You say the most radical things that can be said when one is a Christian today. At this point, especially when you speak of God, of *retrait*, of flame and fire-writing in the promise, in accord with the promise of return towards the land of pre-archi-originarity, it is not certain that you would not receive a comparable reply and similar echo from my friend and coreligionary, the Messianic Jew. I'm not certain that the Moslem and some others wouldn't join in the concert or the hymn. At least all those who in religions and philosophies have spoken of *ruah, pneuma, spiritus* and, why not, *Geist*. (OS; 107, 111; emphasis added)

To which Heidegger, who now breaks the silence, replies:

> But in affirming that Trakl's *Gedicht* – and everything I say along with it – is neither metaphysical nor Christian, I am opposing nothing, especially not Christianity, nor all the discourses of the fall, of malediction, of the promise, of salvation, of resurrection, nor the discourses on *pneuma* and *spiritus*, nor even (I'd forgotten that one) on *ruah*. I'm *simply trying, modestly, discreetly, to think that on the basis of which all this is possible*. (OS, 111-12; emphasis added)

But *who* is, in fact, speaking here? Who is advocating this most matutinal 'earliness' which evades any demarcating 'circle' of positive traditions and resists neutralization of its flaming futurity by any past manifestation – be it *pneuma, spiritus,* or even, 'if you insist', *ruah*? Is it Heidegger – or rather Derrida, the perfect *converso* moving freely in-between worlds and traditions, who speaks Heideggerian better than Heidegger himself and knows exactly what he would have said if he ever broke the silence of his secret and openly addressed *the* question? Or is it Derrida impersonating Heidegger as his *frère*, letting him survive in the Marrano 'ventriloquist manner' and carrying his legacy beyond the public death caused by the scandalous involvement in the Nazi revolution (scandalous already then in 1987, and increasingly more so with every new publication of *Die Schwarze Hefte*)? Only a truly accomplished Marrano, seasoned in the strategies of revealment through concealment, could have forced Heidegger – of all people and all languages 'under the sun' – to talk Hebrew and bring into his discourse on Being 'God, *retrait*, flame, and fire-writing in the promise' (OS, 111), that is, the main ingredients of the Lurianic doctrine of *tsimtsum* as Heidegger's 'unthought debt'.⁴¹ Could it be then that the Marrano alliance with Heidegger announces itself as early as in 'Différance', where Derrida quotes the latter's 'Anaximander's Fragment': 'Being speaks always and everywhere throughout all languages'? Is the (almost) forgotten Being which speaks in all languages under the sun, but has no language of its own the same as the (almost) forgotten Hebrew of *das Früshte*, which also disperses in all speeches, making room for them and allowing them to come to the fore in their difference, but keeps silent itself (*schweigt auf Hebräisch*, as Scholem would have said)? Just as the 'authentic tradition' must be hidden – hidden to the point of being completely lost – so the secretive origin must always be on the verge of oblivion, submerged in hypomnesia. Once again, therefore, we touch the crucial function of forgetting. In the end, Heidegger was right to forget about *ruah*. As a spirit *en retrait* – itself withdrawing in order to let be the other – it should not be recalled in vain.

The problem of forgetting haunts Heidegger, especially in the post-war period, when he continues the process of the 'reversal', *die Kehre*, that began in the late 1930s, by introducing a new motif: *der Entzug des Seins*, 'the withdrawal of Being', which positively cries for a juxtaposition with *tsimtsum*. For Marlene Zarader, it is absolutely clear that, after *die Kehre*, Heidegger is faced with a new task of rethinking his earlier concept of *Seinsvergessenheit*:

> the forgetting of Being, that same Being that he acknowledged very early as not 'being' in the way of an entity, that is, that it was the Other of all entities. But it remained for him to account for this forgetting. If the latter was first attributed to thinking, it was subsequently recognized as proceeding from Being itself: *thinking is only characterized by forgetting because Being unfolds its essence as withdrawal* [...] *Whence the forgetting*. The withdrawal underway, forgetting can be resituated within the essence of Being [*a l'interieur de l'essence de l'etre*], to which the withdrawal gave us access [...] The circle thus closes: Being was forgotten only because it slips away, and it slips away because in evasion lies its unique manner of 'being.' There is therefore no other being than that which withdraws for the benefit of beings. And there is no other God, in the Bible, than the *hidden* God.⁴²

This hiddenness, however, is of a different kind than in the Christian tradition of *deus absconditus*: as with Angelus Silesius, it is not a passive attribution from without, but an attribute of the divine essence active from within. Zarader thus continues: 'the theme of the hidden God nevertheless finds a wholly surprising incarnation, surpassing by far – *even inverting* – the classical idea of a God who hides himself in his creation.

---

[41] Comp. Marlene Zarader, *The Unthought Debt: Heidegger and the Hebraic Heritage*, trans. Bettina Bergo (Stanford: Stanford University Press, 2006 [1999]). In her elaboration on the presence of Hebrew tradition in Heidegger, Zarader admits that she took an inspiration from Derrida's *De l'esprit* (ibid., 112).

[42] Zarader, *The Unthought Debt*, 133–4; emphasis added. Comp. Derrida's comment in *Spurs*: 'Thus, in a thousand ways, has the forgetting of Being [*Seinsvergessenheit*] been represented as if Being (figuratively speaking) were the umbrella that some philosophy professor, in his distraction, left somewhere [...] Forgetting, then, not only *attacks* the essence of Being [*das Wesen des Seins*] inasmuch as it is apparently not distinct from it. It belongs to the nature of Being and reigns as the Destiny of its essence *Zur Seinsfrage*' (S, 148).

This was the doctrine of Tsim-tsum, developed by Isaac Luria, the kabbalist of Safed, around 1550'.[43] This inversion, which as I attempt to prove here, lies also at the core of Derrida's Marrano-messianic reversal, consists in enhancing the benign 'letting-go' aspect of 'the withdrawal for the benefit of beings' that makes forgetting not a grave sin against God but, on the contrary, a legitimate manner in which the gift of being is to be received. In *Given Time*, Derrida links Heidegger's late thinking of Being as *Ereignis* to the meditation on the essence of gift which can be accepted only if the donor hides from sight and allows to be forgotten. This is precisely why *Er-eignis* is always and inescapably also *Ent-eignis*: a de-propriating erasure and a secret that blocks a trope of reversal, attempting to *trace back* the path leading to *das Frühste*.

> After this turning, it will not be a matter of subordinating the question of Being to the question of the *Ereignis*, a difficult word to translate (event or propriation that is inseparable from a movement of dis-propriation, *Enteignen*). This word *Ereignis*, which commonly signifies event, signals toward a thinking of appropriation or of *de-propriation that cannot be unrelated to that of the gift* [...] Heidegger sometimes says that Beyng (*das Seyn*, an archaic spelling that attempts to recall the word to a more thinking – *denkerisch* – mode) is *Ereignis*. And it is in the course of this movement that Being [*Sein*] – which is not, which does not exist as being present/ present being –is signaled on the basis of the gift. (GT, 19)

Yet, all this debt – all the borrowings from the Hebrew tradition: *tsimtsum* as Being's witdrawal, creaturely gift of being as *Ereignis* – remains not only unacknowledged: it is actively fought against. The paradox of late Heidegger *nach der Kehre* is that the more he engages in the Judaic, both orthodox and heterothodox, *topoi*, the less he wants to remember where they came from. And while '*the* (Jewish) question' seemingly disappears from his official discourse, it is, as Derrida proves, always there: the Jew is still mistrusted by Heidegger as 'the principle of metaphysical destruction.'[44] At the same time, however, implicitly and surreptitiously, the Jew becomes also something else which Heidegger refuses to name. Not just a carrier or the secret fire of *ruah* but also a hard-necked *forgetter* whom Heidegger should have recognized as not just an agent of metaphysical destruction, but rather as an agent of Being's own manner of retreating, according to Zarader's formulation: 'The withdrawal underway, forgetting *should* be resituated within the essence of Being.'[45] Just as forgetting should be resituated within the essence of Being – so should the Jew, *the forgetter*, to be resituated within the History of Being (*Seinsgeschichte*). And yet, Heidegger stubbornly resists this logical 'should'. Why?

This question lies at the heart of Elliot Wolfson's magisterial work, *Heidegger and Kabbalah*, which continues Derrida's and Zarader's effort of thinking Heidegger's

---

[43] Ibid., 134; emphasis added.
[44] Martin Heidegger, *Anmerkungen I-V (Schwarze Hefte 1942–1948)*, ed. Peter Trawny (Frankfurt am Main: Vittorio Klostermann, 2015), *Martin Heidegger Gesamtausgabe*, Band 97, 20 (later on as GA and the number of the volume). All quotes in Richard Polt's translation.
[45] Zarader, *The Unthought Debt*, 133.

'unthought debt', by exposing more or less elective affinities between late Heidegger *nach der Kehre* and Kabbalistic reasoning. Wolfson too wants to examine the striking parallel between the withdrawal of Being and the Kabbalistic thought of *tsimtsum* as the originary contraction of *Ein-Sof*, or, in his own idiom, the self-negation of the Supreme Nullity, which results in the emergence of beings. The goal of Wolfson's analysis, in which the affinity between Heidegger and Kabbalah proves deeper and deeper with every page, is to demonstrate that – to paraphrase the title of Robert Anthelme's prosaic fragment, 'Kierkegaard Unfair to Schlegel' – Heidegger is completely and unjustifiedly unfair to Jews. By calling them in *The Black Notebooks* the 'anti-metaphysical agents of the destruction of Being', he cannot be more wrong. In fact, their Kabbalistic piety directed towards *Ein-Sof* as the nothingness beyond the dualism of being and nothing is identical to Heidegger's post-theological project of *Andenken*, which, by combining *Andacht* and *Denken*, constitutes a 'pious thinking of Being'. The hasty accusations against the Jews, formulated in *Schwarze Hefte*, are thus nothing but a grave misunderstanding – which Wolfson's intervention wishes to correct.

I, however, would like to offer a slightly different approach which would place itself simultaneously between and beyond the indignant rejection of Heidegger's *Seinsdenken* as irreparably anti-Semitic, on the one hand – and Wolfson's insistence on the possible reconciliation between Heidegger and the Kabbalistic Jews, on the other. My conjecture is that, while expanding the motif of the *ruah* as the self-erasing origin with the Lurianic *tsimtsum* in the background, Derrida targets what appears as a major aporia in Heidegger's – but also Wolfson's – construct of the originary withdrawal: the never questioned call to remember, recollect, be constantly reminded of the source that withdraws. For, why obsessively recollect what incessantly retreats? Why insist on the reversal of this retreat in 'pious rememberance'? Why not allow the self-erasing ground, that allows everything else, be gently forgotten? At one point Wolfson quotes a Kabbalist saying: *ki nashashani elohim* (God has made me forget) and this amazing sentence could indeed become a motto to Derrida's wrestling with the Marrano aporia of *oublier sans oublier*.

> As David ben Yehudah he-Hasid poetically expressed it, the cause of causes *illat ha-illot* is 'the place to which forgetfulness [*shikhehah*] and oblivion [*nishshayon*] pertain, as in the expression *God has made me forget* [*ki nashashani elohim*] in Genesis 41:51. What is the reason? Because concerning all the gradations and sources their existence should be investigated, searched, and probed from the depth of the supernal Wisdom, and from there one understands one thing from another. However, concerning the cause of causes, there is no aspect in any place to probe, to investigate, or to know of it any knowledge because *it is concealed and hidden in the secret of nothing and the naught*. Therefore, with respect to the matter of comprehension of this place, *forgetfulness pertains to it*.'[46]

---

[46] Elliot Wolfson, *Heidegger and Kabbalah: Hidden Gnosis and the Path of Poiesis* (Bloomington: Indiana University Press, 2019), 114; emphasis added.

This, as we have seen, is also Zarader's point – and, at the same time, a daring argument which should have forced Heidegger to rethink his previous position on the metaphysical Jew as the hateful agent of *Seinsvergessenheit*. Perhaps, it is precisely this type of 'forgetfulness' – *shikhehah* – that not only does not destroy metaphysics but goes along the 'bestowing refusal' of the origin of all beings, which gently withdraws to let them be. On this reading, the metaphysical Jew would emerge not as the obstinate destructor of the metaphysical thinking of Being, but as a positive agent of *Seinlassen*, the letting-be proper, acting in accordance with Being's ordinance. The No of negation and separation, which before excluded the Jew from the history of Being, would now turn into a truly positive and no longer ambivalent principle of *Seinlassen* as the ontological model for all other finite entities to follow in their desire for emancipation, that is, to *be-free* (where *lassen* must also always be *frei-lassen*) – and not just *be-long*, *Seinsgehören*. And if, as Derrida implies in *On the Name*, chiming perfectly with the David the Hasid, that the Jew (and *a fortiori*, the Marrano) 'almost forgets about God' – then all the better, because it happens in accordance with God's own withdrawal. He is not a blasphemer who obliterates God/Being/*Ein-Sof* without a trace; rather, he follows the complex dialectics of obedience in oblivion or listening-to without belonging, which breaks the *continuum* of Heidegger's *Ge-Hören*. This is, indeed, in Heidegger's formulation, the Jews' 'world-historical task'. Thus, when Derrida asks the crucial question: 'How can you remember about God who forgets/abandons himself?' – the best answer is offered by the Marrano 'forgetting without forgetting'.

This, however, is for Heidegger the worst metaphysical nightmare come true: the Marrano, faithful to Being precisely the moment when he 'almost' forgets Being, would be the proper agent of 'letting-be' – while he, Being's most outspoken priest, would betray it, by hindering Being in its 'gentle', *gelassen* and *seinlassend*, withdrawal. While for the Marrano Derrida, the Lurianic *Ur-Sprung* is a discontinuous arche-leap from the infinite to the finite, allowing the world to come to presence as truly separate – for the merely half-marranated Heidegger, it is still a *spring*: the traditional Neoplatonic *fons vitae* which sustains beings in a ceaseless *creatio continua*. And while in the full-fledged Marrano idiom, to get away from the origin (*lekh lekha*) is to wander into the world, stand on one's feet, 'disperse and multiply' – in Heidegger's ultimately Neoplatonic idiom, it is to err through the desert, like a madman who forgot that it is water that keeps him alive. Wolfson's credo sounds similar: 'It is not possible for the light to disappear absolutely, as it is the only thing that is real.'[47]

---

[47] Wolfson, *Heidegger and Kabbalah*, 163. In *The Beginning of Western Philosophy*, the course of lectures run in Freiburg in 1932, Heidegger probes the idea of the 'complete dis-esteeming of Being', and states that, as *complete*, it is simply unthinkable, since it would deprive us of any understanding of beings as such and made impossible our comportment towards them. To be *completely* outside the history of Being – a position attributed to the Jew in *Schwarze Hefte* – would thus equal a *complete* dis-esteeming of Being, which he himself refutes as logically non-viable: 'Our paying no heed to the suppressed question of Being is not a proof against its "being-there" but merely demonstrates that in suppressing it we mean that we could withdraw from it at any time. We can withdraw from it only in the way the wanderer, distancing himself more and more from the spring, semblantly dissolves every relation to it and yet perishes precisely through and on this relation of distancing himself': Martin Heidegger, *The Beginning of Western Philosophy: Interpretation of Anaximander and Parmenides*,

In the name of the nameless: On Frank speculatively

The quote from David the Hasid demonstrates that Derrida's Marrano solution of *oublier sans oublier* – forgetfulness as the most effective means of apophatic iconoclasm – has its Kabbalistic antecedents. In *Giving Beyond the Gift*, Wolfson gives quite a big credit to Derrida's Kabbalistic background, but it is rather unlikely that Derrida knew about Jacob Frank more than it was mediated through Scholem's account. This most (in)famous Polish Marrano who, following the Sabbatian legend, persuaded not a small cohort of the Polish Jews to convert to Catholicism and thus 'forget their God', was not a theologian, but he had his messianic intuitions which, similarly to Wolfson, pushed him beyond the iconophilic 'theomania' – the idolatric belief in the 'God with the Name' or the phallic King-Sovereign of the world, calling himself 'Yehova'. Yet, unlike in Wolfson, it did not install in Frank a new piety of *Ein-Sof* as the highest nameless One and the source of all reality. In Frank's vision, the nameless is to remain nameless, that is, blithely left alone and forgotten for the sake of the living who, on the other hand, no longer should be forgetful of their most vital worldly interests. Just as the numerous Kabbalists before him, Frank does not believe in creation in the voluntarist and nominalist understanding of the term, which involves precisely the all-wilful and all-powerful Creator *with the Name*; although his theological idiom comes from *Zohar*, today we could say that his is a language of the Derridean *Seinlassen* in an inchoate form, where *Ein-Sof* gently withdraws without making any claims on the beings thus let be, even the claims of remembrance and piety. It just lets be and lets go as the nothing that only gives, so it is, says Frank, a high time – a kairotic, truly messianic, time – to finally draw consequences from this originary *tsimtsum*. That means to stop looking back or, in Heidegger's words, still not fully purged from the lingering piety, stop 'looking-out' for the signs of the withdrawn origin. Hence Frank's antinomian message, which he repeats over and over again in his *Words of the Lord*: 'Behold, behold: His religion will be cancelled, but Its honour will stay untouched.'[48] The creationist construct of God the Sovereign, which, for Frank, is a false idolatrous 'garment' of the true nameless deity, will soon pass, but not to be replaced by a new religion 'looking-out' for a new object of piety. What will remain after this cancelling antinomian operation will be the faith in what Frank calls 'life in full': no longer hindered by the remembrance of the *tsimtsem* origin and troubled by the Gnostic desire of *reversio*, but attuned to the rhythm of *Seinlassen* which, by allowing to be, also allows to forget. Thus, by anticipating Nietzsche, Frank deeply believes that there is no true *Lebenlassen* without *Vergessenheit*, but, unlike Nietzsche, he grounds this

---

trans. Richard Rojcewicz (Bloomington: Indiana University Press, 2015), 73. Being's withdrawal, therefore, is a typically tragic situation. A similar intuition appears in David Farrell Krell's *Ecstasy, Catastrophe* (Albany, NY: SUNY University Press, 2015), which focuses on Heidegger's note from *Schwarze Hefte*: 'Das Seyn selbst ist "tragisch".'

[48] Jakub Frank, *Słowa pańskie: Nauki Jakuba Franka z Brna i Offenbachu*, ed. Jan Doktór (Warszawa: Żydowski Instytut Historyczny, 2017), 313.

belief in a powerful theological reading of the Kabbalistic concept of the 'God who made me forget'.

For Frank, it is precisely this licence to forget, which constitutes the antinomian *crux* of his doctrine. On the one hand, it points to the Hidden God or *Ein-Sof*: without-limit, un-de-fined, and, therefore, nameless. It is It (Frank avoids calling *Ein-Sof* with masculine pronouns) who/which generously gives life without expecting anything in return. On the other hand, however, Its concealedness only makes easier to be covered even further by a false theological 'teaching' – akin to Scholem's *Tradierbarkeit* – which looks for more visible and tangible gods (or what Derrida, equally mistrustful to anything that shows itself, calls the luminous *deiwos*). But, says Frank, all these gods – defined, named, spectacular – are merely idols and their cult, YHVH included, is nothing but *avodah zarah*, the betrayal of the true faith. For, the moment the Name appears, there also emerges a narcissistic demand of cult and obedience – and then, subsequently, the whole institutional religion with its codex of dos and don'ts, the aim of which is to worship *Ha-Shem*: the great jealous Name which forbids to cherish anything else apart from itself. Contrary to this, *Ein-Sof* is an infinite abyss from where such narcissistic jealousy is completely absent; as nameless, It cannot require a nomination of Its own, It does not know religion as a sacrificial system of paying God back with awe and respect for the gift of creation.

Frank – the Polish Marrano, de-nominated and with no religious 'fixed abode' – feels thus closer and more faithful to the God-Without-Name than the orthodox Jews whom he brazenly accuses of idolatry, thus reverting the traditional allegation against the *conversos* (see again the passage on Abraham Cardoso in the Introduction). In his 'worship without worship' and 'remembrance without remembrance', he honours the Hidden/Hiding God who withdraws in order to make room for the world and abstains from any cult; the God who gives life without indebting and without marking it with the stain of the original sin, which makes everything living finite, deficient, and destined to death. While it is *Ha-Shem* who watches over the life-death cycle of his believers, so that the gift of life can be returned to Him in a due time – *Ein-Sof*'s primoridial and superior gift is 'life in full': undamaged by the verdict of death. While addressing his last followers in Moravian Brno, where he spent the last days of his life, Frank says:

> You shall be the first who can call themselves people in full – more than an *enosh* (man), as it was before. Before Adam was created, one believed in the groundless *Ensoph*. And no place was called divine, untile there came the One and created Adam, and because of him all became corrupted, and the world was cursed.[49]

---

[49] Ibid., 381–2. In his presentation of Jacob Frank, Paweł Maciejko writes: 'Frank did not seek God; rather, Frank sought the obliteration of God's name in the world': *Sabbatian Heresy*, 143. *Prima facie*, this diagnosis sounds right: Frank indeed wanted to abolish institutional religions as cults of nominated Gods, yet this 'obliteration of God's name' was also result of his own pursuit of *God without Name*, the generous Giver of Life, who would not insist on being worshipped, even remembered. Frank calls Him 'the fourth God': concealed behind the three revealed Gods, his 'deputies' – of life, death, and life eternal after death – and holding the key to the highest secret of

In Frank's Marrano Gnosticism, the 'One' – *Adonai Ehad* of Abrahamic monotheisms with His unpronounceable powerful Name (*Ha-Shem*) – is not a true God, but merely an usurper and minor archon who creates deficient death-destined Adam and thus plunges all nature into a mortal coil. Having been a citizen of Russian empire, Frank calls this archon with the term reserved for the functionaries of the tsarist administration, a 'commissar':

> The world and Adam are not created by the living God, so everybody must die and the world perishes, because it is created by the commissars. But my God is alive and good and wants to make the world in full.[50]

In the next chapter, we shall see that Frank's non-cult of the God-Without-Name, coupled with his deep mistrust in the self-nominated *Melekh ha-olam*, The-Ruler-of-the-World, chimes quite close with Derrida's reading of *Khôra* as the ontotheological equivalent of the Frankist *Einsoph*. Yet, this affinity has its limits too. Although united on the issue of forgetting and the 'harshest impiety' of the 'almost-atheism', Derrida and Frank diverge on the issue of the 'life in full' which, in case of the latter, amounts to an uncompromised demand of life infinite and unscathed that will be granted to us here on earth, once we dare to dress again in 'Esau's skin'. While for the Marrano Frank, the right kind of Judaism is the discarded line of Esau – so his betrayal of the rabbinic orthodoxy merely corrects Jacob's perjury – Derrida remains faithful to Jacob's limping way of the scathed life. And although the issue of 'Esau's skin' will return in our analysis of Derrida's shawl/tallith in Chapter 4, the indemnified vitality standing behind Frank's choice of Esau, the wronged brother, will always remain alien to Derrida's sober finitist view of *la vie la mort*. Yet, the differences notwithstanding, both the Marrano Frank and the Marrano Derrida ascribe to the 'God who has made [them] forget' and, by permitting self-oblivion, allowed the world come to the fore.

This chapter was devoted to the Derridean reconstruction of the faith of the Marranos as the alchemic furnace of the antinomian inversion pioneering the secret evolution of the 'religion of modern times': what began as a defensive reaction to the tragic condition of the historically first 'most severe privation of God', Derrida

---

life infinite on earth. The narrative of four Gods comes from the Frankist document in which Frank tells the history of Judaism and Christianity and announces a new age of the 'Good God': 'It was announced once more in Heaven: "Who is he who wants to go to this world and bring eternal life?" The Lord Sabbatai Tsevi responded: "I shall go." He also went; he raised up nothing and achieved nothing. Thereafter, I was sent that I might bring eternal life into this world. I was given power too, so that I might display the power that was given to me [...]. The world Teüwel [Tevel] is not created by the Good God himself. Similarly, Adam was not created by the Living God. For if Adam and the world had been created by the Living God, then the world would be stable forever and Adam would live eternally; since they were not created by the Good God, every man must die and the world cannot endure. The world and Adam are not created by the Living God; he must die and the world cannot endure, for it is created by a deputy. But my God is alive and is good and seeks to establish a stable world: *und die Menschen will Er derhalten auf der Welt; dus will Gott allein*' ('He will keep the people in this world: this is all he wants'): Jacob Frank, 'Appendix to the Words of the Lord Spoken in Brünn', trans. Paweł Maciejko, in *Sabbatian Heresy*, 159–60.

50 Frank, *Słowa pańskie*, 392.

interprets as a 'paradoxical opportunity' to create a new reflexive faith that would benefit from the death of God as the unscathed Absolute and use it as a chance to return to its roots as 'the religion of the living' and its inner truth of *u-baharta ba-hayim*. The cryptophoric Marrano self is a stage on which this re-turn/*tshuva* occurs, shifting it from the guilt-ridden memory of the loss to the more innocent hope, absolved by God himself who, hiding into the folds of namelessness, made us forget about any religious cult and just let us live beyond the call to sacrifice – as the 'lilies in the field' or Angelus's 'roses without why'. The 'Spanish Marranos' who appear at the very end of *Faith and Knowledge* are designated by Derrida to carry, as well as carry on precisely this task of *oublier sans oublier*: while the 'ontological Marranos' embody the paradox of creation as the true receivers of the nameless gift of being, they also perform the iconoclastic and simultaneously procosmic 'hidden truth' of the Jewish tradition whose godhead withdraws from sight in order to let the world be. In the next chapter, I will focus on the second part of Derrida's title, *Foi et savoir*: 'knowledge'. I will try to show that for Derrida *savoir*, apart from taking the form of modern ontotheology, also leads to a 'metaphysics of modern times', characterized by the radical separation/*coupure* between the origin and the world.

3

The nameless still life

Marrano metaphysics of non-presence

Even in the past the portrayal of nature was probably only authentic as nature morte *[...] The Old Testament prohibition on images has an aesthetic as well as a theological dimension. That one should make no image, which means no image of anything whatsoever, expresses at the same time that it is impossible to make such an image.*
Theodor W. Adorno, Aesthetic Theory, 63.

Both Hegel and Heidegger figure largely in *Faith and Knowledge* – and both as the *hypermnesiac* thinkers who, despite the fact that they constantly talk about the 'death of God' and 'Being's withdrawal', never allow for the weakening of either 'the memory of the Passion' or the 'remembrance of Being'. Both, therefore, regardless of all the differences between them, remain half-way thinkers, ultimately unable to think metaphysically in terms of the radical separation between the origin and the world. While Hegel appears ready to introduce into the language of modern philosophy a self-finitizing vulnerable 'God in pain', he also surreptitiously returns him to his pleromatic sovereignty via the 'axiom of *kenosis*' and the 'Trinitarian machine'.[1] And while Heidegger is prepared to think of 'Being in retreat', he nonetheless insists that we cannot even for a moment 'dis-esteem' Being as the eternal source of existence. For Derrida, this is the main aporia of the 'religion of modern times', which needs to be deconstructed if this religion is to reach, as Hegel himself insisted, a more viable 'form of thought'.

The issue of separation – the true bone of contention between Derrida and Heidegger – comes to the fore most intensely in the former's 1978 essay *Le retrait de la metaphore*. The eponymous retreat of the metaphor is the final result of Heidegger's *Entzug des Seins*, which Derrida interprets, contrary to Heidegger's intentions, as the ultimate incision, cut, *coupure*, 'violent sundering' – or, in Schellingian terms,

---

[1] On the Gnostic/Valentinian genealogy of the motif of 'God in pain', see Cyril O'Regan: 'Thus Gnostic return has to do with the repetition in modern Christian discourses of a narrative focused on the vicissitudes of (divine) reality's fall from perfection, its agonic middle, and its recollection into perfection [...] *It is also to install deipassionism as essential to a vision of the divine*': Cyril O'Regan, *The Gnostic Return in Modernity* (Albany, NY: SUNY Press, 2001), 29; 33; emphasis added.

Abbrechen – between Being and beings. When Being withdraws, it pulls with itself the whole *meta*-phorical order standing behind Western *meta*-physics, grounded in what Thomas Aquinas famously called the principle of analogy. Derrida does not draw on this scholastic discussion, but it is clearly the attack on *analogia entis* that lies behind his critique of metaphors as the tropes of 'turning back' and 'turning over', which create a two-way-street of continuity and communication between the familiar (creatures, beings) and the unfamiliar (God, Being). On Derrida's reading of Being's *retrait*, this umbilical cord which connects the source/origin with the originated beings must be 'violently sundered' (FK, 91): the world is not to be created in its Creator's image and likeness (*imago Dei, tselem Elohim*); it is not to deliver a mirror in which God could see his dim reflection. The only possible relation between Being and beings cannot be thought on the grounds of metaphor/analogy/likeness, but only on the grounds of *catachresis* – the trope of breaking, no turning back and, last but not least, *betrayal*: 'a sort of quasi-catachrestic violence' (RM, 22) which constitutes Derrida's revision of the Schellingian trope of *Abbrechen*, the 'complete breaking-away'.[2]

This betrayal, rejecting the obligation to imitate, implied in the concept of *imago Dei* – also called by Derrida the 'ontological perjury' (ADL, 34) – allows every being as other (*tout autre*) to be wholly other (*tout autre*), that is, liberated from the compulsion to follow the image and the likeness and to break with the participatory metaphorical scheme of *methexis/mimesis*. The withdrawing origin does not ask for imitation, but retreats (*retrait*) into time immemorial – the very opposite of Eliade's *illud tempus*, the time most memorial that can never be forgotten – and, while effacing itself, leaves nothing but a *trait*/trace. Here, retreating and trace leaving is one and the same operation: every *trait* is also a *re-trait*, a 're-cut' which seals the irreversible separation from the withdrawn origin. It is simultaneously a No to the meta-physical/phorical continuum – and a Yes to a singular being that comes to presence as always a completely new figure against the fading ground (which again reminds of the Kabbalistic *tsimtsum* as the 'diminution of light', already used by Derrida in his reading of Hegel in *Glas*):

> From the moment that it withdraws in drawing itself out, the trait is a priori withdrawal, unappearance, and effacement of its mark in its incision. Its inscription [. . .] succeeds only in being effaced [*n'arrive qu'à s'effacer*]. It arrives, happens, and comes about only in effacing itself. Inversely, the trait is not derived. It is not secondary, in its arrival, in relation to the domains, or the essences, or to the existences that it cuts away, frays, and refolds in their re-cut. The *re-* of

---

[2] See again Schelling: 'the origin [*Ursprung*] of the phenomenal world is conceivable only as a complete breaking-away [*Abbrechen*] from absoluteness by means of a leap [*Sprung*]': *Philosophy and Religion*, 26. Catachresis is a trope of break, cut, and leap, but it is still a trope, that is, the form of continuity, even if most paradoxical. This is why Derrida ultimately prefers the figure of *anacoluthon* as a 'non-trope' which fits better the Marrano condition: '*Anakolouthia* designates generally a rupture in the consequence, an interruption in the sequence itself, within a grammatical syntax or in an order in general, in an agreement, thus also in a set, whatever it may be, in a community, let's say, or a partnership, an alliance, a friendship, a being-together: a company or a guild [*compagnonnage*]' (WA, 181).

re-trait is not an accident occurring to the trait. It rises up [*s'enleve*] in allowing any propriety to rise up, as one says of a figure against a ground [. . .] If metaphysics had a unity, it would be the regime of these oppositions which appears and is determined only by way of, by starting out from [*a partir de*], the withdrawal of the trait, the withdrawal of the withdrawal, etc. The 'starting out from' is itself engulfed in it [*s'y abime*]. (RM, 29–30)

'If metaphysics had a unity', therefore, it would have to begin *without* beginning, both in the manner of the Blanchotian *sans* and the Silesian *ohne*; it would have to retreat from the metaphor of the origin and the 'dictation/dictatorship' of the original authority, the commanding Voice and Image that keeps everything that follows in the control, frame, axiomatic derivation: 'can one treat of philosophy itself (metaphysics itself, that is, ontotheology) without already permitting the dictation, along with the pretention to unity and unicity, of the ungraspable and imperial totality of an order? If there are margins, is there still a philosophy, *the* philosophy?', asks Derrida already in 1972, in *Tympan* (M, xvi). The retreat of the metaphor – image, voice, derivation – is thus a gesture inaugurating a new *metaphysics of non-presence*, which constitutes a topological transformation of Derrida's negative *non-metaphysics of presence*: a positive reversal of the Derridean *pars deconstruens*, targeting all traces of continuity/metaphor/analogy/*communio* in Western ontotheology which still treats the Platonic *methexis* as its unquestioned default mode (and which, as we have seen, also proved to be the case with Heidegger, the alleged great 'overcomer of metaphysics'). The metaphysics of non-presence, 'starting from' the abyssal origin-in-withdrawal and its radical 'unappearance', is a new science of separation which cuts the umbilical cord between Being and beings and sets the latter on the journey of dissemination into the proper unknown of the future: the world shall travel through the deserts of destinerrance, always *Fort*, never *Da* – never to be returned to the source or the life-giving 'spring', *fons vitae*. In her brilliant analysis of Derrida's motif of travelling in *Counterpath*, Catherine Malabou points to Derrida's final departure from Heidegger as precisely the result of his thinking to the end of the motif of *Entzug/retrait*, which the latter arrested half-way:

> Derrida follows Heidegger, but distinguishes himself as he follows and retraces. By proposing that Heidegger's text be read on the basis of the motif of the *retrait*, *something that Heidegger himself never configured or organized in the same way*, he is already displacing it. He displaces it toward a thinking of the dissemination of the *trait* that wrenches the path – *Weg* or *Tao* – from what still has to be called its destinal unity, from whatever, within it, resists traveling. Derrida will in fact show that the *Geschick* or *envoi* of being remains dependent upon a traditional logic of destination. That sense of Being never gets lost along the road and always ends up arriving at or being moored to *truth*. In the same manner, it will always be possible for poetry and thinking to recollect themselves or reassemble in the unity of this *envoi* which becomes a putting into operation of their truth. With Heidegger, the originary trait does not end by being effaced. In this sense *the dispensation of being*

still obeys, in its own way, the derivative schema of metaphysics. Given that, the *Be-Wegung* doesn't travel far enough. (CP-M, 133; emphasis added)

Indeed, the whole point here is the freedom to travel: the unstoppable *Be-Wegung* of dissemination which cannot be held in check by a pious remembrance (*Andenken*) of the self-effacing origin. Travel is the very opposite of *nostos*/return which moors beings to the truth of their origin and makes them derivative/epiphenomenal in relation to the only proper source of being: by not being allowed to travel, beings are tied by the uncut umbilical cord which keeps them dependent on the matrix of *creatio continua*. The Many remains merely relative towards the One, and the Other merely relative towards the Same.[3]

This travel arrested midway is the reason why, in *Faith and Knowledge*, the One – the main metaphysical phantasm of all philosophy since Plato – appears as always more-than-One and no-longer-One, *plus d'Un* or *l'Un + n* (FK, 100). If the 'scattered existence' (MCP, 32) is really to be *scattered*, it must also have a multiple self-scattering source. In Luria's system, it is precisely the self-immolating moment of *tsimtsum* that inaugurates self-scattering: the invasion of spacing and distance, from which the dissemination begins. In Derrida, the difference and the distance, made possible by the self-differentiating withdrawal, are the first movement of *khorein*. In the speech called 'Christianity and Secularization', in which Derrida elucidates the most difficult tenets of *Foi et savoir*, he explicitly confirms the intimate link between the 'nameless One', which violently turns on itself (FK, 100) – according to one of the possible definitions of *tsimtsum* as violent self-negation – and the messianic (non-Platonic but also non-Heideggerian[4]) reading of *Khôra*:

> Well, I believe that between this affirmation of the One which does itself violence ... and this motif of the messianic *Khôra*, there is some necessary connection. (CS, 148)

---

[3] In his late lecture on Nietzsche's Zarathustra (1953), while commenting on the section called 'The Convalescent', Heidegger equates 'healing' – becoming whole and sound – with the circular movement of homecoming: 'But what does "the convalescent" mean? "To convalesce" [genesen] is the same as the Greek *nomai, nostos*. This means "to return home"; nostalgia is the aching for home, homesickness. The convalescent is the man who collects himself to return home, that is to turn in, into his own destiny. The convalescent is on the road to himself, so that *he can say of himself who he is*': Martin Heidegger, 'Who Is Nietzsche's Zarathustra?' trans. Bernd Magnus, *The Review of Metaphysics* 20, no. 3 (1967): 412; emphasis added. This could not stand in a greater contrast to Derrida's concept of the 'ontological Marrano' who is for ever out of joints and because of that beyond any possibility of identitarian closure: he, as a metaphysical anacoluth/ unfinished sentence, cannot say of himself who he is – neither where he came from nor where he is heading. See again the quote from *Dissemination*, which refers to writing as a vagrant rogue-Marrano: 'Wandering in the streets, he doesn't even know who he is, what his identity – if he has one – might be, what his name is, what his father's name is' (D, 143).

[4] See also his comment there on Heidegger: 'In the *Contributions to Philosophy*, when Heidegger speaks of the God who comes, I do not know whether he is holding a discourse that has an affinity with what I was trying to say about *khôra* – I'm not sure. The Heideggerian interpretation of the *khôra* has never satisfied me' (CS, 147).

Already in 'Dissemination', devoted to Philip Sollers's novel *Les nombres*, Derrida points to the Lurianic effect of *tsimtsum* as vacating a space-emptiness (*kenoma, tehiru*): 'it uncovers the space of play or the play of space in which transformations are set off and sequences strung out. It is air. *L'air blanc*. Air: the ether in which, from the "beginning," the "One" is caught or *raised*' (DIS, 345). The 'One', therefore, is caught in the self-scattering process from the very beginning as always already *plus d'Un*. The self-disseminating 'no-longer-One' sends itself off as the 'scattered existence', a *being-in-diaspora*, making home out of exile which resulted from the original self-exile of the divine. In Derrida's *diasporic metaphysics of dissemination*, therefore, to be means to be cut from the self-wounded origin whose wound – divisive, yet also open and opening to the multitude of *l'Un + n* – started the process of scattering. Unlike Heidegger, who never stops wondering – in a kind of an amazed horror – at the self-violation of Being which chooses to reveal itself in the distortion and self-erasure, Derrida endorses the violence which the One does to itself as no-longer-One.

But this is also the reason why the model for this exilic/exodic letting-be can no longer be supplied by the Neoplatonic scheme of emanation and the gradual 'diminishing of light', which eventually produces the darkest shadow of the material 'scattered existence'. It calls for a more radical account of the separation. For Derrida, the right model is *writing*: the cosmic *écriture* which wanders away from its 'phallic' origin, disperses and multiplies in the free space of blank cosmic page, separated from the auctorial presence and its commanding voice. This hypothesis is as old as Kabbalah itself: *Sefer ha Zohar*, the first Kabbalistic treatise of Moses de Leon, suggests such departure from the traditional metaphysics of light already in the opening sentence:

> In the beginning – when the will of the King began to take effect, he engraved signs into the heavenly sphere that surrounded him.[5]

While commenting on this fragment, Gershom Scholem claims that the Kabbalistic 'transforming view', announcing a breakthrough in the conception of a new non-Neoplatonic metaphysics, amounts to the intuition that 'all worlds are nothing more than "names recorded" on the scroll of God's essence' (the original German is even more striking in the use of the scriptural metaphor: 'Namen, die auf dem *Papier* von Gottes Wesen *aufgezeichnet* werden').[6] No longer a living presence or voice, God empties himself out into primal 'engraved signs' or the series of 'names recorded' and, in this manner, creates the first transcendental code of differences – we can safely call it the *différance* – from which the manifold will issue and transform the undifferentiated One/Same into differentiated Many/Other.[7] While referring to Sollers's image of the

---

[5] Scholem and de Leon, *The Book of Spendor*, 3.
[6] David Biale, 'Scholem's "Ten Unhistorical Aphorisms on Kabbalah." Text and Commentary', *Modern Judaism* 5, no. 1 (1985): 85.
[7] According to Harold Bloom, the writing offers a necessary respite from the pressure of the living presence: 'Writing, as Derrida tropes it, both keeps us from the void and, more aggressively (as against voicing), gives us a *saving difference*, by preventing that coincidence of speaker with subject that would entrap us in *a presence so total as to stop the mind*': Harold Bloom, *A Map of Misreading* (Oxford: Oxford University Press, 1975), 43; emphasis added.

column of smoke and fire (the traditional representation of YHVH), Derrida himself writes about *différance* as the machine of differentiation which has no meaning in itself apart from inventing the difference:

> The column is nothing, has no meaning in itself. A hollow phallus, cut off from itself, decapitated, it guarantees the innumerable passage of dissemination and the playful displacement of the margins. *It is never itself*, only a writing that endlessly substitutes it for itself, doubling it as of its very surrection. (DIS, 342; emphasis added)

Although the centre is hollowed and emptied – *kenomatic* – and hence no longer 'phallic' (thus akin to *ruah*, the feminine fire of self-transcendence, which is never herself), there is no mention of catastrophe here, either at the stage of God's violent self-negation or at the later, equally violent, stage of breaking of the vessels, which Derrida sees as merely forwarding and intensifying the first move of *différance*. And since there is no catastrophe, there is also no need for redemption understood as *restitutio in integrum*, the undoing of the crisis and making things *whole-again*, safe and sound, returned to their original indemnity: 'pure spacing goes on *forever* and not in the expectation of any Messianic fulfillment' (DIS, 345).

It does not mean, however, that Derrida rejects any form of messianicity, far from it. It only means that he rejects the specific expectations of *fulfillment* or the redemptive completion of the world, mended and rounded in the act of ultimate *tikkun*. The 'scattered existence' writes itself endlessly on, with no fulfilling *telos* in sight, as the black fire of matter on the white fire of the *kenoma/tehiru/Khôra*: the empty space which opened as the originary Wound, the *makom* of the One 'doing violence to itself' (FK, 100). For Derrida, messianicity has nothing to do with completion: *tikkun* as restoration and return. It is rather a 'Khôraic' messianicity of *nursing*, vigilantly assisting, attending, and affirming the continuous birth of the world: 'It is a spacing that is merely *attended*' (DIS, 345; emphasis added). Things fall apart; the centre cannot hold – but this is precisely the way it should be as the way of *différance* 'assisted by the [messianic] discourse' (DIS, 345). The passage from the One infinite 'simple presence' (*metsiut* in Kabbalistic terms) to the finite 'scattered existence', in which One indifferent body is no longer One but begins to envelop in space and time in the infinite series of finite beings, cannot occur but through dissemination conceived as a process of writing.

But when Derrida insists that *Il se fait violence* (FK-F, 100) – the origin does violence to itself – he also inscribes into this figure a motif of circumcision. *It circumcizes itself*. Just as the Lacanian *corps morcelé* disperses under the circumcising blow, so does the infinite body of the primary *Ein-Sof* becomes scattered into ex-istence: the first system of differentials which the Kabbalistic tradition calls *sephirot*, the 'ten signs of creation' forming the Tree of Life, and which, in Derrida's thought, takes the form of *différance*. The *tsimtsem* Origin is here like a voice that fades and, while fading and retreating, allows the writing to assert itself in its own right: rise as a figure/trace/*trait* against the darkening background (RM, 30). For Derrida, therefore, the withdrawal of the commanding voice, which lets the *écriture* be and work through the simple presence as the system of differences, is the gist of the process which Scholem, a propos *tsimtsum*, calls 'liberation of creation'.

Hence, already in 'Différance', Derrida says that *différance* 'maintains our relationship with that which we necessarily misconstrue, and which exceeds the alternative of presence and absence' (M, 20). The reason for this misconstrual is the *image* of the centre/ground which eludes us, but we nonetheless tend to assume that it is surely 'out there', whereas the play of the *sephirot* – the first ten signs of the metaphysical alphabet – is beyond simple presence and absence: they are no-thing in themselves, because they are only insofar as they manifest themselves in singular beings which they allow to emerge as different and differentiated, *tout autre*. Just as the programme/information is no-thing in itself (*ayin*) and becomes some-thing (*yesh*) only when it simulates the event of the play/game, so 'is' the *différance* nothing but the system of differentials that makes possible revealment of all things present, but precisely because of that, it can never be presented as such. Contrary to the Neoplatonic system, therefore, where the highest ground of being 'is generally represented as the calm, present, and self-referential unity' (M, 11), *différance* defers and differs this oneness, by creating a matrix of multiplicity and the ceaseless dynamic of appearances. And just as the Tree of Life is a system of 'delegates', always beginning with *beth-bereshit* leaving the eternally hidden *aleph* behind, so is *différance* a play of 'proxies' that never allows to reach the absent origin:

> If *différance* is (and I also cross out the *is*) what makes possible the presentation of the being-present, *it is never presented as such* [. . .] *différance* remains a metaphysical name [. . .] It differs from, and defers itself; which doubtless means that it is woven of differences, and also that it sends out delegates, representatives, proxies; *but without any chance that the giver of proxies might 'exist,' might be present, be 'itself' somewhere.* (MP, 6; 26; 21; emphasis added)

Derrida's insistence on '*différance* remaining a metaphysical name' makes us immediately rethink his doctrine of grammatology as something more than just a deconstruction of the traditional ontotheology. It paves the way towards a new metaphysics of the *original writing*, which also proposes a new theology of *tsimtsum*: the doctrine of the God-in-retreat, who withdraws into absence and leaves only 'engraved signs' to run the machine of being through the system of *différance*. The sacred *gramme* which forms the arche-writing as the structural DNA of the world constitutes the *machina ex deo* that flies in the face of the traditional metaphysics, based on the conceptual nexus of life, light, presence, and – last but not least – living voice (*phone*). What keeps being in being is not a 'miracle' – of creation, grace, and revelation – but a 'machine': the *machina ex deo* of *différance* as a system of differentiation, iteration, repetition, and the deferral of the end, which indefinitely postpones the apocalyptic endgame.

'Negativity in God, exile as writing, the life of the letter are all already in the Cabala': Derrida states in 'Edmond Jabès and the Question of the Book' (WD, 74). Already at this early stage, Derrida demonstrates fluency in the Kabbalistic arcana as interpreted by Scholem: the 'negative factor' in the Godhead and *tsimtsum* as an act of God's 'exile into himself', which is then followed by 'exile as writing' and, *vice versa*, writing as exile. The exile, however, is not a mortifying condition of death. The deliberately anti-Pauline phrase – *the life of the letter* – which opposes the typically Christian equation of life with the living Spirit, implies a completely different metaphysical model than the *phosocentric* and *iconophilic* Neoplatonic Metaphysics of Light, as well as the *phonocentric* Christian attachment to the idea of the ever-present Voice of the Father.[8] The Kabbalistic intuition that created finite being is nothing but writing, due to which the infinite simple presence ex-scribes itself on the blank space of nothingness, emerges fully in *Of Grammatology*, where Derrida insinuates his new Metaphysics of *Ecriture* into the deconstructive reading of Rousseau:

> *there has never been anything but writing*; there have never been anything but supplements, substitutive significations which could only come forth in a chain of differential references, the 'real' supervening, and being added only while taking on meaning from a trace and from an invocation of the supplement, etc. *And thus to infinity*, for we have read, in the text, that the absolute present, God, that which words like 'real father' name, have always already escaped, have never existed; that what opens meaning and language is writing as the *disappearance of divine presence*. (GRAM, 159; emphasis added)[9]

In the beginning God created nothing – and this creation of the void/*kenoma*/*tehiru*/*makom* in the act of the divine *tsimtsum* turns out to be the greatest possible gift. Contrary to the vitalist intuitions of infinitist metaphysics, it is neither the plenitude of the 'fountain of life' nor the full ontological presence of self-identical highest being, which constitute the creatory *Donum Dei*. In his deconstructive inversion of the 'theological prejudice' spontaneously privileging fullness, presence, nature, voice, and life, Derrida – following the traces of the Kabbalistic counter-imagination – demonstrates that it is actually the very opposite that truly lets beings be, breathe, and live: absence, detachment, fragmentation, space, finite time, counterfeit currency of signs/appearances, and the *techne* of 'writing-out' of the indifferent pleroma of 'simple

---

[8] Also, already at this early stage, Derrida demonstrates his characteristic – Marrano *avant la lettre* – independence from Jabes. Following the latter's diagnosis – 'You are he who writes and is written' (WD, 78) – Derrida states affirmatively: 'Writing is the moment of the desert as the moment of Separation' (WD, 83). While for Jabes, the ecritural exile is a terrible state in between the lost and the promised speech of the living encounter with God 'face to face', Derrida, free from any logocentric nostalgia, parts with Jabes's mournful tone, even to the point of endorsing that *'there is no writing without a lie and writing is the way of God* [...] This way, *preceded by no truth*, and thus lacking the prescription of truth's rigor, is the way through the Desert' (WD, 82–3; emphasis added).

[9] This quote, which originally refers to Rousseau's *Confessions*, is slightly – and deliberately – manipulated in order to enhance its implicit theological context: I substituted 'father' for 'mother' and 'divine' for 'maternal'. Just as Rousseau's writing can only proceed in the absence of his mother, so does the scriptural enterprise of creation can take place only within the empty space made possible by *tsimtsum* as the 'disappearance of the divine presence'.

presence', where no being or life is yet possible. The true gift of creation, therefore, is the freedom of the written sign, constantly falling from grace of the divine presence.[10]

Metaphysics after Auschwitz

Yet, this freedom is possible only due to the concept of the *catachrestic/anacoluthic dissemination*: Derrida's new model of conceiving the relation between the always-retreating ground and beings which spring forth into 'scattered existence' as always already separated – 'violently sundered' (FK, 81) – from their origin. For Derrida, this is a proper realization of Heidegger's idea of letting-be (*Seinlassen, Seinsvermögen*) as a vision of the emergence of beings, alternative to the creationist one, which Heidegger, hindered by his 'theological' bias, was unable to think to the end. At the same time, it is also the only metaphysics which, after Adorno's famous admonition, would be possible after Auschwitz: no longer so optimistic in assuming 'a positive meaning [of being] constituted within itself and orientated towards the divine principle', and no longer so integristic in conceiving the totality of the universe as governed by the all-encompassing One (*plus d'Un*).[11] By accepting Adorno's challenge to seek a new metaphysics which would not be a 'pure mockery in face of the victims and the infinitude of their torment', and choosing, after Hans Jonas, the model of *tsimtsum* as the only one befitting 'God after Auschwitz', Derrida develops his thinking of *Seinlassen* in a strong misreading of Heidegger whom, as we have seen, he deliberately 'marranizes' (or, as Cixous would say, 'marranates'). For, only when transposed to a different model – of scattering, dissemination, and universal diaspora of beings – the Heideggerian idea of *Seinlassen* can become truly effective.

But the Adornian challenge awakes in Derrida also his Marrano guilt of survival, of which we spoke in the first chapter: for him, the new metaphysics of letting-be is not just a conceptual affair, it is also a way of seeking forgiveness for the fact of living-on and still-taking-place – a *metaphysical pardon* which he now associates with the name *Khôra*: 'Being-there [*être-là*]: this would be asking for forgiveness; this would be to be inscribed in a scene of forgiveness, and of impossible forgiveness' (AR, 382). For Derrida, the challenge of a new metaphysics has nothing to do with the

---

[10] This, again, is a traditional Jewish motif: the freedom deriving from the written sign. In *Pirke Aboth*, Rabbi Joshua ben Levi teaches: 'And the tablets were the work of God, and the writing was the writing of God, graven upon the tablets. Read not *charuth* graven but *cheruth* freedom': *Pirke Aboth: The Sayings of the Fathers*, trans. Joseph Hertz (London: Behrman House, 1945), 6;2.

[11] See Adorno's comment: 'It is therefore impossible [. . .] to insist after Auschwitz on the presence of a positive meaning or purpose in being [. . .] The affirmative character which metaphysics has in Aristotle, and which it first took on in Plato's teaching, has become impossible. To assert that existence or being has a positive meaning constituted within itself and orientated towards the divine principle [. . .], would be, like all the principles of truth, beauty and goodness which philosophers have concocted, a pure mockery in face of the victims and the infinitude of their torment' (MCP, 101).

Nietzschean attempt to restore the 'innocence of becoming': it is rather an attempt to relieve becoming of *too much* guilt.

Some commentators claim that it cannot be done and that the challenge set by Adorno is simply too tall. According to Jacob Rogozinski, all that is left to do is to mourn the forever departed metaphysics and preserve its 'exquisite corpse' in an inner crypt (hence the cryptophoric title of his book: *Cryptes de Derrida*). Himself a student of Derrida and a trained psychoanalyst, Rogozinski interprets the Derridean deconstruction as the infinite work of mourning, aporetically torn between the two strategies – introjection and incorporation – where what is mourned is not a departed person, but the whole tradition: the inhabitant of Derrida's crypt is the spectre of metaphysics, which he does not want to resurrect but preserve precisely as dead.

> Deconstruction carries the mourning of metaphysics [. . .] By deconstucting metaphysics, Derrida wished to protect her in himself, to keep her captive in the depths of his labyrinthe, as a precious relic, an enbalmed living dead ('There is solidarity between such thinking and metaphysics at the time of its fall' (ND, 408) – did Adorno also aspire to this melancholy genre?). This was the real passion of Jacques Derrida, the unique love of his life, the only addressee of his *Envois*, and all his writings – *metaphysic was his mad queen*.[12]

As in Adorno, Derrida's 'melancholy science' is the inevitable aftermath of Shoah: 'after Auschwitz' – the section bearing this title opens Adorno's 'Meditations on Metaphysics', which concludes *Negative Dialectics* (ND, 361) – metaphysics is no longer possible. She is thus mourned together with all those who died *la mort sans phrase, la mort sans nom* (G, 155) in the process of impossible mourning which cannot commemorate the nameless and is thus constantly threatened by *amnesie sans reste* (SQ, 83): 'Does not the annihilation of the name announce the failure of all the work of mourning, the ultimate disaster which drowns with it all metaphysics and all dialectics?'[13] Rogozinski is sceptical towards Derrida's own preference of life and constant affirmation of survival: he sees them as defence mechanisms of a thanatological cryptophore, weighed down by the melancholy of nameless death which cannot be properly mourned: 'for how the one who is already dead can decide for life *pour la vie* without forgetting? And how can he preserve the memory without being devoured by death?'[14] According to Rogozonski, this is Derrida's main aporia which puts him in the vicinity of other *je-suis-deja-morts*: Heidegger, Lacan, and Blanchot. His famous last words – *Préférez toujours la vie et affirmez sans cesse la survie* – are nothing but a decoy. The truth which he carries is, in fact, lethal.

A similar claim to Rogozinski was made by David Farrell Krell in his 2000 book on Derrida, *The Purest of Bastards*. In Krell's account, Derrida mourns 'the loss of the confidence' once possessed by the boldest metaphysicians of Western thought

---

[12] Jacob Rogozinski, *Cryptes de Derrida* (Fécamp: Lignes, 2014), 47; 29; emphasis added.
[13] Rogozinski, *Cryptes*, 36.
[14] Ibid., 48.

who daringly ventured towards transcendence. The now elusive object of their failed pursuits is what Krell calls 'ultratranscendence', linked to the 'experience of withdrawal and default':

> such a beyond – let us agree to call it the domain of ultratranscendence – relates in Derrida's *oeuvre* to the theme of the absolute past, the past that never was present [...] Dreams and delusions of either Husserl's 'rigorous science' or Hegel's methodological restitution or Heidegger's circular guideline or Kant's flawless inventory cannot be allowed to undergird and thus subvert the Derridian passage – the *parcours* beyond the empirical realm – toward ultratranscendence. Derrida walks – or limps-in – at the wake (Finn, again) of his predecessors, mourning the loss of the confidence they possessed. The *non plus ultra* of ultratranscendence [...] is not a perfection but an imperfection, an experience of withdrawal and default. The necessity that drives Derrida's thinking of the trace to the yon side of transcendental experience is not victorious; however confident its gesture seems to be, the ultratranscendental experience is fraught [...] For what would it be like to run with concepts that destroy their own names? (PB, 103; 110–11)

The whole of Krell's interpretation of Derrida's *ouevre* is steeped in the language of mourning – the negativity of loss, failure, default, dispersion – but he also notices Derrida's attempt to supplement it with his unique idiom of affirmation, even if that would mean 'attempting the impossible' (PB, 104). Just as Rogozinski, who diagnoses Derrida as a cryptophore, Krell too describes the Derridean mourning as a 'baleful incorporation, rather than successful introjection, of the person (or "object") mourned – that is to say, the cryptic inclusion of the object of prohibited desire in an inaccessible interiority, in an inner sphere that is locked from the inside to the inside' (PB, 130). The cryptophoric condition, which Derrida associates with the 'Spanish Marranos', who encrypted the Jewish God as the object of the officially prohibited desire, cannot be cured, but it nonetheless can pave the way towards a 'mourning affirmation' which occurs precisely in the fiasco of all defence mechanisms, be it reflexive interiorization or cryptohoric introjection: 'the very default of mourning opens a space for the double yes, the *oui* to the *oui* [...] It is the tonality of an affirmation that is always on the verge' (PB, 204). Seeing the frailty and groundlessness of such 'affirmation without issue' as nothing but the reverse of despair, Krell prefers to situate himself on this side of negativity and declare that he feels 'powerless to reconstitute the *Asche* into a *Sache*, powerless to make it all clear for thinking. Labors of mourning do not respond well to cries for clarity' (PB, 146). Yet, in a way, this is precisely what I am trying to do here: to push towards a full messianic inversion in which the Marrano condition of the ashen-like cryptophoric 'incandescent mourning' (PB, 146) can *turn* – that is, pass the 'verge' – into an affirmation of a new metaphysical condition where the 'ultratranscendent', always already withdrawn God is not just 'an imperfection, an experience of withdrawal and default' (PB, 110), but a positive possibility of the gift which constitutes the world. Krell, doubting if such reservedly optimistic reversal is at all possible, tends to perceive the Derridean 'imperfect world' as the Agambenian *limbo*, the ultimately negative neither-nor beyond both redemption and damnation:

> If we are to dwell in neither the heaven of arche-synthesis nor the hell of a complacent objectivism or a smug scientism, would not the imperfect world of Derrida's thought best be designated as an *arche-limbo*? However, in such a limbo, could one ever achieve ecstasy or affirmation? (PB, 116)

But no: the world is not the Agambenian arche-limbo. It is *not* simply dispersed into ashes, cut off from its source, indifferent to anything apart from being-so. If we supplement this negative story with the elements of the Marrano cryptofaith as chiming with the Lurianic paradigm of *tsimtsum*, the whole narrative will begin to reverberate with more affirmative 'yes-laughter', which – as the next chapter should make clear – cannot be reduced to what Krell, mistrustful about the affirmative enterprise, suspects of being 'a kind of shadow play, a snigger at worst, at best a weary and jaded chortle, a kind of secondhand laughter by hearsay, a *oui'-dire*, a *oui-rire*' (PB, 207). The 'yes-laughter' can be truly liberating and ecstatic.

Here I am thus trying to show that a post-Auschwitz metaphysics is possible *after all*: precisely as an *after-all-metaphysics* – not only after Auschwitz, but also after all that which before organized the metaphysical discourse: the Neoplatonic *participatio*, the origin as the One, and the restitutive ideal of *nostos* as homecoming. All this is no longer mourned by Derrida: it is left behind in the gesture of the Marrano separation which, while worked-through by the messianic reversal, eventually turns into a 'lucky break'. The same working-through applies to Derrida's affirmation of survival, which cannot be treated as a mere epiphenomenon towards the lethal Thing buried in his crypt. The Marrano operation of reversal proves precisely the opposite. For Derrida, his *marranismo* offers a therapeutic/redemptive answer to the impossible mourning of nameless deaths, where it is precisely the lack of name and the forgetting that open a new risky game of chances – not just ashes. What thus terrifies him to no end and makes him infinitely guilty in *Glas* and *Shibboleth* gradually loses its traumatic aspect in the 'self-marranating' process of *Durcharbeiten*: the Marrano nameless survival becomes a redemptive counterpart to the Jewish nameless death. Just as in Scholem, therefore, life – survival of the Marrano remnant – becomes a new argument which disturbs and deconstructs the logic of nomination.[15]

This reversal is precisely the reason why Derrida does not conclude *Faith and Knowledge* with the image of the Christian 'exquisite corpse', deposited in the crypt, and adds the second section, no longer in the Latin *italics*, which suggests a way out – an Exodus – out of the realm of a 'certain Christianity' and its *morbidezza* of infinite

---

[15] In their co-written paper, 'Orthobiographies', Yvonne Sherwood and John D. Caputo confirm the seriousness of the messianic anti-thanatological reversal which occurs in Derrida's later writings: 'What is fallen, rises; what is dead, lives on, from the ashes of the absolute end, a future rises – and all this by *écriture* alone [...] Death is always not yet. Even if I am walking death, I am not dead, not yet. The 'not yet' always stirs in writing' (OT, 223; 226).

mourning. This second part is on '*pomegranates*': the fruit which, according to Jewish sources, is still hanging on the branches of the Tree of Life, and still within our reach.

Marrano anabiosis: Crypts and orchards of ontotheology

In the previous chapter, we established that the modern God deposited in the crypt is neither dead nor alive. What is then his ontological status? Before we state the obvious – that he, as a *spectre* emanating from the crypt, belongs not to ontology but *hantologie* – we should first look at what Derrida understands by God's *en-cryption*: his interment and entombment, on the one hand, and his going into hiding, on the other.[16] God is only seemingly dead: reduced to a mummified seed, he is in the state of *anabiosis* – close to death, but only close, in fact *still* surviving, yet with no hope for *anastasis*, the Christian resurrection in full vitality. The Tree of Life, therefore, is *still* secretly growing, like the Mystical Rose on the Grave or the Hegelian *Rose auf dem Kreuz der Gegenwart*, which weaves its delicate organic structure out of the rock of Golgotha. Similarly to the major symbol of the Rosicrucians, which so strongly mesmerized Hegel, the Derridean Rose also takes roots in the crypt and sprouts out in the modest form of '… pomegranates' which Derrida announces with an ellipsis that makes us hold our breath before something truly surprising, unexpected, a pure messianic arrival: a hope of a new *sur-vie*, grown out of the cross/ordeal of the sheer *survie* ad symbolized by the paradisiac *rimonim*. The pomegranates are the traditional Jewish emblems of fertility, expressing a faith that love is as strong as death, which we know from the *Song of Songs*, but, more originally, from the orgiastic funeral rites of ancient Israelites (thus chiming with Jean Genet's *Pompes funebres*, chosen as a mirror image to Hegel's *Phenomenology* in *Glas*). At the very end of his essay, Derrida comes back to the issue of modern ontotheology, which sublated and abstracted the language of old 'living religions' and transformed them into 'religions of the [apparent] death of God'. Contrary to this mortifying view, Derrida points to ontotheology's ambivalent 'double bind' according to which faith may indeed be as strong as death:

> The possibility of radical evil both destroys and institutes the religious. Ontotheology does the same when it suspends sacrifice and prayer, the truth of this prayer that maintains itself, recalling Aristotle one more time, beyond the

[16] Is *Khôra* also a tomb/ crypt of the 'Artisan God'? Is *Khôra* itself a metaphysical cryptophore? In his commentary to *Advances*, the preface which Derrida wrote to Serge Margel's *Le tombeau de dieu artisan*, Philippe Lynes perceptively notices that the term used by both in reference to *Khôra*, 'terre sans terre [earth without earth] in French would be homophonous with *terre s'enterre* [the earth buries or inters itself]. Such a notion lets us read not only Derrida's own description of the *Timaeus* as a tomb sinking into the earth under the weight of the scholarly imprintings on its subject, but also the notion of *Khôra* as a *nonmemory*, something that must let everything become erased in order to receive the Demiurge's imprints': Philippe Lynes, 'Introduction. *Auparadvances*' (ADV, xvii). In that sense, *Khôra* would be another name of the 'God who made me forget' and buried himself in the act of self-erasure: a self-interring God who does not want to be recollected and thus appropriated – as in the Hegelian *Er-innerung* – by any theology: a God-in-crypt who refuses to be – Hegel again – 'resurrected daily' by the pious 'memory of the Passion.'

true and the false, beyond their opposition, in any case, according to a certain concept of truth or of judgement [. . .] Ontotheology en*crypts* faith and destines it to the condition of a sort of Spanish Marrano who would have lost – in truth, dispersed, multiplied – everything up to and including the memory of his unique secret. Emblem of a still life: an opened pomegranate, one Passover evening, on a tray. (FK, 100)

Let's face again this passage which constitutes one of the most cryptic Derridean fragments, deliberately left as a 'fragment' or what Friedrich Schlegel used to call a 'torso': a trace of the once integral religious meaning, now dispersed and incomplete, undergoing a (seemingly) destructive/mortifying process of secularization. We already know that the 'radical evil' of both, religion and ontotheology, consists in the wrong abstraction which creates a 'torso' of an *ab-stracted God*: a radically de-tached *Ab-solutus*, absolved from any relation with the world, elevated/'phallically erected' to the heights of his perfect indifference, as in Aristotle and then in the Aristotelian 'theological absolutism' of Islamic *kalam* and Christian scholastics. This is precisely what Derrida calls the 'indeterminate abstraction' (FK, 55) of God Without Qualities (*theos apoios*), or a Nobodaddy from William Blake's vision, to whom it is impossible to pray and who is completely oblivious to our acts of sacrifice. But if ontotheology not only destroys religious imagery in the deadened concept of the Absolute, but is also faith's 'one chance of survival' (TG, 42), it is because it can also produce a 'determinate abstraction': the notion of the most originary origin (*das Frühste* in Heidegger's idiom) which detaches itself from every place in the world, not because it is an apophatic *Ab-solutus* but because it *gives* place for all place-taking events of the world. Ontotheology, therefore, properly understood, can also *encrypt* faith, by letting it survive in the 'determinate abstraction' of the placeless place-giving origin – just as the 'Spanish Marrano' who seemingly lost his faith, but *in truth* let it survive in secret clandestine forms.

The French phrase, *la grenade entamée*, translated by Samuel Weber as 'opened pomegranate', indeed suggests an opening, a beginning of a new process – of modern secularization as encryption of faith – but it can also mean an indentation which begins an act of consuming a fruit. The paradisiac pomegranates grow on both Edenic trees: the Tree of Life, but also the Tree of Knowledge, and it is from the indentation of the fruit of knowledge that the expulsion and wandering of the first parents begin, before they eventually disperse, multiply, and their progeny takes earth in possession. The indented apple/pomegranate traditionally symbolizes the sin of hubris – of wanting to know more than it is allowed – but not for Derrida. Here it rather means an inauguration of the process of knowing called ontotheology – the once forbidden knowledge of God, now taking the bold form of God's conceptualization – which should end with the whole consummation of the fruit. Once this process is *entamé*, on its way, there is no stopping it: no reversal can make the fruit whole again and return it unscathed to its proper owner. But what happens once the fruit is eaten in full? Then it suddenly turns out that it *was* – *in truth* – the pomegranate from the Tree of Life and that the duplication of the Edenic trees was nothing but the divine trick and deception. To have eaten the fruit of knowledge till the end would thus mean to swallow/internalize also the deepest truth of the Abrahamic tradition: the secret of *Ets Hayim* – and thus regain Paradise.[17]

La grenade entamée, therefore, is also a symbol of SA – 'Saint Augustine', as well as Hegelian *Savoir absolu* – the one thread connecting the paradigmatic thinker of *felix culpa* with the first modern philosopher to see the divine *lapsus* into the world as the most fortunate of events (even if tinged with the sacrificial-redemptive colours of the not fully sublated Christian notion of *kenosis*). Derrida's metaphysics is all about felicity of this fault/fall, *culpa/lapsus*, which eventually loses all lapsarian features: when the origin is left behind and the only way is forward, the whole idea of lapsing from or relapsing back becomes meaningless. On Derrida's reading, the Augustinian phrase *felix culpa* is indeed an encrypted formula for the Absolute Knowledge: once its inner aporia is solved and the guilty memory of lapsing from the origin disappears, all that is left is pure felicity – the *happestance* of constant occurring, of new events coming and going, the 'lucky break' of the Jonasian 'unprejudiced becoming', released from the metaphysical leash: *free at last!* Once we start tasting the pomegranate from the Tree of Knowledge, the SA of the ultimate bite is just there, hidden in SA's secret alchemical formula of *felix culpa*, the happy fault that transmutes everything from crap to gold: from the pathetic excretion of the Absolute, as in Schelling's Gnostic visions of the ignoble beginnings of the world as simply 'thrown away' into a vacuum, to the intended and invented otherness of being realizing itself in the unprejudiced becoming. Hence the Spanish Marranos emerge here as the emblem of the 'first parents', parenting the whole happily faulted modern nation who has only just begun to taste the fruit of knowledge and is determined to eat it further: 'eat it well'.[18]

Abstracted and detached from the living tradition, Marrano is also an allegory of a *still life* (*nature morte*), which locates itself in-between the premodern cult of *Elohim hayim*, on the one hand, and modern atheism which issued from the 'death of God', on the other: seemingly dead, but – *still* – a life; *still*, quiet, restrained, self-withdrawn, and yet – *still* – a life. But if ontotheology can be compared to the Marrano condition, it is because it too is *nature morte*: the nominalist *natura pura* which, deprived of the animating presence of divine grace, transforms into collection of mechanical objects – a dead matter abandoned by God. And yet – *still* – it lives on in the realm of *Verlassenheit*: no longer vitalized by the living Spirit, but nonetheless *un-dead*; not a vitalist pleroma of unbound power, yet – *still* – some kind of deanimated rogue life that does not equal death, but stubbornly survives, against all odds. Ontotheology, therefore, as the *nature morte/natura pura*, depicts the world as *deserted* by the living God, yet also allows God – and the world – to survive in the 'harshest impiety' of desiccated and desertified abstraction. Unlike in the Christian nominalist tradition of

---

[17] Derrida is thus in agreement with Kleist: 'We would have to eat from the tree of knowledge to fall back again into a state of innocence? Most certainly, he replied: That is the last chapter of the history of the world': Heinrich von Kleist, 'On the Marionette Theater', trans. Thomas G. Neumiller, *The Drama Review* 16, no. 3 (1972): 26.

[18] Comp. Jacques Derrida, '*Eating Well*, or the Calculation of the Subject', in *Points. . . Interviews, 1974–1994*, ed. Elisabeth Weber, trans. Peggy Kamuf et al. (Stanford: Stanford University Press, 1995).

natura pura, this abandonment and revealment of a real void – the empty nothing of the space vacated by God – is not univocally negative, as in Pascal's horror vision of empty silent infinite spaces, or rather, not negative at all. Just as in the Dutch masters, whom Derrida evokes, the night that surrounds their collections of objects is a warm penumbral matrix from which they all emerge one by one, each bestowed with the light of its own, radiating from the inside: they *take place* in the night which *gives place* and demands nothing in return. This is not the terrifying void of God's absence, *die Nacht der Erde*, into which the world plunges after *Götterdämmerung*, the Hölderlinian departure of gods; rather a kind of a dark womb which, like the opened pomegranate, grows 'thousands of seeds': the thousand and one life stories taking their singular, hesitant and wandering – *voyou* – paths through the desert (in Latin, pomegranate is *mille granata*, 'thousand seeds').

Derrida's Marrano still life/*nature morte*/*natura pura* should thus be read as the allegory of survival and self-preservation: the Marrano virtue and argument that should not be easily dismissed in the Adornian vein as a miserable predicament of 'life which does not live'.[19] It is quite illuminating to contrast Derrida's empathic feel for the Marrano still life with Adorno's critique of 'mere survival' as life stilled by the defensive strategy of self-deadening, in which the organism reduces its vital signs and begins to mimic the 'motionlessness of surrounding nature.' For Adorno, this archaic strategy reveals the deep paradoxical mechanism of modern enlightenment as the radical disenchantment of nature, due to which the subject mimetically identifies with what terrifies it most: *natura pura* of dead objects scattered in indifferent space and forming an image of the 'absolute alienation'. In modernity, therefore, life does not live because the subject deadens itself in the Pascalian 'petrified terror' of the infinite spaces of *nature morte*, to which he can only feel an 'idiosyncratic aversion':

> The motifs which trigger such idiosyncrasy are those which allude to origin. They recreate moments of biological prehistory: danger signs which made the hair stand on end and the heart stop. In the idiosyncratic aversion individual organs escape the subject's control, autonomously obeying fundamental biological stimuli [. . .] For a few moments they mimic the motionlessness of surrounding nature [. . .] *Space is absolute alienation* [. . .] *Protection as petrified terror is a form of camouflage.* These numb human reactions are archaic patterns of self-preservation: the tribute life pays for its continued existence is adaptation to death.[20]

Derrida would have agreed that such defensive self-deadening and lying *still* is one of the ruses of survival as *Stilleben*, so there is no need to postulate, as Freud did, the hypothesis of a separate death drive. What the father of psychoanalysis took for the distinct activity of Thanatos is, in fact, one of the defence mechanisms of life itself: 'the

---

[19] See the epigraph to Adorno's *Minima Moralia*, deriving from Ferdinand Kürnberger's novel, *Der Amerika-Müde, amerikanisches Kulturbild* (1855): *Das Leben lebt nicht* [Life does not live].

[20] Max Horkheimer and Theodor W. Adorno, *Dialectic of Enlightenment*, trans. Edmund Jephcott (Stanford: Stanfod University Press, 2002), 148; emphasis added.

tribute life pays for its continued existence is adaptation to death'.[21] His own projective identification with *nature morte* – the exteriorized memory of Passover taking the form of the collection of objects scattered in space – indeed suggests a defence of mimicry/mimesis, but he would not brand it as 'aversion' and then reject as a mere remnant of 'biological prehistory' that should be overcome for the sake of a truly 'living life'. Yes, space is absolute alienation, which separates rather than unites, and constitutes the universal condition of the nominalist *natura pura*, deprived of grace and the 'living life', but there is no other, more graceful, nature in store; by claiming that there is no other more living life than *survie*, Derrida consequently rejects all infinitist fantasies that belong to the realm of *l'indemne*, including Adorno's undamaged (*unbeschädigt*) 'living life' (a close avatar of Hegel's *unverletztes Leben*). The Marrano mimesis of *nature morte*, therefore, reveals the truth of the world as a collection of scattered objects – T. S. Eliot's 'heap of broken images' – but not in the plaintive mood of lament over the creaturely 'waste land'. Just as the Dutch *still lives* are not simply vanitative, despite the clichéd reception of the Baroque art, so is the *still life* of nature, 'deadened' by the *khorein*/interspacing, not simply death: it is, *still*, a surviving life – a *life-after-all*. This may not be the 'Triumph of Life' as in the original version of Shelley, to which Derrida devoted his essay on *Borderlines*, but certainly a modest triumph of survival, celebrated as a still life: stilled and lying still, yet – still – a life.

Images can also be – paradoxically – iconoclastic. According to Adorno's *Aesthetic Theory*, the only paintings that obey 'the Old Testament prohibition on images' are precisely still natures which abstain from making a simple copy of the living.[22] This is the reason why I chose Willem Kalf's *Still Life with Ewer, Vessels, and Pomegranate* as the motto-image for the book: the silver tray, the rich oriental vase, and the shape of the glass resembling cups traditionally used for the Passover *kiddush* wine, may indeed suggest a Seder feast held by a post-Marrano Amsterdam Jewry, celebrating the 'invisible' God who is totally absent from the scene. The very centre of this objectual display is occupied by the open pomegranate, exposing 'thousand of seeds', still, but very much alive, and poised on the white silky cloth, which Derrida would have immediately associated with his white silky *tallith*, the 'white night' – warm protective womb-like night – which, in this very painting, does not form a stark contrast with the dark background, but appears rather as its continuation, with its fringes *going gently into that good night*. This is *not* a baroque banal picture of the vanity of vanities, which is the sorry fate of all flesh. On the contrary, Kalf's *pronkstilleven* – named as such to signify the sumptuous luxury of 'earthly delights' – beams with a modest silent affirmation of the finite mode of life which takes place where it was given place and asks for nothing more. Perhaps, its silence is not dissimilar to *die Stille* to which Scholem alludes in his youthful reflections on the Marrano *silenzio*: 'We cannot use our existence as an argument precisely because silence, or more accurately stillness *die*

---

[21] On Derrida's critique of the death drive, see my *Another Finitude*, esp. the chapter 'Derrida's *Torat Hayim*, or the Religion of the Finite Life', 103–44.
[22] See Theodor W. Adorno, *Aesthetic Theory*, trans. Robert Hullot-Kentor (London and New York: Continuum, 1997), 67.

Stille, is the step in which *a life can become an argument*.²³ Seemingly dead, mortified, stilled, the Marrano *nature morte* carries a powerful argument against all traditions of cultured and sublimated *bios*: an argument in favour of life-as-survival, a simple finite *survie* without the grace of immortality. Despite all the plights and dramatic turns of the exodic story which ends up in the uncanny and unhomely desert, Passover is a joyful feast – and so it is for Derrida whose late messianic thinking can indeed be compared to one ceaseless Marrano *Pesach*: a sort of the Messianic Banquet where the righteous, instead of feasting on the meat of Leviathan, consume *la grenade entamée* and thus happily combine the knowledge of life's finitude with faith in its immanent value. Paraphrasing Gebhardt's dictum on the Marrano *fides et ratio*: the Marrano may not have a Catholic faith in immortality or a Jewish knowledge of the Law, but he knows the scathed life of survival and has a faith in this world.

But the Marrano dim memory of the Jewish rite of Passover, here staged as the Dutch (Amsterdam-Marrano?) *nature morte*, suggests also something else – that the God who gives place will be remembered/recalled differently than in the Hegelian 'memory of the Passion': not as the God who fixates his believers on the traumatic image of divine suffering and then demands to be redeemed/repayed by their sacrifice in return, but as the God of Exodus, who truly 'lets his people go' and, absent from the worldly scene, only asks *to be remembered as the God who made them forget*. Recalled dimly, nocturnally as a *trace* which can never be *traced back* to where it came from. Here it is, shown to us openly and plainly, on a silver tray – a 'testimony on display' (TG, 51) – through the collection of objects, which, as Benjamin subtly argued, constitutes a kind of a metonymic external memory as opposed to *Er-innerung*, the internalized 'living' memory based on a metaphor and hence also an image. This form of objectual-yet-iconoclastic memory is thus also a part of the 'retreat of the metaphor' which Derrida sees as the *sine qua non* of a new metaphysics, based no longer on participation and presence, but on separation and absence.

In the very centre of Derrida's Passover collection, there lies an opened pomegranate which shows 'thousand seeds' of stubborn survival – dispersion, multiplication, and dissemination – of Abraham's seed/name. Ontotheology, therefore, would be, by analogy, a survival of God who no longer enjoys full life in the religious 'picture-thinking' (Hegel's *Vorstellungsdenken*) and its mechanical continuation in the ubiquitous tele-evangelism of religions returning onto the world stage, but nonetheless lives on in the shadows of the iconoclastic concept, no longer remembered (*er-innert*) as a living presence and no longer re-collected/re-gathered as the living One:

> Distinct from faith, from prayer or from sacrifice, ontotheology destroys religion, but, *yet another paradox*, it is also what perhaps informs, on the contrary, the theological and ecclesiastical, even religious, *development of faith*. (FK, 53; emphasis added)

---

²³ Scholem, *Lamentations of Youth*, 219.

Once again, Adorno delivers important clues. If we interpret the encrypted life of God seemingly mortified into the idol of ontotheology according to his definition of metaphysics as *die rettende Kritik* (the saving critique), ontotheology will reveal a double aspect of *still life*: destruction of the sacred living presence and its sensuous representation, on the one hand, and a secret rescue of waning faith, preserved in its 'true content' in modern conceptual form, on the other.

> [Metaphysics] is always also an attempt to rescue something which the philosopher's genius feels to be fading and vanishing. There is in fact no metaphysics, or very little, which is not an attempt to save – and to save by means of concepts – what appeared at the time to be threatened precisely by concepts, and was in the process of being disintegrated, or corroded [. . .] Metaphysics is thus, one might say, something fundamentally *modern* – if you do not restrict the concept of modernity to our world but extend it to include Greek history. And it is no accident that metaphysics re-emerges in the High Middle Ages, a period of urban bourgeois culture in which the naive immediacy of Christian faith was already breaking down. (MCP, 19)

It is, therefore, knowledge – a metaphysical iconoclastic science made of concepts – which preserves faith precisely the moment when its fresh naïve imaginary wanes due to the rational critique. Faith, put under the scrutiny of conceptual enlightenment, does not disappear, but wanders into the realm of ontotheology: altered, no longer naïve, yet, in a strange way, all the stronger, ready to disperse, multiply, and disseminate in the form of a universal philosophical abstraction. In the same series of lectures, Adorno states that 'the ancient concepts [of metaphysics] are essentially secularized gods' (MCP, 85), both Greek and Jewish. When translated into the idiom of *Foi et savoir*, this would mean that concepts are gods who might have died for a simple faith, but nonetheless 'resurrect daily' in knowledge (PS, 299). *Ratio*, therefore, is not an enemy of *Fides*: it is its product, made of secularized/whitewashed sacral motives which – like the Derridean still-living inhabitant of the crypt – remain simultaneously dead (killed by rational critique) and alive (preserved in concepts). The concepts are thus nothing but *white metaphors* secretly carrying inside the spectre of once fully alive religious beliefs: *la mythologie blanche*. Just like Marranos who, despite all the forgetting, still carry the latent spark of 'potential Judaism', the concepts are *meta-phoros* – the 'far-fetchers' which carry gods into the realm of knowledge – as well as *crypto-phoros* – the crypts which carry faith in an anabiotic form of a mummified seed, seemingly deadened, but in fact ready to come alive again in the right time. Derrida's metaphysical thinking would be precisely such *kairos* for those whitewashed gods, and particularly for the one called *Ein-Sof*, who, born in the lore of the Kabbalistic faith, wandered into the ontotheological realm of German Idealism, most of all Hegel.

The word 'pomegranate' awakes 'thousand seeds' of possible associations, but there is one particularly telling among them. Undoubtedly, the title of the second part – *et granades* – alludes to Moses Cordovero's *Pardes Rimonim* (*Orchard of Pomegranates*), the fundamental Kabbalistic text, composed in 1648 and published for the first time in Cracow in 1691: it comprises thirty-two sections in which Cordovero comments on *Zohar*, the first system of Kabbalah created by Moses de Leon. The reason why Cordovero chose number 32 is that, according to *Sefer Yetsirah* (the mystical protoplast of the medieval Kabbalah), it represents thirty-two 'wonderful ways of wisdom' which created the whole cosmos on the basis of twenty-two letters of the Hebrew alphabet and ten *sephirot* that constitute the Tree of Life (*Ets hayim*). The reason why the second part of *Faith and Knowledge* is made of fifteen sections also belongs to the realm of symbolic numerology and sends a secret message which was often used by the Iberian *conversos*, well versed in the Spanish Kabbalah, to communicate their forbidden knowledge. Number 15 symbolizes the time of rest, which comes after the violent messianic period of redemption, represented by number 14: hence the 15th of Nisan is celebrated every year as the Feast of Passover, commemorating delivery from Egypt. Made of ten (the letter *yod* symbolizes the Hand of God) and five (the letter *heh* symbolizes the saving power of life), fifteen refers to the cosmic Sabbath: the universal peace of all creatures great and small, returned by *tikkun* to their gentle form of life in the Edenic orchard. It is, therefore, no accident that the Marrano 'memory of Passover' – of Exodus, liberation, and messianic hope – appears in the 14th section of the second part, followed by the last, 15th section, which once again evokes *Khôra* as the 'unique place of the nameless One' (FK, 100). It is the place of ashes and cinders, crypts and orchards: the originary 'forest of the night', *Pardes Khôra*, the Promised Land, and the Garden of Earthly Delights, where life is finally granted a 'Great Pardon' and given a chance to show what it can do: 'we have just enough breath left to ask for pardon, for the Great Pardon, in the languages of the PaRDeS' (C, 243).[24] Nothing can ever eliminate the risk and hazard inscribed into life's essential 'double bind' – its 'painful glory, or glorious pain'.[25]

One can never sufficiently stress this difference: Derrida's vision of *Pardes Khôra* to come and its Marrano revised 'religion of flowers'[26] will always form the very opposite of the triumphant messianic Day of the Lord or 'the day of the phallus' (FK, 83) and its unscathed form of vitality. Derrida does not want to resurrect his godhead (deliberately low key) in its phallic *imago* of the official religions: *It is to remain a colourless white spectre, never again to raise as an image of vital infinite power (or its equally scandalous loss, as in the kenotic passage from God the Father to the Son).*

---

[24] In Derrida's imagination, the eternal *Gan Eden/ Pardes/* orchard, in which everything gets decided, most of all the law of singularity, that allows beings to take place, actually has an address: '13, rue d' Aurelle-de-Paladines, El-Biar, it's still the orchard, the intact PaRDeS, the seamless present which continues you, the imperturbable phenomenon that you will never see age, you no longer grow older, although everything is decided in this garden, and the law...' (C, 247–8). Written as 'PaRDeS', the term alludes also to the three levels of the rabbinic exegesis, the highest of which is *Sod*, the mystery/secret of creation.

[25] 'And yet, that is the painful glory, or glorious pain, of our existence as fallen angels. Call it *yetziat*, 'get thee out', Abraham from Ur, Moses from Egypt, or Jacob into Israel, Yahweh's Promised Land': Harold Bloom, *Fallen Angels* (New Haven: Yale University Press, 2007), 71.

[26] 'Relative to the desert *Gottheit* of negative theology, this desert is the desert in the desert, an extreme of abstraction, where there grows the desert flower of a religion which is "older" than any known religion': Caputo, *The Prayers and Tears*, 155.

The Marrano process of the iconoclastic ontotheologization, therefore, should never be reversed: not only because it preserves faith, but also because it purifies it of its iconophilia and the cult of the unscathed life. While 'naïve' religions succumb to the tendency towards full visibility, which wants to *de-monstrate* the phallic presence of their gods/*deiwos* (think of the *monstrantia*/monstrance: the glorious presentation of the no longer so vulnerable Lamb in the oblate as the climaxing moment of the Catholic mass) – ontotheology makes them invisible within its abstract conceptual folds. It thus *rescues* (*rettet*) faith from falling away from its iconoclastic vocation.[27]

The decision *not* to reverse ontotheology's move away from the 'force of images' marks an important change in Derrida's attitude towards metaphysics as *mythologie blanche*. In his earlier essay from 1971, he sides with Nietzsche and his critique of metaphysical concepts as bland *flatus voci* which could regain their power only if they returned to lively figures and colours of the real world; till then, they remain merely 'worn-out metaphors which have become powerless to affect the senses, coins which have their obverse (*Bild*) *effaced* and now are no longer of account as coins but merely as metal'.[28] For Nietzsche, therefore, the effacement of the image amounts to the loss of validity: no longer a valid currency, now only a piece of metal, the metaphysical concept is also no longer a valid concept, because ultimately it signifies nothing. So, if those concepts are to be given back life, they must, at least partly, recover 'that fabulous scene which brought them into being':

> What is white mythology? It is metaphysics which has effaced in itself that fabulous scene which brought it into being, and which yet remains, active

---

[27] Already Adorno disagrees with Heidegger on the issue of ontotheology, but Derrida goes in his polemic with the author of the concept even further. In 'The Question Concerning Technology', Heidegger talks about the 'danger' of the modern time of *Ge-stell* and the ensuing degradation of the idea of God: 'Thus where everything that presences exhibits itself in the light of a cause-effect coherence, even God can, for representational thinking, lose all that is exalted and holy, the mysteriousness of his distance. In the light of causality, God can sink to the level of a cause, of *causa efficiens*. He then becomes, even in theology, the god of the philosophers, namely, of those who define the unconcealed and the concealed in terms of the causality of making, without ever considering the essential origin of this causality': Martin Heidegger, *The Question Concerning Technology*, 26. For Derrida, however, this very 'danger' also conceals 'salvation' – the Hölderlinian *Rettung* (ibid., 28), carried withing the crypt of the ontotheological abstraction which, for him, is never simply a distortion. Derrida's own comment on Heidegger in 'Christianity and Secularization' echoes the Marrano analogy from *Faith and Knowledge*, by evoking the practice of dissimulation: 'Heidegger deconstructs ontotheology because fundamentally, he says, in ontotheology (and in whatever within ontotheology has infected religion, *whatever has dissimulated religion* by making God a cause or a foundation) there is *no prayer or sacrifice* [. . .] Therefore, Heidegger tries despite everything to awaken, beyond ontotheology, an experience of sacrality of the God who comes, which is not simply the naive belief *Glaube* that he critiques all the time' (CS, 146–7; emphasis added). In the light of what we have said so far, Derrida would not be so eager to restore sacrifice – the gift of blood, which either nourishes the infinite vitality of all 'visible' gods or allows to 'resurrect daily' Christ from his tomb – but he clearly would like to recover a possibility of prayer. Yet, and this is crucial here, *not* on the grave on onthotheology: the ontotheological determinate abstraction, which is a place-giving God-in-retreat, can also be an object of the new 'experience of sacrality'.

[28] Friedrich Nietzsche, 'On Truth and Falsity in their Ultramoral Sense', trans. M. A. Mügge, in *The Works of Friedrich Nietzsche*, vol. 2 (Edinburgh: T.N. Foulis, 1911), 180.

and stirring, inscribed in white ink, an invisible drawing covered over in the palimpsest. (WM, 11)

In *Faith and Knowledge*, Derrida's position will be more nuanced: 'the wear and tear of the symbolic' (WM, 10), which effaces fabulous images from philosophical concepts is now affirmed and juxtaposed with the Marrano 'forgetting without forgetting'. The rule which Derrida applies to the logic of the self-effacing trace of the self-effacing God – 'one can only recall it to oneself in forgetting it [on ne peut se la rappeler qu'en l'oubliant]' (SQ, 49) – is now extrapolated on the currency of ontotheological knowledge which preserves faith in its vestigal form, and also protects it from returning to the devious 'force of images'. Ontotheology, playing with words-coins which erased their iconic origin, is no longer seen as the Nietzschean toothless army of self-effaced metaphors, which can be brought to life solely with the retrieval of their *Einbildungskraft* (imaginative power), but as a vehicle of radical iconoclasm which effectuates *le retrait de la métaphore* of which we spoke at the beginning of this chapter: 'the retreat of the metaphor' as an iconophilic means of imagining gods-*deiwos* in their day, light, and eternal glory. Interestingly, Derrida's reluctance towards these divine 'light-beings' manifests itself already in the earlier essay:

> What is metaphysics? A white mythology which assembles and reflects Western culture: the white man takes his own mythology (that is, Indo-European mythology), his *logos* – that is, the *mythos* of his idiom, for the universal form of that which it is still his inescapable desire to call Reason. (WM, 11)

Yet, the rift between his positions between the 1970s and the 1990s consists in choosing two very different strategies of dealing with the Western seemingly rational 'whitewashing' of the Indo-European tribal myths. While in *Mythologie blanche*, Derrida stakes on the pure deconstructive critique which demonstrates deception hidden behind Western erasure of *mythos* – in *Faith and Knowledge*, he does that, but also adds an alternative: a different, non-Indo-European *myth*, which does not associate its godhead with the 'the day of the phallus', but keeps it in the nocturnal desert as the Lurianic, invisible, and nonrepresentable, God-in-*tsimtsum*. The early diagnosis, therefore, stating that 'metaphysics has effaced in itself that fabulous scene which brought it into being, and which yet remains, active and stirring, inscribed in white ink' (WM, 11) still holds, yet now with a more affirmative intention: ontotheology could not but efface the foundational *fable* of the self-effacing God, which nonetheless remains valid as the very beginning of the story, inscribed there in white invisible ink. *Le retrait de la métaphore* also means that while ontotheological concepts are indeed 'far-fetchers', this transport cannot be reversed: they should rather be considered as *catachreses* – the tropes which can never turn back and trace their figurative origin. They are neither the Nietzschean faded images that can still be reinvigorated, nor the Heideggerian metaphors which must be forced to *turn about* and thus recover the lost sense of piety. They are tropes of no return, which can only turn forward, to the future of the *Khôra-to-come (Khôra ha-ba)*.

But ontotheology is not the only Marrano – secular, worldly, knowledgeable – *afterlife of faith*. In *The Literature in Secret*, Derrida's postscript to the *Gift of Death*, this Marrano role of letting faith survive in the irreligious conditions of modernity is assigned to literature as the 'religious reminder'. Just as ontotheology 'forgets without forgetting' about the 'God of myth', so does literature 'betray without betraying' its religious inheritance: it simultaneously avows and denies the sacred filiation:

> be it understood that literature surely inherits from a holy history within which the Abrahamic moment remains the essential secret (and who would deny that literature remains a religious remainder, a link to and relay for what is sacrosanct in a society without God?), while at the same time denying that history, appurtenance, and heritage. It denies that filiation. It betrays it in the double sense of the word: it is unfaithful to it, breaking with it at the very moment when it reveals its 'truth' and uncovers its secret. Namely that of its own filiation: impossible possibility [...] *Literature can but ask forgiveness for this double betrayal.* There is no literature that does not, from its very first word, ask for forgiveness. *In the beginning was forgiveness. For nothing. For meaning (to say) nothing.* (GD, 157; emphasis added)[29]

While ontotheology deprives the religious experience of the 'fear and trembling', by bleaching the terrifying image of the living God into a still life of a concept, literature reveals the secret of the religious message, by seemingly betraying it: in the beginning was not the 'fear of the Lord', but forgiveness. Just as the Marranos, who uncover the messianic 'choice of life' in their betrayal of the tradition as *tradendum*, the doctrinal 'chain of inheritance' (*shalshelet ha-kabbalah*) – so does literature unearth the mystery of the cosmic pardon, still a glowing cinder among the ashes of betrayed normative religions. The *literary secularization*, therefore, similarly to the ontotheological one – both following the path of the 'Spanish Marranos' – simultaneously betrays religion and secures its religious filiation: it betrays, betrays again, betrays better.[30]

---

[29] See also Derrida's self-commentary in *Paper Machine*: 'Among all the reasons for asking forgiveness from the point one starts writing or even speaking [...] there is also this one: the quasi-sacralization of literature appeared at a point in time when an apparent desacralization of biblical texts had begun. Thus literature, as a faithful unfaithful heir, as a perjured heir, asks for forgiveness because it betrays. It betrays its truth' (PM, 162–3).

[30] Again, it is Michael Naas who seems particularly attentive to Derrida's gnomic, cryptic and simultaneously hyper-condensed Marrano imagery which deliberately avoids full articulation. While commenting on the pomegranate 'still life', he states that 'faith would be a Marrano that eludes this putative self-presence (like a crypt within ontotheology) and opens this seemingly indivisible identity (like a cut pomegranate) [...] Faith would thus be encrypted like a Marrano within religion, given a chance to circulate within a religion only on the condition of hiding or being concealed within it [...] Faith would be encrypted in ontotheology in this way, sublimated, one might say, *forced underground, forced to go by other names or go about in other guises,* able to reveal its true identity only to other members of the same secret community [...] But the Marrano Derrida is evoking here would be a Marrano even to this secret community, a *Marrano of Marranos*, then, a secret even for or to those in on the secret, not unlike the desert within the desert that is *Khôra*. It is in this sense that we must understand why Derrida refers to himself not only as "a sort of Marrano of French Catholic culture" but, in an untranslatable French phrase, as *le dernier des juifs*, that is, as

Pardes Khôra: The garden of earthly delights

In Greek mythology, the pomegranate is a 'bleeding fruit' which was planted by the Furies on the grave of the Theban king, Eteocles: when the pomegranate opens, it exposes a red flesh resembling a wound. Just as the opened/cut pomegranate, which became 'stilled' and 'mortified' as an element of the ontotheological *nature morte*, the once-living God can no longer be the symbol of unscathed vitality, growing an invincible Tree of Life Eternal. Broken internally, self-barred, self-negated, godhead is deeply wounded: cut through, exposing its scathedeness, wound, *blessure*, circumcision. The kenomatic desert source is self-wounded, self-restrained, and self-circumcised: even more *kenotic* than the Christian God, even more *deipassionistic* than in Hegel's description of the modern 'death of God' religion, and even more universally *messianic* than all most radical Jewish, Muslim and Christian messianisms taken all together.

On the one hand, therefore, the second source of religion, protected by ontotheology – *Khôra* – is a wound itself, *l'epreuve*, an ordeal, constant slipping out of being: the open, still-living flesh of the pomegranate. Yet, on the other, it is also still-growing, still-breading the seeds of what is yet to come. The pomegranate is here the same kind of the ambivalent revolving emblem as the ashes which, seemingly dead, can *still* come to life as glowing cinders. Just as the 'Spanish Marranos' exited all forms of institutionalized religions, becoming neither Jewish nor Christian, so does *Khôra* remain outside, *abstracted* from all languages of the sacred:

> *It* will never have entered religion and will never permit itself to be sacralized, sanctified, humanized, theologized, cultivated, historicized. Radically heterogenous to the safe and sound, to the holy and the sacred, it never admits of any *indemnification*. (FK, 58; emphasis added)

And just as Marranos are oblivious and unsure of their past and identity, impure and contaminated – universally despised, yet precisely because of that masters of survival – so is *Khôra*: treated by Plato as metaphysically inferior, reduced by Abrahamic monotheisms to *tohu va-vohu*, *Khôra* constitutes their secret messianic energy without which they turn stale, dead, cultic, too indemnified. It signifies another desert: not the one of a raging jealousy of the One who cannot stand any rivalry, but the one of an original contamination, heterogeneity, always already 'more-than-one'. The pomegranates, therefore, as Michael Naas rightly senses, are here also *grenades*: thrown into the midst of the discussion on religion (which originally took place during the seminar on Capri) in order to explode and 'disperse' the phantasms of the Unscathed One as the daydream of all religions – or rather a nightmare from which Derrida wants to awake – and yet 'multiply' the messianic message, hidden in their secret

---

the "last of the Jews," "the least of the Jews," but also "the most Jewish of Jews," the most because the least, the least became the most, the first because the last, and so on' (MM, 232–3; emphasis added).

core, thanks to the a-theologized idiom of ontotheology.³¹ Thus, if Judaism follows the One as the 'jealous God' who turns the desert into his kingdom (pure absolute Life), and if Christianity follows the One as the 'dead God', who, in the gesture of inverse sovereignty, indebts his believers with the infinite *Schuld* (pure absolute Death) – Marranism can be seen as penetrating deeper beneath those religious fixed identities into the realm of *plus d'Un* as *Pardes Khôra*, where 'scattered existence' tolls with the *survie* of 'unprejudiced becoming', yet, at the same time, is free from any form of sovereign power.

As we have seen, this move was fully affirmed by Jacob Frank who, himself 'a sort of a *marrane* of Polish Catholic culture', wanted to mobilize other *conversos* to become messianic agents of the Hidden *Einsoph*, a truly generous deity which only gives place and 'does not call any place divine', that is, a place that would *belong* exclusively to It as a sacrosanct *illus locus* or a temple.³² The echoes of this unique Marrano 'religion without religion', where space is given freely without any restrictions, can be clearly heard in Derrida's summary of his own re-reading of Plato's *Timaeus*:

> A certain reinterpretation of Plato's *Timaeus* had named *Khôra* (which means locality in general, spacing, interval) another place without age, another 'taking-place,' the irreplaceable place or placement of a 'desert in the desert,' a spacing from 'before' the world, the cosmos, or the globe, from 'before' any chronophenomenology, any revelation, any 'as such' and any 'as if,' any anthro-potheological dogmatism or historicity. But *what would allow these to take place*, without, however, providing any ground or foundation, would be precisely *Khôra*. *Khôra* would *make or give place*; it would *give rise – without ever giving anything* – to what is called the coming of the event. *Khôra* receives rather than gives. Plato in fact presents it as a 'receptacle.' Even if it comes 'before everything,' it does not exist for itself. Without belonging to that to which it gives way or for which it makes place [*fait place*], without being a part [*faire partie*] of it, without being of it, and without being something else or someone other, *giving nothing other, it would give rise or allow to take place. Khôra*:

---

³¹ In French, the title of the section is '. . . *et grenades*': a phrase which involves an ambivalence lost in the English translation, but was well spotted by Michael Naas who in *Derrida From Now On* writes: 'While the latter context [which I have just analysed - A.B.-R.] justifies the translation of grenades by "pomegranates," its context here, in the midst of a text on religion and science, faith and violence, is not so determined as to exclude the other meaning of grenades in French, namely, "grenades." Indeed, Derrida appears to have lobbed this word into the middle of the fifty-two sections of *Faith and Knowledge* in order to gather or, rather, disperse many of the themes of the phantasm we have been following throughout this essay, in order to evoke all the tensions between, precisely, faith and knowledge, nature and culture, the pomegranate of religion and the grenade of techno-science, a symbol of female fertility, of life-giving seed, on the one hand, and an image of masculine violence, of shrapnel-casting death, on the other, the blood-red pomegranate of Persephone, on the one hand, and the army-green hand-held machine of technoscience, on the other': Michael Naas, *Derrida From Now On* (New York: Fordham University Press, 2008), 205. Indeed, the intimate link between pomegranates and grenades constitutes the gist of Derrida's critique of religion: whenever the kenomatic source comes into presence as revealed and is maintained as a revelation by the religious media machine, the innocent fruit hardens into a potential weapon.

³² Frank, *Słowa Pańskie*, 381.

before the 'world,' before creation, before the gift and being, *Khôra* that *there is* perhaps 'before' any 'there is' as *es gibt*... Not foreign to the *salut* as the greeting or salutation of the other, not foreign to the *adieu* ('come' or 'go' in peace), not foreign to justice, but nonetheless heterogeneous and rebellious, irreducible, to law, to power, and to *the economy of redemption*. (R, xiv–xv; emphasis added)

By not lending itself to the religious practice of indemnification, *Khôra* may indeed be 'radically heterogenous to the safe and sound' (FK, 58), which constitutes religion per se – the visible cult of the visible Name – but it is 'not foreign' to messianicity which concerns itself with otherness and justice and attempts to break the vicious circle of redemption with its debit/credit economy of debt and repayment. But, despite the fact that it is called by Derrida a 'second source', it is in fact more original: before any *there is*/*es gibt*; before any coming into presence, being, and life – the pleromatic God-with-the-Name included – *Khôra* already 'is' and patiently *withdraws* from everything that comes into being. Just as *Ein-Sof* in Frank's vision, It/*Khôra* gives rise and allows to take place. Nothing more, nothing less: perfect *Seinlassen*.

What Derrida is thus aiming at is neither dualism nor a synthesis of the two sources, but their constant 'impure' *oscillation* (FK, 59) or *Schweben* – the favourite movement of German Idealism, from Kant to Hegel, which already Luther ascribed to *ruah Elohim*, the Spirit of God hovering over but also reflecting, mirroring, and thus absorbing the image of the watery abysses below. This is not a God who establishes his invincible identity in the gesture of subduing the darkness of *tohu va-vohu*, but rather a God who gives up on the triumphant integrity of the unscathed; cuts/opens himself, like the pomegranate, and exposes to the outmost vulnerability, accident, and chance; *affirms the wound* of the precarious finite life. A Marrano God – unstable and internally dispersed, multiplied: *plus d'Un*, never the One-with-the-Name – who only pretends to be the highest and most perfect *primum ens* of the globalatinized philosophical ontotheology, firmly squatted in the centre of the Kingdom of Being, but in its secret depths is the very opposite: the wound and lack, self-emptying *kenoma*, yet also always in the state of revealing and manifesting itself, which soon or later must inevitably betray the dark source.

In Scholem's account, this tension within the Godhead constitutes the highest *sod*, mystery and secret: on the one hand, the divine is *das Erscheinende*, always 'in the process of revelation', that is, coming into visibility, showing itself; on the other hand, however, 'authentic tradition remains hidden', withdrawing from sight.[33] Derrida takes over this aporia and attempts to solve it through the *Marrano dialectics*. The 'reflecting faith' (FK, 59), which he opposes to the Kantian/Hegelian version, must keep close to the clandestine level of revealability, not contenting itself with any determinate form of revelation. For, even the humblest and most loving God, when fully *revealed* in the articulated set of beliefs, tends to lose the kenomatic aspect of the retreat and assumes the pleromatic aspect of visibility and power. The more he comes into light, the more

---

[33] Scholem, "Zehn Unhistorische Sätze," 264.

he gains presence, the more he fleshes himself out – the more he falls under the rules of 'ontologism', in which all phenomena want to steal the show: be the only thing of light, presence, being, and vitality, and then 'jealously' guard it only for itself. Very much in and from this world, the revealed God cannot but repress the otherworldly source in retreat. Thus, to maintain the abstraction of messianicity means to be faithful to the 'night events' of the hidden and hiding source – and avoid full identification with any overt theology, or, more generally, with any light: be it of the revelation/illumination or of the Enlightenment, either the light of the revealed Faith or the light of the enlightened Knowledge. To be faithful to this original night is, therefore, to be nothing else but a Marrano: a forgetful believer of the self-effacing God in denial. Just as *Khôra* does not enter any explicit theological discourse, so does Marrano stand apart from any *revealed* religion.[34] But it is precisely this separation that brings him closer to the ever-receding non-revealable realm of all revealability as the one properly belonging to a new 'reflecting faith':

> Respect for this singular indecision/oscillation or for this hyperbolic outbidding between two originarities, the order of the 'revealed' and the order of the 'revealable,' is this not at once the chance of every responsible decision and of another 'reflecting faith,' of a new 'tolerance'? (FK, 59)

If so, then the most suitable bearer of such tolerance would indeed be the Marrano as the universal figure of dispersion and contamination, the very opposite of the identitarian purity: the master of survival, the *mischling* being at home nowhere and everywhere, and the new citizen of the globalatinized empire, carrying his 'secret' difference within himself.

As we have seen, Derrida associates the Marrano mode of *survie* with a 'still life': an anabiotic *nature morte*. Neither simply alive nor simply dead, posed in the strange suspension between natural vitality and *arrêt de mort*, it is life *denaturalized* – taken out of nature and its vitalistic sacred, yet, at the same time, arrested in what Lacan calls the 'inversion of the desire': a process in which libido turns away from life and the 'sheeplike conglomerations of the Eros', and aims at the identification with the other, more powerful energy, the death drive.[35] The Marrano still life lies low and still as a 'horizontal' survival, trying to survive the *gigantomachy* between Life and Death, Eros and Thanatos.

This third position in between the two great powers – the one of *survie* represented by the Marrano figure – is precisely the stumbling block which Derrida was looking for in his attempt to jam the machine of religious sublimation as replacing the one unscathed of the infinite Life with another unscathed of the invulnerable Death. This suspension

---

[34] See Naas commenting on the ontologistic rule of presence: 'The sacred or the holy is related not just to sovereign power but to an exuberant, fecund force capable of bringing to life in a spontaneous and automatic way. The phallus effect or the fecund belly rises up of its own accord, self-seeding and self-bearing – like an Immaculate Conception': *Derrida from Now On*, 204. This is why every *revealed* religion, precisely because of the moment of coming-into-light, must necessarily result in the repression of the kenomatic source.

[35] Jacques Lacan, *Ecrits: A Selection*, trans. Alan Sheridan (London: Routledge, 1989), 104–5.

can also be described by the Hegelian term, *die Zerrissenheit* (*arrachement*), which Derrida reuses, but with a changed dispositif. While for Hegel, it served as a critique of Judaism, allegedly accountable for the violent break with nature, hatred for life, and the sin of deracination (Nietzsche and Heidegger merely repeat after young Hegel), for Derrida it denotes a right move – but only provided it does not end up in the 'counter-fetishism' of the thanatic sublimation that creates the 'icy abstraction' of the *more-than-life* deadened Absolute. 'Violent sundering', radical separation, *coupure, catachresis* – yes, but simultaneously *arrested*, caught in the cadre of the 'still life', *nature morte*, content with its aporeticity, not trying to resolve it in the symmetrical sanctification of death. Thus, in *Faith and Knowledge*, right after the section devoted to the 'Jewish question' and the 'Jewish survival', Derrida poises his Marrano ontotheology between the two risky moments of the process of separation which must maintain itself between the two gods – Eros and Thanatos – and represent the profane interests of life finite:

> 1. Violent sundering, to be sure, from the radicality of roots (*Entwürzelung*, Heidegger would say. . .) and from all forms of originary *physis*, from all the supposed resources of a force held to be authentically generative, sacred, unscathed, 'safe and sound' (*heilig*): ethnic identity, descent, family, nation, blood and soil, proper name, proper idiom, proper culture and memory. 2. But also, more than ever, the counter-fetishism of the same *desire inverted*. (FK, 91; emphasis added)

The first moment alludes to the caricature version of Judaism widely sported by 'a certain Christianity' (including Hegel and Heidegger) – the blind and mechanical antithesis towards all living *physis* as the unscathed source of authentic vitality – which Derrida spitefully endorses and intensifies, to the extent of denying, in the Marrano manner, the properly 'separated' ones even the bloodline, proper name, and proper memory. As he himself summarizes young Hegel's view on the Jews: 'Their ownness, their property remains foreign to them, their secret secret: separate, cut, infinitely distant, terrifying' (G, 50). In *Resistances to Psychoanalysis*, 'violent sundering', characteristic of the children of Abraham, appears under the name of *lysis without measure* which eludes repression and forces 'radical forgetting'. While arguing against Lacanian – or, more originally, Hegelian – dogma of the 'return to the Father', Derrida opts for a form of the catachrestic/anacoluthic dissemination which breaks all circularity and

> not only does not come back to the father [. . .] but is exposed to a radical forgetting that no longer belongs to the topic or the economy of repression, destined as it is to chance and to ashes, namely, to a trace without trace: inviolable secret, without depth, without place, without name, without destination, hyperbolytic, excessive destruction, and *lysis without measure, without measure and without return, lysis without anagogy.* (RP, 33; emphasis added)

Nameless energy set on its destinerrance glows in the cinders of the secret, which spell either chance or ashes (as in Shakespeare's 'ashes of my chance'). The secret is without depth, because it is nothing but *absolute separation*: is a trace that cannot be traced back analogically to its origins. All it can do is press forward into futurity: it cannot fixate itself on the past to be remembered and commemorated, but solely the future which can begin to reveal itself only when the past is submitted to 'radical forgetting' and thus no longer overshadows what is yet to come (*ha-ba*). The truly 'sundered', 'separated', and because of that nameless one would thus be the Marrano as the uncanny truth of the Jewish condition: ultimately and decisively cut from *any* form of the original and unscathed gods which populate all past-oriented religions, based on commemorative cults.

> To that which lives without having a name, we will give an added name: Marrano, for example. Playing with the relative arbitrariness of every nomination, we determine this added name [*surnom*], which a name always is, in memory of and according to the figure of the Marrano (of the crypto-judaic, and of the crypto-X in general). (A, 77)

But this is also why only the nameless Marrano can be the figure of the *utterly other*, the faith in whom counteracts the cultic religions of the self-same unscathed: 'The absolute *arrivant* thus has no name and no identity. The imminence of his or her or its coming demands a hospitality without reserve, the opening of the Same to an unassimilable difference' (CP-M, 235).

The crypts, pomegranates, and Eliahu

In *Faith and Knowledge*, all religions of the Greco-Judeo-Christian alliance oscillate between 'swollen' *images* of victorious phallic indemnity, which belong to revealed religions, made *veroffenbart*, manifest, visible, and de/monstrable – and 'self-effacing' *traces* of ultimate vulnerability, left by the kenomatic source in retreat, nocturnal, and resisting visibility. The deconstructive reading, which Derrida undertakes, merely enhances this inner *Schweben* and gives voice to its 'weaker' pole, hidden behind the glorious *insignia* of divine triumph and power. Just as *Khôra* is 'demnity' itself, the very opposite of the whole and sound representations of pleromatic *deiwos*/deities; and just as Jesus, laid down in the crypt and not to be dragged out of it again, is the epitome of the self-deconstructed Christianity, so is also Jacob, Derrida's name bearer, the Hebrew patron of survival as a way of life absolutely contrary to the naturalistic phallic image of vital health.[36] With Jacob's history of deceit, betrayal and struggle with God, which left him with a limp, he is the Derridean human hero personifying

---

[36] Derrida, being named Jacques, also identifies with the biblical Jacob, the younger son who was illicitly blessed with election, but managed to confirm it by his uncanny survival skills: 'I am interested by, interested in the selection or election of me, let us say Jacob, only by curiosity, not of me, for me or by me, but, as ought to go without saying, by the very thing, the other, then, which would have been chosen, blessed, or cursed me, chosen at birth, the moment when the youngest son that I am did not come after the eldest, Rene Abraham, but the second, Paul Moise, dead I know not how or from what a few months before I was conceived, *I who was thus like the twin brother of a*

the impure *scathed life*: life which knows mutilation, brokenness, brush-with-death, damage, *Verletzung*, 'stillness', and the Marrano wandering through the deserts of exile; a life *tsimtsem*, wounded and diminished, yet stubbornly living/limping on. Unlike the Hegelian Jacob, who feels eternally guilty for having wronged his God, the Derridean Jacob proves that 'it is not a sin to limp': he did not kill his God, it is rather God who withdrew from the stage, by granting Jacob the gift of finite life.[37]

But there is yet another name inscribed into this text: Derrida's secret Jewish name, Elie, the close homophone of *élu*, 'the chosen one', and, in Hebrew, Eliahu, the numerical value of which is fifty-two – the total number of the paragraphs of *Faith and Knowledge*. This is Derrida's secret signature that he, following Francis Ponge's practice of cryptograms, already used once in *Envoys*, his love letters which he punctured with fifty-two blank spaces.[38] The reiteration of the secret cryptonym in *Faith and Knowledge* cannot be accidental (we already saw how Derrida uses numerology to convey his 'secret knowledge'): just as his scattered love letters sent in form of postcards, this text is equally personal. It is an invocation to the Marrano God who always fades into the blanks among other gods of visibility (*contre-jour*); the God of the Marrano 'religion without religion' which binds only through unbinding, letting-go, dispersion, and free dissemination. Is this Marrano faith the same as Derrida's secret religiosity to which he alludes in *Circumfession*, when he, after two decades of successful career, admits 'to be bound better and better to' certain religious motifs, but also complains of being 'read less and less well over almost twenty years, like *my* religion about which nobody understands anything' (C, 154; emphasis added)?[39] Each paragraph is an envoy,

---

dead one' (C, 276–7; emphasis added). On many subtleties of Derrida's identification with Jacob see: Bruce Rosenstock, "Derrida's Advent," *Contemporary French Civilization* 30, no. 1 (2006).

[37] When, at the end of *Beyond the Pleasure Principle*, Freud quotes his favorite line from Friedrich Rückert's *Maqams of Al-Hariri* – *Die Schrift sagt, es ist keine Sünde zu hinken!* – he also secretly sides with Jacob and his struggle for the postponement of death which the Hebrew hero agrees to accept, but only later and only on his own terms. On the significance of this hidden 'Marrano-like' hint in Freud, see my *The Saving Lie*, esp. the section 'The Jacob's Way', 151–7. The whole verse goes as follows: 'What we cannot reach flying we must reach limping/It is better to limp than to sink/The Book tells us it is no sin to limp.'

[38] In her contribution to *Other Testaments*, "Secrets and Sacrifices of Scission," Inge-Birgitte Siegumfeldt makes a very convincing discovery about the fifty-two blank spaces with which Derrida interlaces his *Envois* in the *Post Card* as reflecting the numerological value of the Hebrew variant of Elie – Eliahu – being Derrida's secret Jewish name and, at the same time, the name of the guardian of circumcision. 'The associations at once carried and concealed' are thus fitting Derrida's later Marrano self-declaration: '[Deconstruction], Jewish in derivation, is mobilized in the service of all disaffiliation – including dissociation from Judaism in any of its fixed doctrinal forms. It signals the paradox of an origin and an identity that are neither origin nor identity: the notion of the Jew as never 'himself' but cut adrift as the "wandering Jew," captured and undone in dispersion, diaspora. The name is therefore not the site of an embodiment, but (like the name of the Jewish God) points to an identity that is always elsewhere, beyond the reach of definition' (OT, 288).

[39] In 'Christianity and Secularization', a small *addendum* to *Faith and Knowledge*, Derrida states 'that the word *Messiah, messianicity*, I am ready to abandon it at any time, *as soon I will have been understood*' (CS, 143; emphasis added). In the Marrano fashion, therefore, Derrida wants to squeeze the ultimate juice from the Judaic tradition and then abandon it on his way towards a new religion which, perhaps, 'will have no further need of these words' (CS, 148) and will ony focus on the name of *Khôra* as inspiring 'faith [that] is irreducible to every other' (ON, 98). So far, however, because nobody understands him, he must use old notions as 'pedagogical tools' (CS, 143).

a message-prayer sent like a love letter in the bottle: to the God who withdrew, but also to the readers with a plea to read Derrida better and not to dismiss his Marrano revelation as an idiosyncratic whim of no philosophical consequences.

In the next chapter, we shall have a closer look at the 'murky shop' of Derrida's psychotheology from which there emerges *his own private Judaism*: simultaneously singular and universal, like the Marrano he is. We will see how he deals with this self-diagnosis which closely resembles the one uttered by Franz Rosenzweig, soon after his decision *not* to convert to Christianity: 'my life has fallen under the rule of a "dark drive" which I'm aware that I merely name by calling it *my Judaism*'.[40] The question will be: is it, in the case of Derrida, more *my* than *Judaism*, or, perhaps both, *my* and *Judaism* forming a new religious quality? Rosenzweig, himself almost a *converso*, might have sensed that *my Judaism* is a quite dramatic formula which paves the way towards a sort of *marranismo*: a private, secretive, singularly bent '*my* religion'.

---

[40] Franz Rosenzweig, in letter to Friedrich Meinecke, August 30, 1920, in *Briefe und Tagebücher: Band 2*, 680: 'Das Wesentliche ist doch, dass mir die Wissenschaft überhaupt nicht mehr die zentrale Bedeutung besitzt und dass mein Leben seither bestimmt ist von dem "dunklen Drang," dem ich mit dem Namen "mein Judentum," schliesslich eben auch nur einen Namen zu geben, mir freilich bewusst bin.'

4

Two serious Marranos

Derrida and Cixous (with constant reference to Poldy Bloom)

Would anyone care to learn something about the way in which ideas are manufactured? Does anyone have the nerve? [. . .] Well then, go ahead! There's a chink through which you can peek into this murky shop. But wait just a moment, Mr. Foolhardy; your eyes must grow accustomed to the fickle light [. . .] All right, tell me what's going on in there, audacious fellow; now I am the one who is listening [. . .] And the imagined interlocutor, who dared to boldly go where no one has gone before, answers: 'All the sounds are sugary and soft. No doubt you were right; they are transmuting weakness into merit.'

Nietzsche, *The Genealogy of Morality*, 180, emphasis added.

'Here I note what he has confided to us by way of comic Judaism', writes Hélène Cixous (PJD, 34), when she begins to reconstruct the meanders of Derrida's Marrano (non)identification. It is not hard to imagine little Jackie who could not stop thinking about God as Jane Bowles's heroine, young Christina, whose obsessive infatuation with God became a source of a comical nuisance to the rest of the siblings. He could indeed be like the one of *Two Serious Ladies*, who as a child invented a play of 'founding a new religion': an earnest play, a seriously heterodox *para-oide* or a sideway Marrano song out of tune with religious orthodoxies.[1] This is more or less a tone of Hélène Cixous's *Portrait of Jacques Derrida as a Young Jewish Saint*: playful and earnest simultaneously, precisely as Bowles's *Two Serious Ladies* (the gender-bender analogy included). Was it Cixous, herself already toying with the Marrano affinity, who first suggested to Derrida that he should consider calling himself a Marrano too – a 'Jewish Saint' like Teresa of Avila or John of the Cross? Perhaps, this suggestion was already hanging in the air in

---

[1] 'When Sophie came out of the house, Christina was in the act of running backwards and forwards with her hands joined in prayer' and when asked what she is doing, she cheerfully answers: 'I am founding a religion!'.': Jane Bowles, *Two Serious Ladies* (New York: A. A. Knopf, 1943), 6. Comp. Cixous: 'Here's one who, if there's such a thing as faith, has got it. He prays and does not know what he says' (PJD, 86).

their joyful exchange over Leopold Bloom, the paradigmatic literary 'Marrano of the Catholic culture' portrayed by James Joyce. In one of his latest essays, the 'The Last Scene of *Faust*', Adorno states the cryptotheological rule of the Marrano approach to literature, in which also Derrida and Cixous participate: 'To regard profane texts as sacred texts – that is the answer to the fact that all transcendence has migrated into the profane sphere and survives only where it conceals itself.'[2] While for Adorno, it was Goethe's *ouevre*, teeming with 'heterodox theologies'[3] – for our two serious Marranos, it is *Ulysses*, equally rich in exhilarating heresies.

While evoking Celan's *Gespräch im Gebirg*, where he wittily described an encounter (which, in fact, never took place) between Adorno (Big Jew) and himself (Little Jew), Cixous claims that she and Derrida too met on the mountain and that she immediately stepped in the shoes of *Jud Klein* (not because she felt so humble, but also because of the name of her mother, Eve Klein). She also mentions Joyce as the first topic of their conversation, and his creation, the 'true-false Jew Bloom', who, despite all his efforts to assimilate, remained an eternal foreigner in Dublin-Dyoubelong-Doubling (for Paris):

> But through this word and without saying it we came to meet once, on the mountain, yes on a mountain as, one morning in the German language, Celan tells us in his admirable *Gespräch im Gebirg*, the Jew Gross came to Klein the Jew, and, says Celan, Klein, the Jew, bade his stick be silent in front of the Jew Gross's stick. At the foot of the Montagne Sainte-Geneviève, at the corner of the Rue St. Jacques and the year 1963, we came to the meeting as former children of said-to-be-Jews-born-in-Algeria whose book of memories had been inaugurated by similar events, events of war. And in this case Gross is him, Derrida, and Klein is me, and in those days I bade my stick be silent in front of his stick [. . .] So, in the Cafe Balzar, *to rhyme with hazard*, what did Gross and Klein find to talk of? Of exile and Joyce of *phantasmic and literary Judaism*, of the *Jewflight of passages* and of such very tame follies as being a foreigner-in-my-own-country, of circumconniving in the languages of *translinguistic sport*, of philosophical transports [. . .] of the true-false Jew Bloom *put in circulation, in simulation*, in Dyoubelong the uninhabitable Joycian Dublin, doubling for Paris. (PJD, 4–5; 6; emphasis added)

Two serious Marranos: seriously playing their hazardous translinguistic sport within the new discipline of phantasmic literary Judaism which exists only in risky transitions. And the true-false Jew Bloom, put in circulation and simulation, is a 'counterfeit-money': a new coin/coinage of this game.

---

[2] Theodor W. Adorno, *Notes to Literature*, vol. 1, trans. Shierry Weber Nicholsen (New York: Columbia University Press, 1991), 111.
[3] Theodor W. Adorno, *Notes to Literature*, vol. 2, trans. Shierry Weber Nicholsen (New York: Columbia University Press, 1992), 170.

Prayers and laughs of Jacques Derrida: The sacred parody

The theme of election does not appear in late Derrida out of the blue. Already in 1963 (the year of his first meeting with Cixous), in the early text 'Force and Signification', Derrida attempts a prophetic style: a harbinger of what is to come in Derrida's later works where he will no longer hide the messianic aspect of his *différance*. Speaking tentatively, through another prophet, Nietzche, in a typically Marrano ventriloquist manner, Derrida asks:

> Here do I sit and wait, old broken tables around me and also new half tables. When cometh mine hour? – The hour of my descent, of my down-going [. . .] It will be necessary *to descend, to work, to bend in order to engrave and carry the new Tables to the valleys, in order to read them and have them read* [. . .] Behold, here is a new table; but where are my brethren who will carry it with me to the valley and into hearts of flesh? (WD, 35; emphasis added)

Although the Marrano connotation does not yet come into picture here, the Nietzschean description of sitting among the old broken tablets and the new ones, so far inscribed only half-way, fits well Derrida's ambition: the line *Hier sitz ich, forme Menschen nach meinem Bilde*, which derives from Goethe's *Prometheus*, echoes not only in Nietzsche but also in Derrida's aspiration to become a new prophet of the Marrano religion which would mould the new citizens of the world to come, *olam ha-ba*, according to the image/*tselem* of the first fully conscious Marrano subject who chose and embraced his *marranismo* not as a curse but as a chance. He will also go down – bend and descend – to the depths of the despised 'lastness' of the Marrano condition and, following the receipt of the antinomian messianic inversion, attempt to turn this tragic *Untergehen* of *le dernier de juifs* (the tragic hero always *geht unter*, goes down) into a new messianic hope. In all his descents and ascents, Derrida will always have felt chosen, punning on his synagogal name *Elie* as *élu*, 'the elected one' in the midst of 'perdition', as in this confessional moment in 'Abraham, the Other', where he alludes to a narcissistic weakness of fantasizing about himself as a Messiah (or something close to it) on the basis of his secret name:

> *To guard the silence that guards me*, such would be the order – which I understand almost in the religious sense of a community, or rather a non-community, of a *solitude of withdrawal from the world* – the order to which I would have been entrusted forever, almost forever, a bit the way one entrusts or commits an orphan, a pupil of I don't know what nation anymore, even less what nationstate, a lost child – but who perhaps still gives way to the obscure weakness of feeling as if a bit chosen for *this being in perdition [cet être en perdition]. Called, at the risk of a terrifying misunderstanding about the proper name.* (AO, 6–7; emphasis added)

In *La carte postale*, the secret synagogal cryptonym reverberates in *la lettre ellidée*: a 'purloined letter', but also a letter in the word, removed by elision which once again reminds of *Elie* – a silenced name, manifest only in fifty-two blank spaces, just like

Poe's purloined letter hidden in and by a full display: a new Marrano chosenness, contemplated in *silenzio/amidah*, offered on a plate – 'on a Passover tray' – so obvious, and yet so misunderstood, unseen and unused. *Elie* is therefore and elided election, *l'election ellidée*: silenced by the silence that guards the one who carries it – a silent and purloined election which endures in perdition of a prophet who is a lost orphaned child: knows neither his 'brethren' nor 'his hour'. He does not find his new religion by bringing all the good news – the good letter – of revelation with a panache of a typical Jewish Messiah, surrounded by thunders and trumpets. And yet, all this happens, just quietly and imperceptibly: in *eli*-sion and *eli*-psis, silently, as if by omission, visibly and invisibly at the same time. He feels *élu* – called – but at the same time cannot help finding it ridiculous, risking a 'terrifying misunderstanding', precisely as this other Abraham whom Kafka presents as a pathetically comical figure. Derrida's late confession is thus a quasi-comical version of *hineni*, 'here I am', stripped as much as possible from the narcissistic illusions of grandeur: a humble proposal to renew the covenant, this time according to strictly non-identitarian rules. For any identitarian distortion would immediately reawaken the bogey of elective hubris, and with it, the subsequent evils of re-rootedness, nationhood, and racial supremacy. The 'dogmatic caricature' of chosenness belongs to knowledge, not faith:

> I know that perhaps I have not been called, and that perhaps I will never know it is not me who has been called. *Not yet.* Perhaps in a future to come [*avenir*], but not yet. It belongs, perhaps, to the experience of appellation and of responsible response that any certainty regarding the destination, and therefore the election, remains suspended, threatened by doubt, precarious, exposed to the future of a decision of which I am not the masterful and solitary – authentic – subject. Whoever is certain – as was not, precisely, the other, the second other Abraham of Kafka – whoever believes he detains the certainty of having been, he and he alone, he first, called as the best of the class, *transforms and corrupts the terrible and indecisive experience of responsibility and of election into a dogmatic caricature*, with the most fearsome consequences that can be imagined in this century, political consequences in particular [. . .] *The possibility of an originary misunderstanding in destination is not an evil, it is the structure, perhaps the very vocation of any call worthy of that name, of all nomination, of all response and responsibility.* (AO, 31; 34)[4]

---

[4] The theme of election as secret naming returns again and again in *Circumfession* circling round the almost homophony of *ellie/élu*: '*Elie*: my name-not inscribed, the only one, very abstract, that ever happened to me, that I learned, from outside, later, and that I have never felt, borne, the name I do not know, *like a number* [. . .] and in this sense, more than any other, it is the given name, which I received without receiving it in the place where what is received must not be received, nor give any sign of recognition in exchange (the name, the gift), but as soon as I learned, very late, that it was my name, I put into it, very distractedly, on one side, in reserve, a certain nobility, a sign of election, *I am he who is elected* [*celui qu'on elit*]' (C, 84). *Elie* becomes thus an abstract token of an *a-topia* non-inscribed in any register: out of place, radically non-belonging, a cryptonym of an Event that does not belong to any calendar, a 'secret benediction' (C, 84), but also a number (52). While commenting on this fragment, Hélène Cixous emphasizes the belatedness-*Nachträglichkeit* of such *revelection*: 'Matriculated, behind his back [. . .] but in which register exactly (matriculated being

Derrida, therefore, is convinced

> that there should be yet another Abraham: here, then, is the most threatened jewish thought, but also the most vertiginously, the most intimately jewish one that I know to this day. For you have understood me well: when I say 'the most jewish [*la plus juive*],' I also mean 'more than jewish [*plus que juive*].' (AO, 34–5)

The anti-identitarian dance of the 'the hyperbole of this overbidding (the more than, the less and other than)' (AO, 17) here circles, oscillates, *schwebt* – as in the Freudian play, *Fort-Da* – around the impossible identity of the 'jew', which it never touches: a counter-example of all identification as such, 'the intangible Judaic principle' of nomination without nomination. *Hyper-exemplary, more than exemplary, other than exemplary* (AO, 30), being jew strikes against the neat division of universality and particularity, but also against an easy synecdochal substitution of the One for all: a kind of a calling that may paradoxically lead to a new supremacist elected identity above all others. A higher truth of un-truth or the identity of non-identity is precisely the danger to be avoided: a wrong sense of calling leading to the temptation of a self-assured superiority. This is why Derrida can never assert his being Jewish without all those troubling and dissociating particles and adjectives – without, more than, less than, the last, the least – which introduce oscillation in place of the identitarian certainty. Another Abraham – who doesn't know and will never know whether he was called, 'the last in the class' – is a comic figure, stepping directly from the messianic comedy which Benjamin saw as the only genre capable to tell the story of Judaism. In the letter to Scholem from February 1939, the last in their long correspondence on the work of Kafka, Benjamin writes:

> And concerning the friendship with Brod, I think I am on the track of the truth when I say: Kafka as Laurel felt the onerous obligation to seek out his Hardy – and that was Brod. However that may be, I think the key to Kafka's work is likely to fall into the hands of the person who is able to extract the comic aspects from Jewish theology. Has there been such a man? Or would you be man enough to be that man?[5]

That is the question which Cixous could ask Derrida (as well as herself): are you strong enough to laugh at/with Judaism? Our two serious Marranos are also like Laurel and Hardy, the small and the big Jew: they both 'seriously play' with the 'laughter through tears' (AR, 359).

---

derived metaphorically from mater) was he inscribed unknown to everyone, it's one of those stories of belated revelation-election, of *revelection*, one was enrolled without one's knowledge. Suddenly, tardily, the chosen, the elect without knowing it finds himself taken up or off, a sublime and ever-dreadful kidnapping. Benediction strikes' (PJD, 13). It is due to this belated discovery of the name Elie – 'the badge that sets him apart' – that Derrida begins to write his *littérature au secret* under the prohibition of 'openly wearing any Jewish sign' (PJD, 19)).

[5] *The Correspondence of Walter Benjamin and Gershom Scholem: 1932–1940*, trans. Gary Smith and Andre Lefevre (New York: Schocken Books 1989), 595.

To perceive Judaism as a comical religion is not a ridicule. On the contrary, the genre of the sacred parody appears to Derrida as just right to found a new religion – or rather, a *religion without religion*: a religion of the messianic message, which at the same time will be completely free from any solemn cult, piety, and dead-seriousness which traditionally accompany religious beliefs (and have survived in such seemingly post-theological thinkers as Heidegger). The gait will be more 'dancing' (even if a bit clumsy, as in Christina's children play), the 'new tablets' will be lighter and easier to carry, and the whole narrative supporting them will be more of a *fable*, a *game*, or even a *hearsay*, than of a systematic theology. It will, therefore, have a distinctly heterodox – Marrano *picaro/voyou* – sense of humour and it will itself develop like a *picaro* novel, telling the story of a God who partly withdrew into nowhere and partly wandered into the profane, where he encountered curious adventures and took many risks, never tiring of either dangers or chances. And the canvas for this story will be the Lurianic Kabbalah, for sure – yet carefully hidden in the folds of the Marrano-picaresque novel of all times: James Joyce's *Ulysses*.

As we remember from *Faith and Knowledge*, a Marrano is associated by Derrida with Heidegger's ontotheology: the lowest ebb of *Seinsvergessenheit* in which Being-origin becomes eclipsed by beings and, because of that, 'dis-esteemed'. The motif of being sent out on a mission by a 'God who made me forget' culminates in the Marrano ontotheological condition which is neither psychological nor accidental, but structural: it belongs to the ongoing story of *yeses* that proliferate in both, repetition and alteration, fidelity and betrayal. The Marranos are the envoys: they send themselves in great numbers, disperse and multiply into the whole *gamut* – a big 'halo of tender *yeses*' – by perpetuating the 'hear-say' of 'yes-saying': the *ouï-dire* of *ouï-dire*. The hearsay is precisely a story which lost its origin: it had gone through so many echo chambers and mediations, so many cuts, betrayals, and 'absolute renewals', that it simply can no longer point to the place *wo es war*/where *He war*. In his correspondence with Benjamin over Kafka, Scholem says that, for the latter, the talking of God became a kind of a gossip – a hearsay which can no longer trace its source of legitimacy. The same intuition illuminates Derrida's treatment of Leopold Bloom – his favourite and paradigmatic Marrano – in Joyce's *Ulysses*: 'You are hearing me well, the saying *yes* in Joyce but also the saying or the *yes* that is heard, the saying *yes* that travels like a citation or like a circulating rumor, circumnavigating through the labyrinth of the ear, what one only knows through *ouï-dire*, hearsay' (DJ, 49). *Hear Say Yes* in Joyce's Bloom can thus be regarded as an early attempt to reconstruct the same double bind of the miracle and the machine, which later on will emerge in *Faith and Knowledge*. Bloom figures here as the prototype of the latter's 'Spanish Marranos': an envoy – who departed but never arrived (a 'non-arrival') – or a Jewish Ulysses on a secret mission 'to circumcise the Greeks',[6] constantly glued to the telephone – 'His being-there is a being-at-the-

---

[6] While commenting on the scene in *Ulysses* when Leopold Bloom meets for the first time Stephan Dedalus and immediately wants to 'step farther' and become a 'stepfather' to him, Derrida writes: 'You could also have played on the fact that in Hebrew the word for 'stepfather' [...] also names the circumciser. And if Bloom has a dream, it is to have Stephen become part of the family and thus, by way of marriage and adoption, to circumcise the Greek' (DJ, 63).

telephone, a being toward the telephone, in the way in which Heidegger speaks of the being toward death of Dasein' (DJ, 53) – and trying to track the cracking 'message from the Emperor': the no longer living *yes* which became mechanically mediated, worn out, faded, turned into a 'distant call'.

Hello, Israel, are you there? – The Marrano tele-gramo-phony

It is not at all accidental that the telecommunication of *yeses* takes place during Passover, the time of the crossing, also reminding of the first ever Hebrew crosser, Jacob at Penuel.[7] In my reading of Derrida's reading of Joyce, it is Leopold Bloom himself who wanders into the desert of Derrida's *Faith and Knowledge*, composed in its entirety only a whole decade later; it is his Marrano Passover feast that Derrida celebrates at the conclusion of his essay. Bloom, the Irish-Marrano hero of the 'farced Epistle to the Hibruws',[8] is left with nothing but his 'Passover tray', on which there lay displayed remnants of his 'other memory': a *nature morte* as a Benjaminian collection of objects, including the pomegranates, the paradisiac fruit of life. For a cryptophore – and we have already established that the Marranos are cryptophores – the collection is always a favourite mnemonic device in which the secret animation of 'dead' objects reflects better the strange undeadness of the inhabitant of the crypt than a living word of a reflexive memory. Just as Benjamin's collector treats every object in his assembly as an 'encyclopaedia' condensing all there is to know – about the epoch, tradition, and so on – so does Derrida approach the single items of his Marrano collection as 'detached from all its original functions in order to enter into the closest conceivable relation to things of the same kind'.[9] Be it a silver cup, a fruit cut with a small knife – or the tallith: all these objects, separated from their traditional contexts, nonetheless carry the 'other memory' of the tradition. They are parts of Derrida's Marrano *Mnemosyne Project*: his archive of a *different memory*, a tactile 'memoir of the blind'.[10]

---

[7] In the words of another Bloom: 'Like Jacob, we keep passing Penuel, limping on our hips': Harold Bloom, *Breaking the Vessels: The Wellek Library Lectures at the University of California*, ed. F. Lentricchia (Chicago: The University of Chicago Press, 1982), 70.
[8] As Joyce himself described his literary enterprise, adding: 'It is an epic of two races (Israelite-Irish) and at the same time the cycle of the human body as well as a little story of a day (life)': James Joyce, *Letters of James Joyce*, vol. 1, ed. Stuart Gilbert (London: Faber & Faber, 1957), 146.
[9] Walter Benjamin, *The Arcades Project*, trans. Howard Eiland and McLaughlin (Cambridge, MA: The Belknap Press, 1999), [HIa, 2], 205.
[10] I used to have an object like that in my childhood: a lonely little cup, stuck in the back of the closet, because it did not fit more modern sets of glasses used by my parents. I rescued it from its utilitarian oblivion and put on my desk, so I could watch it every day. It was a beautiful thing: slender, on a matt silver leg, with a cup of greenish glass imitating a tulip. I didn't know where it came from and to what 'tray' it once belonged, but it soon became a synecdoche of the forgotten past buried in my parents' dead silence. It completely grew out of its 'original function': I even started to fantasize about its secret animation, as if it were a pet.

The outlines of this Marrano archive – based on the 'memory of Passover' as opposed to the 'memory of the Passion' – appear for the first time in *Ulysses Gramophone*, where it is associated with the great, yet always somehow dysfunctional, system of telephony:

> the first phone call rang with these words from Bloom: 'Better phone him up first' (U. 7.219) in the sequence entitled 'and it was the feast of the passover' (U 7.203). A little earlier, he had repeated, a bit mechanically, like a record, *this prayer, the most serious for a Jew, the one that should never be allowed to become mechanical or be gramophoned*, 'Shema Israel. Adonai Elohenu' (U 7.209). If, more or less legitimately (*for everything is legitimate and nothing is when one borrows some segment in the name of a narrative metonymy*), one singles out this element in the most manifest thread of the story, one can then speak of a telephonic *Shema Israel* between God, who is at an infinite distance (a long distance call, a collect call from or to the 'collector of prepuces' [U 1.394; 9.609]), and Israel. *Shema Israel* means, as you know, call to Israel, listen Israel, hello Israel, address to the name of Israel, a person-to-person call [. . .] *In the beginning, there must have been some phone call.* Before the act, or the word, was the telephone. In the beginning was the telephone. We can hear this *coup de téléphone*, which plays on apparently random numbers and on which there would be much to say, ring all the time. And it opens within itself this *yes* toward which we slowly return, circling around it. There are several modalities or tonalities of the telephonic *yes*, but one of them amounts to simply registering that we are there, present, listening, on the end of the line, ready to answer but without answering anything else for the moment than the readiness to answer (hello, yes: I am listening, I hear that you are there, ready to talk at the moment when I am ready to talk with you). *In the beginning was the telephone, yes, at the beginning of the phone call.* (JD, 51; emphasis added)

'Hear, Israel!' – is a distant call of the transcendence to the immanence, of the separated withdrawn God to the world which answers back: yes, *hineni*. This connection constantly breaks, cuts the message into 'segments' which then become 'cited' and thus even further detached from the origin, forming a broken 'metonymic narrative'. Even the *Shema*, the most sacred Jewish prayer – all the more sacred for the Judaizing Marranos who used to die their martyrological death with 'Sh'ma on their lips'[11] – turns here into a mechanical segment-object of the disjointed collection which falls apart. The centre – far, distant, absent – cannot hold.

What Derrida calls here a 'gramophone effect' (DJ, 56) producing a 'hearsay' – a sequence of first hearing and then repeating, which involves a necessary risk of distortion – is best exemplified by a children's game which must have been known to Kafka, who wrote 'The Message from the Emperor', as *Taubestelephon* and to Derrida as *telephone arabe*, and which the English call *Chinese Whispers*: the 'telephone of the deaf' in which the kids sit in a row and pass on the message through the ear from the first

---

[11] Jonas, *Morality and Mortality*, 133.

to the last one who then says it aloud to the inevitably comical effect. Derrida, highly sensitive to the colonial aspects of his Franco-Jewish-Arabic Algerian childhood, would have been unwilling to hint to this game by its name, but it is nonetheless there as a tacit reference: it is one of the crucial moments of the whole *jeux*. We can go even further and call it a *Marrano telephone*, where Poldy sits at the very end of the 'chain of tradition' (*shalshelet ha-kabbalah*) and repeats its phrases in a mechanical manner, often distorting them into a complete Babelized 'babbling', sowing nothing but confusion. Bloom produces the funniest 'gramophone effect' in the last episode of the book, right before Molly's monologue, where he, together with Stephen, also completely drunk, sings psalms in Latin and praises 'exit *into* the Egyptian bondage'.[12]

It is thus not even about remembering or forgetting, in the first place: it is rather about *decoding*. What one hears immediately becomes a 'hearsay': uncertain and illegitimate, passed on in the *Marrano telephone*, with the origin hidden behind the cloud of static noises – Joyce's acoustic version of the celebrated opening image of the *Zohar*: 'Within the most hidden recess a dark flame issued from the mystery of *Ein-Sof*, the Infinite, like a fog forming in the unformed – enclosed in the ring of that sphere, neither white nor black, neither red nor green, of no color whatever [. . .] nothing beyond this point can be known.'[13] What issues from this mystery and forms like a fog in the unformed is the beginning of a new game:

> before the gramophone, just before, and Elijah's speech as operator of the grand telephone central, the gnome, the 'hobgoblin' speaks in French the croupier's language: 'Il vient! (Elijah, I assume, or the Christ) C'est moi! L'homme qui rit! L'homme primigène! (he whirls round and round with dervish howls) Sieurs et dames, faites vos jeux! (He crouches juggling. Tiny roulette planets fly from his hands.) Les jeux sont faits! (the planets rush together, uttering crepitant cracks) Rien va plus!' 'Il vient', 'rien va plus', in French in the original. (DJ, 66–7)

This is a hazard theology worthy of Pascal (who, by the way, invented modern roulette), but also, as we have seen, of the Marrano Kabbalist, Abraham Cardoso who openly talked about the risks inscribed into the messianic game of redemption, as well as Hans Jonas who, in his version of the Lurianic myth, saw the world as 'the enormous

---

[12] Which, as we have seen in the previous chapter, might not have been just a mistake resulting from the distorted Marrano chain of transmission: Exodus *into* Egypt is, after all, one of the antinomian tenets of the Frankist doctrine which fuses the motif of Jacob's wandering into Egypt and then getting out of Egypt of the whole Jewish nation with Jesus' escape into Egypt as the correction of the latter. Just as Frank chooses the Judaism of Esau, the man of Edom, he also prefers Jesus in Egypt as the alternative version of the Messiah who survives, instead of the one who dies on the cross in Jerusalem.

[13] Scholem and de Leon, *The Book of Splendor*, 3. Speaking about Joyce's primal scene which created him as an artist, Cixous points to the acoustic cloud which fascinated him: 'What the law says frightens but its noise is pretty. Joyce is fixated by the noise of the law. He is someone for whom the secret is audible, which is not the case of Blanchot or Kafka. Joyce writes to the ear, whose secret he tries to surprise. This goes with the fact that he is very myopic': Cixous, *Readings*, 9. Myopia is an important motif of Cixous's stories too: particularly the one called *Savoir/Knowledge*, which opens *The Veils*, the book co-authored with Derrida.

gamble that the first ground, if mind was present then, wagered with creation'.[14] *He comes* and *nothing comes anymore* can apply here both to Elijah the prophet and Jesus the Christian Messiah. This enigmatic *il* who/which 'issues from the mystery' comes as the only envoy – posting – of the withdrawn origin hiding behind the cloud and of which nothing can be known: it will be either 'Him' or nothing. *Les jeux sont faits!* – the universe is forming as a grand scene of a gambling bet in which ladies and gentlemen can put their stakes. Based on the roulette scheme, there will be four options: the red for *yes* and the black for *no*, and then, on the red field, a certain 'number of yeses', and, on the black, many shades of the Gnostic negation. But, while all choices can in the end (if it ever comes) prove victorious, there is only one type of *yes* which, for Derrida, is truly worth risking for. The 'He' of *Il vient!* is announced through Victor Hugo's title as *l'homme qui rit*, a laughing man, and this is precisely what Derrida decides (for in this gamble all is a matter of decision and faith) to hear in the hearsay: '*ouï dire*, "hear say," it was the *oui rire*, "yes laughter"' (DJ, 67) – the *oui rire* of the man *qui rit*.[15]

'For everything is legitimate and nothing is when one borrows some segment in the name of a narrative metonymy' (DJ, 51), says Derrida to justify his decision, not very distant from those skilfull rabbis who engaged in the game of *pilpul*: the holy combinatorics operating on the Hebrew word roots in order to reveal hidden affinities and open new theological vistas. Hélène Cixous admired Derrida (as well as Joyce) for this capacity to play with what she termed as 'nanowords', linguistic 'little beings' invested with an animation of their own:

> How you love the power of little words or the condensation, thunderbolt, cunning in these little beings. You dream of a suitcase word, as one says, a *portmanteau word*, a word for words a miniaturized secret drawer or mirror, light as a feather, quick and clairvoyant as an eagle, little as a *oui*, a *qui*, a *lis*, a *vi*, no bigger than a *J* capable of the whole world a sea/shell for a philosophical kernel, a teetering, needlingword, folding and unfolding, a *nanoword*. A concise key. A comesee. (IJD, 29)

---

[14] Jonas, *Morality and Mortality*, 189.

[15] In another version of the same tale of the origin, Derrida states: 'In the beginning, in principle, was the post' (P, 29). Constantly thinking of Heidegger ('Would this satisfy Martin?', P, 65), Derrida constructs 'a metaphysics of the posts or of postality' which goes against his hypermnesiac system of remembering of and returning to Being: 'To post is to send by "counting" with a halt, a relay, or a suspensive delay, the place of a mailman, *the possibility of going astray and of forgetting* (not of repression, which is a moment of keeping, but of forgetting). The *epokhe* and the *Ansichhalten* which essentially scan or set the rhythm of the "destiny" of Being, or its "appropriation" (*Ereignis*), is the place of the postal, this is where it comes to be and where it takes place (I would say *ereignet*), where it gives place and also lets come to be' (P, 65; emphasis added). The postal model, therefore, not only deconstructs the circularity of Ulysses's path, be it the original Odysseus or his Dublin avatar, but also offers the alternative to the metaphysics in which 'the origin itself remains immune from the drift that it renders possible' (CP-M, 6). In this new vision of the exilic errancy without end, 'travel takes the origin away with it' (CP-M, 12) and exposes it to a 'chance' (CP-M, 4) – precisely as in Cardoso's and then Jonas's 'theology of hazard'.

The sequence – *ouï dire, oui rire, qui rit* – is a brilliant illustration of such linguistic *tsimtsum*, which wants to condense and then carry in the cryptophoric manner the whole *forum/fors* of living linguistic molecules, containing the whole vitality of the otherwise 'sickened' tradition and still capable to make it alive again. Like Paul Celan, another secret carrier (*phoros*) of the *portmanteau* tradition which departed from the world – *Die Welt ist fort, ich muss dich tragen* – Derrida uses his molecules with a similar cunning in view: to carry on in a shell-and-kernel form 'what remains': ashes and seeds at the same time, scattered, disseminated, segmented, simultaneously posthumous and vivifying. These words, therefore, are like Celan's poems-mummies sent off as the envoys to the future with a prospect of a revival. Hélène Cixous, whom I also suspect of being a Marrano cryptophore, joins the other two 'secret sharers' when she avows in *Manhattan*: 'I'm forever remaking myself with these literary molecules I told myself.'[16] The crypt is not sealed tight for ever: those 'magic words' are 'concise keys' which have a power to open the vault – perhaps even come from the kernel/reactor itself, sending a beam of strange energy in the 'unbending rays' (AO, 13) (the Kafkan/Scholemian *strenges Licht des Kanonischen*) – and initiate the process of 'remaking' or the 'absolute renewal'.[17]

Clearly, the crypt cracks a bit when it hears those words 'little as a *oui*, a *qui*'. *Oui, Yes, Yea, Jah* awake its inhabitant – the Benjaminian 'ugly wizened theology' – and make it raise from its tomb, for 'the *yes* implies, Bloom would say, an "implicit believer" to some call by the other' (DJ, 48). *Yes*, therefore, is the word of faith: a 'word for words' which has a capacity to resurrect the banned belief, to make it come – the Blanchotian *vien!* – with the power of the insistent performative invocation. God is no longer there, but he can always come – summoned by *vien!*, he comes, *il vient* – in the form of a spectral *revenant*. In the crucial fragment of *La fable mystique*, devoted to the seventeenth-century Silesian mysticism, de Certeau sketches the succession of such 'yeses' which simultaneously remain faithful and betray the origin, by reinventing it in an ever new language, from Judaism to Christianity, and from Christianity to the modern 'almost-atheism' of Angelus Silesius:

---

[16] Hélène Cixous, *Manhattan: Letters from Prehistory*, trans. Beverly Brie Brahic (New York: Fordham University Press, 2007), 59.

[17] The allusion to Joseph Conrad's novel appears in 'The Night Watch', Derrida's last essay on Joyce, which is devoted to Jacques Trilling, but can also be read as 'not far from a nod toward our friend Hélène Cixous, who was already the author of the first great reading of Joyce in France' (DJ, 89): 'Joyce was our common friend, like a secret between us, turning each of us into a sort of *secret sharer*, to cite the title of a novella on the spectral double, the novella of another foreigner who knew how to make English his own. *The Secret Sharer* is not only "a secret companion" – *un compagnon secret* (as the title of this story of Conrad has been translated into French); I would prefer to speak of an acolyte, a secret guardian, or else – for the syntax of the title, *The Secret Sharer*, allows it, "secret" being at once a noun and an attribute, *the secret of the subject who shares and the secret as the object shared, kept or guarded by the two of them* – a guardian who knows how, in secret, to watch over the secret that is shared: a secret partaker or sharer of the secret' (DJ, 89–90; emphasis added). This cryptophoric image – of Joyce as a secret treasure shared by the two guardians – also emerges in Cixous's portrait of Derrida as a 'Jewish Saint', drawing on the title of Joyce's novel. Besides, Cixous is also an author of the story, 'Aube partagée', which appeared in English as 'Shared at Dawn' in the collection called *Stigmata* and prefaced by Derrida.

Angelus Silesius went even further. He identified the written expression of the Separated (*Jah*, or *Jahve*) with the limitlessness of the 'yes' (*Ja*). In the very place of the sole proper Name (a Name that distances all beings), he installs disappropriation (by a consent to all). The same phoneme (*Ja*) brings together separation and openness, the No-Name of the Other and the Yes of Volition, absolute separation and infinite acceptance. *Gott spricht nur immer Ja* ('God always says only Yes [or: I am]') There is identity between Christ's 'yes' and the 'I am' (the Other) of the burning bush. The Separated is reversed, becoming the exclusion of exclusion. Such is the cipher of the mystic subject. The 'yes,' a figure of 'abandonment' or 'detachment,' is, ultimately, 'interiority.' In that land, a whole population of intentions cries out on all sides 'yes, yes,' like Silesius's God. *Is that space divine or Nietzschean?* (MF, 187; emphasis added)

'Is that space divine or Nietzschean?'; is this 'number of yes' the same as the 'wealth of tender yeses' which Nietzsche attributes to the Abrahamic revelation in *The Genealogy of Morality*? The phrase, 'number of yes', derives from Derrida's 1987 response to *The Mystic Fable*, 'Nombre de Oui', which begins with the double – 'yes, yes' – and then multiplies it into a whole affirmative 'population of intentions'. We will also hear the echo of the Certean *yeses* in the essay on Joyce, written in the similar time (1986), where Derrida will tacitly inscribe the Joycean God in the legacy of Angelus Silesius hearing say yes in the name of God: *Jah-Jahve, Yeah-Yahwa*. Already in Nietzsche, the 'wealth of tender yeses' is a dialectical outcome of affirmation issuing out of negation. Life negated in its natural immediate form becomes complex and 'interesting' precisely thanks to the religious repression; what represses life, but does not kill it, makes it stronger and thus more powerfully affirmative.[18] In de Certeau's rendering, similarly, the Christian mystical *Jah* repeats the proper Name of *Jahve* and, at the same time, alters its signification: it is no longer a self-assertive declaration of absolute independence of 'I-will-be-whenever-I-will-be', but an infinite acceptance of Christ who says the same 'yes' and simultaneously undoes the gesture of separation. The transforming repetition of this 'yes' tells a story of the reversal in the image of God: from the Separated One who 'distances all beings' and 'disappropriates' their will to be, by claiming the supreme and sole being only to Himself – to a fragile departed God who must be welcome into the shelter/crypt of human 'interiority' in order to survive. In this manner, the act of volition – *volo ut sis*, 'I want you to be' – wanders from God to man. It is now the mystic who takes the initiative and 'wants to be Christian' in the absence of God: 'Fundamentally, to be a believer is to want to be a believer.'[19] Thus, just as in Rosenzweig's dialogical grammar of revelation based on the *Song of Songs*, the revelatory encounter

---

[18] Comp. Nietzsche's ambivalent description of the Jewish priest: 'His "no" that he says to life brings a wealth of more tender "yeses" [eine Fülle zarterer Ja's (*sic*)] to light as though by magic; and even when he wounds himself, this master of destruction, self-destruction, – afterwards it is the wound itself that forces him to live...': Friedrich Nietzsche, *On the Genealogy of Morality*, trans. Carol Diethe (Cambridge: Cambridge University Press, 2006), 89.

[19] Michel de Certeau, 'Weakness of Believing', in *The Certeau Reader*, ed. Graham Ward (Oxford: Blackwell, 2000), 231.

is no longer one-sided and asymmetrical: 'Who loves whom? Who wounds whom? Who prays to whom? Sometimes God, sometimes the faithful' (MF, 169–70). The power of the Christian *yes* can reverse all negation and separation; can even undo the death of God and, as Hegel says, 'resurrect Him daily' (PS, 299) in the enclosure of 'interiority'. It is infinite and unscathed: no violence or destruction can touch or thwart the arch-affirmative *volo* which fills the enthusiastic Christian heart.

In his response to the Jesuit, Derrida protests against such Christian monopolization of *Ja-Sagen* and reminds us of not a small number of tender *yeses* that derive from Rosenzweig's *Star of Redemption*. The power to remake religious revelation with the magic 'nanowords' was indeed tested for the first time by Franz Rosenzweig who restlessly searched for the grammar of Judaism's 'absolute renewal', by hoping to awake the sleepy 'survivor' resting in the deep corner of the self. Derrida refers to the ubiquitous presence of *Jah* as *Urwort* in Rosenzweig's *Star* as a proof – against de Certeau – that the Jewish tradition is capable of acknowledging the power of the originary *Yes*. *Ulysses Gramophone* uses Joyce to deliver a further proof, while it again quotes Rosenzweig on the primordial *Yea* as the infinite essence of God: the whole of it can be read as an extended indirect commentary to de Certeau's depiction of the homonymy between *Jah* and *Jahve* in Angelus Silesius, the goal of which is to demonstrate that the Jewish tradition not only contains this form of *Yes*, but also overbids it. This is an absolute Marrano meisterschtück: to show it all through Joyce without mentioning the Kabbalah even once. Nonetheless here it is, on the Passover tray, in the full display despite its anonymity: the *yes-laughter* which pervades Joyce's *ouevre* is nothing but the Kabbalistic *she'a'shuah* – the vibration of divine bliss and laughter, which penetrates the whole creation as something done for no other purpose than pleasure and fun – a motif also present in the Book of Job where God is described as playing with Leviathan.[20] This 'remainder of a quasi-transcendental yes-laughter' (DJ, 80) is here a Joycean 'over-mark' (DJ, 68) which traverses his whole corpus and, simultaneously, a *reshimu/rushum*: the remnant in the form of the divine signature which in the Lurianic Kabbalah constitutes the only trace of the withdrawn God within the created world. While using – for the second time after *Fors* – the ventriloquist metaphor, which later on he will explicitly evoke in his description of the Marranos, Derrida points to a secret Jewish innervation of Joyce's writing:

---

[20] 'The doctrine of *she'a'shua* finds its roots in Moses Cordovero [the 16th century kabbalist from the Safed school], where it connotes, *inter alia*, the activity of *Ein-Sof* before anything existed [and] relates to the first stirrings of divine thought, the self-contemplation of the Infinite, which represents the beginnings of the desire to emanate': Elliot R. Wolfson, *Circle in the Square: Studies in the Use of Gender in Kabbalistic Symbolism* (Albany: State University of New York Press, 1995), 70. In the Lurianic Kabbalah, here represented by Ari's pupil, Israel Sarug, the jouissance is connected to the very idea of creation as an imposition of order on the primordial chaos: 'According to Sarug, the transition from the pre-creative to the creative stage in *Ein-Sof* entailed a stirring of Divine pleasure [*she'a'shua*] at the thought of delineating the worlds-to-be and the rules of justice [*din*] to be imposed': Alexander Altmann, 'Lurianic Kabbalah in a Platonic Key: Abraham Cohen Herrera's *Puerta del Cielo*', in *Jewish Thought in the Seventeenth Century*, ed. Isadore Twersky and Bernard Septimus (Cambridge and London: Harvard University Press, 1987), 31.

Yet, the eschatological tone of this yes-laughter seems to me to be inhabited or traversed, I prefer to say *haunted, joyfully ventriloquized* by an entirely different music, by the vowels of a completely different song. I can hear it too, quite close to the other one, like *the yes-laughter of a gift without debt, light affirmation, practically amnesic, of a gift or an abandoned event*, which is called in classical language 'the work,' a signature lost and without proper name that names and reveals the cycle of reappropriation and domestication of every paraph only to limit its phantasm; and in so doing, in order to introduce the necessary breach for the coming of the other, an other that one could always call Elijah, if Elijah is the name of the unpredictable other for whom a place must be kept, and no longer Elijah the grand operator of the central, Elijah the head of the megaprogramotelephonic network, but the other Elijah, Elijah the other. But this is a homonym, Elijah can always be either one at the same time, *one cannot call on one without risking getting the other*. And one must always run this risk. (DJ, 70; emphasis added)

Alluding to the scene in *Ulysses*, which involves a guy named Elijah running the telepost central, Derrida does here few things at once, by creating a particularly dense palimpsest: overtly engaging in the interpretation of Joyce's laughing signature and presenting it to the audience of learned specialists of Joyce'ology in Frankfurt as a guest speaking with another voice – Elijah being Derrida's synagogal name – he invites them to hear another voice in Joyce's work: the one of Elijah as 'the unpredictable other for whom a place must be kept' and who can be heard as a deep ventriloquist voice hidden in Joyce's belly. As we have seen, Derrida associates this metaphysical hospitality to the other with the *fable* created by Isaac Luria: the story of *tsimtsum*, in which God withdraws for the sake of the other of the world and lets the other be as the other – disseminate further and further into multiplying alterity which is 'assisted' by a 'differential vibration' (DJ, 79), here presented as a generous *yes-laughter*, self-delighted *sha'ashuah*, giving itself lightly without any expectation of return, reappropriation or *restitutio in integrum*. In Derrida's reading of the Lurianic fable, God truly withdraws for good, never to return or to reclaim the whole gamut/gamble of otherness which his contraction made possible in a kind gesture of *Seinlassen*. He, the perfect donor, is the 'God who made me forget': his light affirmation is 'practically amnesic', it lets creatures go without burdening them with the debt of memory. This 'differential vibration [. . .] cannot be stabilized in the indivisible simplicity of one single sending, from oneself to oneself' (DJ, 79): it is not the Hegelian return of the Absolute to itself in the 'the manipulative operation of hypermnesic reappropriation' (DJ, 78), but a genuine 'invention of the other' as envisaged by the Kabbalist named 'Louria': 'This event, which one naïvely calls the first event, can only affirm itself through the confirmation of the other: a wholly other [*tout autre*] event' (DJ, 81).

We also saw that this type of Lurianism is eagerly taken up by the thinkers who went through the incurred oblivion of the Marrano experience: Abraham Cardoso, who coined the antinomian figure of the Torah commanding its followers to be forgotten, as well as Jacob Frank who spoke about *Ein-Sof* as the nameless divinity which does not care about being named or remembered. Derrida goes one step further: while his precursors still maintained the doctrine of the 'redemption through sin', which would put forgetting on the list of transgressions, even if necessary for the fulfillment of the messianic plan – Derrida no longer perceives it as a trespass. In order to join the rhythm of the *différance* as the 'differential vibration' or 'the light, dancing *yes* of affirmation' (DJ, 80), the creature does not have to remember where it came from: it is forgiven in its being 'practically amnesiac' already *in the beginning*. This amnesia, however, is far from problematic, for it also runs a terrible risk of forgetting as an absolute cut which no longer gives rise to 'absolute renewal': a break which tears the thread of the miraculous 'mystic fable' and then results only in an automated series of *yeses* as merely *flatus voci*, mechanical flat noises of a broken 'gramophone effect'. When repetition inscribed in the original *yes* is no longer an *alteration* 'dispersing itself in the multiplicity of unique yet countless sendings' (DJ, 78), but a mechanical punctual break of this delicate continuum, the forgetting becomes quite literal. As we have seen in Chapter 2: instead of the *pious atheism*, which, according to Scholem, characterizes the world that had half-forgotten the withdrawn God, we then simply get an *atheism* – a version of the Enlightenment which bans the fable for good, by discarding it as a mere fiction.[21] This is the integral risk of any 'theology of hazard', which, in Cardoso's opinion, ineluctably pertains to the Lurianic metaphysical narrative: the 'light affirmation' of the gift without debt can indeed liberate creation into a void of pure presence, which reiterates *yes* to itself like a *perpetuum mobile*. When *oubliez sans oubliez* loses its subtle dialectical balance, the whole 'dancing affirmation' stops, together with the music and the song, no longer to be heard and to be passed on as a joyful 'hear-say'.

This is the first risk of the 'gamble': the *atheism* of the pure immanentist presence and its *yes* of a self-repeating mechanism, implying nothing miraculous (*nihil admirabile*). The other, however, equally hazardous, is *theism* – the possessive creationist paradigm which triumphs in the Kafkan ominous formula, *Sein bedeutet Ihmgehören*, 'to be means to belong to Him', always at His miraculous mercy.[22] Both risks are inscribed in the game started with the telephonic beginning, the *hello, yes, are you there?* of the call, for ever withdrawn from presence and fading into a fable-like 'hearsay', which can only be dimly remembered. This memory, however, is also for ever double-bound:

> The *yes* can say itself only if it promises to itself the memory of itself. The affirmation of the *yes* is an affirmation of memory. Yes must preserve itself, and thus repeat itself, archive its voice to give it once again to be heard. This is what I call the gramophone effect. *Yes* gramophones itself and telegramophones itself a priori. The desire for memory and the mourning of the *yes* set into motion the anamnesic machine. As well as its hypermnesic unleashing. (DJ, 56)

---

[21] By answering the question: 'What remains of a fable?', de Certeau writes: 'The spoken word [*parole*] in particular, so closely bound to religious traditions, has evolved, since the sixteenth century, into what its scientific "examiners" and "observers" have for three centuries been designating as the "fable" [...] For the *Aufklärung*, although the "fable" speaks [*fari*], it does not know what it is saying, and one must rely on the writer-interpreter to obtain the knowledge it expresses without knowing it. It is therefore discarded, classed with "fiction," and like all fiction, it is presumed to mask or to have mislaid the meaning it contains' (MF, 12).

[22] 'Das Wort *sein* bedeutet im Deutschen beides: Dasein und Ihmgehören'; 'The German word sein signifies both "to be there" and "to belong to Him"': Franz Kafka, *The Zürau Aphorisms*, trans. Michael Hoffman (London: Harvill Seeker, 2006), 46.

And if Derrida teases the Joyce believers, by claiming that he does not always love Joyce (just as he certainly does not always love God[23]), it is because he can too often hear in him also a 'reactive yes-laughter' of a grand reappropriation which spells the danger of the 'hypermnesic unleashing':

> the Ulyssean circle of sending oneself governs a reactive yes-laughter, the manipulative operation of hypermnesic reappropriation, when the phantasm of a signature wins out, and a signature gathering the sending in order to gather itself by itself. But when, and this is only a question of rhythm, the circle opens, reappropriation is renounced, the specular gathering of the sending can be *joyfully dispersed in the multiplicity* of unique yet countless sendings, then the other yes laughs, the other, yes, laughs. Now, the relation of a *yes* to the Other, of a *yes* to the other and a *yes* to the other *yes*, must be such that the contamination of the two *yeses* remains fatal. *And not only as a threat: but also as a chance.* (DJ, 78; emphasis added)

The phrase 'dispersed in the multiplicity' will then reappear in *Faith and Knowledge* a propose the 'Spanish Marranos who have dispersed, multiplied' (FK, 100) – everything, even up to the memory of their secret, which left them 'practically amnesiac' – but not 'unjoyfully'. The Marrano forgot the original idiom that generously allowed them to forget – and precisely for that reason, they still are part of the 'mystic fable'. More than that: *they* are the true carriers of the fable, the more encrypted – iconoclastic to the point of the cryptophoric anasemia: turned into a song, music, hearsay, rhythm, incantation – the better. And already here, in the *Ulysses* speech, we find the same agonistic juxtaposition which will form the main axis of *Faith and Knowledge*: Hegel's Absolute Knowledge (*Savoir Absolu*) as precisely 'the manipulative operation of hypermnesic reappropriation' versus the joyful dispersion in disseminating polivocity of singular creatures – Rilkean *zahllose Individuen* – let be and let go, made to forget that they were ever made in the first place. We also find here the same double bind of 'the miracle and the machine', which, in the Kabbalistic teaching, so ingeniously applied by Derrida, characterizes every worldly phenomenon as 'duplicated' or 'twinned' in the manner of Jacob and Esau or their *Finnegans Wake* appearance as Shem and Shaun: 'we cannot separate the twin *yeses*, and yet they remain wholly other. Like Shem and Shaun, like writing and the post' (DJ, 79). Everything has a double: simultaneously marked by

---

[23] In an earlier essay, 'Two Words for Joyce', Derrida, writing on *Babel*/confusion, deliberately confuses Joyce with God as the author of the Book of Creation and God with Joyce as the writer aspiring to invalidate all other writers: 'And yet, I'm not sure I love Joyce. Or more exactly: *I'm not sure he is loved*. Except when he laughs – and you'll tell me that he's always laughing [...] I don't know if you can love that, without resentment and without jealousy. *Can one pardon this hypermnesia which indebts you in advance?* In advance and forever it inscribes you in the book you are reading. One can pardon this, this Babelian act of war only if it happens always, from all time, with each event of writing, thus suspending each one's responsibility. One can pardon it only if one remembers too that Joyce himself must have endured this situation' (DJ, 23–4; emphasis added). Even earlier, in 'Violence and Metaphysics', Derrida calls Joyce 'the most Hegelian of modern novelists' (WD, 192), which in his mouth is not exactly a compliment.

the divine trace-signature as the spectral presence/absence of the withdrawn God and fallen on the *sitra ahra*, 'the other side' of the merely mechanical self-repetition:

> The two qualitatively different yes-laughters call out to each other and imply each other irresistibly as soon as they both demand and risk the signed pledge. *One doubles the other: not as a countable presence, but as a specter.* The *yes* of memory, the recapitulating mastery, the reactive repetition immediately duplicates the light, dancing *yes* of affirmation, the open affirmation of the gift. (DJ, 80)

The open affirmation of the gift, which Derrida detects in Joyce read through the Kabbalistic lenses, is also the *yes* which he wants to say to the 'gifts of the demiurge' – against the Gnostic 'Satanic temptation, that of the spirit saying *no*' (DJ, 79). Molly's 'flesh which *stets bejaht*' and from which there flows a soliloquy of endless *yeses* emerges here as the best *pharmakon* against the Mephistophelean *Geist, der stets verneint*, representing the third risk of the metaphysical 'gamble', next to the atheism pure and simple and the 'hypermnesiac' theism.[24] In the game put in motion by the 'gifts of the demiurge', the gift can be: totally forgotten and give way to the automatic self-repetition of the immanence as a self-sufficient machine; totally recalled in the hysterical vision of God the Master who owns and controls everything; totally negated and rejected as a *Gift* – poison responsible for creating the world as 'a defect in the purity of non-being'[25]; and also, in the fourth, for Derrida truly winning option, it can be forgotten without forgetting. It thus can be received, accepted, *dato et accepto*, and then only referred to as a 'hearsay' which never settles itself as a serious theological narrative that necessarily always involves heavy burdens of debt, guilt, and mourning – as in Hegel's *Glauben und Wissen*. If the gift is to be affirmed as a gift, it must be treated lightly, as if imperceptibly, indeed *taken for granted*:

> Before any restitution, symbolic or real, before any gratitude, the simple memory, in truth the mere awareness of the gift, by giver or receiver, annuls the very essence of the gift. The gift must open or break the circle, remain without return, without a sketch, even a symbolic one, of gratitude. (DJ, 24)

The Blanchotian *sans* plays here precisely the role of evading – swerving away from – the absolute purity of any total position: not so much privative as rather contaminative, it points to a dynamic inner negation operative in every stance we take towards the originary gift. *Oubliez sans oubliez* can also be explained as a cryptophoric statement

---

[24] 'Molly gives voice to the flesh (remember that word) which always says "yes" (*stets bejaht*, Joyce recalls, reversing Goethe's words)' (DJ, 57).

[25] Jacques Lacan, *Ecrits* (Paris: Editions de Seuil, 1966), 316. Lacan quotes here Paul Valery's poem *The Sketch of a Serpent* in which the demonic snake, personifying the force of death in the garden of paradise, speaks with the voice of yet another Serpent, the already mentioned Goethean Mephisto: 'Then better 'twere that naught should be/ Thus all the elements which ye/ Destruction, Sin, or briefly, Evil, name/ As my peculiar element I claim': J. W. Goethe, *Faust, Part I*, trans. by Anna Swanwick (New York: Dover, 1994), 42.

playing on the two types of memory, which constitutes the main subject of *Faith and Knowledge*: while the Marrano cryptophore no longer remembers about God in his conscious memory, he had not forgotten Him in the ontological depths of his being. Putting things in the Hegelian manner: the divine Spirit is in his bones.

Does it mean that Bloom, a Marrano carrier of the precious burden of his Jewishness in hyper-Catholic Dublin, is also a cryptophore and that – as in the rapport between Freud and the Wolf Man, described by Abraham and Torok – his crypt resonates with the one of Cixous and Derrida? The rhythmic vibration which he senses in Joyce's writing on Jewish Ulysses indeed resembles a thunder, a seismic stirring, sometimes a growl and sometimes a laughter at the brink of language: a cryptic resonance. Once again playing on the different types of memories – the Hegelian 'hypermnesiac' Odyssey of the phenomenology of Spirit, on the one hand, and the unconscious 'remembering without remembering', on the other – Derrida points to the latter as a form of an indirect recollection, always mediated by the 'postings' arriving from afar 'in the chance form of letters, telegrams, newspapers called, for instance, the Telegraph, long-distance writing, and finally, taken out of a sailor's pocket, postcards whose text at times only displays a phantom address' (DJ, 46). These are envoys, sendings, letters to be encrypted: Shem, the penman, hiding in Shaun, the postman, as in *Finnegans Wake*. While the former remains invisible, the latter erratically carries letters with a blurred 'phantom address': from whom and to whom? – no one can know for sure.

But Molly is not just the *bejahendes Fleisch*, an affirming flesh whose first and last word is always *yes* to the 'gifts of the demiurge'. Molly is not just a perfect creature who, having forgotten (without forgetting) about the origin, found the centre of the universe in her living body 'without why' – as opposed to Poldy who, somewhat farcically obsessed with theological problems of the origin, looses his life in the telegramo-phonic machine. She is also a female version of the Hegelian Spirit – 'the Hebrew *yes* (*ken*) can always inscribe itself in the Shekinah' (PS2, 235) – which, in *Faith and Knowledge*, will be associated by Derrida with the Marrano, self-oblivious, *makom-Khôra*: making room and giving place without expecting anything in return. When Molly says: 'he asked me would I yes to say yes my mountain flower', Derrida notices that it is 'Bloom's name, Flower' (DJ, 75), but does not (yet?) hear *Montefiore* as a possible allusion to the famous surname of the Sephardic Jewry, often popping up in the Marrano archives. A Sephardic hint appears also in the drugstore scene where Bloom is thinking about buying a perfume for Molly: 'What perfume does your? *Peau d'Espagne*. That orangeflower' (DJ, 75). The idea that the scent can be the last and subtlest trace of the spirit – or the last remainder of one's Jewishness, worn only as a whiff of a 'Spanish skin' – will emerge in Derrida's wrestling with Heidegger in *De l'esprit* (1987), yet it is already here that he asks: 'But, is it possible to sign with a perfume?' (DJ, 81) Perhaps, but this could not be the case with the Hegelian Spirit, so seriously set to the task of his hypermnesic reappropriation, but only with the Hebrew Spirit in feminine: *Ruah/Khôra* departing and leaving the world with the scattered tantalizing scent of *Peau de'Espagne*. Signing with the perfume would thus be the lightest and most dancing form of affirmation, fit only for a light-weight story, never for a heavy theological system which, while construing its metaphysics, 'effaces in itself that fabulous scene which brought it into being, and which yet remains, active and stirring, *inscribed in white ink*, an invisible drawing covered over in the palimpsest' (WM, 11; emphasis added). A perfect *fable* would thus not claim anything more solid than a 'hearsay' whose origins were written in the invisible white ink. It would content itself with remaining a 'fabulous' divine comedy of the *Marrano telephone* which, despite its comic features, can still have believers: not the earnest fundamentalist followers who would have been disgusted by such laughable story, but the 'implicit believers' – those who believe without remembering exactly what they believe in (Exodus out or into Egypt?). And, by the way, is not Poldy's term – *implicit believer* – a great name for what he is: a Marrano?

As signing with a scent – or with the milky white invisible ink – *Molly-Ruah-Khôra* forms the very opposite of the male God of Origin. This is yet another playful allusion to the non-binary Kabbalistic *Ein-Sof* who 'leaves an empty space (*tehiru*) in which all things can come into being. Within this space there remains a trace of the Divine, referred to as *reshimu*, which has been compared to the aroma of an empty perfume container or the milk left on the glass of a bottle after it is emptied'.[26] Contrary to this self-erasing milky trace, the signature of the male God of Origin – 'Where it was, *He was*' (DJ, 35) – is a proprietary brand: *Sein bedeutet Ihmgehören*. In an earlier essay, 'Two Words for Joyce', Derrida portrays the angry God, the jealous owner of the house of being, with the help of the two 'magic words': HE WAR.

> I take them from *Finnegans Wake* (258.12): HE WAR. I spell them out: H-E-W-A-R, and sketch a first translation: HE WARS – he wages war, he declares war, he makes war, which can also be pronounced by babelizing a bit (for it is in a particularly Babelian scene of the book that these words rise up), by Germanizing, then, in Anglo-Saxon, HE WAR: he was. *He was he who was.* I am he who is, who am, I am that I am, says Yahweh, supposedly. *Where it was, he was, declaring war.* And it was true. Pushing things a bit, taking the time to draw on the vowel and to lend an ear, it will have been true, *wahr*. That's what can be guarded (*wahren, bewahren*) in truth. God guards. He guards himself thus, by declaring war. He, is 'He,' the 'him,' the one who says 'I' in the masculine, 'He,' war declared, he who was war declared, in declaring war he was he who was and he who was true, the truth as being a war, he who has declared war verified the truth of his truth by war declared, by the act of declaring the war that was in the beginning. Declaring is an act of war, he declared war in tongues (*langues*) and on language and by language, which gave languages, that's the truth of Babel when Yahweh pronounced its vocable, Babel, difficult to say if it was a name, a proper name or a common noun *sowing confusion*. (DJ, 22–3; emphasis added).

'He war – God's signature' (DJ, 37) is the source of all the militant *Unruhe* which Jacob Böhme first attributed to God as *Deus turbae* at the wake of modern mysticism (we

---

[26] Daniel Horwitz, *Kabbalah and Jewish Mysticism Reader* (Lincoln: University of Nebraska Press, 2016), 224.

are still in the vicinity of de Certeau's *Mystic Fable*). He is all being which he guards jealously for himself and wages war on every other who would like to steal being from him. Only He can say 'I am' in the affirmative, say *yes* to Himself and meaningfully use the verb *to be*, without which no language can signify anything; therefore, while to himself He is YHVH, 'I Am That I AM', he is *Babel – Confusion* – to everything else, because he reduces all creatures to dust and ashes and all their languages to meaningless babbling. HE WAR is thus a signature of the God of the 'hypermnesiac appropriation' where 'to be means to belong to him', full stop. It is a signature of the strongest possible sovereign ontological possession.[27]

Yet, the fragment in *Finnegans Wake* where 'the Lord speaks loud' with harsh Anglo-German monosyllables that sound like missiles or lethal molecules of language – *he*, *war*, *wahr* – ends on a different note: the much quieter word *Mummum*: 'the last murmur which closes the sequence, a maternal inarticulated syllabification' (DJ, 37). God speaks loud, but his speech, fully reserved to himself, allows no other language into which his name could be translated: he thus speaks and does not speak, because his private hyper-possessive language not to be shared by anybody else, is, in the end, a private language – and thus another babbling, *confusion*. The triumphant epiphany, therefore, ends in an impasse; the loud hyper-visible God collapses into his over-guarded sameness, and thus lets come to the fore another, less conspicuous, revelation:

> *He war*: it's a countersignature, it confirms and contradicts, effaces by subscribing. It says 'we' and 'yes' in the end to the Father or to the Lord who speaks loud – there is scarcely anyone but Him – but here leaves the last word to the woman who in her turn will have said 'we' and 'yes.' Countersigned God, God who signeth thyself in us, let us laugh, *amen, sic, si, oc, oïl*. (DJ, 39)

Derrida's commentary to the HE WAR fragment can also be read as a variant of a great agon between the two types of *tsimtsum* – the withdrawal in anger versus the withdrawal in kindness – which has divided the Kabbalistic tradition for the last few ages, starting from the two pupils of Isaac Luria: the school of Israel Sarug, which chose the *Din*/severe aspect of *tsimtsum*, later to be found in the Schellingian Gnostic vision of God retreating from the world in disgust – and the school of Hayim Vital, which chose the *Chesed*/kind aspect and *tsimtsum*, later to be found in the Hegelian procosmic vision of God emptying himself out into creation. In Derrida's reading – perhaps influenced by Joyce's theosophical transformation of Böhmian-Schellingian *Deus turbae* into 'He War' – the angry *tsimtsum* is a possessive gesture of God as *Melekh ha olam*, the King of the World, who enters negative theology as the paradigmatic sovereign exception: he cannot be talked about – engenders 'confusion' – because

---

[27] In her presentation at the same colloque, Cixous, while psychoanalysing Joyce as an artist, says openly what Derrida will play with implicitly: 'Joyce situates the structure that can produce what is called "the artist" at an important archetypal level. He puts the artist into rivalry with God since both are creators': Cixous, *Readings*, 8.

he is the exceptional-superlative on all fronts. The kind *tsimtsum*, on the other hand, belongs to *Khôra* as a 'nameless one' (compare again Frank's depiction of *Ein-Sof*) who/which withdraws without asking to be remembered: she/it enters the negative theology as the very opposite of sovereignty and exceptionality, that is, as the most forgettable. If we don't talk about it/her, it is not because we *musn't* – we are forbidden to by God's jealous Name, *Ha-Shem*, that militantly defies all translation – but because we forget to mention, blithely assume, take it/her for granted. It is only when the negative theology of sovereignty reaches its impasse that we can detect the traces of this other 'feminine' absence 'who in her turn will have said *we* and *yes*': the *Khôra* covenant of creatures – her/its 'we' – will be very different than the army gathered by 'He War', capable only of *Zusammenmarschieren*, but never of 'living-together'. *Let us laugh* is here strangely homophonous with *Let there be light*, though perhaps only in English. But some of it can also be heard in Hebrew: *yehi or* – 'let there be light' as the opening vista of the gamble called creation – hides in its folds the joyous Anglo-Saxon *Yea/Jah*. 'Let us laugh' is also a lighter, more comical version of the solemn 'let us rejoice': yes, of course, let's rejoice – *re-Joyce* – but why be so serious about it? In the beginning was a fable; in the beginning was a telephone – the beginning could indeed have been a joke. After all, *joke, jest,* and *jeux* share the same root. Can the 'theology of hazard' be truly serious if it involves a 'gamble'? It must rather be playfully serious and seriously playful – like the figure of Marrano, naturally sliding into a genre of a sacred parody which for Derrida not only is not blasphemous but properly *religiogenic*. If, after Bergson, universe is a machine destined to make gods, it makes them in a comic mode.[28]

Yet, one must be very careful with the distribution of the 'masculine' versus the 'feminine', which, in Derrida, follows both Joyce, very sensitive to the theosophic gender register, and Lacan with his famous two schemes of sexuation. Far from fixing an essence of a true man or a true woman, Derrida rather points to disparate capacities which the 'white mythology' symbolizes via the gender difference. When Derrida says his *yehi or* – 'let us laugh' – it is always in the feminine mode: thinking of Molly who, like Freud's unconscious – *das freudige Unbewusste* – never says no, and of Hélène Cixous, with

---

[28] Derrida's Kabbalistic interpretation of Joyce has a precursor of whom he might have been aware: Jackson I. Cope's '*Ulysses*: Joyce's Kabbalah', that traces the elements of Jewish esoteric doctrines in Joyce's work back to the Dublin milieu of the nineties 'in which flowered Yeats' quondam master MacGregor Mathers, translator-author of the most esoteric addenda to the *Zohar's* pentateuch commentary titled, following Baron von Rosenroth's seventeenth-century Latin selection, *The Kabbalah Unveiled* [...] Later in Joyce's career we will learn that Shem is a sham. And in *Ulysses*, as in Dublin at the turn of the century, shamans, shams and scholars abounded': Jackson I. Cope, '*Ulysses*: Joyce's Kabbalah', *James Joyce Quarterly* 7, no. 2 (Winter, 1970): 94–5. Indeed, Cope's close reading of *Ulysses* demonstrates an ample use of quotes deriving from Mathers's translation. But Cope's angle is different and focuses on the sexual practices of Kabbalah, apparently most significant for the Dublin *shemans*, which are of lesser importance for Derrida. Derrida, however, would have agreed that there is indeed something *sham* in Joyce's take on *Shem*, yet without a critical intention: after all, that's the whole point of his metaphysical 'hearsay-Jewsay'. The universe may be nothing but a 'crap', but, just as in Jonathan Lear's defence of the 'lucky break', this may be an exhilarating respite from theological seriousness – the solemn *tradendum* – thus, perhaps, bringing us closer to the 'truth of the tradition': a 'comical Judaism'.

whom he rejoiced Joyce (*re-Joyced*) and laughed about Poldy Bloom, their favourite Marrano-*picaro*, so comically lost and struggling to survive in the labyrinths of his Irish exile. And it is also in the 'feminine' mode when he speaks in his final text on Joyce, 'The Night Watch', written in 2001, just three years before his death, which contains a declaration of an *auto-tsimtsum* conducted in the gentle manner of *Khôra/ruah*:

> from now on, no more writing, especially not writing, for writing dreams of sovereignty, writing is cruel, murderous, suicidal, parricidal, matricidal, infanticidal, fratricidal, homicidal, and so on. Crimes against humanity, even genocide, begin here, as do crimes against generation. Whence my definition of *withdrawal* [*le retrait*], my nostalgia for *retirement* [*la retraite*]: from now on, before and without the death toward which, as I have written elsewhere, I advance – *to begin finally to love life, namely birth*. Mine among others – notice I am not saying beginning with mine. *A new rule of life: to breathe from now on without writing*, to *take a breath beyond writing*. Not that I am out of breath – or tired of writing because writing is a killer. No, on the contrary, I have never felt so strongly the youthful urgency, dawn itself, white and virgin. *But I want to want*, and decidedly so, I want to want an active and signed renunciation of writing, *a reaffirmed life*. And thus *a life without matricide*. It would be a matter of beginning to love love without writing, without words, without murder. It would be necessary to begin to learn to love the mother – and maternity, in short, if you prefer to give it this name. Beyond the death drive, beyond every drive for power and mastery. *Writing without writing*. The other writing, the other of writing as well, *altered writing, the one that has always worked over my own in silence*, at once simpler and more convoluted, like a counterwitness protesting at each and every sign against my writing through my writing [. . .] I began with a wish. Here is another one, and it may always strike you as being pious, and little more than a pipe dream [*voeu. . . pieux*]: *to write and kill nobody* (signed Ulysses). (DJ, 102–3; emphasis added)

'Signed Ulysses' is a Nietzschean joke (we are still in the scented 'wealth of tender *yeses*', the perfumed aura of the gracefully departed 'feminine' spectre), even if Nietzsche himself was terribly deprived of any sense of humour. Instead of the dead-serious Christ-Dionisos, Derrida chooses the Jewish Ulysses, Leopold Bloom, who also wanted to write and kill nobody and, despite all his preparations to start a noble act of *écriture*, never wrote a single word. Bloom is an impotent author because he abstains from murder; he cannot write when 'writing is a killer'. But can writing be different? Once again, the pretext for this confession is Joyce in his aspect deeply 'unloved' by Derrida, or more precisely, Jacques Trilling's book on Joyce's style of writing as a virtual matricide: Joyce as a writer-murderer, obsessed with the phantasy of sovereign self-begetting – in the manner of Milton's Satan or Harold Bloom's strong poets who dream about being 'navelless' and without parentage.[29] Hence the Arendtian natalistic

---

[29] Jacques Trilling, *James Joyce ou l'écriture matricide* (Belfort: Circé, 2001).

reference to the maternity and birth as the *factum brutum* of life without alibis, that needs to be accepted as a given, that is, as a *gift*, from which will issue an alternative 'writing without writing'.

The Blanchotian construct brings to mind its other applications – 'forgetting without forgetting' and 'religion without religion' – that Derrida also uses in his description of the 'figure of the Marrano' with which he, in 2001, already 'seriously plays'. Could it be that his Ulysses signature belongs to this 'serious play' too? Already at the beginning of the 1980s, in her lectures on Joyce, Hélène Cixous suggested that a true writer must resort to three ruses: *silence, exile, cunning*, necessary to 'the development of the theme of isolation and of a solitude needed to write' (DJ, 10). Without yet alluding to the Marrano condition – a theme that will explicitly appear only later, in her conversations with Derrida in the 1990s – Cixous offers a portrait of a writer that could come straight from Leo Strauss's *Persecution and the Art of Writing*:

> Writers inhabit both the living and the writing worlds. They navigate with difficulty between the two, of which one will always be emphasized more than the other. To be the inhabitant of two worlds brings about a feeling of betrayal. Every exile cannot but think this way since one cannot change countries without being from two countries. This double appurtenance, this double locus is going to lead to the theme of betrayal, a dominant problem in Joyce. It is put into place by the institution of a double world.[30]

In Cixous's Marrano metaphor, the writer is always a double citizen: of the world of living and of the world of writing. He cannot make a move in either of them without betraying the other; when he writes, he cheats life – when he lives, he cheats writing. In consequence, he is illegal in and exiled from both: stuck in an isolated 'elsewhere', he is the eternal 'wandering Jew' who exited the world of living, but never fully arrived into the world of writing. His extreme vulnerability creates a violent 'phantasm of omnipotence' – 'cruel, murderous, suicidal, parricidal, matricidal, infanticidal, fratricidal, homicidal' – but this eloquent veneer merely hides the tacit *homo sacer* sense of being universally banned and excluded: the pressing anxiety of survival, which plays itself out in silence. For Cixous, therefore, Joyce the Terrible – the omnicidal hyper-writer commanding the galaxies of words – will always contain a 'faulted' figure of a weak-bodied, deeply myopic adolescent boy: 'The position of hiding becomes his definitive position [. . .] The reaction – "secret," "defense" – precedes in writing the statement that signifies there has been a fault'.[31] To reach this level of writing, where it 'cunningly' serves the secret and defensive call of *survie*, means also, for Derrida, to find the 'altered writing, the one that has always worked over my own in silence' – the one which not only is not ashamed of survival, but turns it – 'mine among others' – into its *thema regium*. His own private *tsimtsum* – retreat from the phantasy of sovereign power, realized in the omnipotent/omnicidal writing and akin to the 'hypermnesiac

---

[30] Cixous, *Readings*, 10.
[31] Ibid., 6.

Joyce' for whom he had no sympathy – leads him eventually to discover a different *écriture* which was always already there: the one of silence, exile, and cunning. The writing not of a Master, but of a Survivor – a universal Marrano.[32]

Is this a *voeu pieux*, merely a pious wish? Or is this nothing *less* than a *pious* wish? I believe the latter: the new religion of 'Abraham, the Other' with which Derrida seriously plays in all his sacred parodies, starting from *Ulysses Gramophone*, centres on the *survie* which, thanks to the 'literature with secret', metamorphoses into *sur-vie*. It is a religion of the finite life which knows that it advances towards death, but refuses to focus on death as the Heideggerian essence of life. In his confessional postscript to the last essay on Joyce, it is impossible not to hear the echo of Cixous who always tried to pull Derrida to the side of life and who wrote on Kafka in a strangely prophetic anticipation of what was going to happen to her friend twenty years later:

> We have been told that Kafka wanted to live until the very last minute. He was so caught in the death drive that at the moment of agony which lasted several weeks, he was overcome by a terrible desire to live.[33]

Pour vie: The tallith

Life, death, and survival are the three grand themes that constantly recur in the four decades-long conversation between Derrida and Cixous. She, finding herself on the side of life, positions Derrida under the auspices of death: his *la vie la mort* tips the balance towards the precarity of survival, life inescapably tinged with the lethal verdict. Having pursued the enigmas of the primal scene – the birth of a writer – in Joyce and others, Cixous locates it in Derrida's circumcision which constitutes his Blanchotian 'instant of my death':[34] it is precisely the verdict's fatality, the truth-saying of the verdict, which results in the conflation of circumcision and death in Derrida's writing

---

[32] In the later preface to *Stigmata*, Cixous confirms the 'exilic' conception of writing, by pointing to Joyce, but also to Montaigne, another Marrano thinker they often discussed together with Derrida, and links it with a struggle for more life, *pour vie*: 'Language's tricks are the allies of the artist who goes into resistance or exile. Joyce said this a hundred years ago and Montaigne five hundred. Every language artist is an artist of the struggle against the condemnation to death': Hélène Cixous, 'On Stigmatexts of Hélène Cixous', trans. Eric Prenowitz, in Cixous, *Stigmata*, x.

[33] Cixous, *Readings*, 13.

[34] Derrida's comment on Blanchot applies also to himself: 'What Blanchot's text attests to, what it wants to testify to, is, basically, that for the last fifty years, in spite of the anniversary he tells me about, the 20th of July 1994, time has not been measurable. Blanchot has remained the one who remained back there, *undying [demourant] in the same restance* – who died that day, who died without dying, who escaped without escaping [*qui a été sauvé sans se sauver*]; but for how much time? Fifty years? Fifty thousand years? No time. The time of demourance is incommensurable' (D, 82; emphasis added). After the lethal trauma becomes incorporated as the self-defining 'instant of my death', time stands still, wrapping around the bottomless crypt: 'This inexhaustible solipsism is myself before me. Lastingly. [*À demeure.*]' (MO, 2). This is also why Marranos, secretly carrying the enigma of survival, are ageless: 'Is it not possible to think that such a secret eludes history, age, and aging?' (A, 81).

unconscious. This conflation which engenders a defence called 'survival' constitutes one of the most significant aspects of Derrida's Marrano secret: a secret No reacting to fatality of both, circumcision and death – circumcision as death, befalling the subject 'without his consent', and death as circumcision, cutting and depleting the vital organ of life.[35] This also explains a weird temporality of Derrida's act of writing, which he himself compares to weaving the veil from the wrong end: while fending off his future death, he is also fending off against this 'instant of his death' which was determined by his circumcision. This doubly apotropaic defence of survival Cixous names very aptly a 'saving deproximation':

> Before death there is lots of time, just before death there is still time. An infinitesimal space but a space nonetheless. He has always practiced this saving deproximation. Between the Jew and him the Jew they tell him he is, between what, without qualms and without consideration, one is accustomed to term Jewish he has always insisted on introducing the tip [*la pointe*] of a precaution in order to fend off the verdict's fatality, the truth-saying of the verdict, this sense of being condemned and executed that is ineluctably engendered by the incredible circumcision scene. Circumcised without his consent, before any word, before passivity even [...] A day of absolute passivity, which cannot occur save at the expense of the most powerful repression. Day of faith and unreason. Day of amputation [...] *Amputatio* day of thought cut and cutting. Day of judgment and of execution. Circumcision is the first case of a verdict. (PJD, 65; 68)

Although Cixous makes no direct connection with Blanchot, we can nonetheless assume that she points here to the concept of *demeure* which Derrida, in his commentary on Blanchot's story, reserved for the dwelling in between the two deaths, *deux-meure*: 'It is the untranslatable that remains his dwelling place, uninhabitable, it is the word dwelling [*demeure*] that prophesies in his mouth the minute he says it: two always die [*deux...meure*]' (PJD, 119). 'And yet one must go on living', she immediately

---

[35] Derrida's wrestling with his own circumcision as a traumatic intrusion of force, which determined his Jewishness, brings to mind the Catholic concept of 'absolute force', which was applied by the Inquisition in cases of those Marranos who were coerced to accept baptism in a particularly violent manner. When noticing the references to the Provançal *conversos* in the manual for the inquisitors, composed by Bernard Gui, Marina Rustov writes: 'Indeed, Bernard Gui, in discussing the varying degrees of coercion admissible in declaring a conversion to Christianity to be valid, says himself that only if the Jew has been led to the baptismal font by means of "absolute force" is he or she permitted to return to Judaism. In practical application, this clause was obviously a matter of the inquisitor's discretion: *how should one define "absolute"*? Among the *relapsi* Bernard discusses was a German Jew of Toulouse named Barukh who had been baptized on threat of death by a band of *Pas toureaux* during the Shepherds' Crusade; the Inquisition had not allowed him to return to Judaism on the reasoning that the force had not been "absolute" after all': Rustov, 'Yerushalmi and the Conversos', 39; emphasis added. Considering the fact that the Algerian Jews called circumcision a baptism, the *brit milah* executed on the infant Jackie acquires a new dimension: was he dragged to the Jewish font by the 'absolute force'? To whose discretion would it belong to call it absolute? And to what could he *relapse* if he refused the 'validity' of such conversion? Perhaps, it would not be too far-fetched to surmise that, in Derrida's resistance to the forceful act of circumcision, one can sense a frustration of a Marrano who is not allowed by external circumstances to *choose* a faith of his own.

adds (PJD, 119), and in case of Derrida, this imperative of *survie*, living-on, realizes itself in writing: between the two deaths, but also between life and death, testing a new dimension of survival beyond the dualism of living and dying. He thus says:

> 'I posthume as I breathe' – brilliantly inventing the verb *to posthume*, for his own personal usage as a 'survivor' who wants to make liars of life and death. There you have him then he who dies at the top of his lungs, a buried-alive supernatural, who gets wind of a new definition of immortality through the magic of writing [...] He writes as he posthumes. The writing is his survivor, she [*l'ecriture*] survives him. (PJD, 58–9)

Tucked in his *demeure*/dwelling/*Shekhinah*/*Khôra*, safely distanced from both verdicts, Derrida takes his first breath as a freshly born writer and begins to sail under the wings of the magic of writing which, for him, becomes a 'saving lie': 'me, who would be capable of inventing circumcision all by himself, as I do here' (PJD, 61). Cixous's comment on Derrida's primal scene explains why it must have eventually matured in the Marrano strategy of deproximating Judaism:

> invent circumcision, there you have his dream and therefore his gesture. A de-Mosified circumcision, delivered from all genealogy, obedience, alliance. A circumcision unpolluted by legal paternity. Absolute. Absolved. Derridan. Neither gift nor debt. Neither memory nor inheritance. Nor religion. Look at it! He has just invented it, the ageless, faceless infant. He keeps it for himself, alone. (PJD, 61)

Circumcision – *yes, but only on my terms*. This is what Harold Bloom, in *Anxiety of Influence*, calls *apophrades*, 'the return of the dead': the final and highest ratio of the revisionary agon with 'legal paternity', in which the whole tradition, buried in the inner crypt, returns in the form of a *revenant*, renewed and reinvented alongside the poet's idiosyncratic curve. Only the strongest writers are capable of that feat which, in Derrida's case, equals the triumph of his Marrano anxious tactic as the victory over the influence of Judaism: the 'absolute force' of circumcision turned into a wealth of tender significations, or the new 'pronounceable letters' which do not, in fact, lose what they only play to lose.

> Circumcision – I have never spoken of anything but that, consider the discourse on the limit, the margins, marks, marches, etc., the fence, the ring [...], the writing of the body, [...] *the blow and the sewing back up*, whence the hypothesis according to which it's that, circumcision, that, without knowing it, never talking about it or. . . Latin, philosophy, etc., as if imprinted itself on my *language circumcised in its turn*, could not have not worked on me, pulling me backward, in all directions, to love, yes, a word, *milah* [...] the whole lexicon that obsesses my writings, CIRCONSI. . . the point detached and retained at the same time, false, *not false but simulated castration which does not lose what it plays to lose and which transforms it into a pronounceable letter*, I and not I, then always take the most careful account,

in anamnesis, of this fact that in my family and among the Algerian Jews, one scarcely ever said 'circumcision' but 'baptism'. (C, 70–72; emphasis added).

Derrida can thus indeed be seen as a 'Marrano's Marrano' – the Marrano to the second reflective power – who had passed through all the stages of the Bloomian agon with the tradition: the *clinamen* of irony (according to Yovel, the 'marranos of reason' were the first ironists in modern European culture); the *tessera* of completion (Abraham Miguel Cardoso's bold apology of *conversos* as the true messianic agents capable to fulfil universal redemption); the *kenosis* of self-ordeal (Castro's *semitismo atormentado*, full of guilt and self-humbling); the *askesis* of self-limitation (clutching to this-worldly survival, nothing-but-survival, beyond Judaism and Christianity, beyond life and death eternal); the *demonization* of self-importance ('I am the end of Judaism, last of the Jews that I am, advancing in a cloud of eschatological dust', PJD, 85); and, finally, *apophrades*: the 'return of the dead' or reinvention, where the tradition raises like Phoenix from the ashes, 'sown back up', but it is a completely new bird: 'my religion' (C, 154), *my own private Judaism*. Derrida is not the first and not the only one who had gone through those six revisionary ratios: the same can be claimed about Gershom Scholem and Harold Bloom himself, both more 'Marrano' than they would have been willing to declare. The six ratios run the full circle between the trauma of total dispossession ('blow') – the disappearance of the self in the instant of 'absolute passivity, which cannot occur save at the expense of the most powerful repression' (PJD, 68) – and the reparative 'sewing back up', when the inhabitant of the crypt is given a leave and can return, now no longer a threat, but a promise of renewal. Derrida often confesses the primal scene of dispossession (perhaps also explaining Derrida's undying attraction to Heidegger's ambivalent *Er-eignis*) which he sees as determining his birth into a writing life: 'I am overfond of words because I have no language of my own, only false *escarres*, false *foci* (*eskhara*), those blackish and purulent scabs that form around the wounds on my mother's body' (C, 71), which suggests that, for him, his *écriture* would be a mother-substituting, dark and scarred *Shekhinah*, akin to Jacob Frank's beloved Black Madonna from the Częstochowa cloister. And just as often he alludes to his *apophrades* as 'one day when [. . .] I finally know how not to have to distinguish any longer between promise and terror' (MO, 73), that is, to the day when Judaism that gives death (HE WAR) will have metamorphosed into Judaism that gives life (*yehi or: let us laugh*).

Thus, if writing – as Cixous emphasizes, *l'ecriture* in feminine – is for Derrida his survival, his veil woven from the wrong end, spinning a web of a 'saving lie' over the annihilating/amputating verdict of death in circumcision, it is also his 'other *voile*': a sail. His veil is his sail – and he is sailing towards this 'tip [*la pointe*]' where Judaism turns from terror into promise. Derrida gives the report of this journey in 'A Silkworm of One's Own. Points of View Stitched on the Other Veil' (*Un ver a soie. Points de vue piqués sur l'autre voile*), which was first published in 1997 in *Contretemps* (nr 2/3, 1997) and then again in 1998, together with Hélène Cixous's story, *Savoir*, in their common project called *Veils*. But one can also read it as yet another variation on the theme of faith and knowledge: on the absolute difference between *foi* and *savoir absolu*, the

Hegelian SA of the spirit returning to itself after the adventure of alienation without remainder, but also the Augustinian absolute self-introspection which leaves nothing to secrecy.

Cixous's *Savoir* is a little story about a myopic woman who one day undergoes a surgery and begins to see. It forms a quite transparent allegory of Jewish blindness – the Blind-Folded Synagogue is the frequent architectonic topos of *Synagoga et Ecclesia*, not only of the Strasbourg cathedral which inspired Franz Rosenzweig – undergoing Christian conversion. The Jews are myopic: they cannot see and cannot know; they don't touch the wound of Christ and they don't perceive the light of the messianic Day; as Lévinas would have said, they are not tempted by the 'temptation of temptations' which is to see and to know; to stand in the light of *die veroffenbarte Religion*. They belong to the state of absence and withdrawal before the world came to being, 'presence-before-the-world' (V-C, 13); they are the guardians of veils that hide *nothing*, where the apocalyptic tearing of the veil can do nothing, because there is *nothing* to reveal:

> An absolute knowledge [*savoir*] will never accept this unique separation, that in the veiled place of the Wholly Other, nothing should present itself, that there be Nothing there that is, nothing that is present, nothing that is in the present. (V-D, 30)

After the surgery/conversion which removes the myopic veil from her sight, she is at first amazed by the 'miracle of *seeing/with-the-naked-eye*' (V-C, 11) and the constant unstoppable generous flow of the gift of visibility. Soon, however, she discovers that what she saw merely as a sickness (which, just as in Kafka's Hunter Gracchus parabole, 'should be cured in bed') now, in her nostalgic hindsight, turns into a paradoxical merit – *the force of separation*:

> Do not forget me. Keep forever the world suspended, desirable, refused, that enchanted thing I had given you, murmured myopia.
> If I forget thee, oh Jerusalem, may my right eye, etc.
> Ah! I see coming in place of my diffuse reign a reign without hesitation.
> I shall always hesitate. I shall not leave my people. I belong to the people of those who do not see. (V-C, 13)

Yet, 'myopia would not grow again', so there is no coming back to the Jewish people who do not see:

> Only that myopia of a Tuesday in January – the myopia that was going away, leaving the woman like a slow inner sea – *could see both shores*. For it is not permitted to mortals to be on both sides [. . .] Myopia would not grow again, the foreigner would never come back to her, her myopia, so strong a force that she had always called weakness and infirmity. But now its force, its *strange force*, was revealed to her, retrospectively at the very moment it was taken away from her. Nostalgia for

the secret non-seeing was rising. And yet, we want so much to see, don't we? (V-C, 13–14; emphasis added).

Can this passage – about passing – be read as an oblique apology of the Marrano condition? Always in transition, capable to see both shores, and in that manner *see even more* than the Christians swimming in the full light of their revelation; see, but also appreciate the invisible which the seers have never seen, the precreational 'limitless pale nothingness' (V-C, 6) just coming into being, death passing into life? The eternal Passover?

Derrida also writes his response *in passage*. For the first time, he crosses the Atlantic to land in Buenos Aires, which suddenly becomes a synecdoche of his lost – though never properly lived – Marrano Judeo-Spanish life, with all the traces of ladino which his ancestors still spoke in Maghreb, 'one of his forgotten ancestral languages' (V-D, 38). But what causes this flood of displaced memory is his awaiting of the verdict which lets in the repressed memory of the 'original verdict', his circumcision: the first cancer diagnosis which does not come this time, but only seven years later, in 2002, when it indeed will 'drag him down in its fall': 'That's why I've gone so far to wait for the verdict, to the tropics. From Saint James [Santiago] to Saint Paul [Sao Paulo]' (V-D, 38). Escaping to the *tristesse des tropiques*, Derrida plunges into a melancholic self-reflection, where 'Saint Jacques' (Santiago), the 'Jewish saint' (as Cixous calls him), and 'Saint Paul' (Sao Paolo) as Jacques's alter ego and simultaneously an adversary, feature heavily:

> Before the verdict, my verdict, before, befalling me, it drags me down with it in its fall, before it's too late, stop writing. Full stop, period. Before it's too late, go off to the ends of the earth like a mortally wounded animal. Fasting, retreat, departure, as far as possible, lock oneself away with oneself in oneself, try finally to understand oneself, alone and oneself. Stop writing here, but instead from afar *defy a weaving*, yes, from afar, or rather see to its diminution. Childhood memory: raising their eyes from their woolen threads, but without stopping or even slowing the movement of their agile fingers, the women of my family used to say, sometimes, I think, that they had to *diminish*. (V-D, 21)

Contrary to Heidegger's praise of the anagnoretic virtues of 'being-towards-death', Derrida rejects the 'truth-saying' – revelatory – aspect of 'this strange verdict, without truth, without veracity, without veridicity' (V-D, 23): if anything, the 'mortal wound' of the terrified flesh merely occludes the truth even more. But is he looking for another kind of verdict which would truly tear the veil and show the thing itself? Here, as in other places, Derrida demonstrates his mistrust towards the tradition of the apocalypse which always only reveals in destruction and destroys in revelation.[36] He would rather

---

[36] See, for instance, Derrida's essay on the nuclear danger: 'No Apocalypse, Not Now (Full Speed Ahead, Seven Missiles, Seven Missives)', trans. Catherine Porter and Philip Lewis, *Diacritics* 14, no. 2 (1984): 20–31.

side with the other heritage, the one under the auspices of 'interminable diminution' as Derrida's synonym of *tsimtsum*: 'Diminish the infinite, diminish *ad infinitum*, why not? [. . .] We'll have to give up touching as much as seeing, and even saying. *Interminable diminution*' (V-D, 24; emphasis added) and 'reaffirming the veil in unveiling' (V-D, 25). Not so much tearing the veil as rather unweaving the excess of the fabric, and thus making it lighter, softer, less opaque. This diminution will govern the last of Derrida's agons with the tradition: the passage from the sublime Judaism of the Veil to his own private Judaism of the Shawl – the white tallith.

Judaism of the Veil is, as already Hegel stipulated, the sublime religion of separation which veils God in an unapproachable secret. Derrida immediately reminds us that 'the Temple veil was torn on the death of the Messiah, the other one, the ancestor from Bethlehem, the one of the first or second resurrection, *the true-false Messiah* who heals the blind and presents himself saying "I am the truth and the life"' (V-D, 28): Christianity, *die veroffenbarte Religion*, was meant as a cure for the myopic Jews, stuck in their dogma of separation:

> *I know of no other separation in the world*, or that would be commensurable with that one, analogous, comparable to that one which allows us to think nonetheless every other separation, and first of all the separation that separates from the wholly other. Thanks to a veil given by God, and giving here is ordering [*donner c'est ici ordonner*]. Whether or not *this unbelievable separation (belief itself, faith) came to an end with the death of Christ*, will it ever be comprehended, *will it ever be comprehensible in the veiled folds of a Greek aletheia*? No being, no present, no presentation can here be indicated in the indicative. It was, is, shall be, shall have been, should have been for all time *the sentence, the saying of God, his verdict*: by God order (is) given to give the veil, the veil (is) the gift (that it is) ordered to give. Nothing else that is. *God would thus be the name of what gives the order to give the veil, the veil between the holy and the holy of holies*. Now 'God,' the name of God, distinguishes between the artist or inventor of the veil, on the one hand, and the embroiderer on the other [. . .] An absolute knowledge [*savoir*] will never accept this unique separation, that in the veiled place of the Wholly Other, nothing should present itself, that there be Nothing there that is, nothing that is present, nothing that is in the present. (V-D, 30)

Pace Hegel and Heidegger, Derrida defends the specificity of the Jewish *Holy of Holies* as an empty secret: nothing behind the veil. But this is not what he is interested in, not this time. He no longer wishes to be a *Schleiermacher* (V-D, 39), the weaver and the guardian of the veil. The sublime Judaism of the Veil, protecting the 'unscathed' nothingness of the crypt, gives way to another Judaism, much less grandiose: the religion of the *finite life*, here represented by the silkworm. A *manifesto against the shroud* (V-D, 39), as Derrida calls this most intimate text, is set on 'diminished' ideals and virtues: simple patience instead of awaiting miracles and simple return to life instead of resurrection. Awaiting for the medical verdict, which tests his patience to the limit, Derrida, just like Kafka in Cixous's reading, 'is overcome by a terrible desire to live' (V-C, 13) which wants nothing but 'more life': 'the reality of the real, quite simply, if it's possible, ordinary reality finally rendered' (V-D, 87). But the private concreteness of this simple vital desire 'to stay, to remain' (SR, 3) only allows to reveal the secret engine of the deconstructive enterprise, which has always been working behind the scenes to undermine, in the Rosenzweigian manner, the abstract aloofness of philosophical systems. In his mood of 'protestation' against them (V-D, 39), Derrida once again targets Heidegger and returns to the themes of *Faith and Knowledge*. By questioning the sacrificial structure of *Sein-zum-Tode*, which celebrates its existential 'sublime offering', he sees himself rather as 'stretched-toward-other-resurrection' with another deity in sight: not the God who gives veil/shroud/death but a faceless 'unfigurable figure, beyond any holy shroud': the patient, ordinary, scathed and non-sublime, life-affirming *Khôra*.

> *Patience*, yes, the culture of the silkworm, and the quite incomparable patience it demands from a *magnanier*, the sericultivator. Where we're going, before the verdict falls, then, at the end of this time that is like no other, nor even like the end of time, another figure perhaps upsets the whole of history from top to bottom, and upsets even the meaning of the word 'history': neither a history of a veil, a veil to be lifted or torn, nor the Thing, nor the Phallus nor Death, of course, that would suddenly show itself at the last *coup de theatre*, at the instant of a revelation or an unveiling, nor a theorem wrapped up in shroud or in modesty, neither *aletheia*, nor *homoiosis*, nor *adequatio*, nor *Enthüllung*, nor *Unverborgenheit*, nor *Erschlossenheit*, nor *Entdecktheit*, nor *Übereinstimmung*, nor modesty, halt or reticence of *Verhaltenheit*, but *another unfigurable figure, beyond any holy shroud, the secret of a face that is no longer even a face* if face tells of vision and a story of the eye [...] But the resurrection I dream of, for my part, at the ends of the verdict, the resurrection I'm stretched out toward, would no longer have to be a miracle, but the reality of the real, quite simply, if it's possible, ordinary reality finally rendered, beyond fantasy or hallucination. (V-D, 31; 87; emphasis added)

Derrida's passage is thus a deliberate reversal of Cixous's story of coming into the light of *savoir*, but, at the same time, also a subtle move in her direction, closer to her doctrine of and 'for life', beautifully analysed in his lectures on Cixous from 1998, which eventually came out in a posthumous book, *H. C. Pour Vie, c'est a dire*: 'Death would be on my side and life on hers' (HC, 158).[37] While her heroine steps out of the

---

[37] There is a palpable hardening of Derrida's 'taking sides' towards the end of the book, which also shows his – somewhat prodigal – return to the idiom of Heidegger and Blanchot after he had strayed in the regions of pious life-wishing, while awaiting a verdict which then had not yet come: 'I would attempt to be convinced of life by her, preparing myself to receive grace instead of the *coup de grace*, but I am and remain for life *convaincu de mort* (both convicted and convinced of death); convicted, that is to say at fault and accused, found guilty, imprisoned or jailed after a verdict, here a death sentence, but also convinced, convinced by the truth of death, of a true speech (*veridictum*), of a verdict as regards death. She, on her Side [*de son Coté, avec un grand C*], is for life, she is convinced of life for life. Death counts for her, certainly, on every page, but she herself does not count. For me, death counts, it counts, and my days, my hours, and my seconds are numbered [...] The thing is,

pre-creational night of myopic Judaism, Derrida, by diminishing the light of the day (in *Tourner les mots*, he compares this strategy of obfuscation to the filming technic of *contre-jour*, literally: 'against the day'), devolves back into the 'white night' of his protective talisman/tallith, which, as he speculates, could also be his deadly shroud – while going gently, but at the same time not gently at all ('protest, attestation, testament, last will, manifesto'), into that good night, which the medical verdict may have in store for him.[38] He thus reduces himself in the act of *diminution* in which he sheds the shell of the French professor and returns to the kernel of his encrypted Marrano childhood. Diminution, therefore, would also be a partial unweaving of the veil/shroud burying the secret of the Marrano origin: a *genesis without genealogy*. While Cixous's story, *Savoir*, is all about unveiling – the apocalypses of the sudden 'And I saw' in the full light of the day – Derrida's response is about unweaving which does not do the analogical radical apocalyptic trick: it does not let see in the full light, does not bring absolute answer, does not give him a 'face to face' with his origin, and does not promise resurrection. While returning to the Spanish place in which he never was before – in other words, a *prosthesis of origin* – he talks about the 'return to life', but under different auspices than Sao Paulo or Sao Augustine: promising not life immortal, but only *this* life. In the first insight of self-revelation, Derrida sees his work as being neither/nor and, at the same time, both *an Odyssey and a Testament* – just like Leopold Bloom, the paradigmatic literary Marrano for whom home is never exactly home and exile never exactly an exile, he is simultaneously engaged in a childhood-seeking *nostos* and in a proleptic Exodus which projects 'the [prosthetic] memory of what did not take place' (MO, 61) into the future promise, *both* Odyssey and the Testament(s):

Whereas in *diminution*, if I understand right, the work is not undone...

> No, nothing is undone, on the contrary, but I would also like, in my own way, to name the shroud, and the voyage, but a *voyage without return, without a circle* or journey round the world in any case, or, if you prefer, a *return to life that's not a*

I just cannot believe her, as far as life death is concerned, from one side to the other. I just cannot believe her, that is to say: I can only manage to believe her, *I only manage to believe her when she speaks in the subjunctive*' (HC, 158–9; emphasis added). We have, however, seen that in his last essay on Joyce, the power of the 'pious wish' – which Derrida calls Cixou's subjunctive mode of conjuring death away: 'I wish it were not death...' – bounces back with its stubborn faith in life as survival. And the same can be said of the *Death Penalty Seminar*, conducted few years later, when the verdict of the pancreatic cancer already hovers over Derrida's life: here he once again steers away from Heidegger and Blanchot, this time under the wings – the sails and veils – of Montaigne, one of Cixous's favourite life-affirming writers.

[38] It is worth to remember that in *Or Ne'erav* (*The Pleasant Light*) Cordovero links the eponymous pleasant light to the *tsimtsum* as the diminution of the original *Or Ein-Sof*, the blinding light without limits, and then speculates on the etymological link between the word *erav* (pleasant), *erev* (mixed), and *arav* (darkened), which brings him to the following diagnosis of the metaphysical status of the world: '*Malkhut* [the earthly kingdom] was called by past sages "thick light" and due to its thickness it was also rendered "a mixed darkness"': Quot. in Zohar Raviv, *Decoding the Dogma within the Enigma: The Life, Works, Mystical Piety and Systematic Thought of Moses Cordovero* (Saarbrücken: VDM Verlag, 2008), 236. The whole world, therefore, lies in the pleasant shadow of the primordial *Lichtwesen*. This penumbral gentle lighting is also Derrida's favourite.

resurrection, neither the first nor the second, with and without the grand masters of discourse about the Resurrection, Saint Paul or Saint Augustine...
My God, so that's all your new work is, is it, neither an Odyssey nor a Testament...
No, just the opposite, it *is*: I'd like to call them to the witness-stand. (V-D, 22; emphasis added)

Derrida is thus in the passage, in one of his catachrestic travels, searching for the displaced origin in the Hispanophone New World, but he also misses what 'never travels' (V-D, 44) and what he left at home, like a pet animal – his tallith. Just like Molly is for Poldy the unmoved mover of his daily routine, which is both 'an Odyssey and a Testament', the tallith also lies and waits, silently pointing to the other tradition which has nothing to do with the Christian/philosophical game of the impatient veiling and unveiling, truth and un-truth, either in the a/pocalyptic or a/letheic sense of the word:

> A prayer shawl I like to touch more than to see, to caress every day, to kiss without even opening my eyes or even when it remains wrapped in a paper bag into which I stick my hand at night, eyes closed. And it is not an article of clothing, the tallith, although one wears it, sometimes right against one's skin. *Voila* another skin, but one incomparable to any other skin, to any possible article of clothing. It veils or hides nothing, it shows or announces no Thing, it promises the intuition of nothing. Before seeing or knowing [*le voir ou le savoir*], before fore-seeing or fore-knowing, it is worn in memory of the Law [...] before all else, my tallith touches itself. (V-D, 43; 64)

Just as circumcision makes a Jew before *he* can begin to comprehend *his* Jewishness, so does tallith as a 'second skin' compensates for the dramatic loss of the foreskin. Thus, when Cixous writes about Derrida's *écriture* that it weaves for him a 'second skin' – the tallith, in Hebrew also a feminine noun, becomes the visualization of Derrida's defence against the verdict of circumcision, which does not undo the cut itself, but rather undoes – 'diminishes' – its traumatic effect. *Tallith*, deriving from the root *ts-l-l*, is also related to *tsel* (shadow) and *tselem* (likeness): she is thus more than a garment, she grows right into one's flesh ('What is the self? My shawl', V-D, 44). 'Me, who would be capable of inventing circumcision all by himself, as I do here' – is precisely the Derrida wrapped up in his tallith: growing his second skin, like a skin of a pet-animal, against the previous loss of the foreskin, and thus becoming hairy like Esau: 'the tallith hangs on the body like a memory of circumcision' (V-D, 69), but a different, no longer threatening memory of the primal scene which could not have been witnessed by the self.

This may be a far jump, but this was precisely the dream of another Jacob – Jacob Frank – to become like his brother, Esau, and, by reinventing a Judaism of the Esavian line, undo the crookery of Jacob who merely stole the blessing and for that reason was punished by circumcision/castration.[39] In Frank's imagination, the Judaism of Esau,

---

[39] In *Memoirs of the Blind*, written in a similar time, the topic of Jewish blindness returns frequently, also in the context of Jacob's guilt of stealing the blessing from Esau, which may – but also may not – be treated as a Judaic version of the Augustinian *felix culpa*, destined to repeat itself: 'Why a second

preserved as the 'hidden truth' of the tradition, would also undo the castrating effects of circumcision and return the vital immortal powers of *Ein-Sof-Hayim*, limitless Life, to men who were deprived of it by the unjust verdict of the 'commissar' Yahve. Of course, as we have already noticed, Derrida is not Frank: he does not share the latter's desire for the resurrection of life unscathed. But he also dreams about at least partial reversal of the lethal fatality of the circumcising verdict, in which growing the second, animal and Esau-like, skin plays a crucial role: 'God weeping in me, turning around me, reappropriating my languages, dispersing their meaning in all directions [...] as I am someOne that the One God never stops *de-circumcising*' (C, 224; emphasis added). Just as for Frank, Esau-Judaism offers a messianic 'de-circumcising' healing of the life-sucking wound inflicted by Jacob-Judaism – for Derrida, his tallith becomes a *pas pro toto* of the 'diminished' Judaism which gives life and promise instead of death and terror. One can also think here about Walter Benjamin and his version of this opposition: the 'literary' Judaism of Haggadah, represented by the mighty Esavian 'paw', on the one hand – versus the 'traditional' Judaism of Halakhah, represented by the distant legal order of Jacob-Israel.[40]

In Derrida's own literary Haggadah, his tallith is not a veil that *hides*: it is a *hide* that protects. And while the veil *hides* the secret, this *hide* is a product of an inner secretion, a work of the silkworm. Not only the movement is reverse, from inside out as opposed to from the outside in, but also the relationship between passivity and activity. The veil actively conceals the secret which remains a passive object of the operation, laid down in the crypt as if it were dead – whereas the hide/skin is a result of the process of secretion in which the secret revives and, by venturing outward, shows signs of life: 'The secret of the shawl envelops one single body. One might think that it is woven for this one body proper, or even by it, from which it seems to emanate, like an intimate secretion' (V-D, 44). The tallith, therefore, is the secret come alive, no longer threatening, friendly, a furry totem of the other 'diminished' Judaism: 'unlike veil, sail, or canvas, a tallith is primarily animal' (V-D, 69). But not the roaring bull whose wounded raging cry can be heard in Shofar, the ritual blowing of the horn that concludes Yom Kippur liturgy as the divine voice from behind the Veil. She, the silky tallith, always stays home and as such is the living 'prosthesis of the origin': the canny of the uncanny, *das Heimliche des Unheimlichen*.

> So I no longer wear it. I simply place my fingers or lips on it, almost every evening, except when I'm traveling to the ends of the earth, *because like an animal it waits for me, well hidden in its hiding place, at home, it never travels* [...] Fur and skin: the

---

time? Why does this blind man, Jacob, after having himself been chosen or blessed by a blind father, Isaac, why does he in turn invert the natural order of the generations with an eye to obeying divine providence and observing its secret order?' (MB, 100).

[40] See again Benjamin on Kafka: 'His works are by nature parables. But their poverty and their beauty consist in their need to be *more* than parables. They don't simply lie down at the feet of doctrine, the way Haggadah lies down at the feet of Halakhah. Having crouched down, they unexpectedly cuff doctrine with a weighty paw'. Benjamin, *Selected Writings*, vol. 3, 326.

tallith must be something living taken from something living worn by something living. (V-D, 44; 69)

This is important: the livingness, *vivacité* of the tallith, which, for Derrida, is the essential moment of the messianic reversal that turns Judaism of death into Judaism of life, or Judaism as an ancient sacrificial religion into Judaism as faith beyond sovereignty, faith in the ordinary resurrections of simple finite life: 'As the skin comes not from just any animal but from sheep, ewe or ram, it in some sense commemorates an experience one would call sacrificial if the word "sacrifice" were not a bad translation for Korban ("approach," "coming together") and a *translation that moreover takes us back toward the cultures of the veil*' (V-D, 69; emphasis added). Life is not to be sacrificed in the 'sublime offering' which transports the subject beyond life and death – as well as beyond the veil – but itself becomes a new holy of hollies (this time in lower cases), sending a messianic message of *u-baharta ba-hayim*, 'choose to live', to all the living:

> and, leaping with one wingbeat to the eschatalogical term of the story, *the sacrifice of sacrifice, the end of sacrifice in coming together, its unterminated and perhaps interminable sublimation, the coming together of the infinite coming together in the horison of prayer*. (V-D, 70; emphasis added)

This 'coming together' – a new translation of *korban*, usually and wrongly rendered as 'sacrifice' – should thus be understood not as a clash of incommensurables – the infinite and the finite colliding in the apocalyptic explosion – but as *weaving together* a horizontal texture of prayer. *Korban* is not a sacrifice: it is the very end of sacrifice in the 'interminable sublimation' of the more archaic and violent, apocalyptic desire to tear the veil and be one with God. *Korban* as merely 'coming-together' is not a *unio mystica*; it does not promise union, it maintains separation and demands that the mystical drive gets sublimated into a prayer. A prayer 'for life'.

The meditation on the all-white tallith, a 'sign of being chosen' (V-D, 44), ends with the question, deliberately left unanswered, but pregnant with the narcissistic 'infantile presumptuousness' which Derrida, only half-jokingly, derided in himself – Derrida/Derrisa – in *Monolingualism*: 'If there had been one, what color would have been the tallith of someone who said: I am the truth and the life, I have come, they saw me not, I am the coming, etc., so long after another had said, first: here I am?' (V-D, 46). Would Jesus also have the all-white shawl?[41] Especially that the copy of *Shulchan Aruch* – a compendium of the ritual law compiled by Joseph Caro – which he inherited from his father, is 'all-black' (V-D, 67), thus forming a semi-Pauline contrast between the severity of the law and the messianic mercy, represented by the smooth and protective texture of the tallith. In this later circumfession, where tallith serves as a canvas of the *nachträglich* and finally liveable 'memory of circumcision', Derrida allows his secret to secret beyond the walls of the crypt: a revealment which has nothing

---

[41] See a great comment of David Farrell Krell on Derrida's Jesus-like messianic fantasies: 'The purest of bastards believes that he is the Son of God, that God is his mummy. And she is' (PB, 212).

to do with lifting of the veil, which he rejects as too sublime, too apocalyptic, too sacrificial ('. . .this thought of the event without truth unveiled or revealed, without phallogocentrism of the greco-judeo-paulino-islamo-freudo-heideggeriano-lacanian veil, without phallophoria, that is, without procession or theory of the phallus, without veiling-unveiling of the phallus, or even of the mere place, strictly hemmed in, of the phallus, living or dead', V-D, 85). His own personal Judaism – a 'Judaism of one's own' – chooses the intimacy, the 'pleasant light' of the 'white night', of life-protecting tallith over the exacting precision of the law, although, as he himself admits, he is now far from disdaining the 'pharisaic' heteronomy which he fiercely rejected in his childhood. But perhaps he comes to it 'too late': *sero te amavi*, as he repeats after Saint Augustine (V-D, 67), 'I began to love you too late. . .' Like Jacob, only half-covered by his Esavian skin – just enough to get him a blessing from blind Isaac, but not enough to grant him life immortal, dreamt about by Frank who was promising his followers that this time, the second messianic time, Esau's hide will cover their whole bodies – Jacques attempts to reconcile the conflicted twins and position himself in-between the rabbinic Judaism of the mortal wound, on the one hand, and the messianic Judaism of life unscathed, on the other. The tallith – the Kafkan phantastic animal: half-cat and half-lamb – manages to represent both Judaisms and unites them in one reconciling vision of history: the history made possible by the monotheistic invention of the One as the Unique (*ehad*) and, with it, a singular event, the first of which was *matan Torah*, the 'giving of the Law':

> *Liaison or alliance with the unpronounceable.* My tallith does not cover my whole body and leaves me vulnerable. I belong to it and I live in it before claiming it as my property. Perhaps it gives me in secret, I don't know, a roof or protection but, far from assuring me of anything at all, *it recalls me to the mortal wound*. Recalling me thus, everything in it recalls me to the 'One', the 'only once', 'for one only'. Unlike a veil, at least this is what I would like to teach or say in myself, this tallith depends on *the One of the unique*, the singular event whose repetition repeats only, and that's history, the 'once only' of the Law given, the 613 or so commandments that make up the Law (they say that the numerical value of the word designating the fringes of the tallith, the tzitziths, is 600, plus 8 threads and 5 knots, making 613). (V-D, 84; emphasis added)

In Derrida's meditation, therefore, the tallith becomes a new totemic animal: of the traditional Judaism (it is made from sheep, which refers back to the totemic ambivalence between ram and bull, brilliantly psycho-analysed by Theodor Reik in his 'Shofar'[42]); of Derrida's own private Judaism reconciling him with the trauma of circumcision (Esavian 'second skin'); and, last but not least, of Derrida's cryptophoric self which now is no longer dead-secret but live-secreting, where the touch of the tallith works as a trigger allowing for a slight opening of the crypt.

---

[42] See Theodor Reik, 'The Shofar (The Ram's Horn)', in *The Ritual: Psychoanalytic Studies* (Madison, CT: International Universities Press, 1970).

'But I am a worm and not a man': The inner silkworm

Derrida symbolizes this transformation of the buried self into a subtly emanating/leaking self, which reveals 'the truth of the self' (*vrai de soi*) without any apocalyptic veil-lifting and enlightening – that is, still *eu-calyptic*, without violation of the secret – by evoking 'a spectacular homonymy, one that works only in French' (V-D, 58) and that makes 'come together' (*korban*) not only *soi* (self) and *soie* (silk), but also *le voile* (sail) and *la voile* (veil). *Vrai de soi* – the truth-saying verdict of the secret self that ventures out to be found – can thus easily transform into *ver de soie*, the silkworm which secrets and weaves a protective cocoon around itself: a little worm that symbolizes the finite life, the touching finite life which 'touches itself' in the act of auto-affection and knows it's going to die. This allegory has a solid theological background: the line from Psalm 22.6: 'But I am a worm and not a man' (*Mais moi, je suis un ver, et non un homme*) – reverberates in Derrida's projective identification with his *ver de soie*. But not just this biblical source is significant here. The silkworm features large as a metaphor of the soul also in *The Inner Castle or the Mansions* of the most famous Marrano saint, Teresa of Avila:

> When, in the warm weather, the mulberry trees come into leaf, the little egg which was lifeless before its food was ready, begins to live. The caterpillar nourishes itself upon the mulberry leaves until, when it has grown large, people place near it small twigs upon which, of its own accord, it spins silk from its tiny mouth until it has made a narrow little cocoon in which it buries itself. Then this large and ugly worm leaves the cocoon as a lovely little white butterfly. If we had not seen this but had only heard of it as an old legend, who could believe it? Could we persuade ourselves that insects so utterly without the use of reason as a silkworm or a bee would work with such industry and skill in our service that the poor little silkworm loses its life over the task? [. . .] The silkworm symbolizes the soul which begins to live when, kindled by the Holy Spirit, it commences using the ordinary aids given by God to all, and applies the remedies left by Him in His Church, such as regular confession, religious hooks, and sermons; these are the cure for a soul dead in its negligence and sins and liable to fall into temptation. Then it comes to life and continues nourishing itself on this food and on devout meditation until it has attained full vigour, which is the essential point, for I attach no importance to the rest. When the silkworm is full-grown [. . .] *it begins to spin silk and to build the house wherein it must die*. By this house, when speaking of the soul, I mean Christ. I think I read or heard somewhere, either that our life is hid in Christ, or in God (which means the same thing) or that Christ is our life. It makes little difference to my meaning which of these quotations is correct. This shows, my daughters, how much, by God's grace, we can do, by preparing this home for ourselves, *towards making Him our dwelling-place* as He is in the *prayer of union* [. . .] Forward then, my daughters! hasten over your work and build the little cocoon.[43]

---

[43] Teresa of Avila, *The Interior Castle or the Mansions*, trans. from the Autograph of St. Teresa of Jesus by The Benedictines of Stanbrook (London: Thomas Baker, 1921), 130–1; emphasis added.

In Teresa's mystical imagery, the soul is like a silkworm which must bury itself in the white cocoon of Christian teaching in order to die as an ugly caterpillar and be reborn as a beautiful winged butterfly, finally capable to soar higher, towards the union with God. The above fragment is also a great illustration of the *converso* strategy of concealing Jewish motives and mixing them with Christian ones. When Teresa mentions 'prayer of union', it is a clear echo of the Yom Kippur prayers of at-one-ment. And when she says: 'I think I read or heard somewhere, [but] it makes little difference to my meaning which of these quotations is correct', Teresa, cautiously pretending to be an unlearned visionary, encrypts allusions not only to the Psalms of the Hebrew Bible, but also Talmud where God is called *makom*, the dwelling place, then *Merkhabah* mysticism of *heikhalot*, the palaces and their labyrinthine inner chambers that eventually lead to God's throne, and, last but not least, *Zohar* where chambers appear explicitly as divine emanations and *makom* acquires feminine features of *Shekhinah*, the divine dwelling on earth.[44] More than that, in *Zohar* commentary to *Bereshit*, we too find a silkworm metaphor which might have appealed to Teresa (as well as, independently, to Derrida):

> The brightness that it sowed for its honor is similar to the purple seed of the silkworm, for the worm encases itself within its own silk. And from that seed, it prepares for itself a chamber for its own glory and for the benefit of all. With this Beginning, the concealed unknown One created the chamber, and this chamber is called by the name 'Elohim'.

The worm, therefore, is not just a metaphor of the lowly humble condition, as in *Psalms*: here it is attributed also to the Ancient Nameless One who creates himself as 'Elohim' from his own seed 'encased within its own silk'. In *Zohar*, the silkworm represents the powers of autocreation: of becoming something with a name out of a nameless nothing.[45] Teresa – and, as we will see in a moment, Derrida too – combines these two *topoi*: the silkworm symbolizes precarity of a single finite life, but also stands for its self-creative resilience. But, apart from these two powerful sources, the figure of the silkworm appears in the writings of yet another Marrano crucial to Derrida's enterprise, Michel de Montaigne. When discussing the Pythagorean theory of metempsychosis, Montaigne evokes the silkworm in the context of the myth of Phoenix as the intermediary stage of raising from the ashes. What thus raises from the ashes is a completely new being, keeping no continuity with what ceased to be:

---

[44] In her book on Teresa of Avila, Deirdre Green enumerates all those possible influences with a special emphasis on the Zoharic heritage and concludes: '. . .if Teresa *was* aware of the origin of those elements of Jewish mystical tradition found in her writings, she would certainly have kept this knowledge to herself, for fear of more serious persecution from the Inquisition and the terrors that might entail': Deirdre Greene, *Gold in the Crucible: Teresa of Ávila and the Western Mystical Tradition* (Dorset: Element, 1989), 119.

[45] In David Biale's account, this self-creative power was traditionally attributed by the rabbis to the Scripture: 'Like an ancient worm spinning a gossamer of silk out of itself, Scripture seemingly has the power to produce an infinite range of new expressions': David Biale, *What is Judaism?* (New York: W. W. Norton, 2015), 56.

They say that from the ashes of the Phoenix there is born first a worm and then another Phoenix; can anyone think that the second Phoenix is no different from the first? The worm which produces silk for us can be seen dying and shrivelling up: then, from that same body a butterfly appears; that produces another worm: it would be absurd to think it was still the first one. That which once ceases to be no longer exists.[46]

In the Derridean idiom, which combines all those influences, the *ver a soie* is simultaneously the symbol of the self-encased secret and of the emanating secretion that, like a Phoenix rising out of the ashes, creates always something new: a manifest expression which betrays the secret and grows on its grave. It is the symbol of the inward crypt of dark silence and the outward chamber of the first 'pleasant light' in which the self can begin to live and expand. Retreat and bringing forth; contraction and expansion:

The silkworm produced outside itself, before itself, what would never leave it, a thing that was no other than itself, a thing that was not a thing, a thing that belonged to it, to whom it was properly due. It projected outside what proceeded from it and remained at bottom at the bottom of it: outside itself in itself and near itself, with a view to enveloping it soon entirely. *Its work and its being toward death.* The living, tiny but still divisible formula of absolute knowledge. *Absolute nature and culture.* Sericulture was not man's thing, not a thing belonging to the man raising his silkworms. It was the culture of the silkworm qua silkworm. Secretion of what was neither a veil nor a web (nothing to do with the spider), nor a sheet nor a tent, nor a white scarf, *this little silent finite life* was doing nothing other, over there, so close, right next to me but at an infinite distance, nothing other than this: *preparing itself to hide itself, liking to hide itself with a view to coming out* and losing itself spitting out the very thing the body took possession of again to inhabit it, *wrapping itself in white night*. With a view to returning to itself to have for oneself what one is, to have oneself [*s'avoir*] and to be oneself [*s'être*] while ripening but dying thus at birth, fainting to the bottom of oneself which comes down to burying oneself gloriously in the shadow at the bottom of the other: (*Aschenglorie:* ... *grub ich mich in dich und in dich.*) *Love itself. Love made itself make love* right next to the watching dreaming child. (V-D, 89–90; emphasis added)

Now, Derrida, this little silent finite life – the dreaming child, recalling a little box with the miraculous creature in it – is doing exactly the same as his patient worm: inventing a new redemptive language in which he will retell his Marrano condition of cryptophoria as not just deadening, but also enlivening: as not just madness, death, the end of all stories, but also work and love, even new birth; not just miserable *survie*, but also a renewed life of *sur-vie*. In this new idiom of post-traumatic survival,

---

[46] Michel de Montaigne, 'An Apology for Raymond Sebond', in *The Complete Essays*, trans. A. M. Screech (London: Penguin, 2003), 580.

in which life always brushes – 'comes together' – with death, the *crypt transforms into a cocoon*: its walls soften ('I would like to sing the very solitary softness of my tallith, softness softer than softness, entirely singular, both sensory and non-sensory, calm, acquiescent. . .', V-D, 84) and turn into a protective shawl/second skin which watches over *another resurrection*: imago raising out of the caterpillar; *tselem*, the mature self/*soi* ready to be found out, emerging out of the white shadow of the silky *tsel/tallith*. The silkworm's cocoon and the tallith mingle here into one, because the latter's inside lining is usually made of silk – and silk is the very secretion of the secret: 'neither a veil not a web', it is at the same time a shell and a kernel, Frank's *łuspina i orzech* (the wrap and the seed), a crypt and a feeding cocoon, a 'wrapping of a white night' or, equally antithetical, Celan's *Aschenglorie*: the glory of white ashes metamorphosing into glowing cinders or the Zoharic 'purple seeds'. This is also what in Celan's imaginary becomes the highest alchemic transmutation: life coming out of death, which is 'love itself' – *love strong as death*.

But the silkworm allegory can also be read as the ultimate metaphor of the Marrano condition, the way it was suggested by Teresa of Avila: as the secret that comes out and secretes those wraps which simultaneously bury and feed. The phrase 'liking to hide itself with a view to coming out' perfectly mirrors Winnicott's apothegm – 'It is joy to be hidden, but a disaster not to be found' – which, as I suggested already in the Introduction, summarizes the Marrano fate in just one sentence. According to Jacob Frank's doctrine of the shell and the kernel (*łuspina i orzech*), the seeds of the true messianic faith must grow unbothered in protective darkness, hidden from sight and light: this is why the white tallith, which covers to protect, 'belongs to the night' – the silky 'white night'. Stretching the psychoanalytic connection a bit further, *she* is definitely Derrida's *good object* – like, similarly, *Khôra*, whose colour is just as misty and whiteish: a life-death seen as simultaneously *eu-zein* and *eu-thanatein*, glad-living and glad-dying.[47] And just as in the cryptophoric condition, where the self is the

---

[47] We saw with Molly that the figure of a woman emerges in Derrida as a trope of a *double affirmation*: 'yes, yes' – meaning 'yes to life, yes to death'. It is, therefore, a figure of *another finitude* finding an 'infinite pleasure' both in living and in dying. This figure is kept deliberately phantasmatic – surrounded with a messianic halo – and it appears in Derrida's writings as early as 'Law of the Genre', which refers to Blanchot's *Folie de jour*, where *folie* and *filia* come into an intense interplay. Derrida will find *la folie* of this *filia/philia* – a madness and an excess of this double loving affirmation – also in Cixous, especially in his *H.C: That Is To Say, For Life*, being one grand variation on the Blanchotian theme on 'women, the beautiful creatures'. Commenting on the opening lines of Blanchot's story – 'I am neither learned nor ignorant. I have known some joy. This is saying too little: I am living, and this life gives me the greatest pleasure. And death? When I die (perhaps soon), I shall know an immense pleasure. I am not speaking of the foretaste of death, which is bland and often disagreeable. Suffering is debilitating. But this is the remarkable truth of which I am sure: I feel a boundless pleasure in living and shall be boundlessly content to die. . .' – Derrida writes: 'the double negation gives passage to a double affirmation *(yes, yes)* that enters into alignment or alliance with itself. Forging an alliance or marriage-bond ("hymen") with itself, this boundless double affirmation utters a measureless, excessive, immense *yes*: both to life and to death [. . .] the chance and probability of such an affirmation (one that is double and therefore boundless, limitless) is granted to woman. It returns to woman. Rather, not to woman or even to the feminine, to the female genre/gender, or to the generality of the feminine genre but – and this is why I spoke of chance and probability – "usually" to women. It is "usually" women who say *yes, yes*. To life to death. This "usually" avoids treating the

guardian of the crypt, so is the cocoon of *soie* a *soi*: *the self is the secretion of the secret*. It is this 'secretion' which mediates between the total concealment, on the one hand, and the total revealment, on the other: the complete burial of the inhabitant of the crypt and the demolition of the crypt by the apocalyptic full light of redemption and, at the same time, annihilation. Derrida's self is cryptophoric – perhaps even phantomatic, carrying the crypt of their parents' crypt, thus en-crypted to the second power (or, perhaps, even *n*'th power in the Marrano *mise en abime*) – and must remain so: it can only survive in the eucalyptic/well-hidden and myopic/half-blind condition of the 'white night' that merely allows for a spectral, silvery-silky, secretion (remember how, in the Introduction, when referring to Benjamin's metaphor of tradition as the sea and the wave, I compared Derrida's particular form of cresting to 'a singular, delicate, lace-like, foamy structure of a unique *Haggadah*'). All violent dragging into light could only mean, in his case, a death of the self – hence Derrida's stubborn 'resistance to psychoanalysis', as well as his refusal to analyse his liaison with the white tallith any further, in fear that it may bring a terrible *lysis*, a not at all lucky break with what keeps him alive:

> I would like to sing the very solitary *softness* of my tallith [...] a stranger to anything maudlin, to effusion or to pathos, in a word to all 'Passion.' *And yet, compassion without limit, compassion without idolatry, proximity and infinite distance. I love the peaceful passion, the distracted love my tallith inspires in me*, I get the impression it allows me that distraction because it is sure, so sure of me, *so little worried by my infidelities*. It does not believe in my inconstancies, they do not affect it. I love it and bless it with a strange indifference, my tallith, in a familiarity without name or age. As if faith and knowledge, *another faith and another knowledge*, a knowledge without truth and without revelation, were woven together in *the memory of an event to come*, the *absolute delay of the verdict*, of a verdict to be rendered and which is, was, or will make itself arrive without the glory of a luminous vision. My white tallith belongs to the night, the absolute night. *You will never know anything about it, and no doubt neither will I*. (V-D, 84–5; emphasis added)

If the whole circumfession of the silkworm is a feverish oneiric text, this fragment constitutes its true *Traumnabel*: the navel of the dream, the secret of Derrida's *Marrano rêverie*. In this other circumfession of another self – not the hidden traumatized one, but the one venturing out, wanting to be found out – everything appears *in speculum et enigmate* of a dreamy messianic reversal which rubs all rough contours of Judaism, this severe religion of the Law, and, by the softness of the maternal good object, the tallith, returns the 'dreaming child' back to its immemorial origins: the *wo es war* of circumcision as the 'absolute force' imposed from the outside before even

---

feminine as a general and generic force; it makes an opening for the event, the performance, the uncertain contingencies, the encounter' (LG, 222). In Kafka, this privilege of glad-living and glad-dying belongs to the happy pagan, Hunter Gracchus, but only before the *Unglück* happens and he becomes 'undead' as the one inscribed into Jewish religion.

a possibility of either protestation or consent. 'All will be the same, but just a little different', a 'famous rabbi' said about the messianic 'slight adjustment'[48] – and this is precisely what occurs here: the same condition of a 'silent finite life', destined to die and awaiting the verdict, but seen and told differently, backed up with another faith and another knowledge. The tallith – here a synecdoche of Derrida's *maternal Judaism*, a soft 'diminished' compensation to the sublime paternal religion of the Law, which he expected from his mother, Esther, but in vain – grants another access to the lost tradition: patient, compassionate, untroubled by his Marrano strayings and betrayals, indifferently benign (again, like Molly or *Khôra*). But, although *another Judaism*, it is still Judaism: without idolatry, respecting the rule of separation, sober, alien to the Christian theo-dramatic pathos of the tragedy of the cross. Is it possible? Well, in this dream it exists – or, as Cixous calls it, *dreamexists (revexiste)*.[49] The Marrano comes home which is never quite home, but *still...* 'The childman weary, the manchild in the womb. Womb? Weary? He rests. He has travelled' (U, 722).

Speaking about travel and wombs: in the letter to Catherine Malabou, who asked Derrida to reflect on his view on travelling, written on the 10 May 1997 in Istanbul, Derrida describes his encounter with a mysterious Sephardic community (which, as he notices with some enthusiasm, might have been related to the Turkish Sabbatian *donmeh*) and which triggers in him a particularly intense *Marrano rêverie*: a cryptophoric dream of carrying in the inner crypt/womb a larva of a Messiah who is on the verge to be born and who, when turned into a full imago, will have swept away Derrida' aporetic divided self. This impression, equally dreamy and dense as the meditation on the silkworm, could indeed be titled with a paraphrasis on Derrida's essay on the animal that he is/follows: *Messiah donc que je suis*, where the verb *suis*

---

[48] This term, *en geringeres Zurechtstellen*, coined by Walter Benjamin, appears in his essay on Kafka in reference to Gershom Scholem: Walter Benjamin, 'Franz Kafka', in *Illuminations: Essays and Reflections*, trans. Harry Zohn (New York: Schocken Books, 1968), 134.

[49] While discussing Hélène Cixous's own story on *her* tallith (if the tallith, strictly prohibited to be worn by women, can ever be *hers*) as compared to his 'long tender meditation to my tallith' (HC, 155), Derrida suddenly recollects this fortunate verb, *revexister* (HC, 157), which derives from Cixous's short story, 'La Baleine de Jonas' [Jonas's Whale] from the 1967 volume, *Le Prenom de Dieu*. Here, the male hero who inherits the tallith openly avows his cryptophoric condition: 'I contained the lost object, it was inside, and the inside was my being': Hélène Cixous, *Le prenom de Dieu* (Paris: Editions Grasset, 1967), 156. In the reconciliatory mood inspired by his dreamy, soft and gentle, other Judaism, Derrida comments on this story: 'Now I am ready to argue over everything, to argue with her over everything, except a tallith' (HC, 158). Cixous, in her *Portrait*, returns to Derrida's tallith as the silkworm's work of love and identifies it as the key to his imaginative Marrano Judaism, but perhaps also a respite from the restlessness of the Marrano eternal 'passer-by', destined to an endless travelling. Respecting Derrida's prohibition of inquiry into his intimate relation with his tallith/*Khôra/Shekhinah*, Cixous writes: 'I stop without knowing and without seeing. I shall stay with the vision of his astounding union with the white tallith, this *white wedding that belongs to the night*. We shall never know. This was the marvelous tale of the Jew of the night. One can only tell it in French, with a French that surpasses French. Just as he goes beyond the French language, so his Jewish being his Jewish not-being [*son nêtre juif*] his Jewish birth [*son naitre juif*] surpasses (being not being) Judaity Judaism Judaicity Judaica and everything else that might come along with a *j, u,* and *d*, for if as a Marrano he is Jewish at least it is in passing, between the French language, in the turns of French, a passer-by' (PJD, 114; emphasis added).

refers both to being and following/hunting.[50] He is simultaneously the beast and the hunter: the little finite life which wishes to stay away from eschatological events in order to 'have a moment of joy'[51] – and the restless pursuer, terrified of his own potential transformation; a Marrano who blithely forgets his filiation – and a Marrano who cannot stop searching for the secret that is greater and older than him:

> As is often the case, I go looking for exiles and have discovered a very old Sephardic community near here. There are various hypotheses about them [. . .] and I feel, a little like them perhaps, like a survivor, more Marrano than ever. Most often I watch myself traveling without changing places, an immobile voyeur who would analyze what befalls his body in movement with the world. Movie camera without a camera, kinetoscope for a sort of *errance* that is forever encrypted: the always incognito displacement of a secret that I transport without knowing. Even when I speak in front of large crowds, I feel that I transport this secret (I can hear its heartbeat like a child in the womb) but don't understand anything about it. Perhaps it will be told to me while abroad: revelation, bedazzlement, conversion. I fall down backwards, I am born, I die at the moment when, at the end of an unknown alley, I meet the Messiah who will come out of me where he has been hiding for so long. You are giving birth? Think also of a spy charged with a mission. They have confided to this secret agent a message that he can't read, perhaps his own death sentence [. . .] That is why I call myself a 'Marrano': not because of the peregrinations of a wandering Jew, not because of successive exiles, but because of the clandestine search for a secret that is greater and older than me, eschatological, fatal for me, *as me*. That is why I *hunt* it – there is no other word – I am in pursuit of it while making it flee [. . .] It is I who is hunting and I who is pursued. There is someone I would like to save from me by keeping them in me [. . .] Like certain Marranos I would have begun by forgetting, by believing that I have simply forgotten my filiation [. . .] *I am exaggerating, as I always do, with these Messianic scenarios, but they terrify me at the same time* [. . .]. (CP, 14–15: Istanbul, 10.05.1997; emphasis added)

Philosophy as the passion for the veil: *Eucalypse now!*

We have just peeped into the 'murky shop' of Derrida's *psychotheology*: the meandering link between his own cryptophoria, resonating with Cixous's similar condition, for

---

[50] Cixous understands this oscillation between the beast and the Messiah – the larva and the imago, Jew and Jesus – perfectly well, by seeing it as the integral moment of Derrida's Marrano imagination: 'If *Jesuis juif* [If I-am Jewish, if Jesus Jewish], he might say of himself, by way of a joke, it is as wounded [*blessé*] migod mianimal [half-god, half-animal], a sort of striped beast, speaking French as in fables' (TSB, 76).

[51] 'Are not my few days almost over? Turn away from me, so I can have a moment of joy', says Job to God (Job 10.20).

ever ambivalent, double bound, containing both lethal threat and messianic promise; a unique treasure of *das Rettende* to be cautiously guarded, as well as the 'highest danger', *das Gefährlichste*, to be guarded from. In that sense, for Derrida, Marranism, being cryptophoric to the second power, not only does not constitute a deviation from Judaism: it emerges as its intensification which 'transmutes weakness into merit' (see Nietzsche's epigram again). But we also saw that Derrida locates in his Marranism a therapeutic chance, which he immediately universalizes in terms of a new redemption: a new, not so terrifying, messianic scenario thanks to which he – as well as 'we', the secretive community of universal Marranos/cryptophores – can save himself from the tragedy of infinite mourning and turn threat into promise. With the little help of Kafka and especially Joyce, Derrida writes his own divine comedy in which he could *re-joyce* and find 'laughter through tears' (AR, 359): a 'mystical fable' which is not (only) about the tragic cycle of law, trespass, penalty, and exoneration, but (also) about love, laughter, generosity, and letting-be of 'unprejudiced becoming'. And he finds this bright reverse of Judaism in his tallith, a protective 'second skin' and a veil spun by the silkworm, which defends him against the deadly exposure to the 'strong light of the canonical' emanating from the crypt.

But how does this private literary story/Haggadah translate into Derrida's philosophy? In the essay on the 'apocalyptic tone recently adopted in philosophy' – which directly refers to Kant's famous prototype but indirectly to all the contemporary Helpers/ Hasteners of the Apocalypse (Derrida mentions here Heidegger, Blanchot, and Lacan) – Derrida defends deconstruction as a form of enlightenment which uses light against light or, in terms of the *tsimtsum* paradigm, forces light to self-contract and diminish. While it may be true that, in Heraclitus words, 'the lightning steers all' – this flash of light must also be steered: harnessed and made to work for the sake of the world, not against it.[52] The apocalyptic frenzy, therefore, has to be partially *covered*: if it is to bring light and *not* destruction, it must be, in the Hegelian manner, 'held in check' (PS, 118). Derrida's name for this partial covering – the reduction of the light according to the *tsimtsum* paradigm – is the term 'antithetical' to *apokalyptos*, 'fully revealed': it is now *eukalyptos*, 'well covered' and 'well hidden under the avowed desire for revelation' (APO, 23).

On Derrida's account, enlightenment is not a simple secular formation, but a form of an emphatically *procosmic* religious commitment which maintains a complex relation with the apocalyptic lightning of revelation:

> It is difficult to separate the concept of secularization from the concept of *Lumières*, *Illuminisimo*, Enlightenment, or *Aufklärung*, and from the link between the Enlightenment [*Lumières*] of reason (according to Kant, for example) and the light, which is the very element in which revelation, revelations, and above all Judeo-

---

[52] In Hermann Diels's *Fragmente der Vorsokratiker*, this is fragment nr 64: translation slightly altered after Martin Heidegger and Eugen Fink, *Heraclitus Seminar*, trans. Charles Seibert (Evanston: Northwestern University Press, 1993), 4–11, where this aphorism is thoroughly discussed. According to Heidegger and Fink, the Heraclitean lightning is at once fire and logos which governs the rhythm of nature: its *genesis kai phthora*, coming-forth-into-being and perishing.

Christian revelation have been announced and advanced. This connection between the light [*la lumière*] and Enlightenment [*les Lumières*] is already the site of secularization [*sécularisation*]. This is already the analogy that permits *the passage between religion and the world* [*le siècle*], *between revelation and the world*. (CS, 139)

Secularization, therefore, does not announce the age of atheism, but a more gradual passage from the traditional acosmic religion centred around the transcendent God to the modern procosmic 'religion of new times' (Hegelian *Religion der neuen Zeiten*) which decenters the Absolute and focuses on the world as the new arena of eschatological scenarios. As belonging to Enlightenment, deconstruction is always on the side of justice – as Derrida famously claims, deconstruction is conditioned by the 'undeconstructible idea of justice' (SM, 74) – but this is not the otherworldly absolute justice which wishes the world to vanish according to the rule *pereat mundus, sed fiat iustitia*, enthusiastically affirmed by Kant:[53] it belongs to the penumbral lights of *saeculum* or the world (*le siècle*).

Thus, if there is a difference that really makes a difference between Derrida and his philosophical generation, called by him somewhat derisively an 'apocalyptic sect' (APO, 25) it would be this: his suspicion towards the philosophical passion for the Real that longs to tear all the symbolic veils, producing only an 'effect of the real', and bring in the *Kingdom of What Is Really There* – *parousia*, Face-to-Face, Full Light, Ultimate Truth, *jouissance*. Derrida does not belong to this constellation, he does not share the 'passion for the Real'.[54] There is no trace of fetishism of the Real in Derrida's metaphysics of arche-writing, where *différance* constitutes a quasi-transcendental *techne/gramme* of possibilitating the play of phenomenal differences or the 'differential vibration' (DJ, 80), more as a self-iterating code of reality than a hidden Unnameable – somehow *there*, but unreachable – a code to which the hide-and-seek of presence/absence simply does not apply.

For Derrida, the only Real is the 'effect of the Real' in the play of the world, which cannot be put in contrast with any unthinkable *Ding an sich*. The whole point of Derrida's conceptual revolution is thus to go beyond the dualism of the Real and the Effected/Constituted, which plagues transcendental philosophy from Kant, through Heidegger, to Lacan, and to end the *passion de reel*. His faith in the world is, as we have seen in the previous chapter, certainly not naïve, it has a meta-philosophical stake at its core: the overcoming of the oldest and most persistent of philosophy's superstitions, which rejects the phenomenal reality as nothing but a symbolic veil and seeks the noumenal Real as the place of the Truth. Hence, he will always see his own work as

---

[53] While commenting on Kant's ethics, Michael Rosen does not hide his fear of the apocalyptic terror which it openly endorses: 'The austere slogan of retributivism was always: let justice be done although the world perishes (*fiat justitia, pereat mundus*). Kant's position seems even harsher – let justice be done even if we have to create a hell for it to be done in': Michael Rosen, 'Die Weltgeschichte ist das Weltgericht', in *Internationales Jahrbuch des deutschen Idealismus*, ed. F. Rush (Berlin: De Gruyter, 2014), 13.

[54] See most of all, Alain Badiou, *The Century*, trans. Alberto Toscano (Cambridge: Polity Press, 2007), where the 'passion of the real' is the main subject defining the twentieth-century philosophy.

a counter-philosophical practice of writing-on-the-veil and compare himself half-jokingly to all the Schleiermachers and Webers – veil-makers and veil-weavers – that sustain the world in being, contrary to the common philosophical prejudice which accuses them of working for the evil archon or the malicious demon of deception, spinning their treacherous 'veils of Maia'.[55] Let's read again this fragment in the *Veils*, where Derrida evokes the motif of the unrestrained passion for the Real and contrasts it with the alternative paradigm of *tsimtsum* as the 'interminable diminution':

> We'll have to give up touching as much as seeing, and even saying. *Interminable diminution*. For you must know right now: to touch 'that' which one calls 'veil' is to touch everything. You'll leave nothing intact, safe and sound, neither in your culture, nor in your memory, nor in your language, as soon as you take on the word 'veil'. As soon as you let yourself be caught up in it [. . .] nothing will remain, *nothing will remain anymore* [. . .] Finishing with the veil is finishing with self. (V, 24–5; emphasis added)

As well as, we may add, finishing with the world. 'Is that what you're hoping for from the verdict?' (V, 25), asks Derrida himself, or rather the philosopher in himself who sometimes shows signs of impatience with weaving the veils of being. But then, he immediately checks himself – holds his apocalyptic desire 'in check' (PS, 118) – and evokes the patience of the silkworm with which he secretly identifies in his Marrano soul: '*Patience*, yes, the culture of the silkworm, and the quite incomparable patience it demands from a magnanier, the sericultivator' (V, 31). To have faith is thus to exercise the infinite patience of sericultivation that tends to the veils spun by the macrocosmic silkworm which, as we have seen, is one of the names of God in *The Book of Splendor* and which can be comprehended only within the unique theological model of the heterodox 'diminished' Judaism of *tsimtsum*, unlike all the other religious and philosophical traditions *thankful for the veil*:

> *Thanks to a veil given by God*, and giving here is ordering [*donner c'est ici ordonner*]. Whether or not this unbelievable separation (belief itself, faith) came to an end with the death of Christ, will it ever be comprehended, will it ever be comprehensible in the veiled folds of a Greek *aletheia*? No being, no present, no presentation can here be indicated in the indicative. It was, is, shall be, shall have been, should have been for all time the sentence, the saying of God, his verdict: by God order is given to give the veil, the veil (is) the gift (that it is) ordered to give. Nothing else that is. *God would thus be the name of what gives the order to give the veil, the veil between the holy and the holy of holies*. Now 'God,' the name of God,

---

[55] The punning on Schleiermacher and Weber (both Max and Samuel) appears in *Veils*, but also in *Fichus*, where the title word meaning *Halsstück* derives from a dream of Walter Benjamin, in which he imagined that a poetry should be able to metamorphose into a little shawl made of silk. Knowing that Derrida's tallith was also made of silk, we can safely assume that he treated it also as a *fichus*: a veil on which he would leave his signature as the 'silkworm of one's own' and 'the artist of this weaving' (PM, 181).

distinguishes between the artist or inventor of the veil, on the one hand, and the embroiderer on the other. (V, 29; emphasis added)

Let us remember that, in 'Ten Unhistorical Aphorisms on Kabbalah', Gershom Scholem famously defined the Kabbalistic 'transforming view' as the path-breaking intuition that 'all worlds are nothing more than "names recorded" on the scroll of God's essence' ('Namen, die auf dem *Papier* von Gottes Wesen *aufgezeichnet* werden').[56] Derrida's faith follows this hunch which intuits God as the silkworm/inventor of the veil, and also the first embroider. This metaphor dominates the opening paragraph of *Zohar*: 'In the beginning – when the will of the King began to take effect, he engraved signs into the heavenly sphere that surrounded him.'[57] So, indeed, 'thanks to a veil given by God' – *hail to the veil* – without which nothing would have happened, but also 'nothing will remain anymore' (V, 24). If there is a passion here, it is deliberately *oblique*: it is a passion for the veil – *passion de voile* – firmly opposed to the *passion de reel*. What thus Scholem translates as the will of God 'taking effect', Derrida understands literally: the only real is the real effected by the writing on the veil, beyond which, as *Zohar* teaches, 'nothing can be known'.[58] The apocalyptic imagination, both Jewish and Christian, will always focus on the divine 'engravings' as the *writing on the wall* – the warning of the Last Judgment or, as Adorno calls it wittily, 'the always new Menetekel' (ND, 351) – but to those thinking according to the paradigm of 'interminable diminution' (V, 24), they will appear as the very opposite: the letting-be *writing on the veil* which diminishes the infinite splendor of *Or Ein-Sof*, the Light of Lights, and separates it for ever from the 'pleasant light' of the shadowland where being and life become first possible. The defenders of the world, therefore, weave the veil further as 'ordered by God': they are like Sheherazade always differing and deferring the apocalyptic finale.

Indeed, the figure of Sheherazade nicely personifies the abstract rule of *différance* as the Other Sophia of the metaphysics of writing: the self-iterating and self-differentiating arche-writing/'engravings', embroidered on the veil as the Divine Wisdom (*Hohkmah*) or the code for the world which, so Derrida hopes, will turn out to be a *perpetuum mobile*. It is in this *machina ex deo* – the 'red type-ribbon' which envelopes like a Möbius strip, with the 'engravings' on the one side and beings on the other – that we trust, this game/play of the world that, as Derrida wants to believe, will go on for ever: the more mechanical, the better, that is, more assured in its repetition and no longer dependent on the divine caprice, as in Kierkegaard, for whom repetition is always only a sign of God's good will that can be any time revoked. It is precisely this machine of *différance* that allows the miracle of being to persist on and make itself true. In the machine we trust, which means that, for Derrida, faith consists in giving 'thanks to a veil given by God' (V, 29) and in treating the '*effect* of the real' as *real*, full stop.[59]

---

[56] Biale, 'Scholem's 'Ten Unhistorical Aphorisms on Kabbalah', 85.
[57] Scholem and de Leon, *The Book of Spendor*, 3; emphasis added.
[58] Scholem and de Leon, *The Book of Spendor*, 3.
[59] In *Faith and Knowledge*, this self-assuring machine of giving 'without the slightest generosity' (FK, 100) is attributed to *Khôra*. The Kabbalists discovered this affinity too, when they compared the 'engravings' to the Platonic imprints which the demiurge leaves on the primary matter, here

Without this faith, we fall back into the madness of the Cartesian hyperbolic doubt which sees all the '*effects* of the will of the King' as nothing but deception that conceals the true Real. The Derridean-Kabbalistic *God who gives the veil* is definitely not a *deus fallax* of the nominalist theology, deeply entrenched in the thought of Descartes and Kierkegaard. He is a Silkworm of His Own, the originary 'artist of this weaving' (PM, 181), the Arche-Schleiermacher and the Arche-Weber, who spins the yarn of creation as his never-ending signature. Just as in Joyce, therefore, the name of God refers to 'the artist or inventor of the veil, on the one hand, and the embroiderer on the other' (V, 29). The Veil is not what conceals and deceives; the Veil is *das Papier Gottes*, the silky scroll or *fichus* on which God writes the world and the world cannot be any more real than as written: a *Paper Machine*. The Veil, therefore, is not a curse or an obstacle that hinders the view of the Real: it is a gift of being.

The real is thus solely in the effect, the truth is in the mask. The statement from 'The Plato's Pharmacy' – 'Nontruth is the truth. Nonpresence is presence. *Différance*, the disappearance of any originary presence, is *at once* the condition of possibility *and* the condition of impossibility of truth' (DIS, 166) – could thus be read as a Marrano palimpsest which deliberately risks a clash between the two very different idioms: the one, driven by the passion for the Real, which keeps calling all the *effects* as nontruth and nonpresence in expectation of something better, more *an sich*, behind the 'veil of Maya' – and the other, driven by the passion for the Veil, which plays with the old metaphysics and introduces new concepts on its wearied back. What the metaphysical tradition routinely discards as nontruth and nonpresence – the rejected stone of mere appearance and deception – in the Derridean Marrano reversal becomes a solid stuff on which Derrida can build a new sense of presence, truth and reality as the *masks/veils* of the 'will of the King' or his 'desire to create an event' (GT, 157).

Recall once again the image of the blind man in Toledo, reading his book in the Braille alphabet, the embossed engraved signs on the scroll of paper, which so strongly mesmerized Derrida: isn't it also an image of the Ancient Hidden One, immersed in his night, blind, unknown even to itself, who invents the other, by inventing the first alphabet of creation: the 'engravings' on *Papier Gottes*, his 'memoirs of the blind', which he then reads/touches and, while he is caressing the signs, the world springs into being – on the other side? There is no camera that can show what is happening behind the veil, no 'allbrightness' that can penetrate this eternal secret:

> When camera turned towards him and during the filming, he remained himself, in his infinite solitude, turned elsewhere [*ailleurs*], turned towards himself in the inwardness of his secret. *His* secret. A secret of which now and forever we will know that we know nothing. A secret of which we also know, once and for all [*une fois pour toutes*], that it will never come out. (TM, 77)

---

identified with the Wisdom/*Hokhmah* as the 'dough of all creation': see Wolfson, *Heidegger and Kabbalah*, 102.

Just as Derrida touches/reads his white tallith, comparing himself to a silkworm and her to its cocoon – so does the Nameless Silkworm, who started the yarn of creation, touch/read the Braille signs, embroidered on the 'type ribbon' which keeps the world going. The blind man of Toledo is Derrida's ultimate mystical vision which puts him in the line of other Marrano mystics, heterodox on all fronts: the Ancient Blind One, restlessly typing and touch-reading the signs and losing himself in those signs-traces, turned inward, inaccessible to any light. An absolute withdrawal, a perfect *tsimtsum*.

In the next chapter, I will trace the trajectory that leads from Derrida's own *voyage mystique* – from *l'ailleurs*, the 'elsewhere' of the sealed inner secret – back to the world. I will try to show how his own mystical travel becomes a model for the political 'we': a new community of secret sharers who return to the world, but always and only on their own terms.

5

Ana-community

Marrano 'living together'

Everyday opinion sees in the shadow merely the absence of light, if not its complete denial. But, in truth, the shadow is the manifest, though impenetrable, testimony of hidden illumination. Conceiving of the shadow this way, we experience the incalculable as that which escapes representation, yet is manifest in beings and points to the hidden being.
            Martin Heidegger, 'The Time of the World-Picture', in *Off the Beaten Track*, 85.

To guard the silence that guards me, such would be the order – which I understand almost in the religious sense of a community, or rather a non-community, of a solitude of withdrawal from the world . . .
            Derrida, 'Abraham, the Other', 6.

In Chapter 2, we saw that the Marrano religion is neither the 'natural religion' of the one human nature nor the 'revealed religion' of a particular chosen nation (first Jewish, then European-Christian). According to Derrida, it is abstract and because of that universal, but its abstraction must be conceived differently than in Kant's formalism or Hegel-Kojève's sublation into one global and unified 'religion of the Spirit', in which 'the moral law inscribes itself at the bottom of our hearts like a memory of the Passion' (FK, 50). Although close to the radically iconoclastic and unnameable 'desert in retreat', the Marrano religion is not without content: its 'determinate abstraction' urges its followers to wander away from their origins, disperse, multiply, and become universal, for, as Derrida says, 'in uprooting the tradition that bears it, in atheologizing it, this abstraction, without denying faith, liberates a universal rationality and political democracy that cannot be dissociated from it' (FK, 57).

Another abstraction, therefore, allows traditions to wander with it, condensed in a sort of a portable version – as the scroll of the Torah which must compensate for the loss of the Temple and the death of the present God; a piece of parchment that can be carried into all places at all time by anyone, once the connection with the sacred space harbouring the divine pleromatic presence had been broken; 'an opened pomegranate, one Passover evening, on a tray' (FK, 100) or some other 'supporting fragments of memory and custom' (OW, 88), which, like Derrida's tallith, would remind him of the self-absented divine spectre. This type of *Marrano abstraction* indeed uproots and atheologizes, but also secures for the tradition its 'one chance of survival' (TG, 42). While reflecting on Yoseph Yerushalmi in *Archive Fever*, Derrida openly declares that it is only the 'portable' Judaism which is also a proper 'Judaism unterminable': the one capable of infinite survival. When too rooted in its rituals and too caring about its inner purity; when trying too hard to recreate the lost privileged space and time of the Temple and too deeply buried in its archives, Judaism (which here is just an example of any tradition concerned about its living-on) ossifies, dies, and lays itself in the crypt as 'Judaism terminable': the one destined to perish, together with the death of its God. Only this Judaism which wanders away from its own origins, boldly jumps the 'fences around the Torah', raised by the all-too protective guardians,[1] confronts other peoples, marries all languages under the sun, and makes them speak Hebrew, as the Marranos did, allows the tradition to survive. Because tradition, as Scholem noticed, thrives only on *treasons* – and dies from too much awe, piety, and untouchable indemnity.

When contracted-condensed-abstracted to its most dense 'portable' minimum; when shrunk by this radical *tsimtsum* and 'shorn of everything' (MO, 68), the Marrano tradition reveals the teaching of a universal messianic justice:

> This justice, which I distinguish from right, alone allows hope, beyond all 'messianisms,' of a *universalizable culture of singularities*, a culture in which the abstract possibility of the impossible translation could nevertheless be announced. (FK, 56; emphasis added)

Although abstract, the Marrano-messianic universality can be reached only from the particular 'determinate' standpoint, even if it is a point of departure merely to be shaken in the final act of 'burning the archives' and letting them survive in the form of ashes/cinders. This dialectical movement between particularity and universality is what Scholem defines as the very essence of *Tradierbarkeit*: passing on the tradition through its inevitable betrayal. By opening the traditional isolated 'gene pool' to 'mixture' and 'contamination', translation simultaneously preserves it and puts it at risk – yet, this very risk is nothing but *life* itself. All languages and traditions come from different times and places and though all the temples might have been destroyed and all gods might have been dead, some – however impaired – memory of their original particularity lingers, preventing those cultural singularities from dissolving into the Kojèvian 'universal homogenous State', a direct outcome of the Pauline 'certain Christianity'.[2]

---

[1] The first sentence of *Pirke Avoth* (*The Sentences of the Fathers*), the germ-cell of the Talmud, reads: 'Make a fence for the Torah' (1:1).

[2] Kojève explains this link as follows: 'Here again the remote origins of the political idea [of the universal homogenous state] are found in the religious universalist conception that is already present in Ikhnaton and that culminates in St. Paul. It is the idea of the *fundamental equality of all who believe in the same God* [...] For Alexander, the Greek philosopher, no 'mixture' of Masters and Slaves was possible, because they were 'contraries'. Thus, his *universal State*, which did away with races, could not be *homogenous* in the sense of also doing away with 'classes'. For St. Paul, on the other hand, 'the negation [...] of the opposition between pagan Master and Slavery could engender an "essentially" new Christian unity [...] capable of providing the basis not only of the State's

Hegel, Toledo, and universal history

Derrida's alternative strategy of universalization, based on the Marrano 'task of translation' – Reznikoff's 'talking Hebrew' in the Marrano 'ventriloquist' manner, in and through the Global New Latin – has found a fascinating echo in the works of Susan Buck-Morss. Her project, explicitly called 'New Universalism', tries to navigate between the postmodern rejection of the Hegelian universal history and the alternative endorsement of all sorts of 'small narratives', which lead towards the increasing fragmentation of identities and traditions, thus defying any common ground of possible mutual encounters. Convinced, not unlike Derrida, that purity is danger and that cultures thrive on encounters rather than isolation (even though the latter may be more than understandable as the reaction against the abuses of the universalist grand narratives), Buck-Morss proposes that we rethink the idea of a New Universal History: against but also along with Hegel, that is, without the intention of giving up universality altogether. New Universal History would thus amount to a radical revision of Hegelianism, provided it could make room for the heterogeneity of historical lines, tales, events, and sources, that is, for the history imagined as the 'many-headed hydra' rather than just one narrative of the Spirit, heading steadily into one direction.[3] In other words – provided Hegel did not erase the particular trace of his major inspiration, when creating the Master and Slave dialectic, and remembered about the Haitian revolution of Black slaves against their white master, Napoleon. Hence the title in the form of not at all gentle reminder: *Hegel, Haiti, and Universal History*; while it says yes to universal history, it does so only on the proviso that it is mediated through the particular tradition of the Haitian Black rebels whose story will not be erased or sublated into an abstract philosophical scheme. Derrida's rejoinder to Hegel (as well as Kojève) could also be summed up as the paraphrase of Buck-Morss's title. Universal religion – *yes, yes* – but only when taking into account the 'incomplete conversion' of the first historical *marranes*, the seventh century 'Hebrew citizens of Toledo'. This analogy is not at all gratuitous. When Cixous called Derrida 'the Celant, the self-concealed, still a little maroon, fugitive I mean' (PJD, 86), she deliberately created a link between the Haitian maroons and his equally rebellious *marranismo*.

Regarded in this context, the strategy of Philosophical Marranos (the one and only family to which Derrida *nolens volens* belongs), which first confronted the Hegelian universal explicitly, anticipates new universalism *avant la lettre*. Instead of letting their Jewish heritage dissolve into an 'icy wasteland of abstraction' of universal philosophical thought (ND, 4), they – Benjamin, Adorno, Rosenzweig, even Lévinas – turn towards their own Judaic tradition and work upon it to render it universal in the manner of

---

political *universality* but also of its social *homogeneity*': Alexandre Kojève, 'Tyranny and Wisdom', in Leo Strauss, *On Tyranny: Including the Strauss-Kojève Correspondence*, ed. Victor Gourevitch and Michael S. Roth (Chicago: University of Chicago Press, 2000), 172; emphasis added.

[3] See Peter Linebaugh and Marcus Rediker, *The Many-Headed Hydra: Sailors, Slaves, Commoners, and the Hidden History of the Revolutionary Atlantic* (Boston: Beacon Press, 2013).

what we could indeed call, after Buck-Morss, an 'open access'. Instead of sublating their particular ground into one universal Hegelian narrative, they level down the 'fence around the Torah', which guarded the messianic Jewish teaching against the intrusion of the profane, and – as Derrida says in the *Archive Fever* – open the archives to anybody who could use it in the moment of the Benjaminian 'knowability' (*Erkennbarkeit*). This enormous working-through of the Jewish tradition, the goal of which is to make it relevant-recognizable for *anybody, anywhere, anytime*, breaks the seals of restricted admittance and makes it 'citable' in other, distant constellations of thought – which also means, according to the hidden double meaning of the word 'tradition', that they open it to 'betrayal' and 'unfaithfulness'.[4] This is precisely what Buck-Morss calls the 'delicious promiscuity' of non-restricted stocks of traditional archives which, once transformed this way, can produce new configurations of ideas: the process of translation turns their seemingly frozen actuality into a much more plastic and open potentiality (hence, as Samuel Weber called it, numerous Benjamin's-*abilities*: *Erkennbarkeit, Zitierbarkeit, Tradierbarkeit*; knowability, citability, translatability . . .[5]).

The movement, therefore, is double. It consists not only in bursting open the so far sealed archive of *one's own* tradition, in disappropriating it – but also in an attempt to change the so-called universal thought which pretends to be rootless, free of presuppositions and because of that 'pure' and 'proper'.[6] The Hegelian manoeuvre – the sublation of all religions and traditions into one philosophy, leading towards the highest synthesis of the properly universal thought – has to be opposed by the contrary move which proposes *syncresis* instead of *synthesis*. The new universalism would thus resemble the Benjaminian collection, made of heterogenous elements: a collection of languages that mutually foster their 'growth' and indeed 'grow together', as the very notion of *syncresis* suggests.

The 'new historian' and his 'new universal history' must thus be thought as a collection of distinct objects that, although gathered together, never lose their separate status. The *syncresis* of collection allows for a 'togetherness' which is not based on any common denominator or even family resemblance; its ruling trope is not metaphor

---

[4] Comp. Alberto Moreiras's description of the Marrano claim to keep an access to the archive of Jewish tradition: 'I think what we can call the marrano register is the register of our relationship to the archive, what I was calling the total language archive in its relationship with the total archive of languages, that is, if you want, with the geophilosophical totality. It is a perspective, an intended will, an intention: *to work from that marrano will is a way of eluding the traps of identitarianism, but it is also at the same time a political way of accepting the tradition, the archive*. There is a certain belligerence in saying one wants to have a marrano relationship with the archive': Moreiras, *Against Abstraction*, 39; emphasis added.

[5] See Samuel Weber, *Benjamin's-Abilities* (Cambridge, MA: Harvard University Press, 2010).

[6] Buck-Morss says: 'The less we see historical actors as playing theatrically coherent roles, the more universally accessible their human dilemmas become. Perhaps the most deadly blow to imperialism would be to proclaim loyalty to the idea of universal humanity by rejecting the presumption of any political, religious, ethnic, class, or civilizational collectivity to embody this idea as its exclusive and exclusionary possession. To believe in the legitimacy of such an appropriation is political madness. The *loa* of freedom [. . .] cannot be tied down and dragged off as a war trophy, or bought by the highest bidder': Susan Buck-Morss, *Hegel, Haiti, and Universal History* (Pittsburgh: University of Pittsburgh Press, 2009), 145.

but metonymy, a figure of closeness and affinity not built upon an abstract common feature. Collection derives from the primacy of touch over seeing, which, as we have seen, characterizes also Derrida's relationship with his intimate Judaic objects, most of all the tallith. As Benjamin writes in the H section of his *Arcades Project*: 'possession and having are allied with the tactile, and stand in a certain opposition to the optical. Collectors are beings with tactile instincts [. . .] The flaneur optical, the collector tactile'.[7] Unlike metaphor, which involves vertical abstraction, metonymy is the trope of horizontal movement: closer to other elements of the collection, but also away from the place of their origination, which, again, chimes well with Derrida's insistence on traditions being capable of 'wandering away from their origins'.

> What is decisive in collecting is that *the object is detached from all its original functions* in order to enter into the closest conceivable relation to things of the same kind. This relation is the diametric opposite of any utility, and falls into the peculiar category of completeness. What is this 'completeness'? It is a grand attempt to overcome the wholly irrational character of the object's mere presence at hand through its integration into a *new, expressly devised historical system: the collection*. And for the true collector, every single thing in this system becomes an *encyclopedia* of all knowledge of the epoch, the landscape, the industry, and the owner from which it comes [. . .] *Collecting is a form of practical memory*, and of all the profane manifestations of 'nearness' it is the most binding.[8]

Traditions which become objects of this alternative historical system open themselves to a new type of access; they become 'accessible' from the outside by being put together in the new form of an encyclopedic 'assembly',[9] which allows to reshuffle them as if they were items of a spatial collection, and not epochs within a rigidly linear temporal narrative. The result of this *khorein* – arranging different objects in space without collision, but also not randomly – is neither stiff unity nor complete chaos, but rather 'a sort of *productive disorder* [that] is the canon of the collector'[10] and which, despite conventional association of collection with deadness, is also a sign of life – life's impurity which, as Derrida always insists, makes it capable of survival. The elements of the collection become thus synecdoches of the traditions for which they stand: reduced to 'items', traditions contract into 'portable' versions, the *pars pro toto* of the 'all knowledge of the epoch' which, as such, cannot be wholly carried into the 'melange', but still lives on in its parts.

For Derrida, the jewel in the secret collection of his *Judaica* is the tallith whom he touches and caresses as the Benjaminian collector led by the tactile sense of intimacy in darkness. As in *Memoirs of the Blind*, Derrida hurdles his precious objects in the gesture of a blind Jewish patriarch caressing the heads of his sons: 'A prayer shawl I

---

[7] Benjamin, *The Arcades Project*, [H2,5] 206–7.
[8] Ibid., [H1a, 2] 205; emphasis added.
[9] Ibid.
[10] Ibid., [H5, 1], 211.

like to touch more than to see, to caress every day, to kiss without even opening my eyes or even when it remains wrapped in a paper bag into which I stick my hand at night, eyes closed' (V-D, 43). Derrida's tallith is not a symbolic part of the sacramental whole, where the external elements of liturgy complement the internal element of faith. It is not an external symbol of the internal faith, where the two form an integral contemporaneous totality. Derrida's tallith is detached and abstracted from its religious context, and functions as a mnemonic device, the role of which is to remind of the almost-forgotten hidden God. In that sense, it is rather a Benjaminian allegory, taken out of the 'tradition in ruins', than a living sacramental symbol. It is *de-taillé* as a *detail*: a separate item within the collection which the Dutch painting made famous as *nature morte*, with its singular heterogeneous elements emerging as distinct figures from the penumbral retreating background and made more to touch than to see.[11] The Passover tray stylized as a still life – in Chapter 3, we imagined it as Willem Kalf's *Pronkstilleven* – is precisely such a Benjaminian collection in the form of 'practical memory', touch-read in the night, 'eyes closed', as a kind of Braille alphabet of objects. Every Marrano has a collection like that, a beautiful ruin of tradition, which she occasionally touches and caresses: a silver tray with a silver cup – a single survivor of the once functional set of kiddush wine glasses – a little silver dreidel, with which she can no longer play, and sometimes even the tallith that once belonged to the male member of the family, but no longer serves as a means of prayer.

And if Derrida appears very possessive of his tallith – 'my real tallith remains fully mine' (HC, 157) – it is only because he simultaneously knows that such 'details'-*torsos* forming the ruinous collections are, in fact, *spare parts*: the exchangeable elements of traditions partly released from their specific origins. The example given by Susan Buck-Morss indeed suggests that spare *partes pro toto* can be borrowed and used by other traditions to articulate better certain experiences: of loss, dispersion, the 'death of God', detraditionalization, exile, betrayal and survival. Buck-Morss introduces her crucial distinction between the syncretic and the synthetic modes of universalization apropos her description of the Haitian Vodou cults. Already informed by the Scholemian description of the Lurianic Kabbalah, as well as its appropriation by Benjamin in his *Trauerspiel* book (where the Jewish motif of 'breaking of the vessels' that leaves the world, tradition, and humanity in the crisis of exile, is applied to the Christian baroque sensibility), she also uses it freely, very much in the open-access manner of promiscuous 'citability':

> Vodou was constructed out of the allegorical mode of seeing that experiences history as catastrophe. For those who have been defeated by history, whose social relations have been severed, who live in exile, meaning drains out of the objects of a world that has been impoverished by physical distance and personal loss. In Vodou, the collective life of not one but multiple cultures has been shattered,

---

[11] The originally French word, which emerged in the seventeenth century, 'detail', signifies detachment and partition: *de-tail* or *de-taillé* means a cut from the totality. *Detailler* derives from the Latin *talea*, to cut or twig.

surviving as debris and in decay. Emblems are hollowed out; their meanings have become arbitrary. The skull and crossbones – a variant of the pervasive emblem of the deaths-head signifies not merely the transiency of life, but the transiency of meaning, the impermanence of truth itself. The gods are radically distant. They have deserted the living.[12]

Far from representing a unique indigenous African culture, the Vodou emblems lend themselves to an universalizing approach which strikes a chord of resemblance with distant stories of cultural cataclysms which left other traditions in ruin. Here, the spark of 'nearness' or 'elective affinity' runs between the early nineteenth-century narrative of the Haitian Black slaves, the sixteenth-century Isaac Luria's doctrine of the cosmic catastrophe, reacting to the traumatic event of the expulsion of Jews from Spain in 1492, and the twentieth-century Benjamin's *Trauerspiel*, with its mood of the 'permanent catastrophe', this time affecting Christian early modernity – and links them into one collection-constellation: one space/*khôra* in which they can meet and mingle. The seemingly insider story of the messianic Jewry reverberates in the illuminating portrayal of a very remote cult which then reflects back on the Lurianic doctrine itself – and, with its openly pessimistic display of 'debris and decay', challenges the idyllic view of the 'Hassidic stories' we have inherited from Martin Buber. In this constellation, the post-exile Spanish Marranos, the post-pogrom Russian Hassids and Polish Frankists, as well as the post-slavery Black Haitians marry the 'speeches of strangers' in order to convey the experience of the 'death of God', or rather their own particular experiences of the 'deaths of gods' who now are all radically distant and have deserted the living. Thanks to this collecting manoeuvre, both the Lurianic narrative and the Vodou heritage come closer and now 'grow together' in a syncretic approximation, becoming parts – exchangeable spare parts – of the universal history of loss, dispersion, exile, and survival – yet also without giving up on their distinctness.

Buck-Morss's interpretation of both Lurianic Kabbalah and Vodou is a perfect formal example of the new strategy of universalization based on mutual translation, citability, and open access of traditions, handed over to a free and unprotected transmission. But it also offers a very concrete example of what Derrida designates as the true content-message of the new universalism, namely the 'religion of the death of God', where all the origins, sacred groves, and temples had been lost for ever in the sweeping wave of globalized modernization and which the 'returning religion' cannot retrieve despite all its fundamentalist attempts. Yet, in Derrida's interpretation which Buck-Morss shares, this condition of the *universal exile* is not to be lamented. We all, all over the globe – no matter Jew or Greek, European or Haitian – have experienced the same loss of meaning, monolinguality, integrity, rootedness, and the cultic sense of 'the unscathed'. We all have been expelled from the communitarian wombs and scattered in the post-Babelian world, and we all share similar experience of permanent Exodus and wandering

---

[12] Buck-Morss, *Hegel, Haiti. . .*, 127.

through the desert, which, according to Derrida, is now the only possible object of our religious sentiments: 'a memory of Passover' (FK, 100). We all, therefore, participate in the exemplary fate of the Marranos, in the universally shared sense of vulnerability to crisis, catastrophe, and dispersion – but, then, this fate is nothing but *life itself*: life as incalculable risks of constant contamination and exposure, as opposed to the deadness of illusory purity. As Derrida states elsewhere: 'an endless mourning – life itself'.[13] This, however, is not a *negative* experience, which would fix our nostalgic gaze firmly on the past. On the contrary, it is a *new* future-oriented experience, which lends a structure and narrative to the alternative concrete sense of universality and particularity at the same time. The fact *that* we all have lost our unproblematic traditions (if there ever was such a thing) may be common, but *what* we have lost remains particular and as such stubbornly resists abstract universalization. The concrete memory of the deaths of so many gods travels into this universal experience always partly, but never completely, erased. We all are citizens of the global *cosmopolis* which is like one huge 'city of refuge' – where 'the exile [. . .] is always in some way a nonexile, and the home [. . .] is always less than a home'.[14]

Derrida's and Buck-Morss's new universalism uses Benjamin against Hegel, but this gesture may also be seen as the correction of the Hegelian universal history which becomes so easily universal, mostly because – as Benjamin stated it in his theses *On*

---

[13] Derrida, *On Touching*, 35.

[14] Sommer, 'Expulsion as Initiation', 26. In his address given at the conference which took place in Algiers in November 2006 (*Sur les traces de Jacques Derrida*), Marc Goldchmit postulated a renewal of the cosmopolitan idea according to the Derridean hypothesis of the 'absolute Marrano': 'It is a "figureless figure": disfigured, unable to either look like himself or reassemble himself. The resulting impossibility of passing for Jews leads towards *an infinite, potentially universal otherness*, and opens the way to a future idea of cosmopolitics. Such a "figure" renews international law and nations politics, and destabilizes any nationalism, compelling nations to a visitation hospitality irreducible to any invitation and any tolerance. This is perhaps a re-thinking of the Enlightenment, that of a justice disconnected in any sense from truth': Marc Goldschmit, 'Cosmopolitique du marrane absolu', in *Derrida à Alger: Un regard sur le monde*, ed. Mustapha Chérif (Actes Sud/[barzakh], 2008), 143. By refering to Derrida's own words about another cosmopolitanism yet to come in the 'cities of refuge' – 'Being on the threshold of these cities, of these new cities that would be something other than 'new cities', a certain idea of cosmopolitanism, an other, has not yet arrived, perhaps' – Goldschmit convincingly shows that it will have been based on the figureless figure of the universal Marrano as the absolute deconstruction of the identitarian myth: Jacques Derrida, *Cosmopolites de tous les pays, encore un effort!* (Paris: Editions Galilée, 1997), 58; 'On Cosmopolitanism', in *On Cosmopolitanism and Forgiveness*, trans. Mark Dooley and Michael Hughes (London: Rotledge, 2001), 23. Goldschimdt writes: 'The endless errance through the desert without the revealed or objective truth, the errance in and out of oneself, is a mark of the absolute Marrano who represents the trope of the blind and disfigured Jew, of the absolutely non-absolute [. . .] The Marrano is thus the absolute only in the sense that she is always other than herself and that she propagates herself through her infinite alterity. The figure of the Marrano stands for the *abyssal metonymy*, which opens in the chiasm between Judaism and Christianity and which gives the Marrano the strength to multiply secretly on the surface of the earth: *her irreducible singularity contains the universalizing potential*. The Marrano contiguity carries in itself the possibility of a universal contamination which will have go beyond any exemplarity' (ibid., 5; emphasis added). Thus, Godschmit claims, although Derrida tends to be critical of the cosmopolitan idea as 'still implying the rootedness of the political and of democracy in a territory and state', he is not against a 'new International' which would revise cosmopolitanism alongside the Marrano experience, shedding new light on the biblical tradition of the 'Cities of Refuge' (AO, 21).

the Concept of History – it was written by the victors, that is, from the triumphant perspective of the Masters: the world conquerors who spread and multiply without encountering the limit, fracture, or crisis, lead by the 'all-overreaching' Spirit, *der angreifende Geist*.[15] What they, after Benjamin, want to supply is a universal history of victims-Slaves, whose traditions experienced a traumatic break and because of that closed upon themselves, protecting the exclusivity of their respective traumas in the typically narcissistic gesture of small and wounded cultures. But their proposition does not accentuate the moment of catastrophe – be it the expulsion from the Paradise, the shattering of Babel, or the Exile. Fully attuned to the suffering of particular cultures, they nonetheless point to the dangers incipient in such nostalgic pursuit of their lost traditionalist purity. By offering us a new universal idiom of the 'work of mourning', they try to turn the latter into a more positive, proleptic, and life-affirming gesture and thus find an alternative way of 'overreaching' that would not end up in the ultimate deactivation of the original differences. The New Universal History is a Benjaminian *syncretic* collection, made of 'souvenirs' which, although detached from their origins, embody a 'practical memory' – and not the Hegelian s*ynthetic* triumphant grand narrative where particularity becomes irreversibly sublated. It should thus be approached as the Benjaminian-Marrano 'task of the translation' where the particular origin of languages coexists with the ideal of universal communication.

In the end, therefore, the Marrano affair turns out *not* to be a nostalgic-mournful *Trauerspiel*. The Marranos – uprooted from any overt religious identity, atheologized to the limit of the 'almost-atheism', deprived of any cultic piety, and withdrawn into the secret of their 'inner hearts', always on the brink of self-denial and self-oblivion – are *not* the victims of the global modernization, which indeed began with the fifteenth-century 'Marrano experience'. Derrida's intention is to invert this negative image and present the Marranos, the de-nominated people 'without name', as the harbingers of a possible universal and radically iconoclastic faith which will speak simultaneously in the language long forgotten and in the language yet to come. 'On the bottom without bottom of an always virgin impassibility, *Khôra* of tomorrow in languages we no longer know or do not yet speak' (FK, 100) is a heroine of 'an iconoclastic fiction [that] must be thought' (ON, 54) to the very end. All gods might have been sent to their crypts, silenced and no longer representable, but there are still Marrano 'pomegranates', with their 'thousand of seeds' capable to keep on the life of tradition – a *still life*, but still. . .

And the Marranos, indeed, 'disperse and multiply': they disseminate the 'thousand of seeds' which pop out from the wound of the pomegranate/*milgroyn* cut in half. What initially began as a particular condition of the Iberian *conversos* becomes now a universal pattern of a new life that paces the orbit of creation just as fast as the mondialatinized 'certain Christanity', but unlike the latter, 'opening the space of *absolute tolerance* and of a politics that is not a politics of the elect people, the politics of a certain culture, a certain nation, a certain tongue [. . .] opening space for an *effective* universalization' (CS, 144; emphasis added). Faced with the global Christian

---

[15] Walter Benjamin, 'On the Concept of History', in *Selected Writings*, vol. 4, trans. Howard Eiland and Michael W. Jennings (Cambridge, MA: Harvard University Press, 1996–2003), 396.

hegemony, which merely passes for universal, people all over the globe *nolens volens* repeat the experience of the *anusim*, the 'forced ones': they all become new Christians, carrying on the same dim memory of their lost origins.[16] This is the moment of the highest danger – global mankind mourning their destroyed local identities – but also of *das Rettende*, the saving grace of the liberating cut/*coupure*/lucky break. This is why, in *A Taste for Secret*, Derrida the Marrano puts himself forward as the singular *example* of a person without identity, which is not to be mourned, but rather followed as a new form of 'commitment':

> *I'm not one of the family* means [...] do not consider me 'one of you', 'don't count me in', I want to keep my freedom, always [...] This quip also reflects a sort of idiosyncrasy of my own, stemming from my highly unusual family history. The fact is that I have a predisposition to not being one of the family, it wasn't just my choice. I am a Jew from Algeria, from a certain type of community, in which belonging to Judaism was problematic. Belonging to Algeria was problematic, belonging to France was problematic, etc. So all this predisposed me to not-belonging; but, beyond the particular idiosyncrasies of my own story, I wanted to indicate the sense in which an 'I' does not have to be 'one of the family'. *But then*, if we want to look at this statement in another light, the saying 'I am not one of the family' does not simply describe a fact, or way of being. Although I have treated it this way, it can also mean: *I do not want to be one of the family*. 'I am not one of the family' is *a performative, a commitment*. Once we have distinguished the performative [...] The desire to belong to any community whatsoever, the desire for belonging *tout court*, implies that *one does not belong*. I could not say 'I want to be one of the family' if in fact I was one of the family [...] Accounting for one's belonging – be it on national, linguistic, political or philosophical grounds – in itself implies a not-belonging. This can have political consequences: *there is no identity*. There is identification, belonging is accounted for, but this itself implies that the belonging does not exist, that the people who want to be this or that – French, European, etc. – are not so in fact. *And they have to know this!* (TS, 27–8; emphasis added)

To problematize one's belonging, therefore, is not a tragic development; on the contrary, Derrida presents his exemplary Marrano form of non-belonging in the prophetic tone of the evangelical *ecce homo* – take these good news and learn what you really are, as non-identitarian as I am, the 'I' beyond any familial bond. The Marrano universalization is thus also a new *esperanto*: a language of hope, capable to unite global men and women *in* – not despite – their fluid non-identities.[17]

---

[16] Gil Anidjar reminds us that, according to Benzion Netanyahu, the word 'Marrano' does not derive from the Spanish 'pig' but from the Hebrew conjunction of *moumar* (converti) and *anous* (forced): 'Hence the phonological chain in the Latin transcription: *mumar-anus, mumaranus, maranus, marano, marrane*': Anidjar, '*Je te suis vrai...*', 249.

[17] *Esperanto*, an artificial language created in 1887 by Ludwik Zamenhof (Eliezer Levi Samenhof), an assimilated Polish Jew born in Białystok, is indeed a Marrano masterpiece. Most likely its

Into the shadows, away from the sun: Against utopia

Yet, despite the universal language of promise and hope – the *marrano esperanto* of those who lived through and survived the global experiment of modernity – the Marrano community is anything but *utopian*: it is very much located and embodied, yet, at the same time, *spectral*, as a still unrealized messianic possibility, hidden within the folds of the here and now as its open secret: *plus de secret*. Derrida famously attacks the utopian thought – Marxist in particular – for being simultaneously too abstract and too rooted in the necessitarian realm of ontology which remains closed to messianic alternatives. For Derrida, the Marxist utopia is devised as a bold social project, yet, at the same time, too close to the historical actuality of the already existing: just as Plato's ideal republic is a direct derivative of the Platonic ontology, that is, the science of what is and what gives being – so is Marx's vision of the communist society an immediate reflection of his understanding of 'social physis' and its scientific objective laws.

Thus, while the utopian Great Architect builds his vision on the most secure ontological foundations – the Messiah, or any representative of *messianicité*, chooses the rejected stones of the seemingly non-existent secret and the 'impossible'.[18] In Derrida's terminology, however, this 'impossible', which the messianic thought strives for, is not a flat logical impossibility: it is not a simple antithesis to necessity, as, for instance, in the negation of the sentence – 'all men must die' – that would immediately demand nothing short of immortality. It is rather an opening which chips into the seemingly necessitarian closure of ontological thinking that tends to see *what is* as *what must be* and then treat it as a normative model form of the utopian projection of the future.[19] This opening aims at the disclosure of

name derives from the famous *esperanza* of the Iberian *conversos* (the first handbook of the new language was signed by Doktor Esperantus) – a conjecture strengtened by the fact that in 1913 Zamenhof announced a new era of the global unity of mankind under the banner of *homaranismo*: a word combining, in the esperanto manner, the words *homo* ('human being' in Latin, but also 'one' in Greek) and *marranismo*. He thus declared in his new language: *Mi estas Homarano* (I am a homarano): Ludwik Zamenhof, *Declaracio pri Homaranismo* (Represso de Homaro: Madrid, 1913), 5. The surviving Judaic component of *homaranismo* was, for Zamenhof, the Hillelism, i.e. the universal teaching of the neighboury love, which he – in the Marrano vein – refused to call a 'new denomination' and insisted on its universal ethical appeal. However, this is not exactly a realization of Derrida's 'Marrano *rêverie*': while *homaranismo* affirms Marrano universalism, it wants to achieve it in a far too homogenizing manner, by mimicking the unity of the 'Christian Latin global empire'. Hence *esperanto* also belongs to Derrida's *italics*: it is a speech which gives absolute priority to Latin and Roman languages, allowing only for some intrusions from the Slavonic dialects (mostly Polish and Russian).

[18] In the context of Derrida's mistrust towards all sorts of Great Architects and their utopian constructs, see again Derrida's remark from 'Des Tours de Babel': 'The "tower of Babel" does not merely figure the irreducible multiplicity of tongues; it exhibits an incompletion, the impossibility of finishing, of totalizing, of saturating, of completing on the order of edification, architectural construction, system and architechtonics' (AR, 104).

[19] In the discussion with Thomas Assheuer, 'Not Utopia, the Im-Possible', Derrida explains his antipathy towards utopias: 'Utopia has critical powers that we should probably never give up on, especially when we can make it a reason for resisting all alibis and all "realistic" or "pragmatic" cop-outs, but all the same I'm wary of the word. There are some contexts in which *Utopia*, the word at any

what Kierkegaard calls *the possibility of possibilities*: the transcendental reserve of alternatives to the already actualized reality.[20]

In Derrida's own 'white mythology', the figure representing this reserve of possibilities-promises is a *spectre* – a haunting guest, visiting the world from the regions of 'otherwise than being', who can only be approached via the science of *hantologie*. This is how Derrida explains the ontological neither/nor characteristic of the spectral condition in his 'History of the Lie':

> As we know, *phantasma* also named for the Greeks the apparition of the specter, the vision of the phantom, or the phenomenon of the revenant. The fabulous and the phantasmatic have a feature in common: stricto sensu, in the classical and prevalent sense of these terms, they do not pertain to either the true or the false, the veracious or the mendacious. They are related, rather, to an irreducible species of the simulacrum or even of simulation, in the *penumbral light of a virtuality that is neither being nor nothingness*, nor even an order of the possible that an ontology or a mimetology could account for or subdue with reason. *No more than myth, fable and phantasm are doubtless not truths or true statements as such, but neither are they errors or deceptions, false witnesses or perjuries.* (WA, 28; emphasis added)

Now we will see how this 'penumbral light of virtuality', flickering in the shadowland between being and nothingness, enlightens Derrida's politics; how it haunts and simultaneously sustains in being the *body politic* which he calls 'Khôra of the political' (R, 44).

The messianic emerges as the alternative to the utopian for the first time in Derrida's essay from 1997, *Specters of Marx*, and then in the response to his Marxist critics, 'Marx & Sons', from *Ghostly Demarcations*, published two years later. Derrida takes the modern notion of *messianicity without Messiah*, operative already in Lévinas, and turns it into an even stronger, seemingly paradoxical phrase of *messianicity without messianism* (SM, 74). In the Marrano manner refusing to identify with any organized and explicitly named messianic ideology, Derrida speaks in favour of the de-nominated messianic idea of justice which resists full discursive capture. In remaining eternally elusive, it enjoys a modal form of a *ghost/guest*: the messianic spectre of the ultimate justice, which haunts the living who, riveted to the ontological horizon of what already

---

rate, can be too easily associated with dreams, or demobilization, or an impossible that is more of an urge to give up than an urge to action. The "impossible" I often speak of is not the Utopian. Rather, it gives their very movement to desire, action, and decision: it is the very figure of the real. It has its hardness, closeness, and urgency' (PM, 131)

[20] The difference between the mere-possible as fitting neatly the necessitarian view of reality, backed by the power of the *status quo*, and the hyper-possible as exploding this view is well explained by Derrida himself in the dialogue with Elisabeth Roudinesco: 'All responsibility is revolutionary, since it seeks to do the impossible, to interrupt the order of things on the basis of nonprogrammable events. A revolution cannot be programmed. In a certain way, as the only event worthy of the name, it exceeds every possible horizon, every horizon of the possible and, therefore, of potency and power' (FWT, 83).

exists, constantly fall into 'the disgrace of adaptation'.[21] The messianic spectrality, therefore – *hantologie/hauntology* (from the French *hanter*, to haunt) – becomes distinctly opposed to being and *ontology* (even if, when spoken, you can't really hear the difference, as in the original Derridean *différance*).

This homophonic manoeuvre signalizes the asymmetry between ubiquity of being which, according to Parmenides, was, is, and will be – and the elusive modality of 'otherwise than being', to which one has to be especially hospitable and attentive. We could say, following Malebranche, that this particular attention which hears the mute *h* in *hantologie* – being here an equivalent of the Hebrew aleph: the first letter uttered as a breath and, at the same time, a symbol of transcendence – is Derrida's 'natural form of prayer', condensed to the linguistic molecule. When heard and listened to, the mute *h* of the haunting spectre disturbs and disrupts the ontological process of being and does not allow it to rest in its self-repetitive totalities of the seemingly self-evident, self-necessitated, visible, natural, actualized. The mute *h* is in French called *ash* which in Derrida's Babelian idiom immediately translates into those ashes/cinders that remain of the world after the intervention of the fiery *ruah*: the spirit which destroys and rejuvenates simultaneously (interestingly, the *h* in *ruah* is exceptionally *not* mute and as such can indeed be regarded as the characteristic signature of the Hebrew word for 'spirit'). The spectre as the avatar of Spirit/*ruah* is thus a figure of a pure *antinomian* possibility – antinomian, because it goes against the law of the reality principle, that is, against what establishes itself as a powerful law of what is and wants to remain in being: the world's *status quo*. It can only manifest as a *trace*, which cannot find home in the conditions of immanence, for it is only due to this not fully ontologically present dimension of the messianic promise that the spectre can gain distance from *the extant* and press upon it in the name of *the (im)possible*, even if in the form of the haunting threat. In Chapters 1 and 3, we saw how complex this messianic dialectics is, while it alternates between gentle withdrawal of *Seinlassen* and oblivion, on the one hand, and the haunting, 'coming to mind', call of radical justice, on the other: the world is always in the Marrano position of 'betrayal', just because it *is* – but it cannot desist from the demand to *betray better* and simply rest on its laurels. *Khôra* which withdraws and gives *place* is thus the same instance which haunts, by reminding 'us' that the world could still be a *better place* for singular beings, if they learn her way of withdrawing as making room for the 'im-possible' (PM, 131). The spectre, therefore, is the haunting aspect of *Khôra*: 'the experience of the non-present, of the non-living present in the living present, of that which lives on (absolutely past or absolutely to come, *beyond all presentation or representability*)' (MS, 254). Or, in other words: the spectre is the transcendent halo of the immanence, the supranatural hovering over the 'social physis'. If '*Khôra* of the political' is *body politic* in the literal sense of the *body*, the hovering spectre is its spirit-*ruah*.

---

[21] See Adorno, *Minima Moralia*, 111. See also Derrida's 'Injunctions of Marx' (SM, 1–60), which introduces the figure of Hamlet as torn between the allegiance to the haunting fatherly spectre and the simple adaptation to the living present.

In the self-commentary, delivered in the essay 'Marx & Sons', Derrida defends his position of *messianic spectrality* against more materialistically minded, traditional Marxists and their communist utopia (most of all Terry Eagleton and Antonio Negri):

> Nothing would seem to be at a further remove from Utopia or Utopianism, even in its 'subterranean' form, than the messinicity and spectrality which are at the heart of *Specters of Marx* [. . .] Messianicity (which I regard as a universal structure of experience, and which cannot be reduced to religious messianism of any stripe) is anything but Utopian: it refers, in every here-now, to the coming of an eminently real, concrete event, that is, to the most irreducible heterogenous otherness. Nothing is more 'realistic' or 'immediate' than this messianic apprehension, straining forward toward the event of him who/that which is coming. I say 'apprehension,' because this experience, strained forward toward the event, is at the same time a *waiting without expectation* (an active preparation, anticipation against the backdrop of a horizon, but also exposure without horizon, and therefore and irreducible amalgam of desire and anguish, affirmation and fear, promise and threat) [. . .] *Anything but Utopian*, messianicity mandates that we interrupt the ordinary course of things, time and history here-now; *it is inseparable from an affirmation of otherness and justice*. (MS, 248–9; emphasis added)[22]

Here we get all the characteristic elements of Derrida's messianic (as well as deconstructive) position: absolute affirmation of otherness as an attentive anticipation of a coming-possible event and the paradoxical expectation of the non-expected, unbacked by any utopian calculation, staking on the event capable to interrupt the ordinary course of things, or the 'social physis'. There is nothing sure or calculable about the course of history which allegedly leads – through a series of 'historical necessities' – to its utopian goal. Messianic expectation does not believe in *progress*, which sees history as already being on the right track and just needs to be pushed further; but it also does not believe in a *revolutionary change*, for this change is never radical enough; that is, it only overturns one social order and reintroduces another within the untransformed conditions of being. Derrida, therefore, objects to Marx's being 'too ontological', that is, wanting his revolutionary philosophy to stick too close to the actual and the present – 'at the risk of restoring everything to order, to the grand order, *but to order*' (MS, 257). In his attempt to be 'politically realistic', Marx conjures away the most valuable element of his own messianic thought, namely the famous 'spectre of communism' – the very *spirit* of utopia – that was supposed to 'hover over Europe'. In his full-fledged communist system as described in *The Capital*, nothing hovers or haunts anymore; there is no non-immanent dimension which would be able

---

[22] The distinction between the utopian and the messianic may not be, in fact, Derrida's invention. As Menachem Lorberbaum shows in his study on the medieval Jewish political thought, the gap between the two is also a frequent theme in Maimonides: Menachem Lorberbaum, *Politics and the Limits of Law: Secularizing the Political in Medieval Jewish Thought* (Stanford: Stanford University Press, 2002), esp. the chapter 'The Messianic Age and the Utopian Vision', 87–8.

to subvert the mechanisms of being, which in Marx's case are the historical mechanisms of the subsequent economic formations. Derrida says:

> I think it is the most problematic aspect of Marx, namely, the unrestrained, classical, traditional (dare I add 'Platonic'?) desire to conjure away any and all spectrality so as to recover the full physical reality of the process of genesis hidden behind the specter's mask. (MS, 258)

Contrary to this, the spectre is a *normative modality* which always hovers over being, but never coincides with anything fully present, and as such cannot fall prey to physical forces of actuality – for better or for worse. It cannot – should not – be fully realized, but it also cannot – should not – be judged *only* from the perspective of its failed realizations, which tried to 'betray better', but ended up betraying full and simple. As the call to radical justice, the messianic spectre hovers above any historical situation, as, for instance, the disastrous existence of the Communist block, which has no power to invalidate it. The spectre remains separate from the historical process and – here Derrida speaks directly against Negri – there are dark moments in history when it has no 'vessels' at all, no privileged group or class to carry the spark of hope: 'one should not always be one with the people', says Derrida, meaning that one should not always side with the extant social forces and give them full revolutionary credit just because they are. Sometimes one has to withdraw into the spectral 'weakness' that lacks the immanent historicist power: the hiddenness of the inner secret which offers a space of retreat from the pressures of actuality. We shall see in a moment that this is precisely the anti-Marxist position which he shares with Gustav Landauer, Derrida's precursor in the arcana of spectral revolutions.

Should Derrida's hauntology, therefore, be read as the last chapter in the history of the messianic 'powerless power', which guards the purity of the ideal at the expense of its actual efficiency? This may sound as an objection – a typically Hegelian accusation against the political idleness of 'beautiful souls' – but, as I have already argued in Chapter 1, it was not meant that way by Derrida. He would always claim that the betrayal is the necessary form in which the ideal manifests itself on earth – the only question then is the manner in which this treason was committed, as a 'better' or a 'simple' betrayal. But if I invoke the *schöhne Seele* controversy again, it is because it designates the point of the most intense divergence between the utopian and the messianic: while the former insists on the full incarnation of the ideal here and now, in the conditions of historical immanence, the latter resists the temptation to incarnate/immanentize the ideal fully and thus and preserves the alterity of transcendence, which cannot be captured in immanentist terms. Theologically speaking, this opposition may be seen as yet another avatar of the difference between the Jewish mode of revelation, with its antithetical notion of radical transcendence which resists material realization – and the Christian one, with its intended utopia of the divine incarnation which affirms material *phusis* as the place of the potential full embodiment of the sacred ideal. Derrida, by choosing the Marrano option, dialectically mediates between the Judaic rigid dualism (best represented by Lévinas) and the Christian preference of actualization without remainder (best represented by Hegel): while corruption and contamination is inevitable, the deconstructive mind always reminds us to be aware of it. So, again, we are left with the Beckettian imperative: *betray, betray again, betray better...*

Radical community and its traces

But what is this 'we' which Derrida evokes as the non-belonging members of the new community to come, free of the utopian architectonic temptation and open to the messianic horizon of the 'im-possible' justice? Perhaps, the first step to approach it would be to refer to the conception from the outside of the Frankophone sphere: while a lot has been said on Derrida's relation to Blanchot's and then Nancy's versions of 'inoperative community', no one so far associated Derrida with Victor Turner and his seminal work on the difference between *communitas* and *societas*. In fact, Turner's anthropological reflections on liminality and rituals of transgression fit perfectly well Derrida's thinking on the messianicity and its peculiar form of 'we', by giving it a concrete shape. As Turner rightly points out, *communitas* – this special festive moment of bringing down of all social hierarchies, which allows a universal sense of solidarity to come to the fore – cannot be sustained as such: it is only a break, interruption, and temporary release from the pressures of *societas* with its hard laws of hierarchical subjection, differentiation, and identification. *Communitas* comes suddenly as if in a flash and vanishes equally mysteriously. Any attempt to prolong its state of dedifferentiation ends either in violent crisis or confusion: the egalitarian 'treasure of revolution' is soon inevitably lost and once again *societas* cools everything down, by rebinding the released energy into fixed social roles. Yet, despite its elusiveness and effervescence, *communitas* indeed is a 'treasure': in no other state of social life is universal equality and solidarity felt with such intense liberating joy.[23]

The most obvious difference between Derrida and Turner is that the former, by assuming the messianic perspective, teaches that this alternation of *communitas* and *societas* – the momentary flash of freedom followed by the 'restoration of order' – does not have to turn in an idle cycle, as it is portrayed in all anthropological descriptions of traditional carnivals, from Bachtin to Turner. *Communitas* can also become a guiding ideal, but not exactly in the form of a regulative one. In *Rogues*, Derrida says, by pointing to the real effect of *communitas*: 'This impossible is thus not a (regulative) *idea* or *ideal*. It is what is most undeniably *real* and sensible. Like the other. Like the irreducible and non-appropriable *différance* of the other' (R, 84). The intangible presence of radical community is, therefore, also the one of the radical singularity of every other; only seemingly paradoxically, the 'we' is a *community of strangers*, living together neither unified nor completely dispersed, just next to one another as 'place-keepers' in the

---

[23] See most of all Victor Turner, *The Ritual Process: Structure and Anti-Structure* (London and New York: Routledge, 1996).

free space of *Khôra* – and it is precisely this *nextness* as opposed to *oneness*, which, for Derrida is also the sign of real friendship.

Yet, such radical *communitas*, although 'real and sensible' (R, 84), cannot be fully actualized and maintained in its *entelechia*: it does not last in being. Any attempt to make it durable, as Derrida says in agreement with Turner, would only lead to an 'absolute evil' (SM, 220): the ultimate perversion of the fluid freedom granted by the revolutionary moment into a newly fixed order. The goal of the *communitas* fantasy, therefore, is not to become *real* in ontological terms. It is to make possible truly *possible*: to constantly subvert the institutions and laws of *societas*, to undermine them from its 'subterranean' below, make them less rigid and more flexible, less natural and thus more open to historical change. For Turner, this is precisely the epochal difference introduced by modernity: the long-lasting transformation of modern social reality whose laws and institutions – instead of mirroring the hierarchical metaphysics of the universe as in all feudal systems – bend along the curve of the revolutionary ideal of radical equality, fraternity, and liberty. Because of that constant law-bending tendency, modernity is called by Turner *liminoid*, that is, always at the borderline between law and anarchy, hierarchy and carnival, reform and revolution, *societas* and *communitas*.[24] This is precisely what Derrida sees as the messianic promise of the Marrano modernity: not the utopian full actualization of *communitas* as a new *societas*, which is essentially contradictory and because of that infinitely destructive – but the unceasing haunting subversion of all the laws of society, with its rigid hierarchies and identities. Such *communitas* can never become a positive utopian model: it must remain an eternal negativity, the Goethean 'spirit which always says no', or the social *daimonion* of liminoid subversion. Whenever *societas* begins to present itself in feudal terms, as if all its laws and hierarchies came from the divine King of the Universe himself as part and parcel of the created human nature – the *daimonion* of *communitas*, in modernity louder than in any other epoch, raises the voice of protest. This protest, however, fuelling the 'spirit of revolution', must for ever 'exceed every horizon of the possible and, therefore, of potency and power' (FWT, 83). This *ergo*, which implicates the category of the simply possible into the root family of words related to *potestas*, explains why this protest must locate itself in the domain of the *im-possible*. It cannot freeze in any societal representation of power: it must remain deconstructive, constantly working through the delayed destruction of rigid social forms, yet without annihilating them altogether.

In that sense, the subversive-antinomian influence of *communitas* as the ideal of radical justice follows the logic of the Derridean *pharmakon*: when implemented as an antidote, the messianic justice is a healing possibility – when applied as the utopian model of social reality, it turns into a poison. But what is also crucial here is the temporal dimension of the messianic promise: its structural futurity, its *not-yet* or the Blochian *noch-Nicht*. The possibility as possibility must be opposed to the actual as the already existing, but, at the same time, it cannot be opposed to it in a manner of some irresponsible 'subjective fantasy' which can *never* be realized on purely logical

---

[24] Victor Turner, 'From Liminal to Liminoid, in Play, Flow, and Ritual: An Essay in Comparative Symbology', *Rice University Studies* 60, no. 3 (1974): 69.

grounds (as, for instance, the famous childish dream of Saint-Simone, wishing that all melons should grow immediately ripe and sweet). The validity of the messianic expectation locates itself precisely in the realm between *never* and *not-yet*: while the former contains the wish lists of all 'subjective fantasies' that populated the utopian thought of all ages, the latter consists only of the Blochian 'objective fantasies' pointing to the Real-Possible,[25] which, as *communitas*, reveals itself merely in flashes, on the borderline between actuality and possibility, the social immanence and its transcendent lining, the liminal transgressive opening onto the other of *societas*. This is precisely what Derrida means by his metaphor of the spectre: a haunting opening which pierces the fixity of the 'eternal return of the same', breaks the Koheletian curse of 'nothing new under the sun', but also breaks out of the cycle of carnivals and order restorations (which Derrida sees as precisely the cycle still plaguing the utopian thinking where the 'architectonic' desire necessarily betrays the revolutionary, chaotic and lively, moment of *communitas*). While one cannot live and survive in the state of perpetual grace, as Saint Paul famously described the messianic fulfillment,[26] one should neither forget nor neutralize completely those liminal experiences. They constitute the spectral *limes* that gives orientation to our historical and political practice aiming towards just society, where the ideal of justice will survive *in* the laws becoming gradually less rigid and more informed by the egalitarian lesson of *communitas*: the laws that will betray the non-liveable ideal better and better.[27] Hence, once again, the Marrano association: just as the Marrano is a survivor, who chose a 'less bad' life-in-betrayal over against the glorious death, so is the *mundane justice* also a survivor: it inevitably betrays the spirit/spectre of radical *communitas*, yet it also attempts to preserve its spectral memory in the legalistic condition of *societas*.

The main danger to this version of Marrano/messianic dialectics – Judeo-Christian, but *not* Pauline-Christian – is its potential to fall into a static dualism: of, on the one hand, rigid societal hierarchy, which defends against any possibility of subversion, by presenting itself as eternal and natural – and, on the other, the utopian impatience which cannot endure the long durée of reformist dialectics and demands fulfilment

---

[25] In *The Spirit of Utopia*, Bloch formulates the idea of the Real-Possible in terms closely resembling Derrida's 'Im-Possible'. While pointing in a Kabbalistic manner to a secret community of the carriers of the spark (the true *kneset Israel*), he writes: 'We and we alone, then, carry the spark of the end through the course [. . .] And the spark is still open, full of unarbitrary, objective fantasy': Ernst Bloch, *The Spirit of Utopia*, trans. Anthony Nassar (Stanford: Stanford University Press, 2000), 227.

[26] See Letter to Romans 3.21-31.

[27] In his penultimate seminar devoted the death penalty, in the section on psychoanalysis and Theodor Reik, Derrida speaks in favour of *souplesse*: a flexibility which, as I claim here, derives from the fluid element of *communitas* and stays preserved in our attitude towards the law: 'Not that one forgive, since forgiveness is a reaction formation, but that *one become benevolent, tolerant, flexible, in order to avoid the rigidity of the ideal* [. . .] No excessive rectitude in law, in short, no absolute correctness. For inflexibility, rigidness, correction are essential attributes of what is right [. . .] *Flexibility is incalculable*; it is that for which there is no objective rule, as there is for law. But this is perhaps what Reik is suggesting: without an objective rule, one must be benevolent toward the other as other, by finding each time, and this is perhaps what benevolence is, by each time inventing the flexibility, the form and degree of flexibility, of *relaxation of the law*, the good rule (without rule, then) of flexibility. Otherwise we get cruelty; *the inflexible law is what produces cruelty*' (DP2, 205–6; emphasis added).

here and now, by attempting to turn the fantasy of *communitas* into the reality of *societas* (according to the rule of all desire: 'I want it all, I want it now!'). The first danger is the legalistic form of conservatism, which is now adopted by all late modern religious fundamentalisms under the banner of what Derrida, in *Faith and Knowledge*, terms as the 'return to religion'. Suspicious of any kind of subversive anomie, it elevates the concept of the law to the sublime heights of direct divine legislation which cannot *ever* be transgressed; as such it does not even tolerate any kind of exception or carnivalesque respite and, because of that, constitutes a much more rigid and repressive form of *societas* than any premodern social formation. The latter opposite danger is the utopian urge to simply replace society with community: to install the fluid 'promiscuity of all things' as a new rule of social being, which, as I tried to prove here, constitutes a contradiction in terms. There is and can never be any architecture of *communitas*: no Great Architect can construct anything on its an-archaic non-ground, *Un-Grund*, or non-foundation; no 'restoration of order' can be drawn out of this 'drunk and disorderly', ecstatic moment of social coexistence. Which, again, is the lesson we could draw from the life of Saint Paul, who, in order to create a Christian society, had to withdraw from the radicalism of his earlier position on love and grace, and begin to act as the *katechon*: the 'restrainer' introducing new laws.[28]

The dangers, therefore, lie in the simplification: the Marrano fluid dialectics of betrayal/survival deteriorating into a rigid dualism. Yet, despite those potential threats, Derrida maintains that the messianic dialectical game is still worth playing. To 'pluck the living flower of religion' and its central 'objective fantasy' of equality – the true 'specter of Marx'[29] – is to render the fleeting experience of *communitas* operative within the conditions of *societas*, by making the societal laws remember/internalize (*erinnern*) the communal sense of egalitarian dedifferentiation and freedom. The result of this internalization would be an introduction of *new* laws, always more 'bent' and 'supple' and because of that more just. They truly are to be *new*: innovative and liminoid, capable to be inspired by the fleeting memory of the radically communal mode of 'living together'. In this manner, indeed, Derrida's project joins the family of

---

[28] The term *katechon* (in Luther's translation *der Aufhalter*, 'the restrainer') derives from Paul's Second Letter to Thessalonians (2.3-8): 'And you know what is now restraining him, so that he may be revealed when his time comes. For the mystery of lawlessness is already at work, but only until the one who now restrains it is removed.' In *Nomos of the Earth*, Carl Schmitt creates a whole new political theology based on the concept of the *katechon* as the one which withholds the advent of the Antichrist representing the forces of lawlessness and disorder and as such is a true fulfillment of Christian religion; see most of all the chapter 'The Christian Empire as a Restrainer of the Antichrist (Katechon)', *The Nomos of the Earth in the International Law of the Jus Publicum Europaeum*, trans. G. L. Ulmen (New York: Telos Press Publishing, 2003), 59–61. The claim that Paul, unable to wait for the Second Coming any longer, suffered a failure of the messianic nerve and because of that turned towards the figure of the *katechon*, derives from Jacob Taubes, *The Political Theology of Paul*, trans. Dana Holänder (Stanford: Stanford University Press, 2003), 103.

[29] Compare Marx's famous lines on religion: 'Criticism has plucked the imaginary flowers on the chain not in order that man shall continue to bear that chain without fantasy or consolation, but so that he shall throw off the chain and pluck the living flower': Karl Marx, 'A Contribution to the Critique of Hegel's "Philosophy of Right"', in *Critique of Hegel's Philosophy of Right*, trans. Joseph O'Malley (Cambridge: Cambridge University Press, 1970), 131.

similar ones which has grown out of the Blanchotian *unavowable community*, where living together is not founded on any tangible common ground. Derrida's *impossible community* of 'we' stands next to Nancy's *inoperative community* and Agamben's *coming community* as a separate proposition: the unavowable non-ground is the memory/anticipation of the im-possible state of human togetherness called radical *communitas*. Hence the Blanchotian title of Derrida's essay in which he announces his teaching of living together (*vivre ensemble*): 'Avowing – The Impossible'.

Fully aware that this may sound like a heresy in Derridologist circles, I cautiously propose to call Derrida's political position as a *Marrano messianic variant of modern liberalism* – but liberalism widely understood, rather as a mood (in terms of Heideggerian *Einstellung*, general attitude) than the classical doctrine, too often oblivious to the true *libertas* from which it took its name. Frequently declaring sympathy for the republican tradition of the Left, but equally frequently a strong antipathy for any form of realized communism and collectivism, Derrida always was on the side of the modern individual who can exercise her rights to life, liberty, and pursuit of happiness the way she sees it fit, ready to defend them against the totalizing claims coming either from the radical Left or the radical Right.[30] Yet, the manner in which he perceives the individual differs from the classic foundational texts of liberal tradition, invariably presenting it as the Cartesian sovereign *cogito*: an insular *res cogitans*, safely rooted in its self-reflexive and thus fully transparent thinking-being, a new human absolute reflecting the former absoluteness of God.[31] Contrary to this, Derrida's individual derives from the fleeting and effervescent experience of the (im)possible *communitas*: she is neither a self-knowledgeable participant of the social contract nor an abstract insular unit of liberal law, but a living singularity, stripped of her social determinations in the unique moment of the communal *flow*, when all rigid roles and identities become temporarily liquidated. She is thus a *living abstraction* of a 'man without qualities', momentarily deprived of its content – as opposed to the dead 'indeterminate abstraction' of the classical-liberal subject of the rational contract

---

[30] On Derrida's critique of the far too enthusiastic collective spirit of the Parisian 68, see most of all his conversation with Maurizio Ferraris (TS, 50–1). Comp. also his reply to Elisabeth Roudinesco: 'it is true that in *Specters of Marx* I was able to make a gesture from which I had previously thought I should refrain. For many years, for reasons that become more legible in this book (even though they already were in other ways), I could neither subscribe to the Althusserian gesture (a certain return to Marx) nor denounce or critique it from any position that would have been seen as anticommunist, anti-Marxist, or even as that of the communist party. So for a long time I was virtually reduced to silence, a *silence that was also assumed, almost chosen*, but also somewhat painful with regard to what was happening right in front of me' (FWT, 79–80; emphasis added). Could it be yet another dimension – more Straussian this time – of the Marrano *silenzio*?

[31] On the insular absolution of the Cartesian *cogito* as reflecting the same process of the 'indeterminate abstraction' that created God the Absolute, see Derrida's remark in *The Beast and the Sovereign*, where he compares Descartes to Robinson Crusoe: 'the *cogito ergo sum* is a hyperbolic Robinsonade, particularly at the moment of hyperbolic doubt that absolutely insularizes the self-relation of the *cogito sum*, and we could go a long way analyzing this affinity or this analogy between the Philosopher-voyager Descartes and Robinson Crusoe' as the two parallel paradigms of a modern individual imagined as an island of one's own (BS2, 33). This is also the reason why Island and insularity of abstracted absolutes, both divine and human, appear in *Faith and Knowledge* as the third territory next to the Desert and the Promised Land.

and law. As such, she is indeed *individuus*: a no longer divisible absolute kernel of singular existence, singular and universal at the same time – absolutely exemplary. This universalism, therefore, does not annul singular difference, as is the case with the classical-liberal notion of the Cartesian abstract subjectivity – but it also presents this difference in a manner without and beyond the particular qualities: it is not them which make the individual truly indivisible, but solely her status as a *remnant* – a nameless remainder of the societal operation of naming and classifying. This de-nominated remnant, baring the irreducible kernel of singularity, is an exemplary singular: a *universal Marrano*.

The Derridean singular is simultaneously an *arrivant* and a *revenant*: the one coming from the future 'age of friends' in which the inalienable rights will have belonged to truly 'neither Jew, nor Greek', a nameless guest – but also the one who 'comes to mind', constantly reminding us that modern history already knows such a figure of the non-identitarian singularity:

> *To that which lives without having a name*, we will give an added name: Marrano, *for example*. Playing with the relative arbitrariness of every nomination, we determine this added name [*surnom*], which a name always is, in memory of and according to the figure of the Marrano (of the crypto-judaic, and of the crypto-X in general). As we suggested just a while ago, it is said that the history of the Marranos has just come to an end with the declaration by the Spanish court. You can believe that if you want to. (A, 77; emphasis added)[32]

We already know that, against Yerushalmi and the apology of the Spanish Court in 1992, which made all the Marrano rulings in Spain null and void, Derrida wants to maintain Marrano as a valid figure: 'a *universal Marrano*, if one may say, beyond what may nowadays be the finished forms of Marrano culture' (A, 74), because 'in spite of appearances, this exceptional situation[of the *conversos*] is, at the same time, certainly exemplary of a universal structure; it represents or reflects a type of *originary alienation*' (MO, 63) – or the primary non-belonging which, for Derrida, is the crux of a good community.

---

[32] This 'neither/nor' Derrida describes as 'the negativity of just anyone: the friend and non-friend at the same time, a fellow human being and a complete stranger,' while he also pleads that this aporia should not be too easily reconciled, rather maintained as a 'serious' thought underlying any possible 'politics of friendship' (PF, 234). By stressing the non-tangible freedom of radical *communitas*, Derrida distances himself from the letter of the liberal theory of subjective freedom, yet remains loyal to its guiding/haunting spirit of radical singularity which is to be found – only seemingly paradoxically – in the living midst of the radical *communitas* where subjects become 'de-nominated' in the Marrano kind of way and stripped of all 'civil identities': 'If freedom is no longer the attribute of a subject, of a mastery [*maitrise*] or a measure [*metrique*], the unit of calculation can no longer be the *civil identity of a citizen with a patronym*, nor the equality of one person to another, nor the equality of one *ego* to other equal *egos*, nor even, in case one wanted to hold on to the grammatical and ontological power of saying "I," the equality of one conscious, voluntary, and intentional I to another' (R, 52; emphasis added).

It is, therefore, the antinomian Marrano abode of the radical de-nomination, which lends its features to the modern individual – and not the classical-liberal hypostasis of the universal human nature, which remains a wrong kind of 'indeterminate abstraction'. What becomes captured in the structure of the liberal modern law is not a fixed essence of an abstract human being, but a fleeting moment of the communal *flux* which is being remembered and preserved – 'forgotten without being forgotten' – within the structure itself. A moment of the *fluxus* in the *fixus*, therefore: a highly dialectical solution which, according to Victor Turner, makes modern societies permanently *liminoid*, that is, in crisis and on the edge – yet, not necessarily in the negative sense of the encroaching chaos and anomie.[33] The idea that the liberal law is not some eternal law of nature but can always be re-negotiated and re-constituted as a *new* law derives precisely from its liminoid character: the semi-fluid condition which, in the dialectical manner, *er-innert*, that is, preserves and internalizes, the communal experience of the flow. Richard Sennett perfectly spotted the gist of this modern dialectics, which, according to him, is the unique capability to make a 'use of disorder': the utilization of the anarchic subversion of the law in the name of radical justice, but, at the same time, for the sake of the reinvention of the law, which internalizes and memorizes the experience of *crisis* in the form of the internal *critique*.[34] This is also what, according to Yovel, characterizes the 'Marrano experience': the manner in which all those suspect – 'illicit, illogical, immoral' (OW, 348) – vices of betrayal and living in permanent crisis 'without qualities' turn into potential virtues of the 'basic human freedom'. Sennett's felicitous phrase, 'use of disorder', and its potential advantage to the idea of justice brings to mind Derrida's musings on the disjointed tile in the kitchen floor mosaic at his childhood home in El Biar: while at first it irritated him terribly and he, like Hamlet, saw himself as a future tile messiah who would one day set it right, he eventually began to perceive it as a metonymy of the *rogue justice* and simply let it be:

> Hence the return of the law (since the disjointed, misfit tile was *out of joint*, I, after Hamlet, had to say: *I was born to set it right*, it was my duty to repair it, I was born for this. For reestablishment of the law and for rendering justice. But, perhaps, less for setting thing back to order than for becoming an envoy [*la sentinelle*] of disorder, a blind guardian watching over the specters and the crimes?) [. . .] After sixty years, this rogue tile, is still there, surviving. *Who* is this tile? [. . .] Is there any

---

[33] Comp. Turner: 'Liminality may be the scene of disease, despair, death, suicide, the breakdown without compensatory replacement of normative, well defined social ties and bonds. It may be *anomie*, alienation, *angst*, the three fatal "alpha" sisters of many modern myths [. . .], but is both more creative and more destructive than the structural norm': Turner, 'From Liminal to Liminoid', 78. According to Turner, the liminoid formula integrates the negativity of the liminal stage into a modern mode of living, where it becomes a source of creativity – but always inescapably precarious and endangered by destruction.

[34] See Richard Sennett, *The Uses of Disorder: Personal Identity and City Life* (New York: W. W. Norton & Company, 1992). The use of disorder is also the main subject of Derrida's *Rogues*, where the eponimic *rogues/voyous* refer to the 'odd ones' who, becasue of their highly irregular oddity, can never form a well-organized collective.

good in its fault? What was given to us by its fault and what does it consist in? Is there a redemption coming from such *felix culpa*? (TM, 91; 93)

The motif of *felix culpa* is, as we have seen, the one which Derrida shares with Saint Augustine, but there is also a difference: while for the latter, redemption can come only from God himself, for Derrida it must come straight from the *culpa*/fault/defect. This also applies to his reading of Marx: it is the spectre of *communitas* rather than communism – of the intangible experience 'out of joint' surviving despite all odds, rather than a socio-scientific project – that truly haunts modern Europe. The memory of *communitas* is strictly a-temporal and in that sense also properly utopian, non-placeable (as opposed to philosophical utopias which can always be easily located within the structures of being). Bruno Schulz, the famous Marrano of Polish literature, in his messianico-Frankist meditations on the im-possible, delegates this memory/anticipation to the 'thirteenth month, belonging to a non-existent calendar'. It thus comes to mind as the 'unchallenged night' – precisely the non-identitarian and de-nominated night where all cows seem black – to disturb the hierarchy of *societas* in the same way in which the Marrano is always an anachronistic *arrivant* from 'elsewhere' (*d'ailleurs*) who comes to disturb the order of home and exile, us and them:

> How can one have an age among others? How does one calculate the age of a Marrano, for example? Let us figuratively call Marrano anyone who remains faithful to a secret that he has not chosen, in the very place where he lives, in the home of the inhabitant or of the occupant, in the home of the first or of the second *arrivant*, in the very place where he stays without saying no but without identifying himself as belonging to. In the unchallenged night where the radical absence of any historical witness keeps him or her, in the dominant culture that by definition has calendars, this secret keeps the Marrano even before the Marrano keeps it. Is it not possible to think that such a secret eludes history, age, and aging? Thanks to this anachronism, Marranos that we are, Marranos in any case, whether we want to be or not, whether we know it or not, Marranos having an incalculable number of ages, hours, and years, of untimely histories, each both larger and smaller than the other, each still waiting for the other, we may incessantly be younger and older, in a last word, *infinitely finished*. (A, 81; emphasis added)

'Marrano, *for example*' (A, 77), is indeed a perfect *example*: always an anachronistic remnant which belongs only to the night of de-nomination and dedifferentiation, which in Derrida's system bears the name of *Khôra*: 'The *Khôra* is anachronistic; it "is" the anachrony within being, or better: the anachrony of being. It anachronizes being' (ON, 94). It is precisely this association of the Marranos with the ageless night as the self-withdrawing matrix of all finite beings that come out of it one by one, which explains why, in *Aporias*, Derrida juxtaposes universal Marranism with the secret of death: that which finishes us all in the infinite number of ways and bestows our finitude with infinitely unique rogue traits. In *Faith and Knowledge*, this infinite finitude of numberless singulars, always *plus d'un*, was opposed to the finished infinitude of the

One as the Absolute that comprises all being in its perfect form: the complete *Seiendste* or that which exists the strongest in the fullest possible way and cannot die. Contrary to this absolutist closure of finished perfection, the finitude made possible by *Khôra* opens itself to the infinite differentiation thanks to the always unique secret of each and every singular, which is *its* death:

> *death* is always the name of a secret, since it signs the irreplaceable singularity. It puts forth the public name, the common name of a secret, the common name of *the proper name without name*. It is therefore always a shibboleth, for the manifest name of a secret is from the beginning a private name, so that *language about death is nothing but the long history of a secret society*, neither public nor private, semi-private, semi-public, on the border between the two; thus, also a sort of *hidden religion* of the *awaiting* (oneself as well as each other), with its ceremonies, cults, liturgy, or its Marranolike rituals. A universal Marrano, if one may say, beyond what may nowadays be the finished forms of Marrano culture. (A, 74)

But why exactly does death, which finishes 'us' in the infinite number of ways, make 'us' all universal Marranos? Whence this talk of secret societies and crypto-religions with their 'Marranolike rituals'? We saw in Chapter 2 that for Derrida the Marrano-like hidden religion of mortality/finite life constitutes the encrypted secret of the seemingly secular modernity: its secret religious life. In fact, in postulating this shift towards mortality, which made modern Christian thinkers obsess with the 'death of God', he is not far from the findings of one of the best historians of early *modernitas*: Johan Huizinga. In his *Waning of the Middle Ages* (first published in 1924), the *danse macabre* – the dark parade of the plague victims, all, despite their social status, led in one horizontal dance by the skeleton – became the paradigm of radical equality in which death played the role of the Grand Equalizer.[35] In face of death, this 'unchallenged night', everybody appeared dedifferentiated: whether prince or serf, Master or Slave, all were taken equally swiftly by the plague. It was, therefore, the radical *communitas* of death, which shook the feudal hierarchy of the Middle Ages, by demonstrating that – in the eyes of God who gives Death – its hierarchical laws were not set in stone: they were nothing but mere conventions, made fluid – liquidated – by death. The moment of *communitas*, therefore, is not just simply a happy one: it is also deeply ambivalent, lined with a dark apprehension of radical equality in face of death and decay. This ambivalence appeals to Derrida too: to have faith in *Khôra*, this truly 'unchallenged night', is the unspoken Marrano belief in the messianic advent of death as the universal equalizer. In Chapter 1, we saw that the dark *communitas* of death is also a model of Giorgio Agamben's 'coming community', but Derrida's use of mortal equality is different. His aim is to utilize it for the new *societas* of the finite life which will have realized – or, at least, come close to the realization of – the Joachimite prophecy of the

---

[35] See Johan Huizinga, *The Waning of the Middle Ages* (New York: Dover, 2013), most of all chapter 'The Vision of Death', 124–35.

'age of friendship'.³⁶ The 'unchallenged night' is to leave its trace in the 'penumbral light' that will enlighten the horizontal '*Khôra* of the political' (R, 44).

But what really inaugurates modern history is what comes next: the messianic reversal which transforms death into more life. What, in the thirteenth century, started as a bleak *danse macabre* metamorphosed into something much more joyful and positive only one century later: the *love parades* which imitated the democratic form of the death dances, but celebrated love and life instead. Perhaps the word 'instead' is too strong here: as Huizinga and Denis de Rougemont quite rightly notice, Eros wore here a merely thinly disguised mask of Thanatos.³⁷ Free love uniting masters and servants, the universal sense of equalizing friendship, as well as a sense of an ending, of an epochal entropy which were dissolving the feudal society without giving anything tangible instead – all this was exercised by the *morituri* who were walking into death joyfully, enjoying the world's Last Days. In *Sermon on the Song of Songs*, the defining masterpiece of this era of transition, Bernard of Clairvaux describes the newly discovered love passion as an agent of disorder, characteristic of the radical *communitas*: 'What a violent, all-consuming, impetuous love! It thinks only of itself, lacks interest in anything else, despises all, is satisfied with itself! It confuses stations, disregards manners, knows no bounds. Proprieties, reason, decency, prudence, judgment are defeated and reduced to slavery' (79:1).

While imitating the rites of the thanatic equalization, love parades, were, in fact, quite similar to the ancient pagan traditions of funeral orgies. One can clearly see it on the deservedly famous painting of Boticelli, *Primavera*: the love parade celebrating the coming of spring is rendered here in the funeral manner which gives the whole scene its uncanny mesmerizing effect. Even the spring herself resembles the corpse (and not only because she bears the features of the painter's already dead beloved, Simonetta): pale, expressionless, and weirdly static, as if suspended in the air, she is a *transi*, a figure in the in-between state of decomposition, partly a cadaver and partly already a pale haunting spectre. Yet, the early modernity, which once again pulled the vital forces out of the decaying 'Autumn of Middle Ages' – Boticelli's *Primavera* is decidedly autumnal – and, for the first time, made the paradigmatic 'use of disorder', turned the tables for good: the new democratic arrangement of the post-reformational West used the lesson of radical *communitas* to create a new idea of the individual – free, dynamic, 'Marrano-like': no longer determined by social status, now as ready to rise within the social hierarchy as before he was ready to go down and join the fated end of us all. Love, rediscovered by the waning Middle Ages as the equally egalitarian reverse of

---

36 In the fifth chapter of *liber introductorius* to *Expositio in Apocalypsim*, composed in 1186, Joachim da Fiore formulates the outlines of his famous prophecy of the three ages, neatly summarised by the historian of the Franciscan reform: 'The first [age] is in the servitude of slavery, the second in the servitude of sons, the third in freedom. The first in fear, the second in faith, the third in love. The first is the status of bondsmen, the second of freemen, the third of friends': Ernst Benz, *Ecclesia spiritualis: Kirchenidee und Geschichtstheologie der franziskanischen Reformation* (Darmstadt: Wissenschaftliche Buchgesellschaft Darmstadt, 1964), 26.

37 See also Denis de Rougemont, *Love in the Western World*, trans. Mongomery Belgion (New York: Harcourt & Brace, 1940).

death – *love strong as death*, the famous line from the Song of Songs was originally the phrase used during ancient Hebrew funeral rituals – has slowly, but surely, paved its way towards the modern vision of the 'age of friends'.[38]

But, as we have already established, that does not make Derrida a partisan of a sacred anarchy: while justice belongs to the 'ageless' and intangible moment of *communitas*, *societas* needs laws. The dialectical better form of 'betrayal' which makes modern law lies precisely in this novelty – the focus on the singularity as its nominalistic *limes*, or what Rosenzweig calls a 'meta-ethical remnant' and Derrida a 'rogue' (*voyou*). Imagined as a 'universal Marrano', the individual is 'northis northat', for she never coincides with any form or identity, and must be defended against any kind of collective coercion. As such she becomes a legalistic avatar of the *tselem*, a singularity emulating the uniqueness of God, the transcendent *ehad* which transcends any order of general categories and laws.[39] The dialectical evolution of the law, therefore, entails a subsumption of the antinomian element: the role of the law is not to create a general *ethos* of 'parts and wholes', but to protect the 'deviant' meta-ethical singularity in its right *not* to participate in the totality, to remain 'entirely other' (*tout autre*) and

---

[38] The idea that the pro-democratic transformations of early modernity may have something to do with the rediscovery of mortality and finitude and the waning of Middle Ages' belief in eternal absolutes – the experience of death as simultaneously a threat of destruction and a promise of radical equality, as well as a trigger of the 'violent affirmation of survival' (RA, 205) – is well confirmed by Hägglund's interpretation of Derrida's 'democracy to come': 'If one desires democracy, one cannot desire a state of being that is exempt from time. To desire democracy is by definition to desire something temporal, since democracy must remain open to its own alteration in order to be democratic' (RA, 204–5). This accent on mortality brings us back to the Marrano politics of survival outlined in Chapter 1, where we discussed Derrida's protest against any politics based on the sublime 'above' as 'exempt from time' and transcending the dimension of the everyday toil of *survie*.

[39] The link connecting the 'rogue', whom Derrida envisages as the future citizen of the democracy-to-come, also called *voyoucracy*, with the Marrano who distances himself from any communal belonging and preserves his sense of 'shadowy inwardness', has also been noticed by Shmuel Trigano. While criticizing radical republicanism of the French 68', Trigano writes: 'Against what the Marxists say, the limit which separates interiority and exteriority – one of the distinctive features of the Marrano (non)identity – could be affirmed as a positive quality of great importance in safeguarding the human element in politics [. . .] provided that the politics does not constitute a totality of what it means to be human [. . .] The shadowy retreat [*le retrait ombragé*] ("God's image," *tselem Elochim*) which contains the secret of being a human can never be treated as a pretext to the unleashing of violence of the State which would like to *see* what's there. It is a singular human being which is in the centre of the State, but he/she will always be hidden like the Holy of Holies in the Jerusalem Temple – in the heart of the Polis – and never the other way round. The centre of the individual is unreachable [. . .] *This is the teaching which was given to us by the modern experience of Marranism, gradually turned from negative into a positive one*': Schmuel Trigano, 'Le Marranisme, un modèle multidimensionnel', in *Pardes: Etudes et Culture Juives, nr 29 (Le Juif caché: Marranisme et modernité)* (Paris: In Press Editions, 2000), 268–9; emphasis added. See also the great comment of Marc Goldschmit: 'The marrano hypothesis announces itself as the being, the unconscious, and the deconstruction of present democracy - and its future, and its specter beyond its being': *L'hypothèse du Marrane: Le théâtre judéo-chrétien de la pensée politique* (Paris: Editions du Félin, 2014), 11. On the shadowlands of the Marrano 'infrapolitics', see also: Alberto Moreiras, 'Infrapolitical Derrida: The Ontic Determination of Politics beyond Empiricism' (MARS, 116–36). To emphasize a small difference between Moreiras's and my terminology, I choose the term *umbrapolitics* as the politics of the shadows, strictly opposed to the politics of light as absolute visibility, though obviously not against light as enlightenment. In the Latin *umbra*, there should also reverberate the Hebrew *tsel* – 'shadow' which is simultaneously *tselem*, 'God's likeness'.

preserve a distance towards communal belonging.⁴⁰ Before the law always spoke in the name of the ethical whole and preserved its indemnity – now it is supposed to speak in the name of the separated 'Marrano' remnant 'beyond any social bond' (PF, 298) and protect its precarious singular life. This antinomian 'use of disorder', which bends and transforms the law from within, is strictly analogical to the dialectical utilization of apocalypses in Derrida's figure of *différance*. The impatient messianic slogan – 'Lo, I make all things new!' – here becomes harnessed to the most patient of works, which consists in making new laws. 'Lo, I make all laws new!', therefore, constitutes the gist of the Jewish-messianic version of Derrida's revision of Paul: not a sad resignation of a *katechon* but the positive dialectical messianicity inscribed into the very structure of modern legislative process. The old law dies in order to liberate a meta-ethical life which now, patiently and *little by little*, transforms life again into Scripture. As we have seen in Chapter 1, for Derrida, the Benjaminian idea of transforming life back into Scripture means most of all a creation of a new law that would no longer punish/kill life (as in Paul), but become its 'supple' protective expression.⁴¹

By choosing the Marrano *voyou* as the true *tselem Elohim* of his new *voyoucracy*, Derrida places himself firmly on the anti-totalitarian position which combines the best, messianically inspired, elements of both traditions, liberal and leftist. The insistence on the 'awaiting of the impossible' is here the same as the resistance to the 'restoration of order', which allows the moment of *communitas* to linger a little longer in the form of a spectral afterimage. *The leftist spectre hovers over liberal society*: the radical justice, possible only in the unstable conditions of *communitas*, haunts the liberal law-oriented *societas*, yet, at the same time, it is also pushed away – and, with it, 'spectralized' – by this very *societas* which rightly fears totalitarian, all-too-collective closures. To realize *fully* the state of *communitas* here and now equals 'absolute evil' – but not to realize it *at all* is to give up on the ideal of justice, which should remain our constant 'inspiration'.⁴²

---

⁴⁰ According to deconstruction's sacred formula: *tout autre est tout autre*, 'every other is entirely other': see the title of Chapter 4 in Jacques Derrida, *The Gift of Death* (GD, 82–88). On the paradox of the modern law, which commands to recognize the transcendent alterity of the other, see Derrida's comment in *Politics of Friendship*: 'Does not my relation to the singularity of the other *qua* other, in effect, involve the law? Having come as a third party but always from the singularity of the other, does not the law command me to recognize the transcendent alterity of the other who can never be anything but heterogeneous and singular, hence resistant to the very generality of the law?' (PF, 276–7).

⁴¹ Derrida defines the rule of *little by little* when he juxtaposes Shakespeare's *Mercy seasons justice*, falling on it with a gentle rain of Christ's blood, with a similar line in Hugo: 'the gentle [*douce*] law of Christ will finally permeate the legal code and radiate out from there' (quot. in DP1, 201). And comments: 'It is going to irrigate the law, the written legislation. Little by little, Christ, the spirit, the soul, the gentle law, the gentleness of Christ, charity, the blood of Christ, is going to *irrigate the legal code and transform legislative writing* [. . .] the heart is going to transform the written and positive, historical law. *Little by little*, the legal code, written law, historical law, will be irrigated, inspired, vivified, spiritualized, by gentleness, the gentle law of Christ' (DP1, 201; emphasis added). This gentle and fluid law of the heart is here the same as the law of radical *communitas*, which also can be said to *irrigate* and *inspire* the rigid hierarchies of *societas*.

⁴² Derrida summarizes this dialectics in the following way: 'One must constantly remember that this absolute evil (which is, is it not, absolute life, fully present life, the one that does not know death and does not want to hear about it) can take place. One must constantly remember that it is even on the

This *inspiration* must be understood here quite literally as the coming of the spirit in the form of the haunting – *revenant et arrivant* – spectre which is, like Marrano, 'ageless': simultaneously past and future, but never present here and now. It is thus, at the same time, a vigilant anticipation and a living memory of this unique fleeting modality of our 'living together' that cannot last and make itself truly present within the structures of social reality. And although Western metaphysics indeed prioritizes presence – whatever actualizes itself in durable ontological structures – the passing modality of *communitas* should not be deemed as negligeable or *simply* impossible. Lasting, durability – although essential from the point of view of social structures – are not the sole criteria that should govern our political life which not only is but also ought to be 'full of spectres'. Perhaps, this is the true meaning of the 68 slogan – *demandez l'impossible!* – which Derrida sometimes adopts by giving it an ironic spin: yes, demand it precisely as impossible, but not as *simply* impossible, rather as the 'im-possible' which renders all the exciting modern possibilities – of making and un-making of the social law as always *new* – possible in the first place. The non-simply impossible of the radical *communitas* would then constitute the 'quasi-transcendental condition' of the future 'democracy to come', which will have never completely erased its 'objective fantasy': the joyful festivity of life imagined either as the 'Khôra of the political' (R, 44). In *Rogues*, Derrida presents his vision of metaphysical democracy as *voyoucracy* – the infinite differential of beings choreographed by *Khôra*, operating precisely on the grounds of the logic of the non-identitarian remnant: 'the inadequate and improper'.

> In both senses of *différance*, then, democracy is differential; it is *différance, renvoi*, and spacing. That is why, let me repeat, the theme of spacing, the theme of the interval or the gap, of the trace as gap [*ecart*], of the becoming-space of time or the becoming-time of space, plays such an important role as early as *Of Grammatology* and 'Différance.' Democracy is what it is only in the *différance* by which it defers itself and differs from itself. It is what it is only by spacing itself beyond being and even beyond ontological difference; *it is (without being) equal and proper to itself only insofar as it is inadequate and improper*, at the same time behind and ahead of itself, behind and ahead of the Sameness and Oneness of itself. (R, 30–1; emphasis added)

Yet, the democratic differential not only does not preclude community but emerges as the *sine qua non* of the new 'living together' in *Pardes Khôra* which now shows its densely populated reverse as the Garden of Earthly Delights: no longer a desert, it becomes a noisy *place* given to the singularities that blithely disperse and multiply in their differences, free at last from the repressive ideal of oneness and harmony.

basis of the terrible possibility of this impossible that justice is desirable: *through* but also *beyond* right and law' (SM, 220; emphasis original).

'Belonging without belonging': *Specters of Landauer*

Derrida's Marrano dialectics involves a complex movement of withdrawing from and venturing back to the world, precisely as in Winnicott's aphorism which hits the very core of the Marrano condition: 'It is joy to be hidden, but a disaster not to be found.' And he has a powerful precursor in it, Gustav Landauer, the author of *Skepsis und Mystik* and an existentialist anarchist greatly admired by Paul Celan. By drawing on Landauer's reading of Meister Eckhart, which found its poetic expression in Celan's late poems, as well as on Michel de Certeau's defence of the Marrano mystic inwardness, I want to call this other, non-Hegelian, form of dialectics *anacosmic*: 'worldly-again'. Unlike Hegel who criticizes the inward turn of the 'beautiful soul' and praises 'man of action' for his courage to stay in the world no matter what, Landauer intuitively follows the steps of 'mystical Marranos' and advocates a constant oscillation between the inward and the outward: the withdrawal prepares a vantage point from which the self returns to the world in order to find it again – and be found again in it. Landauer, Celan, and Derrida are thus paradigmatic Marranos who retreat into their inner *nowhere/elsewhere*, but never stop longing for the *anacosmic return* – back to the world, but then solely on their own terms.

Landauer's daring reinterpretation of the biblical tradition in terms of anthropological mysticism, laid out in the commentaries on his own translation of Meister Eckhart, as well as in the philosophical treatise on the relation between scepticism and mysticism, influenced the whole next generation of German Jewish thinkers: Buber, Lukacs, Scholem, Arendt, Adorno, and Celan. Although somewhat overshadowed by his ephebes, Gustav Landauer emerges as their indispensable precursor: all the tropes of the progressive theopolitics were originally generated in Landauer's unique genre of *political mysticism* that granted all human beings a divine status and envisaged a future community of god's likenesses/shadows: *tselemim*.

The key to Landauer's political mysticism is his interpretation of Meister Eckhart, which differs strongly from the line of his reception that goes from Novalis through Schopenhauer up to Heidegger. As we have seen in the previous chapters, the latter concentrates on the Eckhartian concept of *Gelassenheit* which, in the Schopenhauerian manner, rings with the quietistic overtones of the nirvanic *Auslöschung*: switching off the active mode of being in the world, which, denounced as deceptive and illusory, appears as an almost Gnostic trap full of disorienting *Verwirrung*, madness. The soul has to withdraw from the snares of the created reality and go down into itself in order to discover the uncreated and eternal spark of impersonal divinity, *Gottheit*, which appears as nothing to the worldly entities but, in fact, is the only true being, the very *natura naturans*: the creative essence of everything that springs into existence. *Nach innen geht der geheimnisvolle Weg*, the mysterious path leads inward, says Novalis after Eckhart:[43] into the deep blue of the Mother Night who shelters and protects from the usurpation of the false *clamor mundi*, the noise of the world.[44]

---

[43] Novalis, *Blütenstaub*, in *Werke in zwei Bänden*, Band 2 (Köln: Könemann, 1996), 103.
[44] See Heidegger, in 'Zeit und Sein', on *die Gelassenheit wartende (nicht hoffende) Abgeschiedenheit*, a 'separation that awaits (without hoping for) a releasment': *Zur Sache des Denkens*, 20.

But although Landauer speaks very highly of Novalis and is very much taken by his coloristic metaphor of medieval Christianity – the deep mystical blue of inchoate intimations as opposed to the full sun of the Hegelian, absolutely revealed, religion – he himself reads Eckhart very differently: through the prophecies of Joachim da Fiore, then mediated by the Rheinland *minnesang* and its hot mystical milieu of the Fraternity of Free Spirits, which feverishly envisaged coming of a *nova era* and an advent of a New Men, defined by their equal participation in the divine.[45] The 'magical blue light' is the colour of Mary and the stained-glass windows of Chartres cathedral; it is the colour of Cusanus's *docta ignorantia* which is a 'form of superior knowledge'; and it is the colour of the Spirit of messianic anticipation which hovers 'above the towns' of the late medieval period, which has already experienced the joys and sorrows of radical *communitas* brought by Black Death:

> In our times, this spirit is represented by Christian rites and Christian symbols. Heaven lingers above the fields on which we labor and above the towns in which we work – the eternity of the spirit and men's equality and divinity fly along soulful ways into blue infinity. Romantics like Novalis knew – felt – that blue was the color of Christianity. A color that signifies the darkness of ignorance rather than the light of knowledge, but that still indicates the direction of yearning and the source of light. It is hard to imagine a picture of Mary, the mother of God, without a blue frame. It is good to be aware of Christianity as a colorful force and to know its color. The further we depart from Christianity, the clearer it becomes that Christianity was not colorless. *It was not a gloomy reflection, but magical blue light*. We must remember this when reading the great minds of those times: from Dionysius to Meister Eckhart to Nicolaus Cusanus; we must remember it when we encounter a form of ignorance [*Unwissen*] that is actually a form of superior knowledge [*Überwissen*]; we must remember it when we encounter a darkness that is actually a light transcending the earth as well as the Gods. The stone towers of the cathedral, rising like trees, reach out to this transcendent reality; *a reality that gave people a special form of inwardness, of yearning, of passion, and of sexuality; a reality that gave people faces, postures, tools, and souls; a reality that filled all their institutions and social entities with a common spirit*.[46]

Landauer names here three theologians of the so-called *via negativa*, where Eckhart (thirteenth century) and Cusanus (fifteenth century) mark the decline of Middle Ages with its slow passage to modernity. He does not mention the twelfth-century Calabrian monk Joachim da Fiore, but it is thanks to this Cistercian that the prophecy of the *nova era*, announcing a reign of the 'common spirit' of universal friendship, begins to incubate in the magical blue atmosphere of the medieval towns. Landauer's choice of Meister Eckhart does not belong to the line of *Gelassenheit* as advocated by Heidegger

---

[45] See Jeanne Ancelet-Hustache, *Master Eckhart and the Rhineland Mystics*, trans. Hilda Graef (London: Longman, 1957).
[46] Landauer, *Revolution*, 129; emphasis added.

who after the *Kehre* decides to withdraw from politics and finds the Eckhartian inner *Ruhe* as a vehicle of liberation from the 'errance of History'. It belongs to the Joachimite line of the free spirit mysticism that is, to use the French formula, very apt in this case, retreats only in order to jump better – *reculier pour mieux sauter* – that is, withdraws only to find a stable vantage point from which it can better attack the worldly realm and abolish its feudal hierarchies of power. The soul must retreat into her blue secret and, thus reinforced, return to the world and 'living together'. Just as she rediscovers the world in the ana-cosmic gesture, she also recognizes a new community of 'we' – the *ana-koine*.

Derrida's insistence on the cohabitation with ghosts and secrets strikes an immediate connection with Landauer's political mysticism. In fact, *Specters of Marx* are a bit of a misnomer: they should rather be called *Specters of Landauer*. In 'Marx & Sons', Derrida speaks about the descendants of Marx, but his description fits even better the 'state of debt' which should rather be due to Landauer: 'There are still sons – and daughters – who, unbeknownst to themselves, incarnate or metempsychosize the ventriloquist specters of their ancestors' (MS, 262). But what is exactly the nature of this influence, of this, as Derrida would have it, *ventriloquism*, which makes so many thinkers after Landauer – Buber, Lukacs, Bloch, Taubes, Arendt – speak with his voice without naming him? Be haunted by him as if he were some kind of a spectre, a ghost residing in their minds, a Stirnerian *Spuk*? Is this a sign of him being forgotten as the precursorial source, or, quite to the contrary, a sign of being ultra-significant, like Marx, ubiquitous in a nameless manner? I would like to believe that the latter is true – and precisely for the reason of Landauer being an eternal adversary of Marx and his materialist-reductive understanding of 'the *spirit* of revolution' (to remind again the title of Derrida's conversation with Roudinesco).

Derrida is a particularly interesting case of Landauer's 'ventriloquist' afterlife. The latter's teaching of *ana-koine*, or the difficult art of how to live together beyond any collectivist pressure of imposed identity and belonging, definitely lies at the core of Derrida's political interventions: most of all, *The Politics of Friendship*, which discusses Joachim's de Fiore prophesy of the universal *amitia* explicitly (1994), *Specters of Marx* (1994), and the late essay, 'Living Together' (1998). None of these works mention Landauer by name, but are nonetheless pervaded by his spirit, or – as Derrida would have put himself – by his spectre. In all these works, we will find a mystico-political variation on the Landauerian theme of *Verbindung der Getrennten* (connection of the separated ones), poised explicitly against the Marxist type of unproblematic collectivism. Its 'mysticism' is undeniable: what Derrida calls a secret/*mysterion* as the essential centre of every singularity is indeed a modernized version of Eckhartian 'free spirit' – a connection which Derrida openly admits in his essay on Heidegger, *Of Spirit*, where he, just as Landauer before, inscribes himself in the lineage of the secularized Christian Spirituals.[47] The Derridean space of freedom is the abstracted 'desert in the desert' (FK, 47) – which Landauer could just as well have described as 'the place of

---

[47] On this, see the lengthy note in which Derrida talks about the 'heretics of *Libre Esprit*', starting from Helvetius, whose 'book *De l'esprit* was burned at the foot of the great staircase of the Palais de Justice

abstraction [. . .], set as the contraction of all of our inner powers and the inclusion of the universe in our sphere of agency'.⁴⁸ Further on, still in the Landauerian vein, Derrida decides to name his position 'paradoxical Marranism' which, by seemingly giving in to the Christian hegemony (e.g. the mystical tradition of Meister Eckhart), remains, in fact, 'more faithful to a certain Jewish vocation', that is, Jewish messianism, than the orthodox Judaism itself.⁴⁹ In 'Living Together', Derrida describes his own version of the ana-communal *vivre ensemble* as a community of strangers: the only form of community that he could have accepted in his Algerian childhood.

> The only belonging, the only 'living together' that he [young Derrida, speaking about himself in the third person – A.B.-R.] judged then bearable and worthy of that name already supposed a rupture with identitarian and totalizing belonging, assured of itself in a homogeneous whole [ensemble]. In a manner as unreflective as reflective, the child felt at his core two contradictory things as to what this 'living together' could signify: on the one hand, that he could betray his own, his close ones, and Judaism, and that he had to avow this within himself, even before others, even before God, but also on the other hand, that by this separation, this rupture, this passage toward a kind of universality beyond symbiotic communitarianism and gregarious fusion, beyond any citizenship, in this very separation, it could be that he was more faithful to a certain Jewish vocation, at the risk of remaining the only, the last, and the least of the Jews [*le seul el le denier des Juifs*], in the most ambiguous sense of this expression with which he played without playing – elsewhere and fifty years later, presenting himself or sometimes also hiding himself as a kind of *paradoxical Marrano who ran the risk of losing even the culture of his secret or the secret of his culture*. For, at the core of this solitude, this child had to begin believing, and he no doubt never finished thinking, that any 'living together' supposes and guards, as its very condition, the possibility of this singular, secret, inviolable separation, from which alone a stranger accords himself to a stranger, in hospitality. *To recognize that one lives together, well then, only with and as a*

---

on 10 February 1759 by order of the Parlement of Paris', and ending with 'the author of the *Mirouer des simples ames*, Marguerite de Porette, who was burned in 1310' (OS, 115–16).

⁴⁸ Gustav Landauer, *Skepticism and Mysticism: On Mauthner's Critique of Language*, trans. David Grunwald (Wrocław: Amazon Fullfilment, 2019), 29.

⁴⁹ The issue of Landauer's Marranism arises apropos his series of lectures on Strindberg's understanding of Christianity, published in 1917 in the magazine *Der Jude*. The Landauerian 'eternal Jew' can indeed be regarded as a Marrano figure: *der Jude, der ewige Jude in immer neuen Gestalten*: Gustav Landauer, 'Strindbergs historische Miniaturen', in Gustav Landauer, *Werkausgabe*, ed. Gert Mattenklott and Hanna Delf, vol. 3 (Berlin: Akademie-Verlag, 1997), 139. Here, the shape-shifting eternal Jew becomes a bearer of the universal Abrahamic promise of redemption, who wanders through the foreign lands of modern Europe (Egypt/Edom) and spreads the messianic spark through the medium of foreign languages and cultures. While Christianity constitutes only one of the changing shapes of the messianic Judaism ('Strindberg's Jesus is Jewish', ibid., 142), 'the messianic [*das Messianische*] starts with the Jews and it ends with the Jews' (ibid., 151). What strengthens the Marrano aspect of fulfilling the messianic vocation in secret and undercover is Landauer's term *die geheime Lenkung*, 'secret tendency', with which he describes the actions of the 'eternal Jew'.

stranger, a stranger 'at home' [chez soi] [. . .] – *here is the justice of a law above laws.* (LT, 28; emphasis added)

This is not just a continuation but also a creative revision of Landauer's motif of 'through separation to community', which leads towards a new *Mit-leben*, 'living together'. By protesting, already as a child, against the 'symbiotic communitarianism and gregarious fusion' of the Sephardic community in his native El Biar, Derrida learns what it means to be a Marrano: the last of the Jews – the despised 'rejected stone' and a misfit – but, at the same time, paradoxically, the first of Jews, because 'more faithful to a certain Jewish vocation' which later on he will understand as the messianic teaching of a good *vivre ensemble*. For Derrida, only the Marrano paradox of simultaneous belonging and non-belonging can carry and preserve the community of friendship, which guards the separation, secrecy, and the inalienable right to be (in) the shadow/*tsel*. What thus eventually emerges from the fusion of Landauer's and Derrida's horizons is a *new science of politics* (to use Voegelin's expression, but with a very different intention) which tries to steer political activity away from the political enthusiasts, always too ready to jump into action and declare their political ideals without ever, even for a second, questioning the communal dimension of life. The *ana-communal* teaching is thus directed precisely against those thinkers, mostly belonging to the firm called by Derrida 'Marx & Sons', for whom being-in-community is the self-evident fact of social *phusis*, which can only be doubted by fantastically minded escapists. The Landauerian spectre is there to remind them, however, that the primary belonging – being physically born into a human community (in this case, a rigidly defined class) – is not a *factum brutum* that cannot ever be probed.[50]

Thus, when today, Alain Badiou still praises communism as a 'paradoxical, passionate, violent love for the communal life'[51] – a primary sense of participation in the common to which everybody belongs and which belongs equally to everybody – Derrida, Landauer inspired, begs to differ and accentuates the need for the secretive withdrawal as the necessary condition of a good ana-community. This fundamental difference is reflected also in their respective views on literature. While Badiou understands literature as the 'poetic desire to make the affairs of life akin to the sky and the earth, the water of the oceans and the bushes burning in the light of the summer evenings, that is, common to all'[52] – Derrida, to the contrary, claims that poetry is possible only as *littérature au secret*, that is, as inflecting the common experiences in

---

[50] While defending himself against the accusations of 'Marx & Sons', who mostly objected to Derrida's alleged neglect of the class-structure in Marx's analysis, Derrida explains that his aim was to create a spectral outline of a new International – an International of Strangers, separated and united at the same time as 'we': 'the point is not to eliminate or deny class affiliations, any more than citizenship or parties, but rather to make an appeal for an International whose essential basis or motivating force would not be class, citizenship, or party' (MS, 252). This 'prophecy' of the International of Friendly Strangers is an essentially Landauerian dream.

[51] Alain Badiou, 'Poesie et communisme', in Alain Badiou, *Que pense le poeme?* (Paris: Editions Nous, 2016), 140.

[52] Ibid., 140.

the medium of singularized idiom, where the phrase *au secret* means also 'solitary confinement' or being 'locked away', radically *getrennt*:

> For the secret of the secret of which we are going to speak doesn't consist in hiding some thing, in not revealing the truth of it, but in respecting the *absolute uniqueness, the infinite separation* of that which *ties* me or exposes me to the unique, to the one as to the other, to the One as to the Other. (GD, 122–3; emphasis added)

This is precisely what Landauer and Derrida have in common: they never see separation as a simple negation of togetherness. The 'infinite separation' – just as the Landauerian *Absonderung* – cuts into the rigid dualism of primary communism and individualistic isolation: paradoxically and dialectically, it becomes a new *tie* that links the subject *au secret* to other subjects *au secret*, thus breaking the continuum of belonging into a series of discrete points (where the words *discrete* and *secret* share the same root). As in Landauer, therefore, the operation of withdrawal does not serve an annihilation of the subject, but a discovery of a new subjectivity, based not on the Cartesian inner light of self-possessive reflection, but on the Eckhartian-Novalisian 'magical blue night' of discretion. This discretion, however, does not break all the ties, but allows the ana-communal turn towards a true relation which now links the singulars in their 'unique', strangely mode. Landauer's thesis that 'the path that leads to fellowship with the world does not lead to the outside, but to the inside of ourselves'[53] chimes thus perfectly well with the Derridean intuition about the secret as something that does not cut us from the world but rather radically transforms the mode of our *in-der-Welt-Sein*: from the compulsory thrownness and primary participation to 'fellowship' and 'friendship', that is, a chosen relation which communicates the freedom to be-in-the-world. The whole point, therefore, is not to drown in the secret as in the bottomless night which, for young Hegel, constitutes the main danger of isolated subjectivity.[54] Spun between the *Geworfenheit* and the retreat into a separated night, the Derridean secret, as well as Landauer's withdrawal, find in the act of separation not a loneliness of an insular self, but a new relational manner of living together. Indeed, the following fragment from Derrida's interview, *A Taste for the Secret*, could have just as well come from Landauer's essay on *Revolution*:

---

[53] Landauer, *Skepticism and Mysticism*, 33.
[54] In his lectures from the period 1805–6, that is, when he was composing *Phenomenology*, Hegel, grappling with the concept of the beautiful soul, portrays it as a night capable of engulfing the whole space outside and drown every external thing, a black hole of nihilizing interiority: 'Man is this night, this empty Nothingness, which contains everything in its undivided simplicity [*Einfachheit*]: a wealth of an infinite number of representations, of images, no one of which precisely attains to the spirit, or even more: which are not as really present. It is the night, the interiority or intimacy [*Innere*] of Nature, which exists here: the pure personal Self': G. W. F. Hegel, *Hegel in 20 Bände*, vol. 20 (Frankfurt am Main: Suhrkamp, 1986), 180–1. In his warning against *die schöhne Seele*, Hegel draws on the mystical notion of subjective inwardness, which he associates with the wrong reception of Eckhart as allegedly advocating a regression into the precreational night of *Indifferenz* where, famously, all cows are black and all differences disappear. Landauer and Derrida are both aware of the dangers of such full nocturnal withdrawal: hence their discourse of blue and penumbral light which lights the way of return to the world and the community.

> Why elect the word 'secret' to say this? Why privilege this word rather than the word *same*, or *logos*, or *being*? The choice is not insignificant: it is a strategy, in a definite philosophical scene, that wishes to insist on separation, isolation. Between this secret and what is generally called secret, even if the two are heterogeneous, there is all analogy that makes me prefer the secret to the non-secret, the secret to the public expression, exhibition, phenomenality. I have a taste for the secret, it clearly has to do with not-belonging; I have an impulse of fear or terror in the face of a political space, for example, a public space that makes no room for the secret. For me, the demand that everything be paraded in the public square and that there be no internal forum is a glaring sign of the totalitarianization of democracy. I can rephrase this in terms of political ethics: if a right to the secret is not maintained, we are in a totalitarian space. Belonging – the fact of avowing one's belonging, of putting in common – be it family, nation, tongue – spells the loss of the secret. (TS, 58–9).

Once again evoking the free spirit of the medieval secret societies and the anarchic sense of liberty, both so very dear to Landauer, Derrida writes about the community to come and its bohemian harbingers,[55] boldly exercising their 'counterpower of countercitizenship':

> *Voyoucracy* is a corrupt and corrupting power of the street, an illegal and outlaw power that brings together into a voyoucratic regime, and thus into an organized and more or less clandestine form, into a virtual state, all those who represent a principle of disorder – a principle not of anarchic chaos but of *structured disorder*, so to speak, of plotting and conspiracy, of premeditated offensiveness or offenses against public order. Indeed, of terrorism, it will be said – whether national or international. *Voyoucracy* is a principle of disorder, to be sure, a threat against public order; but, as a *cracy*, it represents something more than a collection of individual or individualistic *voyous*. It is the principle of disorder as a sort of *substitute order* (a bit like a secret society, a religious order, a sect or brotherhood, a kind of Freemasonry) [. . .] The *voyoucracy* already constitutes, even institutes, a sort of *counterpower or countercitizenship*. (R, 65; emphasis added)

Voyoucracy, therefore, is ana-communal in its very form as a 'structured disorder': it never loses the moment of individual deviation that withdraws from and then plots against the 'public order'. The rogues live together, but not because they share the same identity that would define their belonging to such public entities as nation, race, or gender. The rogues live together as the *revenants* who chose to return to the world

---

[55] One of the most often objections levied against Derrida from the Marxist corners is that his political messianism is elitist and that it invests its hopes in the avant-garde of the chosen few. Here too Landauer is a significant precursor: 'Who are the people who have the strength to no longer partake, you ask? Who are the people ready to create new forms of community? It is the few! [. . .] We need them as role models and shining examples for the whole world. They must realize decency, justice, and beauty': Landauer, *Revolution*, 192.

and share it as a non-identitarian space which welcomes their 'crooked' ways. In his musings on the 'crooked timber of humanity', Kant, similarly, comes to the paradoxical conclusion that the human manner of being sociable is, in fact anti-sociable; *die ungesselige Gesseligkeit* constitutes one of the most significant aspects of our incurable 'crookedness'.[56] In Landauer and Derrida, this *ana*-aspect of return or joining-again becomes inscribed into the very mechanism of *Mit-leben*/living together; a disruption which does not destroy community, but – seemingly paradoxically – makes it better. 'My inner feeling that I am an isolated unit can be wrong – and I declare it so, because *I do not want to be isolated*', writes Landauer.[57] The withdrawal, therefore, is not about some *splendid isolation*, which – in the Emersonian manner – would watch the affairs of the world from the vantage point of a transcendental Oversoul. It is all about *wanting* to come back – yet, not in a humble manner of a prodigal son, but always and only on one's own 'crooked' terms.

Laughter in the dark: Derrida's umbrapolitics

According to Virgil, *exul umbra*, 'the exiled is a shadow' – and although the poet himself, exiled from Rome, saw it as a terrible condition of someone deprived of the light, life, and fame, Derrida – again, in the typically Marrano manoeuvre of reversal which turns vices into virtues and weaknesses into merit – advocates the Marrano-like experience of universal exile as liberating, even exhilarating. We constantly have to remember about the rhetorical register of the 'serious play' in which this joyful liberation of a 'lucky break' is enacted. There is something inescapably parodistic and comical about the rogue's 'crookedness' as 'premeditated offensiveness' (R, 65) against the societal norms: their *queer* moment of singular deviation which parodies the public structure in order to make it more fluid, to remind it that it is constantly undermined by the non-identitarian flow of *communitas*. Rogues, therefore, are *universal queers* just as they are universal Marranos.[58]

---

[56] Immanuel Kant, 'Idea for a Universal History with a Cosmopolitan Aim', trans. Allen Wood, in *Kant's 'Idea for a Universal History with a Cosmopolitan Aim.' A Critical Guide*, ed. Amelie Oxenberg Rorty and James Schmidt (Cambridge: Cambridge University Press, 2009), 13: 'The individual [. . .] constantly oscillates between isolation and participation, when he, more or less reluctantly, returns to being among his fellows, whom he cannot stand, but also cannot leave alone.'
[57] Landauer, 'Through Separation. . .', 97; emphasis added.
[58] What Judith Butler says about the parodistic practices of drag queens, living in the *demi-monde* shadowlands of 'normal' society, can be easily substituted for what Derrida says about the Marrano *para-oide* in which Judaism and Christianity melt into air as distinct identitites. If we replace the word 'gender' with the word 'religion', Butler's argument will read in the following way: 'Practices of parody can serve to reengage and reconsolidate the very distinction between a privileged and naturalized religious configuration and one that appears as derived, phantasmatic, and mimetic – a failed copy, as it were. And surely parody has been used to further a politics of despair, one which affirms a seemingly inevitable exclusion of marginal heresies from the territory of the natural and the real. And yet this failure to become "real" and to embody "the natural" is, I would argue, a constitutive failure of all religious enactments for the very reason that these ontological locales are fundamentally uninhabitable. Hence, there is a subversive laughter in the pastiche-effect of parodic

This is more than just an accidental analogy. The oscillation which Judith Butler's *Gender Trouble* describes – between withdrawal and return – is, similarly to Landauer and Derrida, *ana-communal*. At first, drag parody is a private affair, limited to the region of individual phantasy and idiosyncrasy. Gradually, however, it returns to the world to destabilize fixed identities and expose them as *effects*: not as a passive articulation of natural substance, but as a game that plays with reality and in that manner always creates something new. Parody, therefore, first withdraws into secrecy of the inner play, but only in order to jump better into the political realm which it now wants to 'corrupt'. The camp masquerade reveals itself as the rogue truth of human sexuality, intractable in its non-identitarian depth, which parallels the messianic reversal of the *para-oide* and *oide*: the true song of sexuality is now in the drag and mask, and not in some hidden stable identity. Butler calls it a 'metaleptic reasoning'[59]: the turn in which cause and effect trade places.

We saw that such passage, *from parody to politics*, is the gist of what Derrida calls the rogue *countercitizenship* and its 'corruptive power', and also underlies his Marrano parodies in 'Abraham, the Other', creating an endless *purim* play of *hastaral* concealedness where all wear masks and never take them off: a truly 'serious play' which is also evoked by Butler.[60] What initially seemed as a mimetic 'failed copy' – the Marrano imitating both Christian and Jewish rituals 'without the clue', that is, without substance and identity proper – turns out to be the 'real thing' exposing the parodic nature of *all* rituals, indeed as in Kafka's stories of the Josephine and the nation of mice or the shakals in the temple. The fragmented absurd ritual gestures, which are performed by the Marrano – this troubled drag pretending simultaneously to have become Christian and to have remained Jewish – reveal the truth of the 'intractable' antinomian faith which cannot find full and 'natural' expression in the worldly affairs. Just as gender, so is one's religion *the effect of the natural, the original, and the inevitable*,[61] but only the *effect* – and this revealing self-reflection becomes sufficient to denounce the natural, substantive, and identitarian, foundation of the religious spectacle. The metaleptic reasoning, therefore, allows to revert the situation of despair, routinely ascribed to the Marranos, into a moment of cathartic self-recognition which has a releasing emancipatory effect. 'Is drag/Marrano the irritation of gender/religion, or does it dramatize the signifying gestures through which gender/religion itself is

---

practices in which the original, the authentic, and the real are themselves constituted as effects. The loss of orthodox norms would have the effect of proliferating religious configurations, destabilizing substantive identity, and depriving the naturalizing narratives of compulsory orthodoxy of their central protagonists: "Jew" and "Christian." The parodic repetition of religious ritual exposes as well the illusion of confessional identity as an intractable depth and inner substance': Judith Butler, *Gender Trouble: Feminism and the Subversion of Identity* (London and New York: Routledge, 1990), 146. As we have seen in the previous chapter, the gender-bender games of Joyce and Blanchot are great inspirations for Derrida's own experiments with becoming 'unsexed' and engaging in the feminine genre of saying double *yes* to 'life death' (LG, 222).

[59] Ibid., 145.
[60] Ibid., viii.
[61] Ibid., viii.

established?'⁶² Yes, Butler-Derrida says, the latter is true: this is the Scholemian 'hidden truth' of all authentic traditions.

The right element of the Marrano/rogue/queer living together, therefore, is neither the 'night of the soul', which so terrified Hegel, nor the full sun of the 'heliopolitics' (WD, 111) which scorches all the secrets and drags a naked individual into the public agora of forced belonging: it is the Landauerian 'magical blue light' and the Derridean 'penumbral light' (WA, 28) of the irreducibly singular *tsel/tselem* which can exist only in an *eucalyptic shadow*, hidden away from the apocalypse of truth, law, and order.⁶³ Already in his early essay on Lévinas, *Violence and Metaphysics*, Derrida, following his older colleague, denounces the 'heliocentric' principle of modern philosophy of politics which compels us to live in 'a world of light and of unity' (WD, 111). While referring to Lévinas's essay 'The Time and the Other', Derrida writes:

> In this *heliopolitics* 'the social ideal will be sought in an ideal of fusion [. . .] the subject [. . .] losing himself in a violence and metaphysics collective representation, in a common ideal [. . .] It is the collectivity which says 'us,' and which, turned toward the intelligible sun, toward the truth, experience, the other at his side and not face to face with him [. . .] *Miteinandersein* also remains the collectivity of the with, and its authentic form is revealed around the truth.' (WD, 111–12)⁶⁴

---

⁶² Ibid., viii.

⁶³ In 'Derridapocalypse', Catherine Keller explicitly links Derrida's cryptophilia/*eucalypsis* with his dislike towards the apocalyptic mode of thinking as the blueprint for all totalitarian models: 'In the space of the apocalyptic utopia, the displacement of space itself, darkness, ocean, and death have been eliminated. 'God is the light' of the New Jerusalem, 'and its lamp is the Lamb' (Rev. 21.23). A ghost-white transparency of goodness and security rule: a neon panopticon, shining through the lamb-lamp. For the seven spectral eyes do not just see but shine' (OT, 200). In 'The History of the Lie', while denouncing what he calls 'crypto-politology', Derrida protests against the demands of the instantaneous truth, which he sees as yet another version of the apocalyptic impatience of unveiling. As an example of crypto-politological reasoning, Derrida cites notes of Alexandre Koyre, a Russian emigrant of Jewish descent: 'Koyre seems to consider that any secret is in principle a threat to the *res publica*, indeed to democratic space. This is understandable and in overall conformity with a certain essence of politeia as absolute phenomenality. *Everything must be made to appear in the transparency of the public space and its illumination.* But I wonder if we do not see here signs of the inverse perversion of politicism, of an absolute hegemony of political reason, of a limitless extension of the region of the political. By refusing any right to secrecy, the political agency, most often in the figure of state sovereignty or even of reason of state, summons everyone to behave first of all and in every regard as a responsible citizen before the law of the polis. Is there not here, in the name of a certain type of objective and phenomenal truth, *another germ of totalitarianism with a democratic face*? I could not read without a certain indignant amazement one of Koyre's notes, which, by way of illustrating how one acquires training in secrecy, cryptic codes, and lying, launches a scattershot accusation at Spartans, Indians, Jesuits, and Marranos: "We cite at random the training in lying that was received by the young Spartan and the young Indian; the mentality of the Marrano or of the Jesuit"' (WA, 63; emphasis added).

⁶⁴ Although Lévinas refers here to Heidegger, for Derrida, the paradigmatic heliopolitics is Marxism without ghosts, spectres, and shadows – a diagnosis confirmed by Marx himself who is his notebooks famously compared the modern bourgeois individual to a moth, a creature of night and secret: 'Thus, when the universal sun has set, does the moth seek the lamp-light of privacy [. . .] He who no longer finds pleasure in building the whole world with his own forces, in being a world-creator instead of revolving forever inside his own skin, on him the Spirit has spoken its anathema': quot. in Ernst Fischer, *How to Read Karl Marx*, trans. Ann Bostock (New York: Monthly Review Press,

And instead of this sun-oriented collectivity, he proposes

> a community of nonpresence, and therefore of nonphenomenality. Not a community without light, not a blindfolded synagogue, but a community anterior to Platonic light. A light before neutral light, before the truth which arrives as a third party, the truth 'which we look toward together,' the judgmental arbitrator's truth. Only the other, the totally other, can be manifested as what it is before the shared truth, *within a certain nonmanifestation and a certain absence*. (WD, 112; emphasis added)

This *nonphenomenal community to come* will not be deprived of light – the way in which the Christian prejudice imagines the Jews as blindly following the law and unable to see the true *phos kai zoe*. But it will be a different light, resistant to the *Lichtzwang*, the light-compulsion,[65] instituted by the Platonic topos of the Sun or St John's topos of the Lamb-Lamp, at which we look together: it will be the blue light of the secret – the Marxian 'lamp-light of privacy' – watched secretly by every rogue in separation. Just as the Marrano God, with whom we dealt in Chapter 2, retreats from revealability (*Offenbarkeit*) in order not to become a sunny 'monster' of unscathed vitality and power (the luminous *deiwos*), so does its *tsel/tselem* withdraws from the pressure of phenomenalization in order not to become a clog in the political machine. This is precisely why Derrida needs the figure of the Marrano: the first modern subject who fell out of the indentitarian grids and became an irreducible remnant, invisible to the inquisitory sun of 'heliopolitics'.[66] The new community of 'we' will thus be

---

1996), 39. Is Derrida, who identified with the silk-worm revolving inside his own skin-cocoon, such a bourgeois (or, as Keller suggests, 'crypto-bourgeois', OT, 200) individualist moth? Yes, because he indeed shuns the universal sun – and no, because he still finds pleasure in building the whole world with his own forces, provided they are truly his *own*.

[65] *Lichtzwang/Light Duresse* is the title of Paul Celan's last collection of poems, also written under the auspices of the myth of *tsimtsum* as the good 'diminution of lights': as such, it can be read as a poetic gloss to Derrida's struggle with the apocalyptic light-compulsion of the 'philosophical sect' (APO, 25).

[66] As Erin Graff Zivin rightly points out in her book on Inquisition, the main crime against the Marranos was to force them to come out into the light and 'take a stand within the field of the revealable: as either this or that, Jewish or Catholic, one of us or outsider, friend or foe': Erin Graff Zivin, *Figurative Inquisitions: Conversion, Torture, and Truth in the Luso-Hispanic Atlantic* (Evanston, IL: Northwestern University Press, 2014), 10. What the inquisitional practice targeted, therefore, was the logic of the remnant, represented by the Marrano irreducible difference: the shadowy secrecy of the inner self which resists the 'phenomenalizing demands' telling it to show itself. The anti-heliocentric, anti-apocalyptic, anti-phenomenalist and anti-identitarian principle of Derrida's new politics is also very well described by Patrick Dove who elaborates on Graff Zivin's findings: 'Moving against the grain of a powerful phenomenalism that would define the public or political sphere as a space of unmediated transparency the marrano insists, at the very limits of phenomenal referentiality, on *an inalienable right to secrecy or silence*: secrecy as prior to and irreducible to any identitarian position or content, prior to and irreducible to any ipseity or whatness of a subject. The marrano acts as a *restrainer* against what Derrida describes as the "absolute hegemony of political reason [and] a limitless extension of the region of the political" (WA, 63)': Patrick Dove, 'Two Sides of the Same Coin? Form, Matter, and Secrecy in Derrida, de Man, and Borges' (MARS, 82; emphasis added).

made of universal Marranos: the 'illicit' rogue inhabitants of political shadowlands, who oppose the Platonic-Marxist-utopian politics of sun with their messianic secret-friendly *umbrapolitics*.

> If one were to insist on an unconditional right to the secret against this phenomenalism and this integral politicism and if such an absolute secret had to remain inaccessible and invulnerable, *then it would concern less the political secret than, in the metonymic and generalized figure of the Marrano, the right to secrecy as right to resistance* against and beyond the order of the political, or even of the theologico-political in general. In the political order, this principle of resistance could inspire, as one of its figures, the right to what the United States names with that very fine phrase for the most respectable of traditions, in the case of *force majeure*, where the *raison d'etat* does not dispense the last word in ethics: 'civil disobedience'. (WA, 63–4; emphasis added)

Once again Derrida proves his fidelity to the Jewish-Kabbalistic paradigm of *tsimtsum* as the 'diminution of lights' which defines his Marrano position of a *tsimtsem*, diminished and withdrawn, secret Judaism – over against the Christian apocalyptic paradigm, pressing towards the ultimate *parousia* of the light of lights and the absolute phenomenal transparency of the world and society. Shadow/*tsel*/*tselem* can only live in the shadow, forever avoiding 'the monstrous law of an impossible face-to-face' (C, 171) – just as 'him who has made the shadows his hiding place' (Ps. 18:11).

Conclusion

The purpose of this book was to follow the twists and turns of Derrida's Marrano figuration, meandering through his thinking on the possibilities of a new literature, metaphysics, religion, ethics, and – last but not least – politics. Exile, betrayal, survival, and metaphysics/politics of non-identity emerged as the four pillars of Derrida's Marrano 'normative inversion', in which his *marranismo* was to transform from the tormented form of Judaism (*semitismo atormentado*) into a messianic promise, addressed universally to all 'the others recognized as mortal, finite, in a state of neglect, and deprived of any horizon of hope' (MO, 68). That is, all of us, men and women of the late modern, globalatinized and secularized, era which abandoned all traditional symbolic solutions to the problem of finitude and left us with a *bared life*, a sheer 'survival, the not symbolizable' (WA, 276) on our hands. The Marranos were the first to wrestle with the enigma of survival, split between the death of their tradition and the mystery of living on without a name or form. Derrida's Marrano project aims at overcoming this split thanks to a radical reversal of *survie*, a troublesome remnant fallen out from the symbolic system, into *sur-vie*, the hidden 'truth' of the Abrahamic tradition, which could come to the fore only in the process of 'sickening' of the archives of *tradendum*.

The tragic Marrano condition of a reject 'lower than dust' is thus a shell which conceals a secret kernel: the 'truth' of the religion of finite life as the only viable *Religion der neuen Zeiten*, its one and only chance of survival. It does not promise salvation as a 'convalescence' in which the damage of finitude gets undone and life can return to its unscathed wholeness; as such, it is 'shorn' of the 'proper content' of those religions that attempted to solve the perennial problem of *la vie la mort*. And it does not promise any illumination that would tear down the veils and bring to light 'all things hidden';[67] as such, it is also 'shorn' of the typically religious promise to end all secrets and dispel all shadows. And yet, by addressing 'the Marrano, the not symbolizable' as an 'entirely different other', a living-on remnant-singularity, Derrida's appeal touches the very real of our metaphysical condition which, for much too long, has been 'deprived of any horizon of hope' and sealed in the world without exits and openings, a static *phusis* that exorcized all spectres and shadows:

> There is no salvation here that saves or promises salvation, even if on the hither or the other side of any soteriology, this promise resembles the salvation addressed to the other, the other recognized as an entirely different other [. . .], the other recognized as mortal, finite, in a state of neglect, and deprived of any horizon of hope. But the fact that there is no necessarily determinable content in this promise of the other, and in the language of the other, does not make any less indisputable its opening up of speech by something that resembles messianism, soteriology, or eschatology. It is the structural opening, the messianicity, without which messianism itself, in the strict or literal sense, would not be possible. Unless, perhaps, this originary promise without any proper content is, precisely, messianism. And unless all messianism demands for itself this rigorous and barren severity, this messianicity shorn of everything. Let us never rule it out. (MO, 68)

Once again, Derrida presents his Marrano hypothesis according to the already familiar pattern. As if in the Freudian game of *Fort-Da*, he first projects a distance between messianicity as a promise from all normative theological discourses of 'messianism, soteriology, or eschatology' – but then inverts the whole perspective, by locating the new centre in what before appeared as a de-centred periphery: '*Unless, perhaps*, this originary promise without any proper content is, *precisely*, messianism.' The new *Da* of the messianic religion is the Marrano 'rejected stone': the extimate uncanny hidden truth of the tradition the only role of which was to contain and transmit the idea of the promise given to singular *survie*. And indeed, 'this messianicity shorn of everything', which is never to be ruled out, appears just a moment later as a possible source of a new tradition and new symbolic forms: 'It can also be given over, *without betrayal*, to other inventions of idioms, to other poetics, without end' (MO, 69; emphasis added).

Does this phrase indicate that Derrida's Marrano intervention can heal the Scholemian rift between the 'truth' and the 'transmissibility' of tradition? That it

---

[67] See Lk. 8.17: 'For there is nothing hidden that will not be disclosed, and nothing concealed that will not be known or brought out into the open.'

promises a new tradition that will transmit/betray better the messianic promise itself? Derrida's intention, when he embarked on his Marrano project, could indeed be akin to Scholem's deepest dream: a wish to renew the Abrahamic heritage in such a way that it will no longer bury the messianic promise in the tombs weighed down by the archives of particular identities and nominations. 'Other poetics, without end' – literature, philosophy, metaphysics, politics: *new* symbolic forms that would replace the traditional one, invalidated by the Marrano enigma/miracle of survival – will thus be able to carry on the messianic spectre, and *almost* without betrayal, but only on one condition: that they will be always ready for a new Exodus in the world seemingly without exits.

Bibliography

Abraham, Nicolas and Torok, Maria, *Wolf Man's Magic Word: A Cryptonymy*, trans. N. Rand, Minneapolis, MN: Minnesota University Press, 1986.
Abraham, Nicolas and Torok, Maria, *The Shell and the Kernel*, vol. 1, ed. and trans. Nicholas T. Rand, Chicago, IL: The University of Chicago Press, 1994.
Adorno, Theodor W., *Stichworte: Kritische Modelle 2*, Frankfurt am Main: Suhrkamp, 1969.
Adorno, Theodor W., *Notes to Literature*, vols. 1 & 2, trans. Shierry Weber Nicholsen, New York: Columbia University Press, 1991–92.
Adorno, Theodor W., *Aesthetic Theory*, trans. Robert Hullot-Kentor, London and New York: Continuum, 1997.
Adorno, Theodor W. and Benjamin, Walter, *The Complete Correspondence, 1928–1940*, trans. Nicholas Walker, ed. Henri Lonitz, Cambridge, MA: Harvard University Press, 2001.
Adorno, Theodor W. and Horkheimer, Max, *Dialectic of Enlightenment*, trans. Edmund Jephcott, ed. G. Schmid Noerr, Stanford, CA: Stanford University Press, 2002.
Adorno, Theodor W., 'Negative Dialektik', in *Gesammelte Schriften in 20 Bänden*, Band 6, Frankfurt am Main: Suhrkamp, 2003.
Adorno, Theodor W., *Minima Moralia: Reflections on a Damaged Life*, trans. E. F. N. Jephcott, London: Verso, 2005.
Agamben, Giorgio, *Language and Death: The Place of Negativity*, trans. Karen E. Pinkus and Michael Hardt, Minneapolis, MN: Minnesota University Press, 1991.
Agamben, Giorgio, *The Coming Community*, trans. Michael Hardt, Minneapolis and London: Minnesota University Press, 1993.
Agamben, Giorgio, *Remnants of Auschwitz: The Witness and the Archive*, trans. Daniel Heller-Roazen, New York: Zone Books, 1999.
Agamben, Giorgio, *Potentialities: Collected Essays in Philosophy*, trans. Daniel Heller-Roazen, Stanford, CA: Stanford University Press, 2000.
Agamben, Giorgio, *The Time That Remains: A Commentary on the Letter to the Romans*, trans. Patricia Dailey, Stanford, CA: Stanford University Press, 2005.
Agamben, Giorgio, *Profanations*, trans. Jeff Fort, New York: Zone Books, 2007.
Agamben, Giorgio, *The Use of Bodies: Homo Sacer IV 2*, trans. Adam Kotsko, Stanford, CA: Stanford University Press, 2016.
Altmann, Alexander, 'Lurianic Kabbalah in a Platonic Key: Abraham Cohen Herrera's *Puerta del Cielo*', in *Jewish Thought in the Seventeenth Century*, ed. Isadore Twersky and Bernard Septimus, 1–37, Cambridge-London: Harvard University Press, 1987.
Ancelet-Hustache, Jeanne, *Master Eckhart and the Rhineland Mystics*, trans. Hilda Graef, London: Longman, 1957.
Angelus, Silesius, *Sacred Epigrams from the 'Cherubinic Pilgrim'*, trans. Anthony Mortimer, New York: AMS Press, 2013.
Anidjar, Gil, 'Je te suis vrai (ce qui du marrane m'arrive)', in *l'Herne: Jacques Derrida*, 247–54, Paris: Éditions de l'Herne, 2004.

Assmann, Jan, *Moses the Egyptian: The Memory of Egypt in Western Monotheism*, Cambridge, MA: Harvard University Press, 1997.
Badiou, Alain, *The Century*, trans. Alberto Toscano, Cambridge, MA: Polity Press, 2007.
Badiou, Alain, *Que pense le poeme?*, Paris: Editions Nous, 2016.
Bataille, Georges, 'Sacrifices', in *Œuvres complètes*, vol. 1, 87–96, Paris: Gallimard, 1970.
Benjamin, Walter, *The Correspondence of Walter Benjamin, 1910–1940*, ed. Gershom Scholem and Theodor Adorno, trans. R. Manfred and Evelyn M. Jacobson, Chicago, IL: The University of Chicago Press, 1994.
Benjamin, Walter, *Selected Writings*, vols. 1–4, ed. Howard Eiland and Michael W. Jennings, Cambridge, MA: Harvard University Press, 1996–2006.
Benjamin, Walter, *The Origin of German Tragic Drama*, trans. John Osborne, London: Verso, 1998.
Benjamin, Walter, *The Arcades Project*, trans. Howard Eiland and Kevin McLaughlin, Cambridge, MA: Belknap Press of Harvard University Press, 1999.
Benjamin, Walter and Scholem, Gershom, *The Correspondence of Walter Benjamin and Gershom Scholem: 1932–1940*, trans. Gary Smith and Andre Lefevre, New York: Schocken Books, 1989.
Benz, Ernst, *Ecclesia spiritualis: Kirchenidee und Geschichtstheologie der franziskanischen Reformation*, Darmstadt: Wissenschaftliche Buchgesellschaft Darmstadt, 1964.
Biale, David, *Gershom Scholem: Kabbalah and Counter-History*, Cambridge, MA: Harvard University Press, 1982.
Biale, David, 'Scholem's "Ten Unhistorical Aphorisms on Kabbalah." Text and Commentary', *Modern Judaism* 5, no. 1 (1985): 67–93.
Biale, David, *What is Judaism?*, New York: W. W. Norton, 2015.
Bielik-Robson, Agata, *The Saving Lie: Harold Bloom and Deconstruction*, Evanston, IL: Northwestern University Press, 2011.
Bielik-Robson, Agata, *Jewish Cryptotheologies of Late Modernity: Philosophical Marranos*, London: Routledge, 2014.
Bielik-Robson, Agata, 'Burn After Reading: Derrida as Philosophical Marrano', in *Divisible Derridas*, ed. Victor E. Taylor and Stephen Nichols, 51–70, Aurora, CO: Davies Publication Group, (Emergence), 2017a.
Bielik-Robson, Agata, 'God of Luria, Hegel, Schelling: The Divine Contraction and the Modern Metaphysics of Finitude', in *Mystical Theology and Continental Philosophy*, ed. David Lewin, Simon Podmore, and Duane Williams, 32–50, London: Routledge, 2017b.
Bielik-Robson, Agata, *Another Finitude: Messianic Vitalism and Philosophy*, London: Bloomsbury, 2019.
Bielik-Robson, Agata and Weiss, Daniel H., eds, *Tsimtsum in Modernity: Lurianic Heritage in Modern Philosophy and Theology*, Berlin: de Gruyter, 2020.
Blanchot, Maurice, *L'arrêt de mort*, Paris: Gallimard, 1948.
Blanchot, Maurice, *Writing of the Distaster*, trans. Ann Smock, Lincoln, NE: University of Nebraska Press, 1986.
Blanchot, Maurice, *The Unavowable Community*, trans Pierre Joris, New York: Station Hill Press, 1988.
Blanchot, Maurice, *The Step Not Beyond*, trans. Lycette Nelson, Albany, NY: SUNY Press, 1992.
Blanchot, Maurice, *The Infinite Conversation*, trans. S. Hanson, Minneapolis, MN: University of Minnesotta Press, 1993.

Blanchot, Maurice, *The Work of Fire*, trans. Charlotte Mandell, Stanford, CA: Stanford University Press, 1995a.
Blanchot, Maurice, *Madness of the Day*, trans. Lydia Davis, Barrytown, NY: Station Hill Press, 1995b.
Blanchot, Maurice, *The Instant of My Death*, trans. Elizabeth Rottenberg, Stanford: Stanford University Press, 2000.
Bloch, Ernst, *The Spirit of Utopia*, przeł. Anthony Nassar, Stanford, CA: Stanford University Press, 2000.
Bloch, Ernst, *Atheism in Christianity*, trans. J. T. Swann, London: Verso, 2009.
Bloom, Harold, *A Map of Misreading*, Oxford: Oxford University Press, 1975.
Bloom, Harold, *Breaking the Vessels: The Wellek Library Lectures at the University of California*, ed. F. Lentricchia, Chicago, IL: The University of Chicago Press, 1982.
Bloom, Harold, *The Strong Light of the Canonical: Kafka, Freud and Scholem as Revisionists of Jewish Culture and Thought*, New York: The City College Papers, no 20, 1987.
Bloom, Harold, *Anxiety of Influence: A Theory of Poetry*, Oxford: Oxford University Press, 1997.
Bloom, Harold, *Fallen Angels*, New Haven, CT: Yale University Press, 2007.
Blumenberg, Hans, *The Legitimacy of the Modern Age*, trans. Robert M. Wallace, Cambridge, MA: MIT Press, 1985a.
Blumenberg, Hans, *Work on Myth*, trans. R. M. Wallace, Cambridge, MA: MIT Press, 1985b.
Bowles, Jane, *Two Serious Ladies*, New York: A. A. Knopf, 1943.
Boyarin, Daniel, *A Radical Jew: Paul and the Politics of Identity*, Berkeley, CA: University of California Press, 1994.
Boyarin, Daniel, *Unheroic Conduct: The Rise of Heterosexuality and the Invention of the Jewish Man*, Berkeley, CA: University of California Press, 1997.
Bradley, Arthur, *Negative Theology and Modern French Philosophy*, London: Routledge, 2004.
Bradley, Arthur, *Unbearable Life: A Genealogy of Erasure*, New York: Columbia University Press, 2019.
Buck-Morss, Susan, 'The Flaneur, the Sandwichman and the Whore: The Politics of Loitering', in *Walter Benjamin and the Arcades Project*, ed. Beatrice Hanssen, 33–65, New York: Continuum, 2006.
Buck-Morss, Susan, *Hegel, Haiti, and Universal History*, Pittsburgh, PA: University of Pittsburgh Press, 2009.
Butler, Judith, *Gender Trouble: Feminism and the Subversion of Identity*, London: Routledge, 1990.
Caputo, John D., *The Prayers and Tears of Jacques Derrida: Religion Without Religion*, Bloomington, IN: Indiana University Press, 1997.
Caputo, John D., 'Like a Devilish Knight of Faith', *Oxford Literary Review* 36, no. 2 (2014): 188–90.
Caruth, Cathy, *Unclaimed Experience. Trauma, Narrative, and History*, Baltimore, MD: The Johns Hopkins University Press, 1996.
Castro, Americo, *The Structure of Spanish History*, trans. E. L. King, Princeton, NJ: Princeton University Press, 1954.
Cixous, Hélène, *Le prenom de Dieu*, Paris: Editions Grasset, 1967.

Cixous, Hélène, *Readings: The Poetics of Blanchot, Joyce, Kafka, Kleist, Lispector, and Tsvetayeva*, ed. and trans. Verena Andermatt Conley, Minneapolis, MN: Minnesota University Press, 1991.
Cixous, Hélène, *Manhattan: Letters from Prehistory*, trans. Beverly Brie Brahic, New York: Fordham University Press, 2007.
Cope, Jackson I., '*Ulysses*: Joyce's Kabbalah', *James Joyce Quarterly* 7, no. 2 (Winter, 1970): 93–113.
De Certeau, Michel, 'Weakness of Believing. From the Body to Writing, A Christian Transit', in *The Certeau Reader*, ed. Graham Ward, 214–43, Oxford: Blackwell, 2000.
De Lucena, Juan, *De Vita Beata*, ed. Govert Westerveld, Blanca [Murcia], 2012.
De Rougemont, Denis, *Love in the Western World*, trans. Mongomery Belgion, New York: Harcourt & Brace, 1940.
Derrida, Jacques, 'Feu la cendre', *Anima* 5 (Decembre 1982).
Derrida, Jacques, *Signéponge/Signsponge*, trans. Richard Rand, New York: Columbia University Press, 1984a.
Derrida, Jacques, 'No Apocalypse, Not Now (Full Speed Ahead, Seven Missiles, Seven Missives)', trans. Catherine Porter and Philip Lewis, *Diacritics* 14, no. 2 (Summer, 1984b): 20–31.
Derrida, Jacques and Labarrière, Jean-François, *Altérités*, Paris: Osiris, 1986.
Derrida, Jacques, *Cinders*, trans. Ned Lukacher, Lincoln, NE: Nebraska University Press, 1991.
Derrida, Jacques, '*Eating Well*, or the Calculation of the Subject', in *Points . . . Interviews, 1974–1994*, ed. Elisabeth Weber, trans. Peggy Kamuf et al., 255–87, Stanford, CA: Stanford University Press, 1995.
Derrida, Jacques and Stiegler, Bernard, *Echographies de la television*, Paris: Galilee-INA, 1996.
Derrida, Jacques, Foreword to Hélène Cixous, *Stigmata*, trans. Eric Prenowitz, London: Routledge, 1998.
Derrida, Jacques, *Cosmopolites de tous les pays, encore un effort!*, Paris: Editions Galilée, 1997.
Derrida, Jacques, 'Littérature au secret: une filiation impossible', in *Donner la mort*, 163–209, Paris: Galilée, 1999.
Derrida, Jacques, 'On Cosmopolitanism', in *On Cosmopolitanism and Forgiveness*, trans. Mark Dooley and Michael Hughes, 1–24, London: Rotledge, 2001a.
Derrida, Jacques, 'On Forgiveness: A Roundtable Discussion with Jacques Derrida', in *Questioning God*, ed. John D. Caputo, Mark Dooley, and Michael Scanlon, 52–72, Bloomington, IN: Indiana University Press, 2001b.
Derrida, Jacques, 'The Becoming Possible of the Impossible: An Interview with Jacques Derrida' in *Passion for the Impossible: John D. Caputo in Focus*, ed. Mark Dooley, 21–33, Albany, NY: SUNY Press, 2003.
Derrida, Jacques, *On Touching – Jean-Luc Nancy*, trans. Christine Irizarry, Stanford, CA: Stanford University Press, 2005a.
Derrida, Jacques, 'Epoche and Faith', in *Derrida and Religion: Other Testaments*, ed. Yvonne Sherwood and Kevin Hart, 27–51, New York and London: Routledge, 2005b.
Derrida, Jacques, 'Final Words', trans. Gila Walker, in *The Late Derrida*, ed. W. J. T. Mitchell and Arnold I. Davidson, Chicago, IL: The University of Chicago Press, 2007a.
Derrida, Jacques, 'Confession et Circumfession', in debate with Richard Kearney, in *Des confessions*, Paris: Stock, 2007b.

Derrida, Jacques, *The Animal That Therefore I Am*, trans. David Wills, New York: Fordham University Press, 2008.
Derrida, Jacques, *Athens, Still Remains*, trans. Pascale-Anne Brault and Michael Naas, New York: Fordham University Press, 2010.
Derrida, Jacques, 'Faxitexture', trans. Laura Bourland, in *Anywhere*, ed. Cynthia Davidson, New York: Rizzoli International Publications, 2015.
De Spinoza, Benedict, *The 'Ethics' and Other Works*, ed. and trans. Edwin Curley, Princeton, NJ: Princeton University Press, 1994.
De Spinoza, Benedict, *Theological-Political Treatise*, ed. Jonathan Israel, Cambridge, MA: Cambridge University Press, 2007.
De Vries, Hent, *Philosophy and the Turn to Religion*, Baltimore, MD: Johns Hopkins University Press, 1999.
De Vries, Hent, *Religion and Violence: Philosophical Perspectives from Kant to Derrida*, Baltimore, MD: Johns Hopkins University Press, 2002.
De Vries, Hent, *Minimal Theology: The Critique of Secular Reason in Adorno and Lévinas*, Baltimore, MD: Johns Hopkins University Press, 2005.
Di Cesare, Donatella, *Heidegger, die Juden, die Shoah*, Frankfurt am Main: Vittorio Klostermann, 2016.
Dickinson, Colby, 'The Logic of the "As If" and the Existence of God: An Inquiry into the Nature of Belief in the Work of Jacques Derrida', *Derrida Today* 4, no. 1 (2011): 86–106.
Drob, Sanford L., *Kabbalah and Postmodernism: A Dialogue*, New York: Peter Lang, 2009.
Dunkelgrün, Theodor and Maciejko, Paweł, eds, *Bastards and Believers: Jewish Converts and Conversion from the Bible to the Present*, Philadephia, PA: University of Pennsylvania Press, 2020.
Eliade, Mircea, *The Sacred and the Profane: The Nature of Religion*, trans. William R. Trask, New York: Harcourt, Brace & World, 1959.
Engel, Amir, *Gershom Scholem: An Intellectual Biography*, Chicago, IL: University of Chicago Press, 2017.
Fackenheim, Emil L., *Jewish Return into History: Reflections in the Age of Auschwitz and a New Jerusalem*, New York: Schocken, 1980.
Fackenheim, Emil L., *To Mend the World: Foundations of Post-Holocaust Jewish Thought*, Bloomington, IN: Indiana University Press, 1994.
Feld, Edward, 'Spinoza the Jew', *Modern Judaism* 9, no. 1 (Febuary, 1989): 101–19.
Fischer, Ernst, *How to Read Karl Marx*, trans. Ann Bostock, New York: Monthly Review Press, 1996.
Frank, Jacob, *Rozmaite adnotacja, przypadki, czynności i anekdoty pańskie [Various Adnotations, Cases, Deeds, and Anegdotes of the Lord]*, ed. Jan Doktór, Płońsk: Tikkun, 1992.
Frank, Jacob, *Słowa pańskie: Nauki Jakuba Franka z Brna i Offenbachu*, ed. Jan Doktór, Warszawa: Żydowski Instytut Historyczny, 2017a.
Frank, Jacob, 'Appendix to the Words of the Lord Spoken in Brünn', in *Sabbatian Heresy: Writings on Mysticism, Messianism, and the Origins of Jewish Modernity*, trans. Paweł Maciejko, 157–60, Waltham, MA: Brandeis University Press, 2017b.
Freud, Sigmund and Breuer, Joseph, *Studies in Hysteria*, trans. James Strachey, London: Penguin, 2004.
Gebhardt, Carl, *Die Schriften des Uriel da Costa*, ed. Carl Gebhardt, Amsterdam: M. Hertzberger, 1922.
Goethe, J. W., *Faust, Part I*, trans. Anna Swanwick, New York: Dover, 1994.

Goldish, Matt, 'Patterns in Converso Messianism', in *Millenarianism and Messianism in Early Modern European Culture: Jewish Messianism in the Early Modern World*, ed. M. Goldish and R. H. Popkin, 41–64, Haague: Kluwer Academic Publishers, 2001.

Goldschmit, Marc, 'Cosmopolitique du marrane absolu', *Derrida à Alger: Un regard sur le monde*, ed. Mustapha Chérif, Actes Sud/ [barzakh] (2008): 143–4.

Goldschmit, Marc, *L'hypothèse du Marrane: Le théâtre judéo-chrétien de la pensée politique*, Paris: Editions du Félin, 2014.

Greene, Deirdre, *Gold in the Crucible: Teresa of Ávila and the Western Mystical Tradition*, Dorset: Element, 1989.

Gutkind, Erich, *Choose Life: The Biblical Call to Revolt*, New York: Henry Shuman, 1952.

Handelman, Susan A., *The Slayers of Moses: The Emergence of Rabbinic Interpretation in Modern Literary Theory*, Albany, NY: SUNY Press, 1982.

Hammerschlag, Sarah, *The Figural Jew: Politics and Identity in the Postwar French Thought*, Chicago, IL: Chicago University Press, 2010.

Hammerschlag, Sarah, 'The Last Jewish Intellectual: Derrida and His Literary Betrayal of Lévinas', in *Jews and the Ends of Theory*, ed. Shai Ginsburg, Martin Land, and Jonathan Boyarin, 88–107, New York: Fordham University Press, 2019.

Hamacher, Werner, *Pleroma – Reading in Hegel*, trans. Nicholas Walker and Simon Jarvis, Stanford, CA: Stanford University Press, 1998.

Harnack, Adolf von, *Marcion: Das Evangelium vom fremden Gott: Eine Monographie zur Geschichte der Grundlegung der katholischen Kirche*, Leipzig: J. C. Heinrichs'sche Buchhandlung, 1924.

Hägglund, Martin, *Dying for Time: Proust, Wolf, Nabokov*, Cambridge, MA: Harvard University Press, 2012.

Hegel, G. W. F., *Science of Logic*, trans. A. V. Miller, London: Allen and Unwin, 1969.

Hegel, G. W. F., *On Christianity: Early Theological Writings by Friedrich Hegel*, trans. T. M. Knox; with an introduction, and fragments trans. Richard Kroner, Gloucester, MA: Peter Smith, 1970.

Hegel, G. W. F., *Aesthetics: Lectures on Fine Art*, trans. T. M. Knox, Oxford: Clarendon Press, 1975.

Hegel, G. W. F., *Faith and Knowledge*, trans. Walter Cerf and H. S. Harris, Albany, NY: State University New York Press, 1977.

Hegel, G. W. F., *Hegel in 20 Bände*, vol. 20, Frankfurt am Main: Suhrkamp, 1986.

Hegel, G. W. F., *The Encyclopaedia Logic (With the Zusätze)*, trans. T. F. Geraets, W. A. Suchting, H. S. Harris, Indianapolis: Hackett Publishing Company, 1991.

Hegel, G. W. F., *Philosophy of Right*, trans. S. W. Dyde, Kitchener, ON: Batoche Books, 2001.

Hegel, G. W. F., *Lectures on the Philosophy of Religion (The Lectures of 1827 – One Volume Edition)*, trans. R. F. Brown, Oxford: Oxford University Press, 2006.

Hegel, G. W. F., *Philosophy of Mind*, trans. W. Wallace and A. V. Miller, rev. and ed. Michael Inwood, Oxford: Clarendon Press, 2007.

Heidegger, Martin, *Der Satz vom Grund*, Pfullingen: Günther Neske, 1957.

Heidegger, Martin, *Gelassenheit*, Pfullingen: Günther Neske, 1959.

Heidegger, Martin, *Discourse on Thinking*, trans. John M. Anderson and E. Hans Freund, New York: Harper & Row, 1966.

Heidegger, Martin, 'Who Is Nietzsche's Zarathustra?' trans. Bernd Magnus, *The Review of Metaphysics* 20, no. 3 (March, 1967): 411–31.

Heidegger, Martin, *On The Way to Language*, trans. Peter D. Hertz, New York: Harper & Row, 1971a.

Heidegger, Martin, *Poetry, Language, Thought*, trans. Albert Hofstadter, New York: Harper, 1971b.
Heidegger, Martin, *The Question Concerning Technology and Other Essays*, trans. William Lovitt, New York: Garland Publishing, 1977.
Heidegger, Martin, *The Principle of Reason*, trans. Regina Lilly, Bloomington, IN: Indiana University Press, 1991.
Heidegger, Martin and Fink, Eugen, *Heraclitus Seminar*, trans. Charles Seibert, Evanston, IL: Northwestern University Press, 1993.
Heidegger, Martin, *Pathmarks*, ed. William McNeill, Cambridge, MA: Cambridge University Press, 1998.
Heidegger, Martin, *Introduction to Metaphysics*, trans. Gregory Fried and Richard Polt, New Haven, CT: Yale University Press, 2000.
Heidegger, Martin, *Off the Beaten Track*, trans. Julian Young and Kenneth Haynes, Cambridge, MA: Cambridge University Press, 2002.
Heidegger, Martin, *Zur Sache des Denkens (1962–1964)*, ed. Friedrich-Wilhelm von Herrmann, *Gesamtausgabe*, vol. 14, Frankfurt: Vittorio Klostermann, 2007.
Heidegger, Martin, *Überlegungen XII-XV (Schwarze Hefte 1939–1941)*, ed. Peter Trawny, *Gesamtausgabe*, vol. 96, Frankfurt am Main: Vittorio Klostermann, 2015a.
Heidegger, Martin, *The Beginning of Western Philosophy: Interpretation of Anaximander and Parmenides*, trans. Richard Rojcewicz, Bloomington, IN: Indiana University Press, 2015b.
Heidegger, Martin, *Anmerkungen I-V (Schwarze Hefte 1942–1948)*, ed. Peter Trawny, *Gesamtausgabe*, vol. 97, Frankfurt am Main: Vittorio Klostermann, 2015c.
Hess, Moses, *The Holy History of Mankind and Other Writings*, trans. Shlomo Avineri, Cambridge, MA: Cambridge University Press, 2004.
Hollander, Dana, *Exemplarity and Chosenness: Rosenzweig and Derrida on the Nation of Philosophy*, Stanford, CA: Stanfod University Press, 2008.
Horkheimer, Max and Adorno, Theodor W., *Dialectic of Enlightenment*, trans. Edmund Jephcott, Stanford, CA: Stanfod University Press, 2002.
Horwitz, Daniel, *Kabbalah and Jewish Mysticism Reader*, Lincoln, NE: University of Nebraska Press, 2016.
Huizinga, Johan, *The Waning of the Middle Ages*, New York: Dover, 2013.
Idel, Moshe, 'Infinities of Torah in Kabbalah', in *Midrash and Literature*, ed. G. H. Hartman and S. Budick, 141–57, New Haven, CT: Yale University Press, 1986.
Idel, Moshe, *Old Worlds, New Mirrors: On Jewish Mysticism and Twentieth-Century Thought*, Philadelphia, PA: University of Pennsylvania Press, 2010.
Idziak-Smoczyńska, Urszula, 'Deconstruction between Judaism and Christianity', in *Judaism in Contemporary Thought: Traces and Influence*, ed. Agata Bielik-Robson and Adam Lipszyc, 139–54, London: Routledge, 2014.
Jaron, Steven, *Edmond Jabes: The Hazard of Exile*, Oxford: Oxford University Press, 2003.
Jay, Martin, *Permanent Exiles: Essays on the Intellectual Migration from Germany to America*, New York: Columbia University Press, 1985.
Jonas, Hans, *Mortality and Morality: A Search for the Good after Auschwitz*, trans. Lawrence Vogel, Chicago, Evanston, IL: Nortwestern University Press, 1996.
Jonas, Hans, *The Gnostic Religion*, Boston, MA: Beacon Press, 2001.
Joyce, James, *Letters of James Joyce*, vol. 1, ed. Stuart Gilbert, London: Faber & Faber, 1957
Joyce, James, *Ulysses*, New York: Vintage International, 1990.

Kamuf, Peggy, *To Follow: The Wake of Jacques Derrida*, Edinborough: Edinborough University Press, 2010.
Kant, Immanuel, 'Idea for a Universal History with a Cosmopolitan Aim', trans. Allen Wood, in *Kant's 'Idea for a Universal History with a Cosmopolitan Aim'. A Critical Guide*, ed. Amelie Oxenberg Rorty and James Schmidt, 9–23, Cambridge, MA: Cambridge University Press, 2009.
Kepel, Gilles, *The Revenge of God: The Resurgence of Islam, Christianity and Judaism in the Modern World*, London: Polity Press, 1994.
Kermode, Frank, *The Art of Telling: Essays on Fiction*, Cambridge, MA: Harvard University Press, 1972.
Kleist, Heinrich von, 'On the Marionette Theater', trans. Thomas G. Neumiller, *The Drama Review* 16, no. 3 (1972): 22–6.
Kojève, Alexandre, 'Tyranny and Wisdom', in Leo Strauss, *On Tyranny: Including the Strauss-Kojève Correspondence*, ed. Victor Gourevitch and Michael S. Roth, 135–76, Chicago, IL: University of Chicago Press, 2000.
Krell, David Farrell, *The Tragic Absolute: German Idealism and the Languishing of God*, Bloomington, IN: Indiana University Press, 2005.
Krell, David Farrell, *Ecstasy, Catastrophe*, Albany, NY: SUNY University Press, 2015.
Kristeva, Julia, *Powers of Horror: An Essay on Abjection*, trans. Leon S. Roudiez, New York: Columbia University Press, 1982.
Kristeva, Julia, *Revolution in Poetic Language*, trans. Leon S. Roudiez, New York: Columbia University Press, 1984.
Kristeva, Julia, *Tales of Love*, trans. Leon S. Roudiez, New York: Columbia University Press, 1987.
Lacan, Jacques, *Écrits: A Selection*, trans. A. Sheridan. London: Routledge, 1989.
Lacan, Jacques, *The Ego in Freud's Theory and in Technique of Psychoanalysis: The Seminar of Jacques Lacan 1954–1955: Book 2*, ed. Jacques Alain-Miller, trans. Sylvana Tomaselli, New York: Norton, 1991.
Lacan, Jacques, *Seminar XX: Encore: On Feminine Sexuality, the Limits of Love and Knowledge*, ed. Jacques-Allain Miller, trans. B. Fink, New York and London: W. W. Norton & Company, 1998.
Landauer, Gustav, 'Strindbergs historische Miniaturen', in trans. Gustav Landauer, *Werkausgabe*, ed. Gert Mattenklott ad Hanna Delf, Band 3, 139–51, Berlin: Akademie-Verlag, 1997.
Landauer, Gustav, *Revolution and Other Writings: A Political Reader*, ed. and trans. Gabriel Kuhn, Pontypool: The Merlin Press Ltd, 2010.
Landauer, Gustav, *Skepticism and Mysticism: On Mauthner's Critique of Language*, trans. David Grunwald, Wrocław: Amazon Fullfilment, 2019.
Lear, Jonathan, *Happiness, Death, and the Remainder of Life*, Cambridge, MA: Harvard University Press, 2000.
Leibovici, Martine, 'Le rêverie marrane de Jacques Derrida', in *Les marranismes: De la religiosité cachée à la société ouverte*, ed. Jacques Ehrenfreud and Jean-Philippe Schreiber, 253–78, Paris: Demopolis, 2014.
Lévinas, Emmanuel, *Otherwise than Being or Beyond Essence*, trans. Alphonso Lingis, The Hague: Martinus Nijhoff, 1981.
Lévinas, Emmanuel, 'The Trace of the Other', trans. Alphonso Lingis, in *Deconstruction in Context: Literature and Philosophy*, ed. Mark C. Taylor, 345–59, Chicago, IL: University of Chicago Press, 1986.

Lévinas, Emmanuel, 'Ethics and Politics', in conversation with Alain Finkielkraut, *The Lévinas Reader*, ed. Sean Hand, 289–97, Oxford: Blackwell, 1989.

Lévinas, Emmanuel, *Nine Talmudic Readings*, trans. Annette Aronowicz, Bloomington, IN: Indiana University Press, 1990.

Lévinas, Emmanuel, *Totality and Infinity: An Essay on Exteriority*, trans. Alphonso Lingis, Dordrecht: Kluver Academic Publishers, 1991.

Lévinas, Emmanuel, *In the Time of the Nations*, trans. Michael B. Smith, Bloomington, IN: Indiana University Press, 1994.

Lévinas, Emmanuel, *God, Death, and Time*, trans. Bettina Bergo, Stanford, CA: Stanford University Press, 2001a.

Lévinas, Emmanuel, *Is It Righteous to Be?: Interviews with Emmanuel Lévinas*, Stanford, CA: Stanford University Press, 2001b.

Linebaugh, Peter and Rediker, Marcus, *The Many-Headed Hydra: Sailors, Slaves, Commoners, and the Hidden History of the Revolutionary Atlantic*, Boston, MA: Beacon Press, 2013.

Liska, Vivian, *German Jewish Thought and Its Afterlife: A Tenuous Legacy*, Bloomington, IN: Indiana University Press, 2017.

Lorberbaum, Menachem, *Politics and the Limits of Law: Secularizing the Political in Medieval Jewish Thought*, Stanford, CA: Stanford University Press, 2002.

Löwith, Karl, *Meaning of History: The Theological Implications of the Philosophy of History*, Chicago, IL: University of Chicago Press, 1957.

Löwy, Michael, *Redemption and Utopia: Jewish Libertarian Thought in Central Europe: A Study in Elective Affinity*, trans. Hope Heaney, London: Verso, 2017.

Lynes, Philippe, 'Introduction. Auparadvances', in Jacques Derrida, *Advances*, trans. Philippe Lynes, ix–xvii, Minneapolis, MN: University of Minnesota Press, 2017.

Maciejko, Paweł, *Mixed Multitude: Jacob Frank and the Frankist Movement, 1755–1816*, Philadelphia, PA: Pennsylvania University Press, 2011.

Maciejko, Paweł, ed., *Sabbatian Heresy: Writings on Mysticism, Messianism, and the Origins of Jewish Modernity*, Waltham, MA: Brandeis University Press, 2017.

Magee, Alexander Glenn, *Hegel and the Hermetic Tradition*, Ithaca, NY: Cornell University Press, 2008.

Maimonides, Moses [Moshe ben Maimon], 'Epistle on Conversion or a Treatise on Martyrdom', (Heb.) in *Epistles*, ed. M. D. Rabinowitz, Jerusalem: Rav Cook Institute, 1981.

Maiorino, Giancarlo, *At the Margins of the Renaissance: Lazarillo de Tormes and the Picaresque Art of Survival*, Philadelphia, PA: The University of Pennsylvania Press, 2003.

Malabou, Catherine, *The Future of Hegel: Plasticity, Temporality, and Dialectics*, London: Routledge, 2005.

Mannheim, Karl, *Ideology and Utopia: An Introduction into Sociology of Knowledge*, trans. Louis Wirth and Edward Shils, London: Routledge, 1936.

Manteuffel, Tadeusz, 'W oczekiwaniu ery wolności i pokoju. Historiozofia Joachima z Fiore', *Przegląd Historyczny* 60, no. 2 (1969): 233–56.

Margel, Serge, *Le Tombeau du dieu artisan: Sur Platon*, Paris: Editions de Minuit, 1995; English translation: *The Tomb of the Artisan God: On Plato's Timaeus*, trans. Philippe Lynes, Minneapolis, MN: Minnesota University Press, 2019.

Marx, Karl, *Critique of Hegel's Philosophy of Right*, trans. Joseph O'Malley, Cambridge, MA: Cambridge University Press, 1970.

Mendes-Flohr, Paul, 'The Spiritual Quest of the Philologist', in *Gershom Scholem: The Man and His Work*, 1–28, Albany, NY: SUNY Press, 1997.

Meskin, Jacob, 'The Role of Lurianic Kabbalah in the Early Philosophy of Emmanuel Lévinas', *Lévinas Studies* 2 (2007): 49–77.

Milbank, John and Žižek, Slavoj, *The Monstrosity of Christ: Paradox or Dialectic?*, ed. Creston Davis, Cambridge, MA: MIT Press, 2011.

Milesi, Laurent 'Jacques Derrida in Secret(s)', in *Secrets, Mysteries, Silences*, ed. Ruth Evans, Therence Hughes and Georges Letisser, 113–24, Nantes: Publications CERCI-CRINI, 2005.

Moingt, Joseph, 'L'ailleurs de la théologie in Michel de Certeau. Le voyage mystique', *Recherches de Science Religieuse* 76, no. 3 (1988): 365–80.

de Montaigne, Michel, *The Complete Essays*, trans. A. M. Screech, London: Penguin, 2003.

Moreiras, Alberto, *Against Abstraction: Notes from an Ex-Latin Americanist*, Austin, TX: University of Texas Press, 2020.

Naas, Michael, *Derrida From Now On*, New York: Fordham University Press, 2008.

Naas, Michael, *Miracle and Machine*, New York: Fordham University Press, 2012.

Nancy, Jean-Luc, *Corpus*, trans. Richard Rand, New York: Fordham University Press, 2008.

Nancy, Jean-Luc, *Dis-enclosure: The Deconstruction of Christianity*, trans. Bettina Bergo, New York: Fordham University Press, 2008.

Negri, Antonio, 'The Specter's Smile', in *Ghostly Demarcations: A Symposium on Jacques Derrida's Specters of Marx*, ed. Michael Sprinker, 5–16, London: Verso, 2008.

New Oxford Annotated Bible, ed., Bernhard W. Anderson, Bruce Manning Metzger and Roland Edmund Murphy, Oxford and New York: Oxford University Press, 1991.

Nietzsche, Friedrich, 'On Truth and Falsity in their Ultramoral Sense', trans. M. A. Mügge, in *The Works of Friedrich Nietzsche*, vol. 2, 171–92, Edinburgh: T.N. Foulis, 1911.

Nietzsche, Friedrich, *Unpublished Writings from the Period of Unfashionable Observations*, trans. Richard T. Gray, Stanford, CA: Stanford UniversityPress, 1995.

Nietzsche, Friedrich, *Human All too Human: A Book for Free Spirits*, trans. Marion Faber and Stephen Lehman, Loncoln, NE: Bison Books, 1996.

Nietzsche, Friedrich, *The Birth of Tragedy*, trans. Roland Speirs, Cambridge, MA: Cambridge University Press, 1999.

Nietzsche, Friedrich, *Gay Science*, trans. Josefine Nauckhoff, Cambridge, MA: Cambridge University Press, 2001.

Nietzsche, Friedrich, *On the Genealogy of Morality*, trans. Carol Diethe, Cambridge, MA: Cambridge University Press, 2006.

Nirenberg, David, *Anti-Judaism: The Western Tradition*, New York: W.W. Norton, 2013.

Novalis, 'Blütenstaub', *Werke in zwei Bänden*, Band 2, Köln: Könemann, 1996.

O'Regan, Cyril, *The Gnostic Return in Modernity*, Albany, NY: SUNY Press, 2001.

Pirke Aboth: The Sayings of the Fathers, trans. Joseph Hertz, London: Behrman House, 1945.

Popkin, Richard H., *Isaac La Peyrere (1596–1676): His Life, Work, and Influence*, Leiden: Brill, 1987.

Raviv, Zohar, *Decoding the Dogma within the Enigma: The Life, Works, Mystical Piety and Systematic Thought of Moses Cordovero*, Saarbrücken: VDM Verlag, 2008.

Rilke, Rainer Maria, *The Notebooks of Malte Laurids Brigge*, trans. Burton Pike, Urbana-Champaign: Dalkey Archive, 2008.

Reik, Theodor, *The Ritual: Psychoanalytic Studies*, prefaced by Sigmund Freud, Madison, CT: International Universities Press, 1970.

Révah, Israël Salvador, 'Les Marranes', *Revue des études juives* 118 (1959–60): 29–77.

Reznikoff, Charles, *The Poems of Charles Reznikoff: 1918–1975*, ed. C. Reznikoff and S. Cooney, Jaffrey, NH: Black Sparrow Books, 2005.
Rogozinski, Jacob, *Cryptes de Derrida*, Fécamp: Lignes, 2014.
Rosen, Michael, 'Die Weltgeschichte ist das Weltgericht', in *Internationales Jahrbuch des deutschen Idealismus*, ed. F. Rush, 256–72, Berlin: De Gruyter, 2014.
Rosenberg, Harold, *The Tradition of the New*, Boston, MA: Da Capo Press, 1994.
Rosenstock, Bruce, 'Messianism, Machismo, and Marranism', in *Queer Theory and the Jewish Question*, eds. Daniel Boyarin, Daniel Itzkovitz and Ann Pellegrini, 199–227, New York: Columbia University Press, 2003.
Rosenstock, Bruce, *New Men: Conversos, Christian Theology, and Society in Fifteenth-Century Castile*, Papers of the Medieval Hispanic Research Seminar nr 39, London: University of London, 2002.
Rosenstock, Bruce, 'Derrida's Advent', *Contemporary French Civilization* 30, no. 1 (2006): 75–90.
Rosenzweig, Franz, *Briefe und Tagebücher: Band II*, ed. Rachel Rosenzweig, Edith Rosenzweig-Scheinmann, and Bernhard Casper, Haag: Martinus Nijhof, 1979.
Rustov, Marina, 'Yerushalmi and the Conversos', *Jewish History* 28, no. 1 (2014): Special Issue: From History to Memory: The Scholarly Legacy of Yosef Hayim Yerushalmi, 11–49.
Schelling, Friedrich Wilhelm Joseph, *Philosophy and Religion*, trans. Klaus Ottmann, Putnam: Spring Publications, 2010.
Schmitt, Carl, *The Nomos of the Earth in the International Law of the Jus Publicum Europaeum*, trans. G. L. Ulmen, New York: Telos Press Publishing, 2003.
Scholem, Gershom and De Leon, Moses, *The Book of Spendor: Basic Readings from the Kabbalah*, New York: Schocken, 1963.
Scholem, Gershom, 'Zehn unhistorische Sätze über Kabbalah', in Gershom Scholem, *Judaica 3: Studien zur jüdischen Mystik*, 235–42, Suhrkamp: Frankfurt am Main, 1973.
Scholem, Gershom, *On Jews and Judaism in Crisis: Selected Essays*, ed. Werner Dannhauser, New York: Schocken Books, 1976.
Scholem, Gershom, *Major Trends in Jewish Mysticism*, New York: Schocken, 1995.
Scholem, Gershom, 'Die Theologie des Sabbatianismus im Lichte Abraham Cardosos', in Gershom Scholem, *Judaica 1*, 120–48, Frankfurt am Main: Suhrkamp, 1997.
Scholem, Gershom, *Tagebücher nebst Aufsätzen und Entwürfen bis 1923: 2 Halbband 1917–1923*. Frankfurt am Main: Suhrkamp, 2000.
Scholem, Gershom, *Lamentations of Youth: The Diaries of Gershom Scholem, 1913–1919*, ed. and trans. Anthony David Skinner, Cambridge, MA: Belknap Press of Harvard University Press, 2008.
Schulte, Christoph, *Zimzum: Gott und Weltursprung*, Frankfurt am Main: Suhrkamp, 2014.
Sennett, Richard, *The Uses of Disorder: Personal Identity and City Life*, New York: W. W. Norton & Company, 1992.
Shakespeare, Steven, *Derrida and Theology*, New York: Continuum, 2009.
Shakespeare, William, *The Works of Shakespeare: Collated with the Oldest Copies, and Corrected*, London, 1723.
Sherwood, Yvonne, 'Specters of Abraham', in *Judaism in Contemporary Thought: Traces and Influence*, ed. Agata Bielik-Robson and Adam Lipszyc, 26–38, London: Routledge, 2014.

Simms, Norman, *Masks in the Mirror: Marranism in Jewish Experience*, London & New York: Peter Lang, 2006.
Sommer, Benjamin D., 'Expulsion as Initiation', in *Beginning/ Again: Towards a Hermeneutics of Jewish Texts*, ed. Aryeh Cohen and Shaul Magid, 23–48, New York: Seven Bridges Press, 2002.
Strauss, Leo, *Persecution and the Art of Writing*, New York: Free Press, 1952.
Taubes, Jacob, *The Political Theology of Paul*, trans. Dana Holänder, Stanford, CA: Stanford University Press, 2003.
Teresa of Avila, *The Interior Castle or the Mansions*, trans. from the Autograph of St. Teresa of Jesus by The Benedictines of Stanbrook, London: Thomas Baker, 1921.
Trigano, Schmuel, 'Le Marranisme, un modele multidimensionnel', in *Pardes: Etudes et Culture Juives*, no. 29 (*Le Juif caché: Marranisme et modernité*), 260–74, Paris: In Press Editions, 2000.
Turner, Victor, *The Ritual Process: Structure and Ani-Structure*, Michigan: Aldine Pub. Co, 1969.
Turner, Victor, 'From Liminal to Liminoid, in Play, Flow, and Ritual: An Essay in Comparative Symbology', *Rice University Studies* 60, no. 3 (1974): 53–92.
Thurschwell, Adam, 'Cutting the Branches for Akiba: Agamben's Critique of Derrida', in *Politics, Metaphysics, and Death: Essays on Giorgio Agamben's 'Homo Sacer'*, ed. Andrew Norris and Thomas Carl Wall, 173–97, Durham, NC: Duke University Press, 2005.
Trilling, Jacques, *James Joyce ou l'écriture matricide*, Belfort: Circé, 2001.
Twersky, Isadore, 'Maimonides', in *Understanding Rabbinic Judaism: From Talmudic to Modern Times*, ed. Jacob Neusner, 187–2012, Eugene, OR: Wipf and Stock, 2003.
Valery, Paul, *Selected Writings*, New York: New Directions Books, 1950.
Vital, Hayyim ben Joseph, *The Tree of Life: Hayyim Vital's Introduction to the Kabbalah of Isaac Luria – The Palace of Adam Kadmon*, trans. Donald Wilder Menzi and Zwe Padeh, Northvale, NJ and Jerusalem: Jason Aronson, 1999.
Voegelin, Erich, *Science, Politics and Gnosticism: Two Essays*, Washington, DC: Regnery Publishing, 1997.
Voegelin, Erich, *Modernity Without Restraint: The Political Religions, The New Science of Politics, and Science, Politics, and Gnosticism, w Collected Works of Eric Voegelin*, vol. 5, Kansas City, MO: University of Missouri Press, 1999.
Weber, Max, *Ancient Judaism*, trans. Hans. H. Gerth and Don Martindale, New York: Free Press, 1952.
Weber, Samuel, *Benjamin's-Abilities*, Cambridge, MA: Harvard University Press, 2008.
Weil, Simone, *An Anthology*, ed. Sian Miles, London: Penguin Classics, 2005.
Winnicott, Donald Woods, *Playing and Reality*, London: Routledge, 1971.
Wittgenstein, Ludwig, *Culture and Value, A Selection from the Posthumous Remains*, ed. G.W. von Wright and H. Nyman, trans. P. Winch, Oxford and Cambridge, MA: Blackwell Publishers, 1998.
Wolfson, Elliot R., *Circle in the Square: Studies in the Use of Gender in Kabbalistic Symbolism*, Albany, NY: SUNY Press, 1995.
Wolfson, Elliot R., 'Assaulting the Border: Kabbalistic Traces in the Margins of Derrida', *Journal of the American Academy of Religion* 70, no. 3 (2002), 475–514.
Wolfson, Elliot R., *Alef, Mem, Tau: Kabbalistic Musings on Time, Truth, and Death*, Berkeley, CA: University of California Press, 2006.
Wolfson, Elliot R., *Giving Beyond the Gift: Apophasis and Overcoming Theomania*, New York: Fordham University Press, 2014.

Wolfson, Elliot R., *Heidegger and Kabbalah: Hidden Gnosis and the Path of Poiesis*, Bloomington, IN: Indiana University Press, 2019.
Wolf, A., trans. and ed., *The Correspondence of Spinoza*, London: Routledge, 2019.
Wyschogrod, Edith, *Spirit in Ashes: Hegel, Heidegger and the Man-Made MA Death*, New Haven, CT: Yale University Press, 1985.
Wyschogrod, Edith, 'Crossover Dreams', *Journal of the American Academy of Religion* 54 (1986): 543–7.
Yerushalmi, Yosef Hayim, *From Spanish Court to Italian Ghetto: Isaac Cardoso; A Study in Seventeenth-Century Marranism and Jewish Apologetics*, New York: Columbia University Press, 1971.
Yerushalmi, Yosef Hayim, *Freud's Moses: Judaism Terminable and Interminable*, New Haven, CT: Yale University Press, 1991.
Yovel, Yirmiyahu, *Spinoza and Other Heretics: The Marrano of Reason*, Princeton, NJ: Princeton University Press, 1989.
Yovel, Yirmiyahu, *Spinoza and Other Heretics: The Adventures of Immanence*, Princeton, NJ: Princeton University Press, 1989.
Zamenhof, Ludwik, *Declaracio pri Homaranismo*, Madrid: Represso de Homaro, 1913.
Zarader, Marlene, *The Unthought Debt: Heidegger and the Hebraic Heritage*, trans. Bettina Bergo, Stanford, CA: Stanford University Press, 2006.
Žižek, Slavoj, 'The Lamella of David Lynch', in *Reading Seminar XI: Lacan's Four Fundamental Concepts of Psychoanalysis*, ed. Richard Feldstein, Bruce Fink, and Maire Jaanus, 205–20, Albany, NY: State University of New York Press, 1995.
Žižek, Slavoj, *Maximilien Robespierre, Virtue and Terror*, London: Verso, 2007.
Žižek, Slavoj, *Absolute Recoil: Towards a New Foundation of Dialectical Materialism*, London: Verso, 2012.
Žižek, Slavoj, *Less than Nothing: Hegel and the Shadow of Dialectical Materialism*, London: Verso, 2014.

Index of names and terms

Abraham, Abrahamic 5, 7, 12, 13, 23, 24, 26, 31, 35, 37, 40, 48–9, 56, 58, 62, 74, 85, 96, 105, 112, 113, 134, 151, 154, 156, 159–60, 164, 171–3, 177, 180, 192, 219, 250, 255, 258, 260
Abraham, Nicolas 6, 9
absolute 34, 55, 61, 64, 67, 76, 86, 96, 98, 103–9, 111–13, 119–22, 135, 150–1, 164, 182, 194, 213, 238, 242
Adorno, Theodor W. 43–4, 54, 100, 121, 122, 137, 145–6, 152–5, 157, 170, 215, 221, 231, 247
Agamben, Giorgio 25, 52–3, 62, 81–2, 87–92, 148, 238, 242
Altmann, Alexander 181
anarchism/anarchy 46, 73, 90, 235, 240, 244, 247, 253
Ancelet-Hustache, Jeanne 248
Angelus Silesius 121–3, 128, 179–81
Anidjar, Gill 57–60, 228
antinomianism/antinomian 13, 20, 26–7, 30–1, 45–9, 60–1, 64–9, 73–6, 81–2, 85–6, 89–92, 97, 118, 132–4, 171, 177, 182, 231, 235, 240, 244–5, 255
apocalypsis/apocalyptic 5–6, 19, 39, 70, 72, 116, 143, 196–7, 200, 203–5, 209, 212–15, 243, 245, 256–8
  vs. eucalyptic 209, 211, 256
apophatic 40–2, 95, 105, 108, 124–6, 132, 150
assimilation 19, 28–30, 43, 55, 58, 170, 228
Assmann, Jan 20, 33
atheism 12, 23, 36, 37, 95–6, 104, 107–8, 111–13, 115, 122, 134, 151, 179, 183, 185, 213, 227
  a-theism 95, 108
  pious 96, 183

Augustine of Hippo 1, 9, 11, 14, 23, 41, 85, 151, 196, 200–1, 204, 241

Badiou, Alain 213, 251
Bataille, Georges 44, 104
Benjamin, Walter 28, 32, 38, 43, 52–5, 60, 82, 87–8, 95, 96, 126, 154, 173–5, 179, 202, 209–10, 214, 221–7, 245
Benz, Ernst 243
betrayal 4, 25–7, 29, 32, 34, 37–8, 51–2, 60, 67–9, 86, 93, 123–4, 131, 133–4, 138, 159, 162, 165, 174, 179, 191, 210, 224, 231, 236–7, 240, 244, 258–60
  as 'better betrayal' 51, 69–79, 85, 88, 90, 231–4
  as perjury 2, 4, 67–9, 72–4, 76, 85–6, 124, 134, 138
  as treason (Marrano as a traitor) 11, 52, 63–4, 67, 73–5, 84, 86, 220–2, 233
Biale, David 30, 141, 206, 215
Blanchot, Maurice 15, 36–7, 39, 44, 47, 55–6, 77–8, 91–3, 97, 100, 106, 139, 146, 177, 179, 185, 191–3, 199, 200, 208, 212, 234, 238, 255
Bloch, Ernst 104, 235–6, 249
Bloom, Harold 18, 27, 141, 156, 175, 190, 194–5
Bloom, Leopold 170, 174–5, 177, 186–7, 190, 200–1
Bowles, Jane 169
Boyarin, Daniel 25, 65, 83–6
Bradley, Arthur 78
Buck-Morss, Susan 221–6
Butler, Judith 254–6

calling
  as accusation 53, 59
  as election 8–12, 24, 173

Index Of Names And Terms

Caputo, John D.   22, 23, 37–8, 93, 148, 156
Cardoso, Abraham Miguel   26, 30–3, 68, 113, 133, 177–8, 182–3, 195
Caruth, Cathy   63
Castro, Americo   8, 13–14, 195
Catholicism/Catholic   1–2, 5–7, 13–14, 19–20, 23, 30–1, 37, 40, 42, 54, 59, 64, 79–80, 83–4, 86, 101, 132, 154, 157, 159, 161, 170, 186, 193, 257
Celan, Paul   3, 10, 16, 43, 67, 170, 178, 208, 221, 247, 257
Christ   2, 25, 80, 101, 157, 180, 190, 196, 198, 205, 214, 245
Christianity/Christian   1–2, 4–9, 13–15, 17–19, 22–3, 25, 28, 31–2, 37, 42, 53, 63–5, 67–8, 80–1, 83–4, 90, 93, 96–107, 109–22, 126–7, 134, 137, 140, 144, 148–51, 155, 157, 160, 164–7, 178–81, 193, 195–7, 201, 206, 210, 213, 215, 219–21, 224–9, 233, 237, 248–50, 254–8
  Christianizers   37
  Judeo-Christian   32, 104, 165, 236
  New Christian   2, 8, 13–14, 28, 63, 228
  Protestant   19, 96, 124
Cixous, Helene   6–8, 11–12, 16, 19, 21, 23, 26, 37–8, 40, 43, 53–4, 67, 86, 145, 169–79, 186, 188–201, 208, 210–11, 221
community   2, 12, 16, 19, 44, 60, 66, 106, 110, 113, 138, 159, 171, 210–12, 217, 228, 234, 236, 239, 242, 246–54, 257
  as ana-community   219, 251
  as *communitas*   234–48, 254
conversion/convert (*converso*)   1, 7–8, 18–20, 24, 28–32, 42, 51–3, 56–9, 64–7, 79–85, 90, 127, 133, 156, 161, 167, 193, 195–6, 206, 211, 221, 227, 229, 239, 257
  as *tshuva*   20–1, 40, 135
Cope, Jackson L.   189
Cordovero, Moses   155–6, 181, 200
creation/creaturely   12, 30, 35–6, 46, 86, 98, 105–6, 113–14, 119–24, 128–9, 132–5, 142–5, 153, 156, 162, 170, 178, 181–4, 188–9, 197, 200, 206, 216–17, 227, 245, 252
crypt   5, 7, 11, 13, 27, 41, 45, 49, 59, 62, 92, 96, 148–9, 155–7, 159, 169–70, 179–80, 192–5, 198–202, 206–12, 220, 227
crypto-Judaism/crypto-Jewish   4, 8, 29, 47, 95, 148, 165, 239, 242
cryptophoria   6, 9–10, 15, 110, 112, 135, 146–7, 184–6, 204, 207–12
crypto-religion   242
cryptotheology   26, 79, 123, 170
encryption   49, 59, 62, 64, 96–7, 101, 107–8, 149–51, 155, 159, 175, 179, 184, 186, 200, 204, 211, 242

death
  death drive   56, 110, 116, 152–3, 163, 190, 192
  of God   23, 96–104, 121, 123, 135, 137, 149, 151, 160, 181, 224–5, 242
  martyrological   29, 64–8, 77–9, 83, 86, 92–3, 176, 236
  symbiosis with   87, 91–3
de Certeau, Michel   13–16, 29, 179–83, 188, 247
deconstruction   19, 21–3, 33, 35, 43, 57, 74, 77–8, 104, 109, 111, 115–16, 143, 166, 212–13, 226, 244–5
de Leon, Moses   47, 141, 156, 177, 215
de Lucena, Juan   1
democracy   61, 77, 219, 226, 244, 246, 253
  As *voyoucracy*   77, 244–6, 253
de Montaigne, Michel   25, 77–9, 192, 200, 206–7
de Rougemont, Denis   243
desert   5, 23, 30, 33, 41–2, 47, 79, 86, 88, 96, 102–8, 131, 138–9, 144, 151–66, 175, 219, 225–6, 238, 246, 249
de Vries, Hent   76, 95
diaspora/diasporic   5, 14, 20, 23–6, 35, 141, 145, 166
Dickinson, Colby   25
différance   23, 39–40, 42, 45, 62, 75, 122, 128, 141–3, 171, 183, 213–16, 231, 234, 245–6

dissemination 39–40, 62–3, 105, 109, 111–13, 124, 139–42, 145, 154–5, 164, 179, 182, 184, 227
Dunkelgrün, Theodor 2, 17

ecriture 35, 63, 141–4, 148, 190–5, 201
Edom 31, 39, 177, 250
Egypt 20, 33, 250
　Exodus out of 30, 35, 40, 82, 98, 156, 177, 187
Eliade, Mircea 34, 109, 138
Elijah 9–10, 79, 177–8, 182
Engel, Amir 28
Esau 134, 177, 184, 201–2
eschatology 85, 116, 182, 195, 211–13, 259
Esther 32, 210
event 21, 86, 91, 114, 117–18, 143, 161, 172, 182, 184, 204, 209, 216, 230, 232
　As *Ereignis* 59, 129, 195
exile/exilic 5, 22, 25, 28, 30, 32–7, 43, 61, 93, 95, 126, 141–4, 166, 170, 178, 190–2, 200, 211, 224–7, 241, 254, 258

Fackenheim, Emil 65–6
fall 33, 127, 137, 142, 146, 151, 197
　as *felix lapsus/culpa* 5, 11, 151, 241
Feld, Edward 79
Fischer, Ernst 256
forgetting 12, 36, 67–8, 92, 95, 123–4, 128–31, 134, 146–8, 155, 158–9, 164–5, 177–8, 185–8, 191, 211
　as *Gelassenheit* 123, 247–8
　as hypomnesia 11, 126
　as oblivion 11–13, 28, 82, 92, 109, 122–4, 128–34, 150, 160, 175, 182, 186, 227, 231
Frank, Jacob 20, 31, 46, 82, 132–4, 161, 177, 182, 201–2, 204
Frankism/Frankist 20, 29–31, 134, 177, 225, 241
Freud, Sigmund 4, 15, 20, 41, 43–4, 48, 82, 99, 152, 166, 173, 186, 189, 259

Gebhardt, Carl 7, 154
gender 83, 169, 189, 208, 253–5

gift 11, 36, 45, 59, 86, 107–9, 114–18, 122–4, 129, 133, 135, 143–5, 157, 162, 166, 172, 182–3, 185, 191, 194, 196, 198, 214, 216
God
　Christian 4, 160
　Godhead (as *Ein-Sof*) 106–7, 114, 116, 120, 130–3, 142, 155, 162, 177, 181, 187, 189, 200, 202, 215
　Jewish 4, 64, 66, 110, 116, 124, 147, 166
　Marrano 36, 162, 166, 257
Goethe, J. W. 170, 171, 185, 235
Goldish, Matt 29, 32
Goldschmit, Marc 226, 244
Graff Zivin, Erin 5, 42, 257
Greene, Deirdre 206
guilt 30, 64, 83–6, 98–9, 109, 114, 116, 123–4, 135, 185, 195, 201
　of survival 66–74, 145–6

Haggadah 38, 82, 202, 209, 212
Hägglund, Martin 76, 95, 111–13, 244
Halakhah, halakhic 65–6, 80, 202
Hamacher, Werner 119
Hammerschlag, Sarah 23, 25, 69
Handelman, Susan A. 22
hantology (*hantologie*) 149, 230–1
　haunting 45, 55, 58, 67, 72, 182, 230–6, 239, 241, 243–6, 249
Hastara (concealment) 4–5, 32, 39, 108, 127, 209, 255
　veil/veiling/unveiling 5, 15, 39, 41, 51, 66, 86, 117, 193, 195–204, 207–8, 211–16, 256, 259
Hegel, G. W. F. 4, 22, 40, 72–7, 93, 95–124, 137–8, 147, 149, 151–5, 160, 162, 164, 166, 181, 184–8, 196, 198, 212–13, 219, 221–2, 226–7, 234, 247–8, 252, 256
Heidegger, Martin 15, 39, 42, 59, 62, 78, 82, 99, 105, 107, 115, 123–32, 137, 139–40, 145–7, 150, 157–8, 164, 170, 174–5, 178, 186, 192, 195, 197–200, 212–13, 216, 219, 238, 247–9, 256
Heresy, heretic 22, 118, 122, 238, 249
Hess, Moses 34

Index Of Names And Terms

history   20, 25, 30, 46, 47, 55, 63, 90, 114–22, 129, 131, 134, 150, 159, 192, 199, 204, 221–8, 230–2, 239, 241–3, 249
Hollander, Dana   43
hope   10, 15, 20, 28–31, 44, 47–9, 60, 65, 67, 72, 80, 83–4, 90, 98, 135, 149, 156, 171, 215, 220, 228–9, 233, 247, 253, 258–9
  as *esperanza*   81, 84, 228–9
Horkheimer, Max   152
Horwitz, Daniel   187
Huizinga, Johan   242–3

iconoclasm   95–6, 99–107, 110, 124, 132, 135, 153–8, 184, 219, 227
Idel, Moshe   32, 36
identity/identitarian   2–7, 12–13, 17–18, 23–7, 30, 35, 37, 40–1, 45, 48, 53, 63–4, 73, 80–2, 86, 92, 124–6, 160–6, 172, 180, 221–2, 226–8, 235, 238–9, 249–50, 255, 260
  identity politics   17–18
  non-identity   16–20, 95, 127, 140, 159, 172–3, 239–41, 244–6, 253–4, 257–8
Idziak-Smoczyńska, Urszula   23
immanence/immanent   20, 72–5, 80–1, 108, 112, 124, 154, 176, 183–5, 231–3, 236
Islam   30–1, 37, 41, 120, 150, 204

Jacob   5, 47, 79, 86–7, 98, 134, 156, 165–6, 175, 177, 184, 201–2, 204
Jaron, Steven   25
Jay, Martin   43
Joachim da Fiore   242–3, 248–9
Jonas, Hans   37, 64, 113, 145, 151, 176–8
Joyce, James   12, 16, 40, 86, 101, 103, 106, 115, 119, 124, 170, 174–92, 200, 212, 216, 255
Judaism   2, 7–8, 10–15, 18–30, 45–8, 51, 59–61, 64–6, 74, 76, 79–80, 83–7, 92–3, 95, 119, 129, 134, 141, 155, 161, 164, 166–7, 170, 179, 181, 193–5, 198, 200–6, 209–10, 212, 214, 220, 221, 223, 226–9, 233, 239, 250, 254, 258

comic   169, 173–4
Judaizers   8, 80, 84, 177, 189
justice   19, 45–6, 49, 69–76, 162, 181, 213, 220, 226, 230–6, 240, 244–6, 252–3

Kabbalah/Kabbalistic   5, 10, 19, 26–32, 86, 105, 107, 114, 129–33, 138, 141–4, 155–7, 159, 174, 177, 181–9, 215–16, 224, 236, 258
Kafka, Franz   5, 8, 11, 15, 19, 23, 27–8, 43, 46, 53–5, 58, 62, 74, 88, 90, 172–9, 183, 192, 196, 198, 202, 204, 209, 212, 255
Kamuf, Peggy   16, 151
Kant, Immanuel   74, 98–9, 110, 112, 116, 119, 147, 162, 212–13, 219, 254
Kenoma, kenomatic   103–10, 113, 141–4, 160–5
Kenosis/kenotic   98–108, 113–25, 137, 151, 156, 160, 195
Kepel, Gilles   102–3
Kermode, Frank   6
Khora   12, 15, 45, 47, 61, 78, 104–8, 113, 125–6, 134, 140, 142, 145, 149, 156–66, 186–90, 194, 199, 208, 210, 215, 225, 227, 230–1, 235, 241–2, 246
Kleist, Heinrich von   151
Kojève, Alexandre   90, 219–21
Krell, David Farrel   6, 20, 63, 132, 146–8, 203
Kristeva, Julia   53, 58–9

Lacan, Jacques   39, 60–1, 83, 90, 106, 116, 142, 146, 163–4, 185, 189, 212–13
Landauer, Gustav   34, 233, 247–56
law/legal   1–2, 7, 12, 17, 24, 26, 31, 33, 37, 39, 45–9, 57–9, 63, 69–76, 80–2, 88, 90, 92, 99, 127, 156, 162, 177, 203–4, 212, 219, 226, 229, 231, 234–46, 251, 256–8
  Jewish   46, 49, 59, 64–6, 72–6, 80–2, 90, 154, 201, 204, 209–10, 232
Lear, Jonathan   85–6
Leibovici, Martine   9

Letting-Be (*Seinlassen*) 45–6, 123, 131–2, 141, 145, 162, 182, 212, 215, 231
Lévinas, Emmanuel 15, 40, 45, 69–76, 106, 126, 196, 221, 230, 233, 256
life
   as bare/ bared 52–3, 87–92
   choice of (*u-baharta ba-hayim*) 31, 55, 64, 66, 73, 83, 135, 159, 203
   as *conatus* 66–72, 76, 79–82, 88, 90
   as mere life 52, 81, 87–8
   as more life 29, 52–3, 68, 79, 81, 87, 109, 192, 199, 243
   as New Scripture 55–6, 60, 64, 88–93, 206, 245
   preservation of 70, 76, 88–9, 152
   as still life (*nature morte*) 62–3, 68, 137, 150–5, 159, 163–4, 224, 227
   as *vita nuova* 77–9
liminal/liminality/liminoid 81, 234–7, 240
Linebaugh, Peter 221
Liska, Vivian 43
Lorberbaum, Menachem 232
Löwy, Michael 19, 26, 43
Luria, Isaac, Lurianic 30, 32, 37, 105–7, 113–16, 120–31, 140–1, 148, 158, 174, 177, 181–3, 188, 224–5
Lynes, Philippe 149

Maciejko, Paweł 2, 17, 31, 133, 134
Magee, Alexander Glenn 121
Maimonides, Moses 64–5, 232
Maiorino, Giancarlo 81–2
Malabou, Catherine 21–2, 43, 82, 98, 113, 116, 139, 210
Mannheim, Karl 18
Margel, Serge 149
Marrano, *see also* betrayal; conversion; crypt, crypto-Judaism; God; Judaizers; Messiah; modernity; picaro; religion; survival
   experience 13, 17, 28, 35, 43, 78–9, 81, 86–8, 90, 105, 162, 226–7, 240
   faith 96, 131, 166
   non-identity 6, 86, 127

   as remnant 17–18, 22, 25, 31, 48, 51–2, 62, 68, 77, 87, 92, 100, 124, 148, 153, 175, 181, 239, 241, 244–6, 257–9
   secret/secrecy 3–7, 10, 16, 26, 28, 40–1, 48–9, 57–61, 107, 125, 193, 196, 251, 255–8
   theology 16, 26, 30–2, 51, 93
   universalism 3, 5, 17–19, 25, 36, 43, 61, 88, 96, 192, 212, 226, 229, 239, 242–4, 254, 258
Marx, Karl, Marxism 118, 229–33, 237–8, 241, 244, 249, 251, 253, 256–8
Meister Eckhart 14–15, 123, 247–52
Mendes-Flohr, Paul 28
Messiah 58, 64, 229–30, 240
   Christian 31, 80, 178, 198
   Jewish 80, 172
   Marrano 8, 31–2, 54, 171–2, 177, 210–11
messianism/messianic 32, 45–7, 84, 107, 160, 220, 230, 232, 250, 253, 259
   messianicity 10–13, 16, 46–9, 52, 62, 105–7, 113, 142, 162–3, 166, 230–4, 245, 259
   reversal 20, 29, 35, 57–9, 63, 93, 124, 129, 148, 203, 209, 243, 255
metaphysics 15, 16, 26, 95, 113, 122–3, 131, 135, 147–51, 154–7, 178, 186, 213–16, 235, 240, 258–60
modernity 69, 77–9, 88, 110, 121, 152, 155, 159, 225, 229, 235, 242–4, 248
   Marrano 88, 235
monotheism/monotheistic 81, 134, 160, 204
Moreiras, Alberto 53, 57, 90, 222, 244
Moses 20, 27, 80, 156
mourning 22–3, 66, 72, 86, 96–9, 109, 146–9, 183–5, 212, 226–8
mysticism/mystical 14–16, 27–8, 31, 41, 119, 121–2, 125, 149, 156, 179–80, 183–4, 187–8, 203, 206, 212, 217, 247–50

Naas, Michael 66, 98, 106, 159–63
Nancy, Jean-Luc 104, 115–16, 234, 238

Index Of Names And Terms

Negri, Antonio 51, 121, 232–3
Neoplatonism 14, 42, 106, 131, 141, 143–4, 148
Nietzsche, Friedrich 29–30, 39, 69, 98, 102, 104, 110, 112, 115, 123, 126, 132, 140, 146, 164, 167–9, 171, 180, 190, 212
Nirenberg, David 2
Novalis 247–8, 252

Ofrat, Gideon 22–3, 83, 85
ontology 34, 45, 51–2, 59, 62, 70–5, 79, 112, 114–15, 119, 122, 131, 135, 138, 140, 144, 149, 163, 186, 188, 229–32, 235, 239, 246, 254
ontotheology 35–6, 51, 62, 75, 79, 99–104, 107, 109, 117–18, 126, 134–5, 139, 143, 149–51, 154–64, 174
O'Regan, Cyril 137
orthodoxy, orthodox 22, 26, 64–5, 78–80, 83, 96, 118, 129, 133–4, 169, 250, 255

passion 209
  as Hegelian memory of 97–101, 104, 109, 114–15, 118, 124, 137, 149, 154, 176, 219
  for the Real 213–16
  for the Veil 211, 215
Passover 62, 98, 116, 153–4, 156, 172, 175–6, 188, 224, 226
Paul, Pauline 4, 18, 25, 62–3, 68, 70, 80, 98, 144, 197, 200–3, 220, 236–7, 245
persecution 2, 9, 31, 70, 83, 101, 206
Picaro 13, 37–8, 62, 81–2, 86, 174, 190
  as *voyou* 20, 61–4, 77–8, 81, 152, 174, 240, 244–6, 253

rabbi/rabbinic 6, 8, 18–19, 22, 47, 64–5, 69, 74, 78, 83–6, 134, 145, 156, 178, 204, 208, 210
Raviv, Zohar 200
redemption 11, 20, 32, 36, 64, 80, 92, 102, 104, 116, 122, 143, 156, 162, 177, 181–2, 195, 209, 212, 241, 250
Rediker, Marcus 221
Reik, Theodor 204, 236

religion
  Marrano 38, 95, 171, 219
  'of modern times' 95–6, 99, 107, 134, 137
  religiosity 18, 96, 102, 110–13, 166
  without religion 36–8, 55, 95, 161, 166, 174, 191
remembrance 36, 62, 132–3, 140
  as hypermnesia 36, 124, 137, 178, 182–91
  as *Zakhor* 36, 46, 48–9
Revah, Israel Salvador 8
revelation 6–7, 11, 25, 27, 30, 40, 86–9, 92–3, 107, 143, 161–3, 167, 172–3, 180–1, 188, 197–200, 209–13, 233
  revealability (*Offenbarkeit*) 4, 105–7, 162–3, 257
Reznikoff, Charles 42, 221
Rilke, Rainer Maria 184
Rogozinski, Jacob 146–7
Rosen, Michael 213
Rosenstock, Bruce 8, 166
Rosenzweig, Franz 12, 43, 70, 87, 107, 167, 180–1, 196, 199, 221, 244
Rustov, Marina 193

sacrifice 44, 52–3, 64, 66–8, 71, 74, 76–81, 85, 89, 99–107, 110, 114–19, 124, 135, 149–50, 154, 157, 203
  as *auto da fé* 7, 46–7, 79
  sacrificial logic 52, 66–7, 76, 87, 90, 100, 110, 114–15
salvation 22, 76, 80, 92, 102, 104, 127, 157, 259
Schelling, Friedrich Wilhelm Joseph 32–4, 86, 120, 137–8, 151, 188
Schmitt, Carl 76, 237
Scholem, Gershom 26–38, 42–3, 45–6, 49, 54–5, 59, 60, 62, 68, 70, 73, 75, 88, 92–3, 96–7, 118, 120, 125, 128, 132–3, 143, 148, 153–4, 162, 173–4, 177, 179, 183, 195, 210, 215, 220, 224, 247, 256, 259–60
Scotus, Duns 121
secularization/secular 7, 28, 31, 69, 96, 104, 123, 150, 155, 159, 212–13, 242, 249, 258

Sennett, Richard 240
separation 44–5, 86, 98, 113, 119, 131, 135–41, 148, 154, 163–4, 180–1, 196–8, 203, 210, 214, 247, 250–3, 257
   as catachresis 22, 138, 145, 158, 164, 201
   as cut (*coupure*) 22–3, 83–6, 90, 93, 135, 137, 164, 228
   in Landauer (*Absonderung*) 252
   as lucky break 85–6, 148, 151, 189, 209, 228, 254
Sephardic 5, 19–20, 42, 66, 186, 210–11, 251
Shakespeare, William 47
Shekhinah 194–5, 206, 210
Sherwood, Yvonne 23, 148
Shoah 47, 65–6, 69, 146
silence 27–31, 39, 42, 70, 127, 153, 171–2, 175, 190–2, 207, 219, 227, 238
   silenzio 27–30, 42, 79, 153, 172, 238
   stillness (*Stille*) 28, 34, 152–4, 160, 166, 224, 257
Simms, Norman 4
sin 32, 81, 84–5, 101, 104, 109, 129, 150, 164, 166, 182, 185
   original 83–5, 133
Sollers, Philippe 141
Sommer, Benjamin D. 33–5, 43, 126, 226
Spinoza, Baruch 5, 7, 51, 76–82
spirit 45–7, 125, 144, 151, 162, 186, 205, 249, 256
   in Hegel 98–9, 108, 219, 221, 227
   in Heidegger 118, 125–6
   as *ruah* 45–7, 124–30, 142, 162, 186–7, 190, 231
   as spectre 23, 51, 126, 185, 232–3, 237, 240, 244, 247, 249
Strauss, Leo 221
survival (*survie*) 12–13, 23, 29–30, 37, 44, 51–6, 60–70, 83–96, 108, 111, 114, 145–6, 148, 150, 152–4, 160–5, 191–5, 200, 207, 220, 223–5, 237, 244, 258–60, *see also* life, choice of
   enigma of 63, 93, 192, 258

subject as survivor 66–7, 71–2, 78, 87, 90–2, 181, 194, 211, 236
   as *sur-vie* 52, 56, 78, 87, 92–3, 149, 192, 207, 258

Talmud/Talmudic 22, 27, 54, 58, 65, 105–6, 206, 220
Taubes, Jacob 237, 249
Teresa of Avila 13–14, 28, 41, 169, 205–8
theology 23, 30, 41, 69, 95, 103–4, 107, 121–4, 143, 149, 156–7, 163, 173–4, 179, 188–9, 216, 237, *see also* crypt, cryptotheology
   of risk (hazard) 13, 15, 30, 92, 113, 177–8, 183, 189
Thurschwell, Adam 87
Torok, Maria 6, 9–10, 112, 186
totalitarianism/totalitarian 3, 88, 245, 253, 256
tradition
   chain of (*shalshelet ka-kabbalah*) 10, 27, 30, 93, 159, 177
   hidden 27–31, 97, 103, 107, 127, 135, 202, 256, 259
   as the Truth versus the Teaching 26–8, 35, 46–7, 55, 69, 89, 92, 118, 159, 258
transcendence 15, 20, 27, 46, 56, 72–5, 80, 108, 110–12, 122, 141–2, 170, 176, 181, 213, 230–3, 236, 244–8, 254
   ultratranscendence 147
trauma/traumatic 9–10, 20, 39, 43–4, 50, 60, 63, 70, 79, 95, 100–1, 148, 154, 192–5, 201, 204, 207–9, 225, 227
Trigano, Schmuel 244
Trilling, Jacques 179, 190
Tsevi, Sabbatai 30–1, 46, 134
   Sabbatian 20, 26, 30–2, 132, 210
Tsimtsum (contraction) 36, 64, 70, 96, 105–6, 113–16, 120, 123–32, 138–45, 148, 158, 179, 182, 188–91, 198, 200, 212–17, 220, 257–8
   as diminution of light (*contre-jour*) 97, 138, 141, 166, 197–8, 200–2, 210–15, 257

as retreat (*retrait*)   70, 96–8, 102–9, 117, 129–30, 137–9, 142–3, 145, 154, 157–8, 162–5, 188, 191, 197, 207, 219, 224, 233, 244, 247–9, 252, 257–8
Turner, Victor   234–5, 240
Twersky, Isadore   65, 181

umbrapolitics   244, 254, 258

Valery, Paul   16, 185
Vital, Hayyim ben Joseph   188
Voegelin, Erich   110, 251

Weber, Elisabeth   12, 21, 43, 151
Weber, Samuel   150, 214, 222
Winnicott, Donald Woods   34, 40–1, 45, 208, 247

witness/witnessing   6, 36, 64–8, 72, 91–3, 96, 201, 241
  as martyr   64, 67, 79, 92–3
Wittgenstein, Ludwig   1, 16, 42
Wolfson, Elliot   24–5, 105, 108, 124, 130–2, 181, 216
Wyschogrod, Edith   124

Yerushalmi, Yosef Hayim   8, 38, 47–8, 193, 220, 239
Yom Kippur   62, 83–8, 202, 206
  as *Yom Coupure*   23, 85–6, 93
Yovel, Yirmiyahu   2, 7, 17–18, 80–1, 83–4, 86, 88, 90, 195, 240

Zamenhof, Ludwik   228–9
Zarader, Marlene   128–9
Žižek, Slavoj   61, 76, 104

www.ingramcontent.com/pod-product-compliance
Lightning Source LLC
Chambersburg PA
CBHW052214300426
44115CB00011B/1687